I0646646

CCNA Wireless

Official Exam Certification Guide

Brandon James Carroll

Cisco Press

800 East 96th Street

Indianapolis, IN 46240

CCNA Wireless Official Exam Certification Guide

Brandon James Carroll

Copyright© 2009 Cisco Systems, Inc.

Published by:
Cisco Press
800 East 96th Street
Indianapolis, IN 46240 USA

Printed in the United States of America

First Printing October 2008

Library of Congress Cataloging-in-Publication Data:

Carroll, Brandon.
  CCNA wireless official exam certification guide / Brandon James Carroll.
    p. cm.
  ISBN 978-1-58720-211-7 (hbk. : CD-ROM)
  1. Wireless LANs--Examinations--Study guides. 2. Electronic data
processing personnel--Certification--Study guides. I. Title.
  TK5105.78C37 2009
  004.6'8076--dc22

                                  2008038512

ISBN-13: 978-1-58720-211-7

ISBN-10: 1-58720-211-5

Warning and Disclaimer

This book is designed to provide information about the 640-721 Implementing Cisco Unified Wireless Networking Essentials (IUWNE) certification exam. Every effort has been made to make this book as complete and as accurate as possible, but no warranty or fitness is implied.

The information is provided on an "as is" basis. The authors, Cisco Press, and Cisco Systems, Inc., shall have neither liability nor responsibility to any person or entity with respect to any loss or damages arising from the information contained in this book or from the use of the discs or programs that may accompany it.

The opinions expressed in this book belong to the author and are not necessarily those of Cisco Systems, Inc.

Trademark Acknowledgments

All terms mentioned in this book that are known to be trademarks or service marks have been appropriately capitalized. Cisco Press or Cisco Systems, Inc., cannot attest to the accuracy of this information. Use of a term in this book should not be regarded as affecting the validity of any trademark or service mark.

Corporate and Government Sales

The publisher offers excellent discounts on this book when ordered in quantity for bulk purchases or special sales, which may include electronic versions and/or custom covers and content particular to your business, training goals, marketing focus, and branding interests. For more information, please contact:

U.S. Corporate and Government Sales
1-800-382-3419
corpsales@pearsontechgroup.com

For sales outside the United States please contact:
International Sales
international@pearsoned.com

Feedback Information

At Cisco Press, our goal is to create in-depth technical books of the highest quality and value. Each book is crafted with care and precision, undergoing rigorous development that involves the unique expertise of members from the professional technical community.

Readers' feedback is a natural continuation of this process. If you have any comments regarding how we could improve the quality of this book or otherwise alter it to better suit your needs, you can contact us through email at feedback@ciscopress.com. Please make sure to include the book title and ISBN in your message.

We greatly appreciate your assistance.

Publisher: Paul Boger

Executive Editor: Brett Bartow

Managing Editor: Patrick Kanouse

Senior Development Editor: Christopher Cleveland

Project Editor: Mandie Frank

Editorial Assistant: Vanessa Evans

Book and Cover Designer: Louisa Adair

Composition: Mark Shirar

Associate Publisher: Dave Dusthimer

Cisco Representative: Anthony Wolfenden

Cisco Press Program Manager: Jeff Brady

Copy Editors: Karen A. Gill, Gayle Johnson

Technical Editors: Bobby Corcoran, Robert Marg

Proofreader: Sheri Cain, Water Crest Publishing, Inc.

Indexer: Tim Wright

Americas Headquarters
Cisco Systems, Inc.
San Jose, CA

Asia Pacific Headquarters
Cisco Systems (USA) Pte. Ltd.
Singapore

Europe Headquarters
Cisco Systems International BV
Amsterdam, The Netherlands

Cisco has more than 200 offices worldwide. Addresses, phone numbers, and fax numbers are listed on the Cisco Website at **www.cisco.com/go/offices.**

CCDE, CCENT, Cisco Eos, Cisco Lumin, Cisco Nexus, Cisco StadiumVision, the Cisco logo, DCE, and Welcome to the Human Network are trademarks; Changing the Way We Work, Live, Play, and Learn is a service mark; and Access Registrar, Aironet, AsyncOS, Bringing the Meeting To You, Catalyst, CCDA, CCDP, CCIE, CCIP, CCNA, CCNP, CCSP, CCVP, Cisco, the Cisco Certified Internetwork Expert logo, Cisco IOS, Cisco Press, Cisco Systems, Cisco Systems Capital, the Cisco Systems logo, Cisco Unity, Collaboration Without Limitation, EtherFast, EtherSwitch, Event Center, Fast Step, Follow Me Browsing, FormShare, GigaDrive, HomeLink, Internet Quotient, IOS, iPhone, iQ Expertise, the iQ logo, iQ Net Readiness Scorecard, iQuick Study, IronPort, the IronPort logo, LightStream, Linksys, MediaTone, MeetingPlace, MGX, Networkers, Networking Academy, Network Registrar, PCNow, PIX, PowerPanels, ProConnect, ScriptShare, SenderBase, SMARTnet, Spectrum Expert, StackWise, The Fastest Way to Increase Your Internet Quotient, TransPath, WebEx, and the WebEx logo are registered trademarks of Cisco Systems, Inc. and/or its affiliates in the United States and certain other countries.

All other trademarks mentioned in this document or Website are the property of their respective owners. The use of the word partner does not imply a partnership relationship between Cisco and any other company. (0805R)

About the Author

Brandon James Carroll, CCNA, CCNP, CCSP, is one of the leading instructors for Cisco security technologies in the country, teaching classes that include the CCNA, CCNP, and CCSP courses, numerous CCVP courses, and custom developed courseware. In his eight years with Ascolta, Brandon has developed and taught many private Cisco courses for companies such as Boeing, Intel, and Cisco. He is a certified Cisco instructor and the author of *Cisco Access Control Security*, in addition to several Quick Reference Sheets.

Prior to becoming a technical instructor for Ascolta, Brandon was a technician and an ADSL specialist for GTE Network Services and Verizon Communications. His duties involved ISP router support and network design. As a lead engineer, he tested and maintained Frame Relay connections between Lucent B-STDX and Cisco routers. His team was in charge of troubleshooting ISP Frame Relay to ATM cut-overs for ADSL customers. Brandon trained new employees at Verizon to the EPG in ADSL testing and troubleshooting procedures and managed a Tekwizard database for technical information and troubleshooting techniques. He majored in information technology at St. Leo University.

About the Technical Reviewers

Bobby Corcoran, CCNA, is a systems engineer responsible for the design, configuration, implementation, and support of LAN, WAN, wireless, voice, and security infrastructures for a health care organization, including two acute care hospitals and several ancillary health care facilities. His recent wireless experience includes the migration of a multicampus Cisco SWAN to CUWN architecture. Bobby holds a bachelor's degree in business administration from Southern Oregon University.

Robert Marg is a wireless consulting systems engineer with Cisco. In his position at Cisco, he is a technical leader in wireless and mobility and has worked closely with enterprise, commercial, federal and transportation marketing, and product management teams to develop and deliver solutions for numerous customers and various transportation and federal agencies. Robert holds a bachelor's degree in bacteriology from the University of Wisconsin-Madison.

Dedication

I would like to dedicate this book to all those engineers out there who are going to spend many hours away from friends and family just to learn this material, advance their careers, and accelerate the network world. It's because of you that I have done the same in writing this book.

Acknowledgments

I would like to thank Brett Bartow for giving me another wonderful opportunity to work on this book and to work with a handful of exceptional people.

I'd also like to thank my technical editors, Robert Marg and Bobby Corcoran, for the extremely difficult task that they underwent and for the continued support. Thanks for responding to all my extra emails! You truly have made this a better book.

I would like to give special recognition to Christopher Cleveland, Dayna Isley, Andrew Cupp, Mandie Frank, and all the good people at Cisco Press, for keeping this publication on track.

In addition, I would like to thank Ascolta Training for giving me the opportunity to explore areas of technology that I really love. And I want to recognize Ted Wagner and Kevin Marz for their constant encouragement and support. Finally, thanks to Tony DeSimone, William Kivlen, Jack Wood, Kevin Masui, and the other instructors at Ascolta for being there when I needed to bounce ideas off of someone.

Contents at a Glance

Contents

Icons Used in This Book

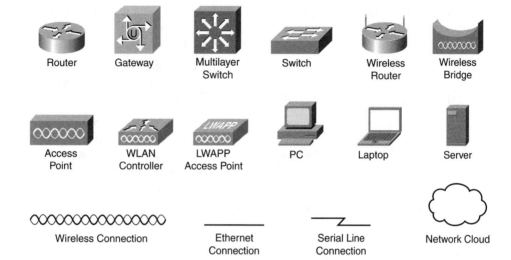

Command Syntax Conventions

The conventions used to present command syntax in this book are the same conventions used in the IOS Command Reference. The Command Reference describes these conventions as follows:

- **Boldface** indicates commands and keywords that are entered literally as shown. In actual configuration examples and output (not general command syntax), boldface indicates commands that are manually input by the user (such as a **show** command).

- *Italic* indicates arguments for which you supply actual values.

- Vertical bars (|) separate alternative, mutually exclusive elements.

- Square brackets [ ] indicate optional elements.

- Braces { } indicate a required choice.

- Braces within brackets [{ }] indicate a required choice within an optional element.

Foreword

CCNA Wireless Official Exam Certification Guide is an excellent self-study resource for the Cisco IUWNE (640-721) exam. Passing the IUWNE exam validates the knowledge and skills required to successfully secure Cisco network devices.

Gaining certification in Cisco technology is key to the continuing educational development of today's networking professional. Through certification programs, Cisco validates the skills and expertise required to effectively manage the modern enterprise network.

Cisco Press exam certification guides and preparation materials offer exceptional—and flexible—access to the knowledge and information required to stay current in your field of expertise or to gain new skills. Whether used as a supplement to more traditional training or as a primary source of learning, these materials offer users the information and knowledge validation required to gain new understanding and proficiencies.

Developed in conjunction with the Cisco certifications and training team, Cisco Press books are the only self-study books authorized by Cisco, and they offer students a series of exam practice tools and resource materials to help ensure that learners fully grasp the concepts and information presented.

Additional authorized Cisco instructor-led courses, e-learning, labs, and simulations are available exclusively from Cisco Learning Solutions Partners worldwide. To learn more, visit http://www.cisco.com/go/training.

I hope that you find these materials to be an enriching and useful part of your exam preparation.

Erik Ullanderson
Manager, Global Certifications
Learning@Cisco
May 2008

Introduction

Welcome to the world of Cisco Certified Network Associate (CCNA) Wireless! As technology continues to evolve, wireless technologies are finding their way to the forefront. This clearly indicates the progression from a fixed wired type of connectivity to a more fluid, mobile workforce that can work when, where, and how they want. Regardless of your background, one of the primary goals of the new CCNA Wireless certification is to introduce you to the Cisco Unified Wireless Network (CUWN).

In June 2008, Cisco announced new CCNA specialties, including CCNA Security, CCNA Wireless, and CCNA Voice. These certifications, released 10 years after the initial CCNA, represent the growth of Cisco into new and emerging industries. Certification candidates can now specialize into specific areas of study. Figure I-1 shows the basic organization of the certifications and exams used to achieve your CCNA Wireless certification.

Figure I-1   *Cisco Certifications and CCNA Wireless Certification Path*

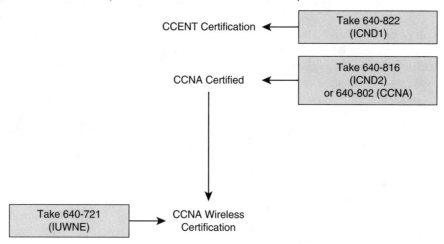

As you can see from the figure, a traditional CCNA certification is a prerequisite before you venture into the CCNA Wireless certification.

Goals and Methods

The most important and somewhat obvious goal of this book is to help you pass the Implementing Cisco Unified Wireless Networking Essentials (IUWNE) exam (640-721). In fact, if the primary objective of this book were different, the book title would be misleading; however, the methods used in this book to help you pass the IUWNE exam are designed to also make you much more knowledgeable about how to do your job.

This book uses several key methodologies to help you discover the exam topics that you need to review in more depth so that you can fully understand and remember those details and prove to yourself that you have retained your knowledge of those topics. This book does not try to help you pass by memorization but helps you truly learn and understand the topics. The CCNA Wireless exam is the foundation for Cisco professional certifications to come, and it would be a disservice to you if this book did not help you truly learn the material. Therefore, this book will help you pass the CCNA Wireless exam by using the following methods:

■ Helping you discover which test topics you have not mastered

■ Providing explanations and information to fill in your knowledge gaps

■ Supplying exercises and scenarios that enhance your ability to recall and deduce the answers to test questions

■ Providing practice exercises on the topics and the testing process via test questions on the CD

In addition, this book uses quite a different style from typical certification-preparation books. The newer Cisco certification exams have adopted a style of testing that essentially says, "If you do not know how to do it, you will not pass this exam." This means that most of the questions on the certification exam require you to deduce the answer through reasoning or configuration rather than just memorization of facts, figures, or syntax from a book. To accommodate this newer testing style, I have written this book as a "real-world" explanation of Cisco wireless topics. Whenever possible, key concepts are explained using real-world examples rather than showing tables full of syntax options and explanations, which are freely available at Cisco.com. As you read through this book, you will definitely get a feeling of, "This is how I can *do* this" rather than, "There is the general syntax I need to memorize," which is exactly what you need for the newer Cisco exams.

Who Should Read This Book?

This book is designed to provide a twofold purpose. The primary purpose is to tremendously increase your chances of passing the CCNA Wireless certification exam. The secondary purpose is to provide the information necessary to deploy a CUWN and a Cisco Mobility Express (CME) network as part of the Smart Business Communications System (SBCS). The new Cisco exam approach provides an avenue to write the book with both a real-world and certification-study approach at the same time. As you read through this book and study the configuration examples and exam tips, you will truly understand how you can deploy a wireless network, while at the same time feel equipped to pass the CCNA Wireless certification exam.

Strategies for Exam Preparation

Strategies for exam preparation will vary depending on your existing skills, knowledge, and equipment available. Of course, the ideal exam preparation would consist of building a small wireless lab with a 2106 wireless LAN controller and an 1131AP, as well as a Cisco Mobility Express (CME) 526 controller and 521 AP. You would also need a switch and a few wireless clients so that you could work through configurations as you read through this book. However, not everyone has access to this equipment, so the next best step you can take is to read through the chapters in this book, jotting notes down with key concepts or configurations on a separate notepad. Each chapter begins with a "Do I Know This Already?" quiz designed to give you a good idea of the chapter content. In some cases, you might already know most of or all the information covered in a given chapter.

After you have read this book, look at the current exam objectives for the CCNA Wireless exam listed on the Cisco website (http://www.cisco.com/certification). If you see areas shown in the certification exam outline that you would still like to study, find those sections in the book and review them. When you feel confident in your skills, attempt the practice exam included on the book CD. As you work through the practice exam, note the areas where you lack confidence, and review those concepts or configurations in the book. After you have reviewed the areas, work through the practice exam a second time and rate your skills. Keep in mind that the more you work through the practice exam, the more familiar the questions will become and the less accurate the practice exam will measure your skills. After you have worked through the practice exam a second time and feel confident with your skills, schedule the real IUWNE (640-721) exam through VUE (www.vue.com). You should typically take the exam within a week from when you consider yourself ready to take it so the information is fresh in your mind.

Cisco exams are difficult. Even if you have a solid grasp of the information, many other factors play into the testing environment (stress, time constraints, and so on). If you pass the exam on the first attempt, fantastic! If not, know that this is happens to many people. The next time you attempt the exam, you have a major advantage: You have experienced the exam firsthand. Although future exams might have different questions, the topics and general "feel" of the exam will remain the same. Take some time to study areas from the book where you felt weak on the exam. You must wait a certain period between attempts, so use that time to make yourself more prepared in the areas in which you scored low.

640-721 IUWNE Exam Topics

Table I-1 lists the exam topics for the 640-721 IUWNE exam. This table also lists the book parts where each exam topic is covered.

Table I-1 *Exam Topics for 640-721 IUWNE Exam*

Book Part(s) Where Topic Is Covered	Exam Topic
Describe WLAN fundamentals	
Part I	Describe basics of spread spectrum technology (modulation, DSS, OFDM, MIMO, Channels reuse and overlap, Rate-shifting, CSMA/CA)

Table I-1   *Exam Topics for 640-721 IUWNE Exam*   *(continued)*

Book Part(s) Where Topic Is Covered	Exam Topic
Part I	Describe the impact of various wireless technologies (Bluetooth, WiMAX, ZigBee, cordless phone)
Part I	Describe wireless regulatory bodies, standards and certifications (FCC, ETSI, 802.11a/b/g/n, WiFi Alliance)
Part I	Describe WLAN RF principles (antenna types, RF gain/loss, EIRP, refraction, reflection, ETC)
Part I	Describe networking technologies used in wireless (SSID —> WLAN_ID —> Interface — >VLAN, 802.1Q trunking)
Part I	Describe wireless topologies (IBSS, BSS, ESS, Point-to-Point, Point-to-Multipoint, basic Mesh, bridging)
Part III	Describe 802.11 authentication and encryption methods (Open, Shared, 802.1X, EAP, TKIP, AES)
Part I	Describe frame types (associated/unassociated, management, control, data)
Install a basic Cisco wireless LAN	
Part II	Describe the basics of the Cisco Unified Wireless Network architecture (Split MAC, LWAPP, stand-alone AP versus controller-based AP, specific hardware examples)
Part II	Describe the Cisco Mobility Express Wireless architecture (Smart Business Communication System — SBCS, Cisco Config Agent — CCA, 526WLC, 521AP - stand-alone and controller-based)
Part II	Describe the modes of controller-based AP deployment (local, monitor, HREAP, sniffer, rogue detector, bridge)
Part II	Describe controller-based AP discovery and association (OTAP, DHCP, DNS, Master-Controller, Primary-Secondary-Tertiary, n+1 redundancy)
Part II	Describe roaming (Layer 2 and Layer 3, intra-controller and inter-controller, mobility groups)
Part II	Configure a WLAN controller and access points WLC: ports, interfaces, WLANs, NTP, CLI and Web UI, CLI wizard, LAG AP: Channel, Power
Part II	Configure the basics of a stand-alone access point (no lab) (Express setup, basic security)
Part II	Describe RRM

Table I-1 *Exam Topics for 640-721 IUWNE Exam* *(continued)*

Book Part(s) Where Topic Is Covered	Exam Topic
Install Wireless Clients	
Part II	Describe client OS WLAN configuration (Windows, Apple, and Linux.)
Part II	Install Cisco ADU
Part II	Describe basic CSSC
Part II	Describe CCX versions 1 through 5
Implement basic WLAN Security	
Part III	Describe the general framework of wireless security and security components (authentication, encryption, MFP, IPS)
Part III	Describe and configure authentication methods (Guest, PSK, 802.1X, WPA/WPA2 with EAP- TLS, EAP-FAST, PEAP, LEAP)
Part III	Describe and configure encryption methods (WPA/WPA2 with TKIP, AES)
Part III	Describe and configure the different sources of authentication (PSK, EAP-local or -external, Radius)
Operate basic WCS	
Part III	Describe key features of WCS and Navigator (versions and licensing)
Part III	Install/upgrade WCS and configure basic administration parameters (ports, O/S version, strong passwords, service vs. application)
Part III	Configure controllers and APs (using the Configuration tab not templates)
Part III	Configure and use maps in the WCS (add campus, building, floor, maps, position AP)
Part III	Use the WCS monitor tab and alarm summary to verify the WLAN operations
Conduct basic WLAN Maintenance and Troubleshooting	
Part III	Identify basic WLAN troubleshooting methods for controllers, access points, and clients methodologies
Part III	Describe basic RF deployment considerations related to site survey design of data or VoWLAN applications, Common RF interference sources such as devices, building material, AP location Basic RF site survey design related to channel reuse, signal strength, cell overlap

Table I-1   *Exam Topics for 640-721 IUWNE Exam   (continued)*

Book Part(s) Where Topic Is Covered	Exam Topic
Part III	Describe the use of WLC show, debug and logging
Part III	Describe the use of the WCS client troubleshooting tool
Part III	Transfer WLC config and O/S using maintenance tools and commands
Part III	Describe and differentiate WLC WLAN management access methods (console port, CLI, telnet, ssh, http, https, wired versus wireless management)

How This Book Is Organized

Although you can read this book cover to cover, it is designed to be flexible and allow you to easily move between chapters and sections of chapters to cover just the material that you need more work with. If you do intend to read all the chapters, the order in the book is an excellent sequence to use.

Part I, "Wireless LAN Fundamentals," consists of Chapters 1 through 9, which cover the following topics:

- **Chapter 1, "Introduction to Wireless Networking Concepts":** This chapter discusses the basics of wireless networking along with some of the challenges you may face. It is intended to be an introductory chapter to what you will be covering in chapters to come.

- **Chapter 2, "Standards Bodies":** This chapter focuses primarily on the standards bodies involved in wireless technology.

- **Chapter 3, "WLAN RF Principles":** This chapter discusses WLAN transmissions along with some of the influences on WLAN transmissions. You will also learn how to determine your signal strength and determine what may be influencing your wireless deployment.

- **Chapter 4, "WLAN Technologies and Topologies":** This chapter covers the various wireless topologies that you may come across, from Wireless Personal Area Networks (WPAN) to wireless LANs (WLAN). It also offers a further look at 802.11 topologies, including Ad-hoc mode and Infrastructure mode. In addition, you get a look at roaming and some vendor-specific topologies.

- **Chapter 5, "Antennae Communications":** This chapter focuses on antennas. It covers everything from how antennas work to how they are regulated. It even discusses the different types of antennas that Cisco offers.

- **Chapter 6, "Overview of the 802.11 WLAN Protocols":** This chapter examines each of the 802.11 protocols, including 802.11a, 802.11b. 802.11g, and even 802.11n.

- **Chapter 7, "Wireless Traffic Flow and AP Discovery":** This chapter disusses how traffic flows in a wireless network and shows you the various headers and communications. You will also learn how a client discovers an AP.

- **Chapter 8, "Additional Wireless Technologies":** This chapter takes into account the other wireless technologies that are seen in the market today, including Bluetooth, ZigBee, and WiMax.

- **Chapter 9, "Delivering Packets from the Wireless to Wired Network":** This chapter dives into the flow of a packet. You will actually experience the journey of a packet as it travels from the wireless to the wired network.

Part II, "Cisco Wireless LANs," which focuses primarily on configuration and consists of Chapters 10 through 16, covers the following topics:

- **Chapter 10, "Cisco Wireless Networks Architecture":** This chapter discusses the CUWN architecutre and the devices involved.

- **Chapter 11, "Controller Discovery and Association":** In this chapter, you will learn how an AP discovers a controller and associates with it. You will also learn what steps to take to provide controller redundancy.

- **Chapter 12, "Adding Mobility with Roaming":** This chapter discusses how clients roam, how the controllers are configured to support roaming, and all that is involved in asymmetric roaming, symmetric roaming, and mobility anchors.

- **Chapter 13, "Simple Network Configuration and Monitoring with the Cisco Controller":** This chapter is your first configuration chapter that gets into allowing client access. In this chapter, you will learn how to build a WLAN with open authentication.

- **Chapter 14, "Migrating Standalone APs to LWAPP":** This chapter discusses the process of migrating a standalone AP to LWAPP using various tools.

- **Chapter 15, "Cisco Mobility Express":** This chapter discusses the Mobility Express solution for small environments. In this chapter, you will learn how to configure the Cisco 526 controller and 521 AP.

- **Chapter 16, "Wireless Clients":** This chapter discusses the Windows wireless clients with the Wireless Zero Configuration utility, the Apple Airport utility, and the Linux Network Configuration utility. You will also learn how to set up the Aironet Desktop Utility (ADU) and the Cisco Secure Services Client (CSSC). Finally, you will learn about the Cisco Compatible Extensions Program (CCX).

Part III, "WLAN Maintenance and Administration," which consists of Chapters 17 through 20, covers the following topics:

- **Chapter 17, "Securing the Wireless Network":** This chapter discusses the various methods of securing wireless networks. This chapter covers the many EAP methods, 802,.1x, Wired Equivalent Privacy (WEP), and Wi-Fi Protected Access (WPA)/WPA2.

- **Chapter 18, "Enterprise Wireless Management with the WCS and the Location Appliance"**: This chapter introduces the Wireless Control System (WCS) that can be used to manage large depolyments with many controllers.

- **Chapter 19, "Maintaining Wireless Networks"**: This chapter discusses the management side of things. Here you learn how to perform mainentance tasks, including upgrades.

- **Chapter 20, "Troubleshooting Wireless Networks"**: This chapter discusses troubleshooting techniques for wireless networks using the various tools that are available. You will learn to use the command-line interface (CLI) of the controller as well as the WCS.

In addition to the 20 main chapters, this book includes tools to help you verify that you are prepared to take the exam. Chapter 21, "Final Preparation," includes guidelines that you can follow in the final days before the exam. Appendix A, "Answers to the 'Do I Know This Already?' Quizzes," will help you verify your knowledge based on the self-assessment quizzes at the beginning of each chapter. The Glossary helps to navigate you through the many terms associated with wireless networking. Also, the CD-ROM includes quiz questions and memory tables (refer to Appendix B and C on the CD-ROM) that you can work through to verify your knowledge of the subject matter.

Cisco Published 640-721 IUWNE Exam Topics Covered in This Part

Describe WLAN fundamentals

- Describe basics of spread spectrum technology (modulation, DSS, OFDM, MIMO, Channels reuse and overlap, Rate-shifting, CSMA/CA)

- Describe the impact of various wireless technologies (Bluetooth, WiMAX, ZigBee, cordless phone)

- Describe wireless regulatory bodies, standards and certifications (FCC, ETSI, 802.11a/b/g/n, WiFi Alliance)

- Describe WLAN RF principles (antenna types, RF gain/loss, EIRP, refraction, reflection, ETC)

- Describe networking technologies used in wireless (SSID —> WLAN_ID —> Interface — >VLAN, 802.1q trunking)

- Describe wireless topologies (IBSS, BSS, ESS, Point-to-Point, Point-to-Multipoint, basic Mesh, bridging)

- Describe frame types (associated/unassociated, management, control, data)

Part I: Wireless LAN Fundamentals

This chapter covers the following subjects:

Wireless Local-Area Networks: A brief history of wireless networking and some of the basic concepts.

How Bandwidth Is Achieved from RF Signals: The frequency spectrum used in RF transmissions.

Modulation Techniques and How They Work: How binary data is represented and transmitted using RF technology.

CHAPTER 1

Introduction to Wireless Networking Concepts

Perhaps this is the first time you have ever delved into the world of wireless networking. Or maybe you have been in networking for some time and are now beginning to see the vast possibilities that come with wireless networking. Either way, this chapter can help you understand topics that are not only tested on the CCNA Wireless exam but provide a good foundation for the chapters to come. If you are comfortable with the available frequency bands, the modulation techniques used in wireless LANs, and some of the standards and regulatory bodies that exist for wireless networking, you may want to skip to Chapter 2, "Standards Bodies."

This chapter provides a brief history of wireless networks and explores the basics of radio technology, the modulation techniques used, and some of the issues seen in wireless LANs.

You should do the "Do I Know This Already?" quiz first. If you score 80 percent or higher, you might want to skip to the section "Exam Preparation Tasks." If you score below 80 percent, you should spend the time reviewing the entire chapter. Refer to Appendix A, "Answers to the 'Do I Know This Already?' Quizzes" to confirm your answers.

"Do I Know This Already?" Quiz

The "Do I Know This Already?" quiz helps you determine your level of knowledge of this chapter's topics before you begin. Table 1-1 details the major topics discussed in this chapter and their corresponding quiz questions.

Table 1-1 *"Do I Know This Already?" Section-to-Question Mapping*

Foundation Topics Section	Questions
Wireless Local-Area Networks	1–2
How Bandwidth Is Achieved from RF Signals	3–6
Modulation Techniques and How They Work	7–10

1. Which of the following accurately describes the goal of RF technology?

   a. To send as much data as far as possible and as fast as possible

   b. To send secure data to remote terminals

   c. To send small amounts of data periodically

   d. To send data and voice short distances using encryption

2. Which of the following is a significant problem experienced with wireless networks?

   a. Infection

   b. Policing

   c. Transmission

   d. Interference

3. Which two of the following are unlicensed frequency bands used in the United Stated? (Choose two.)

   a. 2.0 MHz

   b. 2.4 GHz

   c. 5.0 GHz

   d. 6.8 GHz

4. Each 2.4-GHz channel is how many megahertz wide?

   a. 22 MHz

   b. 26 MHz

   c. 24 MHz

   d. 28 MHz

5. How many nonoverlapping channels exist in the 2.4-GHz ISM range?

   a. 9

   b. 3

   c. 17

   d. 13

6. The 5.0-GHz range is used by which two of the following 802.11 standards? (Choose two.)

   a. 802.11

   b. 802.11b/g

   c. 802.11n

   d. 802.11a

7. Which three of the following modulation techniques do WLANs today use? (Choose three.)

   a. OFDM

   b. AM

   c. FM

   d. DSSS

   e. MIMO

8. DSSS uses a chipping code to encode redundant data into the modulated signal. Which two of the following are examples of chipping codes that DSSS uses? (Choose two.)

   a. Barker code

   b. Baker code

   c. Complementary code keying (CCK)

   d. Cypher block chaining (CBC)

9. DSSS binary phase-shift keying uses what method of encoding at the 1-Mbps data rate?

   a. 11-chip Barker code

   b. 8-chip CCK

   c. 11-chip CCK

   d. 8-chip Barker code

10. With DRS, when a laptop operating at 11 Mbps moves farther away from an access point, what happens?

   a. The laptop roams to another AP.

   b. The laptop loses its connection.

   c. The rate shifts dynamically to 5.5 Mbps.

   d. The rate increases, providing more throughput.

Foundation Topics

Wireless Local-Area Networks

Although wireless networking began to penetrate the market in the 1990s, the technology has actually been around since the 1800s. A musician and astronomer, Sir William Herschel (1738 to 1822) made a discovery that infrared light existed and was beyond the visibility of the human eye. The discovery of infrared light led the way to the electromagnetic wave theory, which was explored in-depth by a man named James Maxwell (1831 to 1879). Much of his discoveries related to electromagnetism were based on research done by Michael Faraday (1791 to 1867) and Andre-Marie Ampere (1775 to 1836), who were researchers that came before him. Heinrich Hertz (1857 to 1894) built on the discoveries of Maxwell by proving that electromagnetic waves travel at the speed of light and that electricity can be carried on these waves.

Although these discoveries are interesting, you might be asking yourself how they relate to wireless local-area networks (WLANs). Here is the tie-in: In standard LANs, data is propagated over wires such as an Ethernet cable, in the form of electrical signals. The discovery that Hertz made opens the airways to transfer the same data, as electrical signals, without wires. Therefore, the simple answer to the relationship between WLANs and the other discoveries previously mentioned is that a WLAN is a LAN that does not need cables to transfer data between devices, and this technology exists because of the research and discoveries that Herschel, Maxwell, Ampere, and Hertz made. This is accomplished by way of Radio Frequencies (RF).

With RF, the goal is to send as much data as far as possible and as fast as possible. The problem is the numerous influences on radio frequencies that need to be either overcome or dealt with. One of these problems is interference, which is discussed at length in Chapter 5, "Antennae Communications." For now, just understand that the concept of wireless LANs is doable, but it is not always going to be easy. To begin to understand how to overcome the issues, and for that matter what the issues are, you need to understand how RF is used.

How Bandwidth Is Achieved from RF Signals

To send data over the airwaves, the IEEE has developed the 802.11 specification, which defines half-duplex operations using the same frequency for send and receive operations on a WLAN. No licensing is required to use the 802.11 standards; however, you must follow the rules that the FCC has set forth. The IEEE defines standards that help to operate within the FCC rules. The FCC governs not only the frequencies that can be used without licenses but the power levels at which WLAN devices can operate, the transmission technologies that can be used, and the locations where certain WLAN devices can be deployed.

Note: The FCC is the regulatory body that exists in the United States. The *European Telecommunications Standards Institute* (ETSI) is the European equivalent to the FCC. Other countries have different regulatory bodies.

To achieve bandwidth from RF signals, you need to send data as electrical signals using some type of emission method. One such emission method is known as Spread Spectrum. In 1986, the FCC agreed to allow the use of spread spectrum in the commercial market using what is known as the industry, scientific, and medical (ISM) frequency bands. To place data on the RF signals, you use a modulation technique. Modulation is the addition of data to a carrier signal. You are probably familiar with this already. To send music, news, or speech over the airwaves, you use *frequency modulation* (FM) or *amplitude modulation* (AM). The last time you were sitting in traffic listening to the radio, you were using this technology.

Unlicensed Frequency Bands Used in WLANs

As you place more information on a signal, you use more frequency spectrum, or band-width. You may be familiar with using terms like *bits*, *kilobits*, megabits, and gigabits when you refer to bandwidth. In wireless networking, the word *bandwidth* can mean two different things. In one sense of the word, it can refer to data rates. In another sense of the word, it can refer to the width of an RF channel.

Note: This book uses the term *bandwidth* to refer to the width of the RF channel and not to data rates.

When referring to bandwidth in a wireless network, the standard unit of measure is the Hertz (Hz). A Hertz measures the number of cycles per second. One Hertz is one cycle per second. In radio technology, a *Citizens' Band* (CB) radio is pretty low quality. It uses about 3 kHz of bandwidth. FM radio is generally a higher quality, using about 175 kHz of bandwidth. Compare that to a television signal, which sends both voice and video over the air. The TV signal you receive uses almost 4500 kHz of bandwidth.

Figure 1-1 shows the entire electromagnetic spectrum. Notice that the frequency ranges used in CB radio, FM radio, and TV broadcasts are only a fraction of the entire spectrum. Most of the spectrum is governed by folks like the FCC. This means that you cannot use the same frequencies that FM radio uses in your wireless networks.

As Figure 1-1 illustrates, the electromagnetic spectrum spans from Extremely Low Frequency (ELF) at 3 to 30 Hz to Extremely High Frequency (EHF) at 30 GHz to 300 GHz. The data you send is not done so in either of these ranges. In fact, the data you send using WLANs is either in the 900-MHz, 2.4-GHz, or 5-GHz frequency ranges. This places you in the Ultra High Frequency (UHF) or Super High Frequency (SHF) ranges. Again, this is just a fraction of the available spectrum, but remember that the FCC controls it. You are locked into the frequency ranges you can use. Table 1-2 lists the ranges that can be used in the United States, along with the frequency ranges allowed in Japan and Europe.

The Entire Electromagnetic Radio Spectrum										
ELF	SLF	ULF	VLF	LF	MF	HF	VHF	UHF	SHF	EHF
3 Hz	30 Hz	300 Hz	3 kHz	30 kHz	300 kHz	3 MHz	30 MHz	300 MHz	3 GHz	30 GHz
30 Hz	300 Hz	3 kHz	30 kHz	300 kHz	3 MHz	30 MHz	300 MHz	3 GHz	30 GHz	300 GHz

Figure 1-1   *Electromagnetic Spectrum*

**Key
Topic**

Table 1-2   *Usable Frequency Bands in Europe, the United States, and Japan*

Europe	USA	Japan	Frequency
2.4 GHz	900 MHz		
	2.4 GHz ISM		2.0–2.4835 GHz
		2.4 GHz	2.0–2.495 GHz
CEPT A	UNII-1	5.15–5.25 GHz	5.15–5.25 GHz
CEPT A	UNII-2		5.25–5.35 GHz
CEPT B	UNII-2 Extended		5.47–5.7253 GHz
	ISM		5.725–5.850 GHz
		5.0 GHz	5.038–5.091 GHz
		4.9 GHz	4.9–5.0 GHz

Table 1-2 clearly shows that not all things are equal, depending on which country you are in. In Europe, the 2.4-GHz range and the 5.0-GHz range are used. The 5.0-GHz frequency ranges that are used in Europe are called the Conference of European Post and Telecommunication (CEPT) A, CEPT B, CEPT C, and CEPT C bands. In the United States, the 900-MHz, 2.4-GHz ISM, and 5.0-GHz Unlicensed National Information Infrastructure (UNII) bands are used. Japan has its own ranges in the 2.4- and 5.0-GHz range. The following sections explain the U.S. frequency bands in more detail.

900 MHz

The 900-MHz band starts at 902 MHz and goes to 928 MHz. This frequency range is likely the most familiar to you because you probably had a cordless phone that operated in this range. This is a good way to understand what wireless channels are. You might have picked up your cordless phone only to hear a lot of static or even a neighbor on his cordless phone. If this happened, you could press the Channel button to switch to a channel that did not have as much interference. When you found a clear channel, you could make your call. The channel you were changing to was simply a different range of frequencies. This way, even though both your phone and your neighbor's were operating in the 900-MHz range, you could select a channel in that range and have more than one device operating at the same time.

2.4 GHz

The 2.4-GHz range is probably the most widely used frequency range in WLANs. It is used by the 802.11, 802.11b, 802.11g, and 802.11n IEEE standards. The 2.4-GHz frequency range that can be used by WLANs is subdivided into channels that range from 2.4000 to 2.4835 GHz. The United States has 11 channels, and each channel is 22-MHz wide. Some channels overlap with others and cause interference. For this reason, channels 1, 6, and 11 are most commonly used because they do not overlap. In fact, many consumer-grade wireless devices are hard set so you can choose only one of the three channels. Figure 1-2 shows the 11 channels, including overlap. Again, notice that channels 1, 6, and 11 do not overlap.

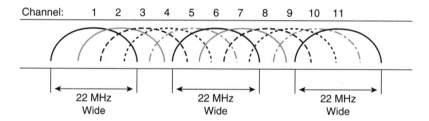

Figure 1-2 *2.4-GHz Channels*

With 802.11b and 802.11g, the energy is spread out over a wide area of the band. With 802.11b or 802.11g products, the channels have a bandwidth of 22 MHz. This allows three nonoverlapping, noninterfering channels to be used in the same area.

The 2.4-GHz range uses *direct sequence spread spectrum* (DSSS) modulation. DSSS is discussed later in this chapter in the section "DSSS." Data rates of 1 Mbps, 2 Mbps, 5.5 Mbps, and 11 Mbps are defined for this range.

5 GHz

The 5-GHz range is used by the 802.11a standard and the new 802.11n draft standard. In the 802.11a standard, data rates can range from 6 Mbps to 54 Mbps. 802.11a devices were not seen in the market until 2001, so they do not have quite the market penetration as 2.4-GHz range 802.11 b devices. The 5-GHz range is also subdivided into channels, each being 20-MHz wide. A total of 23 nonoverlapping channels exist in the 5-GHz range.

The 5-GHz ranges use *Orthogonal Frequency Division Multiplexing* (OFDM). OFDM is discussed later in this chapter in the section "OFDM." Data rates of 6, 9, 12, 18, 24, 36, 48, and 54 Mbps are defined.

Modulation Techniques and How They Work

In short, the process of *modulation* is the varying in a signal or a tone called a *carrier signal*. Data is then added to this carrier signal in a process known as *encoding*.

Imagine that you are singing a song. Words are written on a sheet of music. If you just read the words, your tone is soft and does not travel far. To convey the words to a large group, you use your vocal chords and modulation to send the words farther. While you are singing the song, you encode the written words into a waveform and let your vocal cords modulate it. People hear you singing and decode the words to understand the meaning of the song.

Modulation is what wireless networks use to send data. It enables the sending of encoded data using radio signals. Wireless networks use modulation as a carrier signal, which means that the modulated tones carry data. A modulated waveform consists of three parts:

Amplitude:	The volume of the signal
Phase:	The timing of the signal between peaks
Frequency:	The pitch of the signal

Wireless networks use a few different modulation techniques, including these:

DSSS

OFDM

Multiple-Input Multiple-Output (MIMO)

The sections that follow cover these modulation techniques in further detail.

DSSS

DSSS is the modulation technique that 802.11b devices use to send the data. In DSSS, the transmitted signal is spread across the entire frequency spectrum that is being used. For example, an access point that is transmitting on channel 1 spreads the carrier signal across the 22-MHz-wide channel range of 2.401 to 2.423 GHz.

To encode data using DSSS, you use a chip sequence. A chip and a bit are essentially the same thing, but a bit represents the data, and a chip is used for the carrier encoding. Encoding is the process of transforming information from one format to another. To understand how data is encoded in a wireless network and then modulated, you must first understand chipping codes.

Chipping Codes

Because of the possible noise interference with a wireless transmission, DSSS uses a sequence of chips. When DSSS spreads information across a frequency range, it sends a single data bit as a string of chips or a *chip stream*. With redundant data being sent, if some of the signal is lost to noise, the data can likely still be understood. The chipping code process takes each data bit and then expands it into a string of bits.

Figure 1-3 illustrates this process for better understanding.

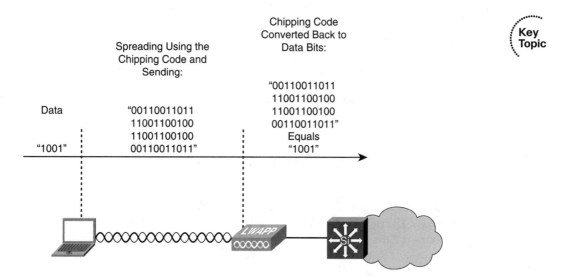

Key
Topic

Figure 1-3 *Chipping Sequence*

As the laptop in the figure sends data over the wireless network, the data must be encoded using a chip sequence and then modulated over the airwaves. In the figure, the chipping code for the bit value of **1** is expanded to the chip sequence of 00110011011, and the chipping code for the bit value of **0** is 11001100100. Therefore, after the data bits are sent, **1001** creates the chip sequence.

00110011011	11001100100	11001100100	00110011011
1	0	0	1

You can decode this chip sequence back to the value of 1001 at the receiving access point. Remember, because of interference, it is still possible that some of the bits in the chip sequence will be lost or inverted. This means that a 1 could become a 0 and a 0 could become a 1. This is okay, because more than five bits need to be inverted to change the value between a 1 and a 0. Because of this, using a chipping sequence makes 802.11 networks more resilient against interference.

Also, because more bits are sent for chipping (carrier) than there is actual data, the chipping rate is higher than the data rate.

Barker Code

To achieve rates of 1 Mbps and 2 Mbps, 802.11 uses a Barker code. This code defines the use of 11 chips when encoding the data. The 11-chip Barker code used in 802.11 is 10110111000. Certain mathematical details beyond the scope of this book make the Barker code ideal for modulating radio waves. In the end, and for the exam, each bit of data sent is encoded into an 11-bit Barker code and then modulated with DSSS.

Complementary Code Keying

When you are using DSSS, the Barker code works well for lower data rates such as 1-Mbps, 2-Mbps, 5.5-Mbps, and 11-Mbps. DSSS uses a different method for higher data rates, which allows the 802.11 standard to achieve rates of 5.5 and 11 Mbps. Complementary code keying (CCK) uses a series of codes called complementary sequences. There are 64 unique code words. Up to 6 bits can be represented by a code word, as opposed to the 1 bit represented by a Barker code.

DSSS Modulation Techniques and Encoding

Now that the data has been encoded using Barker code or CCK, it needs to be transmitted or modulated out of the radio antennas. You can think of it this way:

- Encoding is how the changes in RF signal translate to the 1s and 0s.
- Modulation is the characteristic of the RF signal that is manipulated.

For example, amplitude modulation, frequency modulation, and phase-shift keying are modulations. The encoding would be that a 180-degree phase shift is a 1, and 0-degree phase shift is a 0. This is binary phase-shift keying. In 802.11b, the data is modulated on a carrier wave, and that carrier wave is spread across the frequency range using DSSS. 802.11b can modulate and encode the data using the methods seen in Table 1-3.

Key Topic

Table 1-3 *DSSS Encoding Methods*

Data Rate	Encoding	Modulation
1	11 chip Barker coding	DSSS Binary Phase Shift Keying
2	11 chip Barker coding	DSSS Quadrature Phase Shift Keying
5.5	8 chip encoding 8 bits CCK coding	DSSS Quadrature Phase Shift Keying
11	8 chip encoding 4 bits CCK coding	DSSS Quadrature Phase Shift Keying

One method of modulation that is simple to understand is amplitude modulation. With amplitude modulation, the information sent is based on the amplitude of the signal. For example, +5 volts is a 1, and –5 volts is a 0. Because of external factors, the amplitude of a signal is likely changed, and this in turn modifies the information you are sending. This makes AM a "not-so-good" solution for sending important data. However, other factors, such as frequency and phase, are not likely to change. 802.11b uses phase to modulate the data. Specifically, in 802.11b, BPSK and QPSK are used.

BPSK

Remember that phase is timing between peaks in the signal. Actually, that needs to be expanded further so you can really grasp the concept of BPSK and QPSK. To begin, look at Figure 1-4, which shows a waveform. This waveform, or motion, is happening over a period of time.

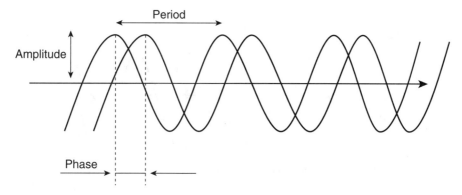

Figure 1-4 *Waveform*

Figure 1-4 illustrates the next step in determining phase. The phase is the difference between the two waveforms at the same frequency. If the waveforms peak at the same time, they are said to be *in-phase*, or 0 degrees. If the two waves peak at different times, they are said to be *out-of-phase*. Phase-shift keying (PSK) represents information by changing the phase of the signal.

BPSK is the simplest method of PSK. In BPSK, two phases are used that are separated by 180 degrees. BPSK can modulate 1 bit per symbol. To simplify this, a phase shift of 180 degrees is a 1, and a phase shift of 0 degrees is a 0, as illustrated in Figure 1-5.

802.11 also uses quadrature phase-shift keying (QPSK), which is discussed in the following section.

QPSK

In BPSK, 1 bit per symbol is encoded. This is okay for lower data rates. QPSK has the capability to encode 2 bits per symbol. This doubles the data rates available in BPSK while staying within the same bandwidth. At the 2-Mbps data rate, QPSK is used with Barker encoding. At the 5.5-Mbps data rate, QPSK is also used, but the encoding is CCK-16. At the 11-Mbps data rate, QPSK is also used, but the encoding is CCK-128.

OFDM

OFDM is not considered a spread spectrum technology, but it is used for modulation in wireless networks. Using OFDM, you can achieve the highest data rates with the maximum resistance to corruption of the data caused by interference. OFDM defines a number of channels in a frequency range. These channels are further divided into a larger number of small-bandwidth subcarriers. The channels are 20 MHz, and the subcarriers are

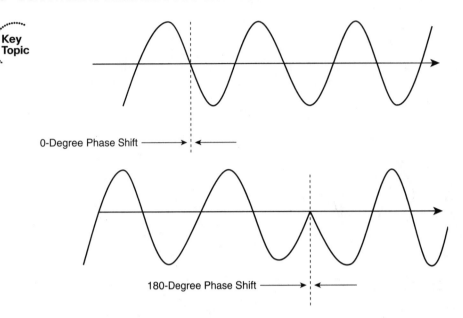

Figure 1-5   *Encoding with Phase Shifting*

300 kHz wide. You end up with 52 subcarriers per channel. Each of the subcarriers has a low data rate, but the data is sent simultaneously over the subcarriers in parallel. This is how you can achieve higher data rates.

OFDM is not used in 802.11b because 802.11b devices use DSSS. 802.11g and 802.11a both used OFDM. The way they are implemented is a little different because 802.11g is designed to operate in the 2.4-MHz range along with 802.11b devices. Chapter 2, "Standards Bodies," covers the differences in the OFDM implementations.

MIMO

MIMO is a technology that is used in the new 802.11n specification. Although at press time, the 802.11n specification had not yet been ratified by the IEEE, many vendors are already releasing products into the market that claim support for it. Here is what you need to know about it, though. A device that uses MIMO technology uses multiple antennas for receiving signals (usually two or three) in addition to multiple antennas for sending signals. MIMO technology can offer data rates higher than 100 Mbps by multiplexing data streams simultaneously in one channel. In other words, if you want data rates higher than 100-Mbps, then multiple streams are sent over a bonded channel, not just one. Using advanced signal processing, the data can be recovered after being sent on two or more spatial streams.

With the use of MIMO technology, an access point (AP) can talk to non-MIMO-capable devices and still offer about a 30 percent increase in performance of standard 802.11a/b/g networks.

Dynamic Rate Shifting

Now that you have an idea of how data is encoded and modulated, things will start to get a little easier. Another important aspect to understand, not only for the exam but for actual wireless deployments, is that the farther away you get from the access point, the lower the data rates are that you can achieve. This is true regardless of the technology. Although you can achieve higher data rates with different standards, you still have this to deal with.

All Cisco wireless products can perform a function called dynamic rate shifting (DRS). In 802.11 networks, operating in the 2.4-GHz range, the devices can rate-shift from 11 Mbps to 5.5 Mbps, and further to 2 and 1 Mbps depending on the circumstances. It even happens without dropping your connection. Also, it is done on a transmission-by-transmission basis, so if you shift from 11 Mbps to 5.5 Mbps for one transmission and then move closer to the AP, it can shift back up to 11 Mbps for the next transmission.

This process also occurs with 802.11g and 802.11a. In all deployments, DRS supports multiple clients operating at multiple rates.

Sending Data Using CSMA/CA

Wireless networks have to deal with the possibility of collisions. This is because, in a wireless topology, the behavior of the AP is similar to that of a hub. Multiple client devices can send at the same time. When this happens, just like in a wired network where a hub exists, a collision can occur. The problem with wireless networks is that they cannot tell when a collision has occurred. If you are in a wired network, a jam signal is heard by listening to the wire. To listen for a jam signal, wireless devices need two antennas. They can send using one antenna while listening for a jam signal with the other. Although this sounds feasible, especially because MIMO technology defines the use of multiple antennas, the transmitting signal from one antenna would drown out the received signal on the other, so the jam signal would not be heard.

To avoid collisions on a wireless network, carrier sense multiple access collision avoidance (CSMA/CA) is used. You are probably familiar with carrier sense multiple access collision detect (CSMA/CD), which is used on wired networks. Although the two are similar, collision avoidance means that when a device wishes to send, it must listen first. If the channel is considered idle, the device sends a signal informing others that it is going to send data and that they should not send. It then listens again for a period before sending. Another way to supplement this is using request to send (RTS) and clear to send (CTS) packets. With the RTS/CTS method, the sending device uses an RTS packet, and the intended receiver uses a CTS packet. This alerts other devices that they should not send for a period.

Exam Preparation Tasks

Review All Key Concepts

Review the most important topics from this chapter, noted with the Key Topics icon in the outer margin of the page. Table 1-4 lists a reference of these key topics and the page number where you can find each one.

Table 1-4   *Key Topics for Chapter 1*

Key Topic Item	Description	Page Number
Figure 1-1	The electromagnetic spectrum	10
Table 1-2	The usable frequency bands for WLANs in the United States, Europe, and Japan	10
Figure 1-2	The 2.4-GHz channels	11
Figure 1-3	Understanding chipping sequences	13
Table 1-3	DSSS encoding methods	14
Figure 1-5	Phase-shift encoding and how it works	16

Complete the Tables and Lists from Memory

Print a copy of Appendix B, "Memory Tables," (found on the CD) or at least the section for this chapter, and complete the tables and lists from memory. Appendix C, "Memory Tables Answer Key," also on the CD, includes completed tables and lists to check your work.

Definition of Key Terms

Define the following key terms from this chapter, and check your answers in the Glossary:

FCC, IEEE, ETSI, bandwidth, Hz, ISM, UNII, channels, DSSS, OFDM, amplitude, phase, frequency, chipping code, Barker code, CCK, BPSK, QPSK, MIMO, DRS, CSMA/CA, RTS, CTS

This chapter covers the following subjects:

Wireless Standards and Regulatory Committees: Looks at the wireless regulatory committess and some of their requirements.

Wi-Fi Certification: Discusses how Wi-Fi devices are certified for interoperability.

CHAPTER 2

Standards Bodies

It took a long time for wireless to come together as we know it today. If it weren't for the standards bodies and committees, there's no telling where the technology would be. In this chapter, you will look at the standards bodies as well as the bodies that regulate the airwaves.

Take the "Do I Know This Already?" quiz first. If you do well on the quiz, you may want to skim through this chapter and continue to the next. If you score low on the quiz, you should spend some time reading through the chapter. These standards are important because they are something you will deal with on a day-to-day basis in wireless networking. Refer to Appendix A, "Answers to the 'Do I Know This Already?' Quizzes" to confirm your answers.

"Do I Know This Already?" Quiz

The "Do I Know This Already?" quiz helps you determine your level of knowledge of this chapter's topics before you begin. Table 2-1 details the major topics discussed in this chapter and their corresponding quiz questions.

Table 2-1 *"Do I Know This Already?" Section-to-Question Mapping*

Foundation Topics Section	Questions
Wireless Standards and Regulatory Committees	1–8
Wi-Fi Certification	9–10

 1. The FCC regulates wireless usage in which of the following countries?

  a. United States of America

  b. United Arab Emirates

  c. United Kingdom

  d. Europe, Asia, and Asia

2. True or false: The U.S. complies with ETSI standards of EIRP.

   a.   True

   b.   False

3. What is the maximum EIRP for point-to-multipoint in Europe? (Choose all that apply.)

   a.   20 dBm

   b.   17 dBi

   c.   17 dBm

   d.   36 dBm

4. The FCC regulates EIRP in the U.S. to a maximum of _____ for point-to-point and _____ for point-to-multipoint.

   a.   36 dBm, 36 dBm

   b.   30 dBm, 17 dBm

   c.   17 dBm, 36, dBm

   d.   36 dBm, 17 dBm

5. The IEEE committees work on which of the following wireless standards? (Choose all that apply.)

   a.   802.11a

   b.   802.11g

   c.   802.11x

   d.   802.1q

   e.   802.11b

6. True or false: The IEEE is a regulatory body in the U.S. that controls the usage of wireless frequencies.

   a.   True

   b.   False

7. In Europe, can a professional installer increase the gain on wireless antennas?

    a. Yes, provided that he or she decreases the transmit power using a 1:1 ratio.

    b. No; this is illegal.

    c. Only with a wavier.

    d. Antennas don't have anything to do with gain.

8. The FCC regulates that professional installers maintain what ratio of gain to transmit power when increasing the gain of an antenna?

    a. 3:1

    b. 1:1

    c. 6:1

    d. 1:3

9. Which organization certifies interoperability for wireless equipment?

    a. Wi-Max Alliance

    b. IEEE

    c. Wi-Fi Alliance

    d. FRF.12

10. Certification of wireless equipment includes which protocols and standards for interoperability? (Choose two.)

    a. 802.11a/b/g

    b. IPsec

    c. WPA/WPA2

    d. Zigbee

Foundation Topics

Wireless Standards and Regulatory Committees

Many people benefit from the availability of wireless Internet access as they travel to various parts of the world. Without regulatory committees and organizations to ensure the proper use and interoperability of equipment, it's likely that people could not connect from place to place. To ensure that certain rules governing the use of wireless RF are adhered to, numerous country-specific organizations and global committees monitor standards and usage. This chapter discusses some of them.

FCC

The Federal Communications Commission (FCC) is an independent agency in the United States that regulates communication methods. It is held directly responsible by Congress. It is the FCC in the United States that governs the frequency ranges that can be used without a license, the transmit power of devices, the types of devices that can be used indoors as well as outdoors, and how the various types of hardware can be used. The FCC exists because of the Communications Act of 1934.

Note: The FCC website is http://www.fcc.gov.

When it comes to the FCC and Cisco wireless, it's important to know the requirements defined in *FCC - Part 15 - Antenna Requirements*. This federal requirement states that antennas must use a unique nonstandard connector that cannot be acquired easily. The reason for not being acquired easily is to ensure that home users and noncertified installers cannot easily deploy an antenna that goes beyond the regulated values. For this reason, Cisco uses a connector known as the Reverse-Polarity-Threaded Neil-Concelman (RP-TNC) connector, as shown in Figure 2-1.

Figure 2-1   *RP-TNC Connector*

What makes this connector unique is that the center contacts are reversed so that you can't use a store-bought antenna with a Cisco wireless device. If you did so, you might violate the FCC regulatory requirements.

In addition to the antenna rules, the FCC defines power output rules that must be followed. There are rules for everyday people to follow, and rules for people who are considered professionals in the field. A professional has a little more leeway than someone who buys a wireless device at the local electronics store. To get an idea of these rules, you can look at the 2.4-GHz EIRP Output Rules. Effective Isotropic Radiated Power (EIRP) is a way to measure the amount of energy radiated from an antenna. EIRP is an important concept to understand, especially when you're dealing with regulatory bodies. It's important that the EIRP not exceed that mandated by the governing bodies. These rules are designed for point-to-point scenarios as well as point-to-multipoint. The point-to-point rules are as follows:

■ You can have a maximum of 36-dBm EIRP.

■ You can have a maximum of 30-dBm transmitter power with 6-dBi gain of antenna and cable combined.

■ You are allowed a 1:1 ratio of power to gain.

For point-to-multipoint scenarios, you are allowed the same maximum EIRP and the same maximum transmitter power and antenna gain; however, you can exceed the 36-dBm EIRP rule using a 3:1 ratio of power to gain.

Table 2-2 compares the FCC maximum requirements for point-to-point to the Cisco maximum.

Table 2-2 *FCC Antenna Requirements Versus Cisco Standards for Point-to-Point Environments*

	Transmitter Power	Maximum Gain	EIRP
FCC Maximum	30-dBm	6-dBm	36-dBm
Cisco Maximum	20-dBm	36-dBm	56-dBm

Table 2-3 compares the FCC maximum requirements for point-to-multipoint to the Cisco maximum.

Table 2-3 *FCC Antenna Requirements Versus Cisco Standards for Point-to-Multipoint Environments*

	Transmitter Power	Maximum Gain	EIRP
FCC Maximum	30-dBm	6-dBm	36-dBm
Cisco Maximum	20-dBm	36-dBm	36-dBm

ETSI

The European Telecommunication Standards Institute (ETSI) is the not-for-profit organization that standardizes the frequencies and power levels used in Europe as well as many other countries. The European Commission (EC) recognizes ETSI as an official European Standards Organization. Many of the mandates for wireless usage come from the EC. Then, ETSI defines various standards based on these mandates. According to the ETSI website, the ETSI has almost 700 members in 60 countries.

Similar to the FCC, the ETSI has 2.4-GHz EIRP output rate standards that you should be familiar with. The ETSI's rules, however, are different from the FCC's rules. ETSI defines 20-dBm EIRP on point-to-multipoint and on point-to-point with 17-dBm maximum transmit power with 3-dBi gain. In a way, this is easier to remember, because these numbers are the same value for both point-to-point and point-to-multipoint connections. Of course, a professional installer can increase the gain as long as he or she lowers the transmit power below 17 dBm at a ratio of 1:1. Therefore, a professional installer could drop the transmit power by 1 dBm and increase the gain by 1 dBm and still stay within the guidelines.

Table 2-4 compares the Cisco standards to the ETSI standards for EIRP. The table shows the governing body maximum transmitted power, maximum gain, and EIRP compared to that of the Cisco integated antennas. You can see that the Cisco antenna has a transmit power of 17 dBm and a maximum gain of 2.2 dBi and ends up with an EIRP of 19.2 dBm, which is lower than the 20 dBm allowed by the governing bodies. If you reduced the transmit power to 15 dBm and increased the maximum gain to 5 dBi, the resulting EIRP would be 20 dBm, which is still within the guidelines of the governing body. Likewise, reducing the transmit power to 13 dBm and increasing the gain to 7 dBi keeps the EIRP at 20 dBm—within the guidelines.

Key Topic

Table 2-4   *Cisco Versus ETSI EIRP Standards for Point-to-Point and Point-to-Multipoint Environments*

	Transmitter Power (dBm)	Maximum Gain (dBi)	EIRP (dBm)
Governing Body Maximum	17	3	20
Cisco Integrated Antennas	17	2.2	19.2
Reduced Tx Power	15	5	20
Reduced Tx Power	13	7	20
Reduced Tx Power	7	13	20
Reduced Tx Power	0	20	20

IEEE

The Institute of Electrical and Electronics Engineers (IEEE) is a not-for-profit organization that has more than 370,000 members globally. It has 319 sections in ten geographic areas. It has defined more than 900 standards and has another 400 in development.

Note: For a history of the IEEE, see http://ieee.org/web/aboutus/history/index.html.

The IEEE's "Wireless Standards Zone" is dedicated to standards that are related to wireless technology. Here you can find information about the 802 protocols, such as the following:

- **802.11:** The Working Group for Wireless LAN

- **802.15:** The Working Group for Wireless PAN

- **802.16:** The Working Group for Broadband Wireless Access Standards

Note: You can find the Wireless Standards Zone at http://standards.ieee.org/wireless/ and an overview of the aforementioned working groups at http://standards.ieee.org/wireless/overview.html.

This book focuses mainly on the 802.11a, 802.11b, 802.11g, and 802.11n protocols. These protocols are for wireless LANs.

Wi-Fi Certification

Into the arena of interoperability testing enters the Wi-Fi Alliance. The Wi-Fi Alliance is a not-for-profit organization that certifies the interoperability of more than 4200 products. The Wi-Fi Alliance was formed in 1999 and currently has more than 300 members in more than 20 countries. What makes this organization different from the ETSI, FCC, and IEEE is that it gives its seal of approval to devices that plan in interoperability. The next time you're at the electronics shop, flip over one of the wireless products; you might find it to be Wi-Fi Certified. If so, you will notice that the 802.11a, 802.11b, and 802.11g protocols are certified if the device can use them as well as security protocols such as WPA and WPA2. Usually, the label has a checkmark next to what the device is certified for.

Note: The Wi-Fi alliance can be found at http://www.wi-fi.org.

Exam Preparation Tasks

Review All the Key Topics

Review the most important topics from this chapter, denoted with the Key Topic icon. Table 2-5 lists these key topics and the page number where you can find each one.

Table 2-5 *Key Topics for Chapter 2*

Key Topic Item	Description	Page Number
Table 2-2	FCC antenna requirements versus Cisco standards (point-to-point)	25
Table 2-3	FCC antenna requirements versus Cisco standards (point-to-multipoint)	25
Table 2-4	Cisco versus ETSI EIRP standards (point-to-point and point-to-multipoint)	26

Complete the Tables and Lists from Memory

Print a copy of Appendix B, "Memory Tables," (found on the CD) or at least the section for this chapter, and complete the tables and lists from memory. Appendix C, "Memory Tables Answer Key," also on the CD, includes completed tables and lists to check your work.

Definition of Key Terms

Define the following key terms from this chapter, and check your answers in the glossary:

FCC, IEEE, ETSI, W-Fi Alliance, EIRP

This chapter covers the following subjects:

Characteristics of Wireless Networks:
Provides a review of wireless transmissions.

Influences on Wireless Transmissions:
Covers the different elements that can affect wireless transmissions.

Determining Signal Strength Influences:
Describes how to determine your signal strength and what might be influencing your wireless deployment.

CHAPTER 3

WLAN RF Principles

In wireless technologies, you need to understand what influences act on wireless transmissions. This chapter reviews the characteristics of wireless transmissions and the influences that act on them, sometimes causing problems. Some of the material covered in the first section, "Characteristics of Wireless Networks," is a review of information you learned in Chapter 1, "Introduction to Wireless Networking Concepts." If you are comfortable with your knowledge of this information, you can just review the key topics at the end of this chapter.

The second section of this chapter covers influences on wireless transmissions. These are usually drawbacks, so you should become familiar with them. The third part of this chapter discusses ways to determine signal strength and other influences on wireless signals.

You should do the "Do I Know This Already?" quiz first. If you score 80% or higher, you might want to skip to the section "Exam Preparation Tasks." If you score below 80%, you should spend the time reviewing the entire chapter. Refer to Appendix A, "Answers to the 'Do I Know This Already?' Quizzes" to confirm your answers.

"Do I Know This Already?" Quiz

The "Do I Know This Already?" quiz helps you determine your level of knowledge of this chapter's topics before you begin. Table 3-1 details the major topics discussed in this chapter and their corresponding quiz questions.

Table 3-1 *"Do I Know This Already?" Section-to-Question Mapping*

Foundation Topics Section	Questions
Characteristics of Wireless Networks	1–3
Influences on Wireless Transmissions	4–9
Determining Signal Strength Influences	10–11

1. Which of the following best describes a frequency that is seen 1 million times per second?

   a.   1 Hz

   b.   1000000 Mb

   c.   1 joule

   d.   1 MHz

2. What does amplitude measure?

   a.   Distance from high crest to high crest horizontally in a waveform

   b.   Distance between two access points

   c.   Distance from low crest to midspan in a waveform

   d.   Height of wave from lowest crest to highest crest

3. EIRP is calculated using which of the following formulas?

   a.   EIRP = transmitter power – cable loss + antenna gain

   b.   EIRP = interference – cable loss + antenna gain

   c.   EIRP = cable gain – cable loss + antenna gain

   d.   EIRP = transmitter loss + cable loss + antenna gain

4. Metal desks, glass, light fixtures, and computer screens can contribute to which influence on wireless transmissions?

   a.   Scattering

   b.   Refraction

   c.   Reflection

   d.   Absorption

5. Carpet, human bodies, and walls can contribute to which influence on wireless transmission?

   a.   Scattering

   b.   Refraction

   c.   Reflection

   d.   Absorption

6. In the Free Path Loss model, objects that are farther away from a transmitter receive the same amount of signal as those that are closer to the transmitter. True or False?

   a.   True

   b.   False

7. If a signal is being spread about by microparticles, it is experiencing which influence on wireless transmissions?

   a. Scattering

   b. Spreading

   c. Scarring

   d. Splitting

   e. Refracting

8. Multipath causes which of the following issues? (Choose all that apply.)

   a. Redundant connectivity

   b. The signal becoming out of phase, which can potentially cancel the signal

   c. The signal being received by multiple devices in the path, causing security concerns

   d. Portions of the signal being reflected and arriving out of order

9. Scattering is caused by humidity. True or False?

   a. True

   b. False

10. For line of sight (LOS) transmissions, what can determine where signals can become out of phase?

    a. Free Path Zone

    b. EIRP

    c. Fresnel Zone

    d. Phase Zone

11. Link budget is used to do which of the following? (Choose two.)

    a. Account for all the receivers on a link

    b. Account for all the gains and losses

    c. Determine how much money you can spend on a wireless deployment

    d. Factor in EIRP and attenuation for a transmission

Foundation Topics

Characteristics of Wireless Networks

Many influences can act on a wireless transmission. For that reason, it is important to understand what is actually involved in a wireless transmissions so you know exactly what is being affected. This section reviews what a wavelength is, how frequency it is used in wireless transmission, and what the purpose of amplitude is. In addition, it covers how Effective Isotropic Radiated Power (EIRP) is calculated and what it defines.

Review of Wavelength

A *wavelength* is the distance between successive crests of a wave. This is how wavelength is measured. Most people have seen examples of sound waves. By measuring the distance between the crest of each wave, you can determine the wavelength. This is a distinctive feature of radio waves that are sent from a transmitter. Thinking back to what was discussed in Chapter 1, the waveform takes on a form called a *sine wave*.

The waveform starts as an AC signal that is generated by a transmitter inside an access point (AP) and is then sent to the antenna, where it is radiated as a sine wave. During this process, current changes the *electromagnetic field* around the antenna, so it transmits electric and magnetic signals.

The wavelength is a certain size, measured from one point in the AC cycle to the next point in the AC cycle. This in turn is called a *waveform*. Following are some quick facts about waveforms that you may relate to:

- AM radio waveforms are 400 to 500 meters long.

- Wireless waveforms in wireless LANS are only a few centimeters.

- Waveforms sent by satellites are approximately 1 mm long.

Review of Frequency

Because the term *frequency* is thrown around quite a bit in wireless networking, you need to have a clear understanding of it. Frequency, as discussed in Chapter 1, determines how often the signal is seen. It is the rate at which something occurs or is repeated over a particular period or in a given sample or period. It is insufficient to say that frequency is how often a signal is seen. If you are going to measure frequency, you need a period of time to look at it. Frequency, which is usually measured in seconds, is the rate at which a vibration occurs that constitutes a wave; this can be either in some form of material, as in sound waves, or it can be in an electromagnetic field, as you would see in radio waves and light.

Because frequency refers to cycles, following are some quick facts to help you to understand how it is measured:

- 1 cycle = 1 Hz

- Higher frequencies travel shorter distances

- When a waveform is seen once in a second = 1 Hz

- 10 times in a second = 10 Hz

- 1 million times in a second = 1 MHz

- 1 billion times in a second = 1 GHz

These are useful numbers that you can see throughout wireless networks.

Review of Amplitude

The vertical distance between crests in the wave is called *amplitude*. Different amplitude can exist for the same wavelength and the same frequency. Amplitude is the quantity or amount of energy that is put into a signal. Folks like the FCC and European Telecommunications Standards Institute (ETSI) regulate the amplitude.

Note: You can find a neat visualization of amplitude at http://id.mind.net/~zona/mstm/ physics/waves/introduction/introductionWaves.html.

What Is Effective Isotropic Radiated Power?

When an access point sends energy to an antenna to be radiated, a cable might exist between the two. A certain degree of loss in energy is expected to occur in the cable. To counteract this loss, an antenna adds gain, thus increasing the energy level. The amount of gain you use depends on the antenna type. Note that both the FCC and ETSI regulate the power that an antenna radiates. Ultimately, Effective Isotropic Radiated Power (EIRP) is the power that results. EIRP is what you use to estimate the service area of a device.

To calculate EIRP, use the following formula:

EIRP = transmitter output power – cable loss + antenna gain

Influences on Wireless Transmissions

Now that you clearly understand wireless transmissions and what is involved, it is a good time to discuss the influences on wireless signals. Some influences can stop a wireless signal from propagating altogether, whereas others might simply shorten the transmission distance. Either way, you should be aware of these factors so you can plan and adjust your deployment accordingly. In this section, you learn about the Free Path Loss model, absorption, reflection, scattering, multipath, refraction, and line of sight.

Understanding the Free Path Loss Model

To understand *Free Path Loss*, you can think of jumping smack into the middle of a puddle. This would cause a sort of wave effect to spread in all directions away from you. The closer to you that the wave is, the larger it is. Likewise, the farther away from you that wave travels, the smaller it gets. After a certain distance, the wave widens so much that it just disappears.

You might recall learning that an object that is in motion stays in motion until something stops it. But nothing stops the wave. It just disappears. This is where you get the term *free*. Take a look at Figure 3-1, and you can see that as the wave—or, in this case, the radiated wireless signal—travels away from the source, it thins out. This is represented by the bold dots becoming less and less bold.

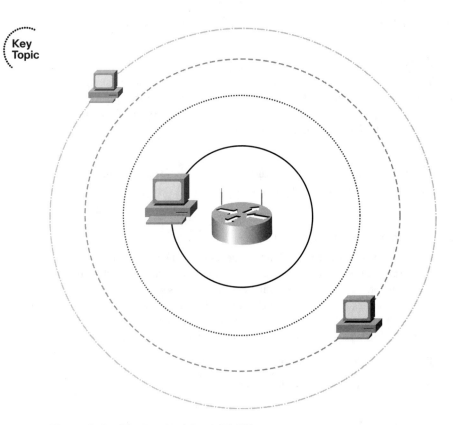

Figure 3-1   *The Free Path Loss Model*

You might also notice that the farther away the signal gets from the center, the sparser the dots are. Figure 3-1 has a single transmitting device (you could relate that to an access point) and many receiving devices. Not all the receiving stations get each one of the dots or signals that the transmitter sent. A device closer to the transmitter usually gets a more concentrated signal, and a receiver farther away might get only one dot.

Determining the range involves a determination of the energy loss and the distance. If you place receivers outside of that range, they cannot receive wireless signals from the access point and, in a nutshell, your network does not work.

Understanding Absorption

Earlier in this chapter, you learned that amplitude allowed a wave to travel farther. This can be good, because you can cover a greater area, potentially requiring fewer access points for your wireless deployment. By removing or reducing amplitude in a wave, you essentially reduce the distance a wave can travel. A factor that influences wireless transmission by reducing amplitude is called *absorption*.

An effect of absorption is heat. When something absorbs a wave, it creates heat in whatever absorbed the wave. This is seen in microwaves. They create waves that are absorbed by your food. The result is hot food. A problem you can encounter is that if a wave is entirely absorbed, it stops. While this effect reduces the distance the wave can travel, it does not change the wavelength or the frequency of the wave. These two values do not change as a wave is absorbed.

You might be asking what some possible sources of absorption are. Walls, bodies, and carpet can absorb signals. Relate it to sound. If you had really loud neighbors who were barbecuing outside your bedroom window, how could you deaden the sound? You could hang a blanket on the window or board up the window. Things that absorb sound waves also absorb data waves.

How can this affect your wireless deployment? Looking at Figure 3-2, you can see an office that has just been leased and ready to move in. After a quick site survey, you determine that four APs will provide plenty of coverage. This is because you cannot see absorption. Nothing causes the issue.

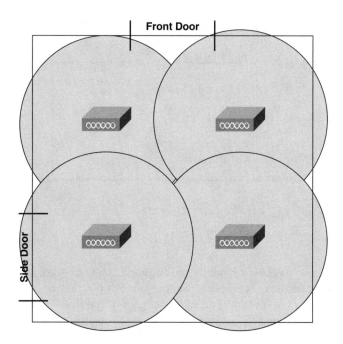

Figure 3-2 *Absorption Before Office Move-In*

Now look at Figure 3-3, which shows the same office after move-in. Notice that with the furniture, cubicle walls, and other obstacles, the four APs that you originally thought would be sufficient no longer provide the proper coverage because of the signal being absorbed. This is an illustration of absorption.

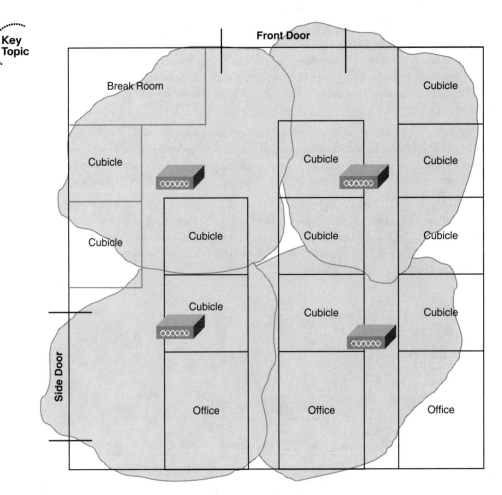

Figure 3-3 *Absorption After Office Move-In*

Understanding Reflection

Although absorption causes some problems, it is not the only obstacle that you are going to encounter that will affect your wireless deployments. Another obstacle is *reflection*. Reflection happens when a signal bounces off of something and travels in a different direction. This can be illustrated by shining a flashlight on an angle at a mirror, which causes it to reflect on an opposite wall. The same concept is true with wireless waveforms. You can see this effect in Figure 3-4, where the reflection of the signal is reflected at the same angle that it hits the mirror. You can also relate this to sources of interference in an office environment. Although offices do not usually have mirrors lying around, they do have other objects with similar reflective qualities, such as monitors and framed artwork with glass facing.

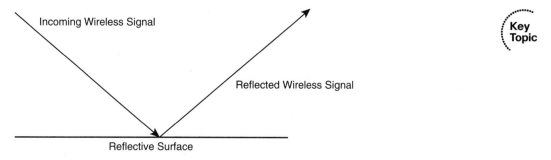

Figure 3-4 *The Reflection Issue*

Reflection depends on the frequency. You will encounter some frequencies that are not affected as much as others. This is because objects that reflect some frequencies might not reflect others.

Understanding Multipath

Multipath is what happens when portions of signals are reflected and then arrive out of order at the receiver, as illustrated in Figure 3-5.

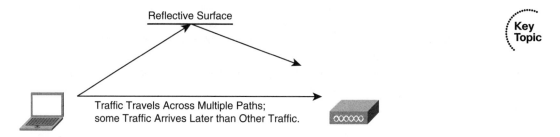

Figure 3-5 *The Multipath Issue*

One characteristic of multipath is that a receiver might get the same signal several times over. This is dependent on the wavelength and the position of the receiver.

Another characteristic of multipath is that it can cause the signal to become out of *phase*. When you receive out-of-phase signals, they can cancel each other out, resulting in a null signal.

Understanding Scattering

The issue of wireless signals scattering happens when the signal is sent in many different directions. This can be caused by some object that has reflective, yet jagged edges, such as dust particles in the air and water. One way to illustrate the effects would be to consider shining a light onto a pile of broken glass. The light that is reflected shoots off in many different directions. The same is true with wireless, only the pile of glass is replaced with microparticles of dust or water.

On a large scale, imagine that it is raining. Large raindrops have reflective capabilities. When a waveform travels through those microparticles, it is reflected in many directions. This is *scattering*. To visualize this, notice that Figure 3-6 involves a waveform traveling between two sites on a college campus. During a heavy downpour of rain, the wireless signal would be scattered in transit from one antenna to the next.

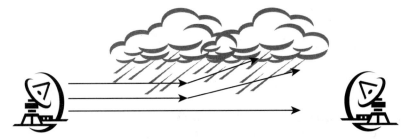

Figure 3-6   *Wireless Signal Scattering*

Scattering has more of an effect on shorter wavelengths, and the effect depends on frequency. The result is that the signal weakens.

Understanding Refraction

Refraction is the change in direction of, or the bending of, a waveform as it passes through something that is a different density. This behavior causes some of the signal to be reflected away and part to be bent through the object. To better understand this concept, Figure 3-7 demonstrates the effect of refraction. A waveform is being passed through a glass of water. Notice that, because the glass is reflective, some of the light is reflected, yet some still passes through.

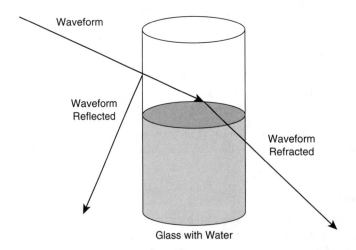

Figure 3-7   *The Refraction Issue*

The waveform that is passed through the glass is now at a different angle.

Note: You can find a neat Java-based example of refraction at http://www.phy.hk/wiki/englishhtm/RefractionByPrism.htm.

Because refraction usually has the most effect on outdoor signals, dryness refracts away from the earth (as seen in dust particles), and humidity refracts toward the earth.

Understanding Line of Sight

As an object travels toward a receiver, it might have to deal with various obstructions that are directly in the path. These obstructions in the path cause many of the issues just discussed—absorption, reflection, refraction, scattering. As wireless signals travel farther distances, the signal widens near the midpoint and slims down nearer to the receiver. Figure 3-8 illustrates where two directional antennas are sending a signal between the two points. The fact that it appears to be a straight shot is called *visual line of sight (LOS).* Although the path has no obvious obstacles, at greater distances the earth itself becomes an obstacle. This means that the curvature of the earth, as well as mountains, trees, and any other environmental obstacles, can actually interfere with the signal.

Figure 3-8   *Directional Antennas and Line of Sight*

Even though you see the other endpoint as a direct line, you must remember that the signal does not. The signal in fact widens, as illustrated in Figure 3-9. What was not an obvious obstruction in Figure 3-8 is more clearly highlighted in Figure 3-9.

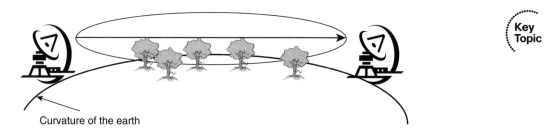

Curvature of the earth

Figure 3-9   *Directional Antennas and LOS with Obstructions*

When you plan for LOS, you should factor in the closest obstacle.

Key Topic

Determining Signal Strength Influences

Although it might seem hopeless to deploy a network that is susceptible to various forms of interference, you can fight back. To fight back, you need to know what tools are available out there for you to determine signal strength, noise levels, and potential sources of interference in the path. This section discusses these tools.

The Fresnel Zone

To give you a little background, Augustin-Jean Fresnel was a French physicist and civil engineer who lived from 1788 to 1827. He correctly assumed that light moved in a wavelike motion transverse to the direction of propagation. His assumption, or claim, was correct. Because of his work, a method for determining where reflections will be in phase and out of phase between sender and receiver is based on his name. This method determines what is called the *Fresnel zone*.

Here is how Fresnel did it. First he divided the path into zones. The first zone should be at least 60 percent clear of obstructions. To visualize this, you can think of the shape of a football, which is wider in the middle. However, with the Fresnel zone calculation, you use an equation to determine what the size of the ball is at the middle. This helps to determine the width that a wave will be so you can make sure that no obstacles are in the path.

Note: While at the CCNA wireless level, you should not need to calculate the Fresnel zone. You can find the actual formula at http://en.wikipedia.org/wiki/Fresnel_zone#Determining_Fresnel_zone_clearance.

Also, you can find an online Fresnel zone clearance calculator at http://www.terabeam.com/support/calculations/fresnel-zone.php.

Note: Indoor signals are too short to be affected.

Figure 3-10 illustrates the height an antenna would need to be at different distances to overcome this. For example, for a 2.4-GHz system, at 7 miles you need to have the antennas mounted at 45 to 50 feet.

Although this is just an example, the numbers are pretty close, and at least you can get more of a visual of what you are up against in the real world. Again, do not spend too much time on this in preparation for the CCNA wireless exam, because it is not a concept you will be tested on.

Received Signal Strength Indicator

The Received Signal Strength Indicator (RSSI) measurement uses vendor-specified values. Because of this, you cannot rely on it to compare different vendors. In the end, all this gives you is a grading of how much signal was received.

Keep in mind that the measurement is vendor specific, so the scale that is used might vary. For example, one vendor might use a scale of 0 to 100, whereas another might use a scale

2.4 GHz Systems			
Wireless Link-Distance in Miles	Approximate Value "F" (60% Fresnal Zone at 2.4 GHz)	Approximate Value "C" Earth Curvature	Value "H" Antenna Mounting Height with No Obstructions
1	14	3	17
5	31	5	36
10	43	13	56
15	53	28	81
20	61	50	111
25	68	78	146
5 GHz Systems			
1	9	3	12
5	20	5	25
10	28	13	41
15	35	28	63
20	40	50	90
25	45	78	123

Figure 3-10 *Sample Bridge Calculator*

of 0 to 60. The scale is usually represented in dBm, so the two scales would not match up. It is also up to the vendor to determine what dBm is represented by 0 and what dBm is represented by 100.

One tool that is used in wireless networks to give RSSI values is called Network Stumbler.

Note: You can find the free Network Stumbler software at http://www.netstumbler.com/.

RSSI is acquired during the preamble stage of receiving an 802.11 frame. RSSI has been replaced with Receive Channel Power Indicator (RCPI), which is a functional measurement covering the entire received frame with defined absolute levels of accuracy and resolution. To gain these measurements, you can use a CB21AG card and the Aironet Desktop Utility (ADU), which are covered in Chapter 16, "Wireless Clients." The CB21AG card is the most widely adopted card used by Airmagnet and OmniPeek.

Signal-to-Noise Ratio

Signal-to-noise ratio (SNR) is the term used to describe how much stronger the signal is compared to the surrounding noise that corrupts the signal. To understand this, suppose you walk into a crowded park with many screaming kids and speak in a normal voice while on the phone. The odds are that the noise is going to be so loud that the person on the other end will not be able to distinguish your words from all the noise around you that is also being transmitted over the phone. This is how the wireless network operates. If the outside influences are causing too much noise, the receivers cannot understand the transmissions.

When the software that runs your wireless card reports this measurement, it is best to have a higher number, but this is also built on the RSSI value, so it is vendor determined.

Note: You can explore SNR levels in the Network Stumbler application previously mentioned. Remember that the values are valid only for the Network Stumbler application. Other applications might report different SNR values.

Link Budget

Link budget is a value that accounts for all the gains and losses between sender and receiver, including attenuation, antenna gain, and other miscellaneous losses that might occur. This can be useful in determining how much power is needed to transmit a signal that the receiving end can understand.

The following is a simple equation to factor link budget:

Received Power (dBm) = Transmitted Power (dBm) + Gains (dB) − Losses (dB)

Exam Preparation Tasks

Review All Key Concepts

Review the most important topics from this chapter, noted with the Key Topics icon in the outer margin of the page. Table 3-2 lists a reference of these key topics and the page number where you can find each one.

Table 3-2 *Key Topics for Chapter 3*

Key Topic Item	Description	Page Number
Figure 3-1	The Free Path Loss model	36
Figure 3-3	The absorption issue	38
Figure 3-4	The reflection issue	39
Figure 3-5	The multipath issue	39
Figure 3-9	Line of sight	45

Definition of Key Terms

Define the following key terms from this chapter, and check your answers in the Glossary:

wavelength, frequency, amplitude, EIRP, Free Path Loss, absorption, reflection, multipath, phase (in-phase/out-of-phase), scattering, refraction, line of sight, SNR, link budget

This chapter covers the following subjects:

General Wireless Topologies: Discusses wireless LAN topologies from a high-level perspective.

Original 802.11 Topologies: Discusses wireless network topologies defined by the IEEE.

Vendor-Specific Topology Extensions: Explains how vendors extend network topologies.

CHAPTER 4

WLAN Technologies and Topologies

When you work in a wireless network, you can encounter a number of technologies and deployment options. Sometimes your situation calls for a peer-to-peer connection, and other times you will want to connect to users who are in another room or on another floor, yet on the same network. In this chapter you will learn what these networks are and when they are appropriate. You will also look at which types of equipment are appropriate for certain situations and environments.

Use the "Do I Know This Already?" quiz to gauge whether you should read the entire chapter or if you should simply jump to the "Exam Preparation Tasks" section and review. If in doubt, read through the whole chapter!

"Do I Know This Already?" Quiz

The "Do I Know This Already?" quiz helps you determine your level of knowledge of this chapter's topics before you begin. Table 4-1 details the major topics discussed in this chapter and their corresponding quiz questions.

Table 4-1 *"Do I Know This Already?" Section-to-Question Mapping*

Foundation Topics Section	Questions
General Wireless Topologies	1–7
Original 802.11 Topologies	8–20
Vendor-Specific Topology Extensions	21–26

1. Which of the following topologies can be used with clients closer than 20 feet?

    a. WLAN

    b. WWAN

    c. WPAN

    d. WMAN

2. True or false: A WLAN uses 802.16b.

   a. True

   b. False

3. What topology is most often seen in a LAN and is designed to connect multiple devices to the network?

   a. WMAN

   b. WPAN

   c. WLAN

   d. WWAN

4. In what frequency ranges does a wireless LAN operate? (Choose two.)

   a. 2.2 GHz

   b. 2.4 GHz

   c. 2.4 MHz

   d. 5 GHz

   e. 5 MHz

5. What type of speed can you expect from a WMAN?

   a. Broadband

   b. WAN

   c. Ethernet

   d. Dialup modem

6. What is the name of the common WMAN technology?

   a. WiMAN

   b. WiMAX

   c. Wi-Fi

   d. WiNET

7. True or false: Deploying a WWAN is relatively inexpensive, so it's common for enterprise customers to deploy their own.

   a. True

   b. False

8. Which of the following are 802.11 topologies for LANs? (Choose all that apply.)

   a. Adsense

   b. Ad hoc

   c. Infrastructure

   d. Internal

9. What does BSS stand for?

   a.   Basic Service Signal

   b.   Basic Service Separation

   c.   Basic Service Set

   d.   Basic Signal Server

10. If an AP is not used in a wireless network, this is called which of the following?

   a.   Independent Basic Service Set

   b.   Solitary Service Set

   c.   Single-Mode Set (SMS)

   d.   Basic Individual Service Set

11. For two devices to communicate without an access point, you must define which of the following?

   a.   A group name

   b.   A password

   c.   A network number

   d.   A key

12. True or false: When operating in infrastructure mode, an AP is operating in full-duplex mode.

   a.   True

   b.   False

13. What device does an access point act as to connect wireless clients to a wired network?

   a.   Hub

   b.   Bridge

   c.   Router

   d.   Repeater

14. What is another name for wireless clients?

   a.   Stations

   b.   End nodes

   c.   Clients

   d.   Mobile APs

15. An access point is what kind of device?

   a.   Support device

   b.   Network device

   c.   Perimeter device

   d.   Infrastructure device

16. What is the name for the area of coverage offered by a single access point?

    a. VSA

    b. MSA

    c. TSA

    d. BSA

17. When more than one AP connects to a common distribution, what is the network called?

    a. Extended Service Area

    b. Basic Service Area

    c. Local Service Area

    d. WMAN

18. Clients connect to which of the following to access the LAN via a wireless AP?

    a. SSID

    b. SCUD

    c. BSID

    d. BSA

19. When one area exists, what is the name of the service set advertised by an AP?

    a. BBSM

    b. BSUP

    c. BSSID

    d. SSIG

20. Using MBSSIDs indicates which of the following?

    a. More than one AP is advertising SSIDs.

    b. More than one SSID is being advertised by one AP.

    c. The AP sees more than one SSID.

    d. There are multiple MACs on one SSID.

21. What can you use to connect an isolated wired network to a LAN?

    a. WLAN

    b. WGB

    c. Repeater

    d. Hub

22. Cisco offers which types of wireless bridges? (Choose two.)

   a.   aWGB

   b.   bWGB

   c.   uWGB

   d.   cWGB

23. For topologies where cable lengths prohibit placing an AP in certain locations, what solution can be used?

   a.   Install a new switch that's closer.

   b.   Install a hub instead.

   c.   Install a repeater.

   d.   Install a wireless client.

24. How much overlap is needed with an AP when a wireless repeater is used?

   a.   10 to 15 percent

   b.   100 percent

   c.   50 percent

   d.   40 to 80 percent

25. True or false: Outdoor mesh networks support only point-to-point topologies.

   a.   True

   b.   False

26. Mesh deployments are appropriate when _____ is a major concern.

   a.   Connectivity

   b.   Security

   c.   Cost

   d.   Speed

Foundation Topics

General Wireless Topologies

When you're talking about wireless topologies, there are a number of ways it could go. If you are talking about how your wireless network looks next to your wired network, you are most likely talking about a wireless local-area network (WLAN). The goal of a WLAN versus a wireless personal-area network (WPAN) is quite different. The following sections discuss the purpose of each network type, what they try to accomplish, and what types of wireless technologies you might encounter there. Figure 4-1 shows the various wireless topologies.

Key
Topic

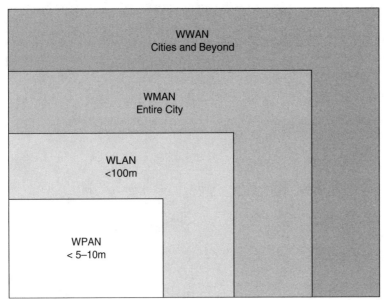

Figure 4-1 *Wireless Topology Overview*

WPAN

If you were to consider all the options, a WPAN would be the solution to choose if you wanted to wirelessly connect to something that is very close to you. It seems funny to put it that way, because if something close to you needs to be networked, you might as well just walk over and grab it, right? Wrong. Even though this is called a network, its form can mislead you into thinking that it's not a networking technology. What forms are we talking about? Headsets, headphones—even a mouse.

A WPAN has the following characteristics:

■ The range is short—about 20 feet.

- Eight active devices

- Unlicensed 2.4-GHz spectrum

- Called a piconet

A WPAN is a network that is designed to operate within a 20-foot range. The most common WPAN is Bluetooth. In a Bluetooth network, you communicate on the 2.4-GHz spectrum. Thinking about how many people have Bluetooth headsets and mice and such, you would expect a lot of interference, but that's not the case. Bluetooth uses Frequency Hopping Spread Spectrum (FHSS). Although this book doesn't discuss FHSS, it's good to understand that even though Bluetooth operates on the same frequency as 802.11b and 802.11g, they don't interfere *as much as* another AP in the same frequency spectrum would, but they *do* interfere. The fact that Bluetooth communicates with a shared hopping sequence in a local area is what makes it a *piconet*.

Bluetooth piconets consist of up to eight active devices but can have many inactive devices. WPANs usually fall into the unlicensed 2.4-GHz spectrum and are standardized by the 802.15 IEEE workgroup. A WPAN study group was formed in 1998, and two months later a Bluetooth Special Interest Group (SIG) was formed. Shortly thereafter the study group became the IEEE 802.15 group. The Bluetooth SIG has more than 9000 members and continues to further the technology.

Note: You can find out more about the Bluetooth SIG at http://www.bluetooth.com/Bluetooth/SIG/.

WLAN

WLANs are designed for a larger area than that of a WPAN. These can scale from very small home offices to large enterprise networks. The fact that they are local-area means that the organization where the WLAN exists also manages and probably owns the equipment. WLANs have the following characteristics:

- 2.4-GHz or 5-GHz spectrum.

- A larger range than a WPAN—close to 100 meters from AP to client.

- To achieve further distance, more power output is required.

- It's not personal; rather, more clients are expected.

- WLANs are very flexible, so more than eight active devices/clients are expected, unlike a WPAN.

Normally you find a mix of dual-band wireless access points, laptops, and desktops in a WLAN. A WLAN operates in either the 2.4-GHz spectrum for 802.11b/g or the 5-GHz spectrum for 802.11a. Of the protocols seen in WLANs, 802.11b was the first to really get market penetration. Others, such as the 802.11a, have followed. Now the 802.11a, b, g, and n WLAN standards are commonly found in networks around the world. The frequency spectrums used by 802.11a/b, g, and n are all unlicensed.

Because WLANs cover larger areas, they require more power output than a WPAN. The issue to watch in WLANs is that you don't exceed the power rules that the government sets forth. For example, in the U.S., the Federal Communications Commission (FCC) mandates radiated power levels.

WLANs are designed to give mobile clients access to network resources. For this reason, a WLAN expects to see multiple users. In addition to wireless users, there are wireless print servers, presentation servers, and storage devices. You end up with many devices connecting to each other or sharing information with each other, usually over a common distribution system such as the local-area network. This makes WLANs much more complex than WPANs.

What makes WLANs flexible is the fact that the APs and clients are dual-band. This makes it easy to deploy different transmission methods in different areas, and most clients can still operate.

WMAN

A wireless metropolitan-area network (WMAN) covers a large geographic area and has the following characteristics:

■ Speeds decrease as the distance increases.

■ Close to broadband speeds versus Ethernet speeds.

■ Used as a backbone, point-to-point, or point-to-multipoint.

■ Most well-known is WiMax.

WMANs are used as backbone services, point-to-point, or even point-to-multipoint links that can be a replacement for technologies such as T1 and T3. Sometimes, a WMAN can use unlicensed frequencies. However, this isn't always a preferred solution, because others could use the same frequency, thus causing interference. Instead, many prefer to use a licensed frequency range; however, this requires payment for exclusive rights.

It's normal for the speeds in a WMAN to decrease with distance. This places them in a closer category to broadband than to Ethernet. The most widely known WMAN is WiMax (802.16b). WiMax can be used to offer last-mile access as an alternative to broadband services such as DSL or cable connections. WiMax is an excellent solution where facilities or distance are a limitation. With WiMax, you pay a service provider for access, because the cost of deployment is normally very high.

Note: Cisco offers a WiMax solution; however, this is not covered in this book. For more information on the Cisco WiMax solution, visit http://www.cisco.com/go/wimax.

WWAN

A wireless wide-area network (WWAN) covers a large geographic area. WWANs have the following characteristics:

■ Low data rates

■ Pay-for-use

- High cost of deployment

Because they cover a large geographic area, WWANs usually are very expensive to deploy. To better understand what a WWAN is, consider your cellular service. Your cell service is a WWAN and probably offers data access as well as voice access. The data rates are probably around 115 kbps, although some providers offer higher data rates. The most widely deployed WWAN technologies are Global System for Mobile Communication (GSM) and Code Division Multiple Access (CDMA). Payment for data access or even voice access is typically based on usage.

Original 802.11 Topologies

Although the previous sections discussed network topologies that you might encounter, it was a very general discussion. You also need to understand the original topologies, defined by the 802.11 committees, including the following:

- Ad hoc mode

- Infrastructure mode

The following sections give more details on these topologies.

Overview of Ad Hoc Networks

When two computers want to communicate directly with one another, they do so in the form of an *ad hoc* network. Ad hoc networks don't require a central device to allow them to communicate. Rather, one device sets a group name and radio parameters, and the other uses it to connect. This is called a *Basic Service Set (BSS)*, which defines the area in which a device is reachable. Because the two machines don't need a central device to speak to each other, it is called an *Independent Basic Service Set (IBSS)*. This type of ad hoc network exists as soon as two devices see each other. Figure 4-2 shows an ad hoc network.

Each computer has only one radio. Because there is only one radio, the throughput is lower and acts as a half-duplex device, because you can't send and receive at the same time.

You don't have much control in these networks, so you're stuck when it comes to methods such as authentication. In addition, you need to address who starts the conversation and who decides on the order of communication, to name just a couple issues.

Network Infrastructure Mode

In wireless networks, an access point acts as a connection point for clients. An AP is actually a cross between a hub and a bridge. Here's why:

- There is one radio, which cannot send and receive at the same time. This is where the AP is likened to a hub. It's a half-duplex operation.

- APs have some intelligence that is similar to that of a bridge. That is how an AP can see a frame and decide to forward it based on MAC addresses.

What is different on an AP versus a bridge is that wireless frames are more complex. Standard Ethernet frames have a source MAC address and a destination MAC address. Wireless frames can have three or four MAC addresses. Two of them are the source and destination MAC addresses, and one is the AP's MAC address that is tied to a workgroup.

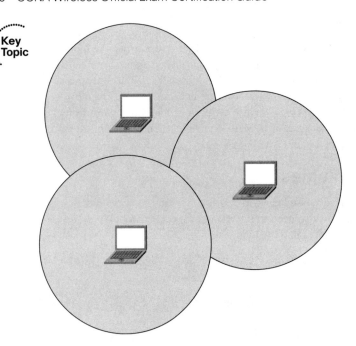

Key
Topic

Figure 4-2   *Ad Hoc Network*

The fourth that could be present is a NEXT_HOP address in the event that you are using a workgroup bridge (WGB).

An AP is actually just one type of wireless station. This terminology could cause some confusion between an AP and a client on a network, so to differentiate between them, a client is called a *station (STA)*, and an AP is called an *infrastructure device*.

So what does a typical wireless topology look like? Of course, wireless clients are associated with an AP. In the wireless space, the coverage area of the AP is called a *Basic Service Area (BSA)*, which is also sometimes known as a *wireless cell*. They mean the same thing. When only one AP exists, this coverage area is called a BSA, as shown in Figure 4-3. That AP then usually has an Ethernet connection to an 802.3 LAN, depending on the function of the AP.

Note: Some APs can function in a repeater mode, in which they don't need an Ethernet connection.

Assuming that the AP has an Ethernet connection, it bridges the 802.11 wireless traffic from the wireless clients to the 802.3 wired network on the Ethernet side.

The wired network attached to the AP's Ethernet port is a path to a wireless LAN controller (or controller for short). The client traffic is passed through the controller and then is forwarded to the wired network, called the *distribution system*. The distribution system is how a client accesses the Internet, file servers, printers, and anything else available on the wired network.

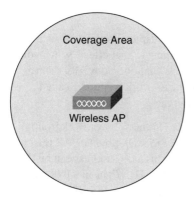

Figure 4-3 *Basic Service Area*

When more than one AP is connected to a common distribution system, as shown in Figure 4-4, the coverage area is called an *Extended Service Area (ESA)*.

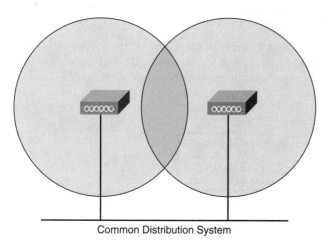

Figure 4-4 *Extended Service Area*

Why would you want more than one AP connected to the same LAN? There are a few reasons:

■ To provide adequate coverage in a larger area.

■ To allow clients to move from one AP to the other and still be on the same LAN.

■ To provide more saturation of APs, resulting in more bandwidth per user.

This process of a client moving from one AP to another is called *roaming*. For roaming to work, the APs must overlap. You might wonder why they need to overlap, because interference in a wireless network is a common issue. The reason for the overlap is so that a client can see both APs and associate to the one with the stronger signal. As soon as the signal from the associated AP hits the threshold built into the client, the client looks for another AP with a better signal.

Service Set Identifiers

Think about how you connect to a wireless network. On your laptop, you might see a popup that says "Wireless networks are available" or something to that effect. When you look at the available networks, you see names. On older Cisco autonomous APs, the network was called "Tsunami." On a store-bought Linksys, the network is actually called "linksys." So the client sees a name that represents a network.

On the AP, the network is associated with a MAC address. This network or workgroup that your clients connect to is called a *Service Set Identifier (SSID)*. So on an AP, the SSID is a combination of MAC address and network name. This MAC address can be that of the wireless radio or another MAC address generated on the AP. When an AP offers service for only one network, it is called a *Basic Service Set Identifier (BSSID)*. APs offer the ability to use more than one SSID. This would let you offer a Guest Network and a Corporate Network and still use the same AP. When the AP has more than one network, it is called a *Multiple Basic Service Set Identifier (MBSSID)*. You can think of it as a virtual AP. It offers service for multiple networks, but it's the same hardware. Because it's the same hardware and the same frequency range, users on one network share with users on another and can collide if they send at the same time.

Now let's return to the roaming discussion. To get roaming to work, the BSA of each AP must overlap. The APs also need to be configured for the same SSID. This enables the client to see that the same network is offered by different MAC addresses, as illustrated in Figure 4-5.

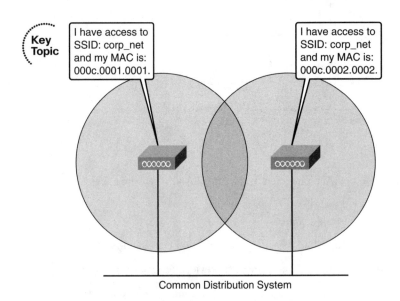

Figure 4-5   *Wireless Roaming*

When a client roams and moves from one AP to the other, the SSID remains the same, but the MAC address changes to the new AP with a better signal.

Another issue to consider when roaming is the possibility of interference between the two overlapping APs. Even though they offer the same SSID, they need to be on different *channels*, or frequency ranges, that do not overlap. This prevents *co-channel interference*, which should be avoided. The 2.4 spectrum allows only three nonoverlapping channels. You must consider this fact when placing APs.

Vendor-Specific Topology Extensions

The vendor-specific topology extensions are an enablement of additional network functionality by way of vendor-defined protocols, devices, and topologies. In this section you will learn how workgroup bridges, wireless repeaters, outdoor wireless bridges, and wireless mesh networks through the use of wireless controllers can enhance the functionality and capability of your wireless deployment.

Workgroup Bridges

You will most likely have times when you have an isolated network that needs access to the rest of the network for access to the server farm and the Internet. You might not be able to run an Ethernet cable to the isolated network, or you might not own the property so you can't drill holes in the walls, and so on. In this scenario, you would use a WGB topology such as the one shown in Figure 4-6.

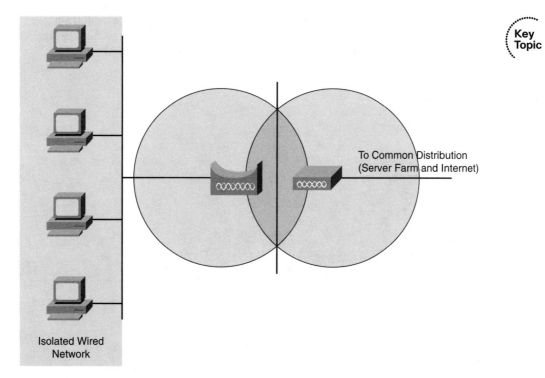

Key
Topic

Figure 4-6   *Workgroup Bridge Topology*

Notice that the WGB is used to bridge a wired network to an AP that connects to a distribution system.

Cisco offers two types of workgroup bridges:

■ **Autonomous Workgroup Bridge (aWGB):** The aWGB was originally just called a workgroup bridge, but Cisco later changed the name when it introduced the Universal WGB. The aWGB is supported in IOS AP version 12.4(3G)JA and later. The aWGB connects only to upstream Cisco APs, and the AP sees multiple Ethernet clients.

■ **Universal Workgroup Bridge (uWGB):** The uWGB is supported on IOS AP version 12.4(11)XJ and later. It allows bridging to upstream non-Cisco APs and appears as a single client.

Repeaters

Recall that in an Extended Service Set (ESS), multiple APs connect clients. This is all well and good until you have clients roaming about who get into areas where coverage is necessary but not possible. The solution of a WGB doesn't work, because a WGB connects users who are wired. An example is a worker at a warehouse who carries a barcode scanner or even a wireless Cisco IP Phone. There are scenarios where you can't run a cable into a location to install an AP. This is where you want to use a *wireless repeater*. A wireless repeater is simply an AP that doesn't connect to a wired network for its connectivity to the distribution network. Instead, it overlaps with an AP that does physically connect to the distribution network. The overlap needs to be 50 percent for optimal performance. Figure 4-7 shows an example. A repeater is allowing a client to connect to the network when in fact the client would normally be out of the service area of the AP.

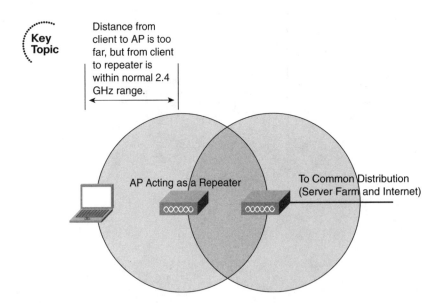

Figure 4-7 *Wireless Repeater Topology*

You can get APs that act as a repeater as well, which is how the Cisco solution works. The catch is that you need a Cisco AP as the upstream "root" device, and only one SSID is supported in repeater mode. Additionally, the overall throughput is cut in half for each repeater hop.

Outdoor Wireless Bridges

When you have two or more LANs within a few miles of each other and you want to link them, you can use a wireless bridge. Because you are "bridging," the technology works at Layer 2. This means that the LANs do not route traffic and do not have a routing table.

You can connect one LAN directly to another in a point-to-point configuration, as shown in Figure 4-8, or you can connect many LANs through a central hub, as shown in Figure 4-9.

Key
Topic

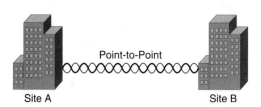

Point-to-Point

Site A   Site B

Figure 4-8   *Point-to-Point Wireless Bridge Topology*

Key
Topic

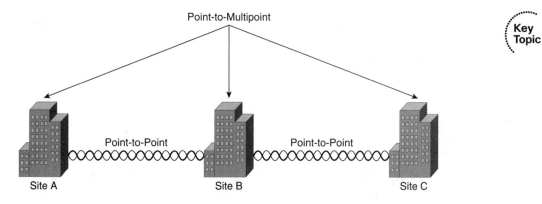

Point-to-Multipoint

Point-to-Point   Point-to-Point

Site A   Site B   Site C

Figure 4-9   *Point-to-Multipoint Wireless Bridge Topology*

Each end of a point-to-multipoint topology would have to communicate through the hub if it wanted to communicate with the others. Cisco offers the Cisco Aironet 1300 series wireless bridge and the Cisco Aironet 1400 series wireless bridge. When using a 1400 series, you can bridge only networks, but if you use a 1300 series, you can allow clients to connect as well as bridge networks. The 1300 series operates in the 2.4-GHz range, and the 1400 series operates in the 5-GHz range.

Outdoor Mesh Networks

As you can see, bridges are a good way to connect remote sites. However, suppose that you are operating in a point-to-multipoint topology, and the central site experiences congestion. Who suffers? Just the central site? Just the remote site? No; the answer is everyone. When two remote sites communicate through a central site, the central site makes all the difference.

Assume that the central site goes down, as shown in Figure 4-10.

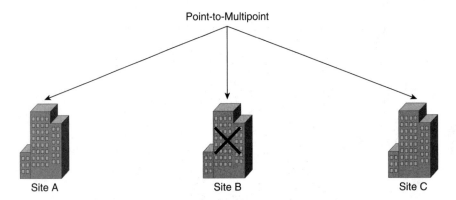

Figure 4-10   *Wireless Bridge Issues*

Now the remote sites can't communicate with each other or the central site. This can be a major issue to contend with. The solution is to deploy a mesh network such as the one illustrated in Figure 4-11.

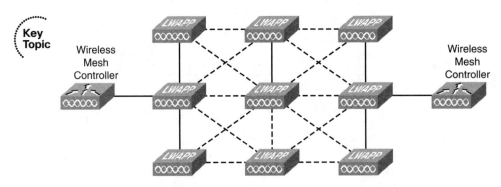

Figure 4-11   *Wireless Mesh Solution*

The mesh solution is appropriate when connectivity is important, because multiple paths can be used. The IEEE is currently working on a mesh standard (802.11s). However, the solution discussed here is a Cisco solution in which a wireless controller, also shown in Figure 4-11, is involved.

When you have a mesh network, some *nodes* (another term for APs in a mesh network) are connected to a wired network. Some nodes simply act as repeaters. A mesh node repeats data to nearby nodes. More than one path is available, so a special algorithm is used to determine the best path. The alternative paths can be used when there is congestion or when a wireless mesh node goes down.

Exam Preparation Tasks

Review All the Key Topics

Review the most important topics from this chapter, denoted with the Key Topic icon. Table 4-2 lists these key topics and the page number where you can find each one.

Table 4-2   *Key Topics for Chapter 4*

Key Topic Item	Description	Page Number
Figure 4-1	Wireless topology overview	52
Figure 4-2	Ad hoc network	56
Figure 4-3	Basic service area	57
Figure 4-4	Extended service area	57
Figure 4-5	Wireless roaming	58
Figure 4-6	Workgroup bridge topology	59
Figure 4-7	Wireless repeater topology	60
Figure 4-8	Point-to-point wireless bridge topology	61
Figure 4-9	Point-to-multipoint wireless bridge topology	61
Figure 4-11	Wireless mesh solution	62

Definition of Key Terms

Define the following key terms from this chapter, and check your answers in the glossary:

WPAN, SIG, WLAN, IEEE, WMAN, WiMax, WWAN, GSM, CDMA, ad hoc, infrastructure, distribution system, BSS, IBSS, STA, infrastructure device, BSA, ESA, roaming, SSID, BSSID, MBSSID, co-channel interference, WGB, aWGB, uWGB, repeater, node

This chapter covers the following subjects:

Principles of Antennas: Covers antenna concepts.

Common Antenna Types: Describes omnidirectional and directional antennas.

Antenna Connectors and Hardware: Looks at some of the connectors used in wireless deployments as well as other common hardware.

CHAPTER 5

Antenna Communications

In any wireless network, the capability to propagate the signal is key. Without that capability, the whole concept of a wireless network falls apart. In this chapter, you will learn about antenna principles, along with some common antenna and connector types.

You should take the "Do I Know This Already Quiz?" first. If you score 80 percent or higher, you may want to skip to the section "Exam Preparation Tasks." If you score below 80 percent, you should review the entire chapter.

"Do I Know This Already?" Quiz

The "Do I Know This Already?" quiz helps you determine your level of knowledge of this chapter's topics before you begin. Table 5-1 details the major topics discussed in this chapter and their corresponding quiz questions.

Table 5-1 *"Do I Know This Already?" Section-to-Question Mapping*

Foundation Topics Section	Questions
Principles of Antennas	1–7
Common Antenna Types	8–16
Antenna Connectors and Hardware	17–20

1. Which of the following are types of polarization? (Choose all that apply.)

    a. Vertical

    b. Horizontal

    c. Nautical

    d. Circular

2. All Cisco antennas use what type of polarization?

    a. Linear

    b. Circular

    c. Magnetic

    d. Perpendicular

3. In an electromagnetic wave, where is the magnetic wave found in relation to the electric wave?

    a. Parallel to the electric wave.

    b. At a 45-degree angle to the electric wave.

    c. Perpendicular (at a 90-degree angle).

    d. There is no magnetic wave.

4. How many antennas are used with diversity?

    a. Three

    b. Four

    c. One

    d. Two

5. What does diversity listen to when choosing a better antenna to use?

    a. The destination MAC address

    b. The preamble

    c. The data

    d. The source MAC address

6. How far apart should antennas be placed when using diversity?

    a. 2 meters

    b. Two wavelengths

    c. One wavelength

    d. 1 meter

7. True or false: Two antennas using diversity can cover two areas.

    a. True

    b. False

8. What are the main families of antennas? (Choose all that apply.)

    a. Omnidirectional

    b. Unidirectional

    c. Directional

    d. Yagi

9. In relation to sending a linear waveform, the horizontal plane (H-plane) is also called what?

    a. Vertical plane

    b. Azimuth

    c. Axis

    d. Linear plane

10. To display the coverage from top to bottom, what plane is represented?

    a. A-plane

    b. E-plane

    c. C-plane

    d. Airplane

11. The 2.2 dipole antenna is designed for what type of deployment?

    a. Indoor omnidirectional

    b. Indoor directional

    c. Outdoor point-to-point

    d. Outdoor omnidirectional

12. Which antenna is considered a "special" omnidirectional antenna?

    a. AIR-ANT1728

    b. AIR-ANT3338

    c. AIR-ANT2485P-R

    d. AIR-ANT3213

13. A yagi antenna is best used in what setting or settings? (Choose all that apply.)

    a. Warehouse where multiple antennas are lined up

    b. Conference room

    c. Point-to-point over long distances

    d. Long hallways

14. True or false: A parabolic dish antenna uses a wide RF path.

    a. True

    b. False

15. For mounting reasons, what can be changed on a parabolic antenna?

    a. Polarity

    b. Diversity

    c. Shape

    d. Radiation pattern

16. The AIR-ANT3213 uses how many antennas?

    a. Two

    b. Four

    c. Six

    d. One

17. Cisco uses which types of connectors? (Choose all that apply.)

   a. SMA

   b. N-connector

   c. RP-TNC

   d. TNC

18. To lower the amount of energy being sent to the antenna, which of the following devices could be used?

   a. Amplifier

   b. Attenuator

   c. Lightning arrestor

   d. Fiber-patch

19. To increase the amount of energy, which of the following devices could be used?

   a. Amplifier

   b. Attenuator

   c. Lightning arrestor

   d. Fiber-patch

20. True or false: Lightning arrestors are designed to withstand a full lightning strike.

   a. True

   b. False

Foundation Topics

Principles of Antennas

If someone asked you what the most important part of a wireless network is, what would you say? I'd have to say the antenna. Why? Without it, you have a nice little AP that can offer network services for anyone within about 3 feet. But that's not what you want. You want to make sure that your space is properly covered. You need antennas to do this. In fact, you need the *right* antennas to do this. In this section you will learn about the factors involved in dealing with antennas, which include *polarity* and *diversity*.

Polarization

The goal of an antenna is to emit electromagnetic waves. The electro portion of the term electromagnetic describes the wave and that it can move in different ways. The way that it moves is its polarization. There are three types of polarization:

- Vertical
- Horizontal
- Circular

As shown in Figure 5-1, *vertical polarization* means that the wave moves up and down in a linear way. *Horizontal polarization* means that the wave moves left and right in a linear way.

The third type of polarization, *circular polarization*, indicates that the wave circles as it moves forward, as illustrated in Figure 5-2.

The electric field is generated by stationary charges, or current. There is also a magnetic field—hence the term electromagnetic. The magnetic field is found perpendicular (at a 90-degree angle) to the electric field. This magnetic field is generated at the same time as the electric field; however, the magnetic field is generated by moving charges. Cisco antennas are always vertically polarized in wireless networks. This makes the electric field vertical. Why is this important? The importance is that the antenna is designed to propagate signals in a certain direction. Here is where installation errors can hurt you. For example, if you have a long tube-like antenna, it would face up/down. If you placed it flat instead, the signal would propagate in a different direction and would end up degraded.

Although this is not a huge factor in indoor deployments, it can be in outdoor deployments. Usually other factors degrade your wireless signal propagation on indoor deployments.

Diversity

By now you should understand what the multipath issue is. Traffic takes different paths because of the obstacles in the wireless path. One way to deal with multipath issues is to use two antennas on one AP. *Diversity* is the use of two antennas for each radio to increase the odds that you receive a better signal on either of the antennas.

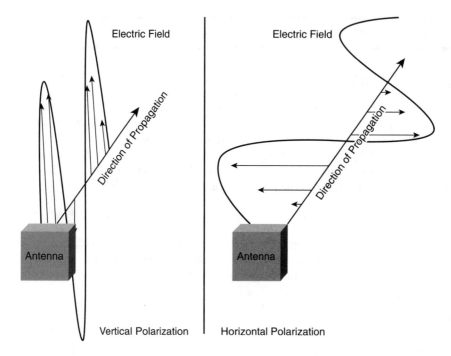

Figure 5-1   *Vertical and Horizontal Polarization*

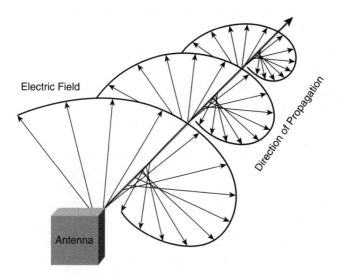

Figure 5-2   *Circular Polarization*

Here is how it works: The two antennas are placed one wavelength apart. When the AP hears a preamble of a frame, it switches between the two antennas and uses an algorithm to determine which antenna has the better signal. After an antenna is chosen, it is used for the rest of that frame. You can switch antennas and listen to the preamble because it has no real data. As soon as the real data gets there, it uses only one of the antennas.

Most of the time this happens with a single radio in the AP and two antennas connected to it. This is important because the two antennas cover the same area. You wouldn't try to cover two different areas with the same radio. Additionally, the antennas need to be the same. If you used a weaker antenna on one side versus the other, the coverage area would not be the same.

Common Antenna Types

The two main types of antennas are directional and omnidirectional. In this section you will learn the difference between the two types and look at some of the antennas that Cisco offers. Both send the same amount of energy; the difference is in how the beam is focused. To understand this, imagine that you have a flashlight. By twisting the head of the light, you can make the beam focus in a specific area. When the beam has a wider focus, it doesn't appear to be as bright. While you twist the head of the light, you never change its output. The batteries are the same. The power is the same. The light is the same. You simply focus it in different ways. The same goes for wireless antennas. When you look at a directional antenna, it appears to be a stronger signal in one direction, but it's still emitting the same amount of energy. To increase power in a particular direction, you add gain.

The angles of coverage are fixed with each antenna. When you buy high-gain antennas, it is usually to focus a beam.

Omnidirectional Antennas

There are two ways to determine the coverage area of an antenna. The first is to place the AP in a location and walk around with a client recording the signal-to-noise ratio (SNR) and Received Signal Strength Indicator (RSSI). This could take a really long time. The second method is a little easier. In fact, the manufacturer does it for you. Figures 5-3 and 5-4 show different views of the wireless signal. Figure 5-3 shows how the wireless signal might propagate if you were standing above it and looking down on the antenna.

Note: We say "might" because these values are different for each type of antenna.

This is called the *horizontal plane (H-plane)* or *azimuth*. When you look at an omnidirectional antenna from the top (H-plane), you should see that it propagates evenly in a 360-degree pattern.

The vertical pattern does not propagate evenly, though. Figure 5-4 shows the *elevation plane (E-plane)*. This is how the signal might propagate in a vertical pattern, or from top to bottom. As you can see, it's not a perfect 360 degrees. This is actually by design. It's what is known as the "one floor" concept. The idea is that the signal propagates wider from side to side than it does from top to bottom so that it can offer coverage to the floor it is placed on rather than to the floor above or below the AP.

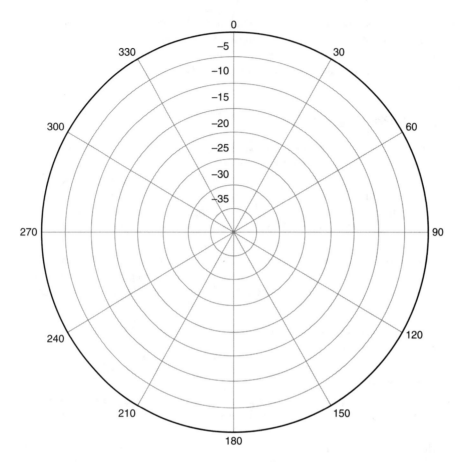

Figure 5-3 *H-plane*

Another way to look at this is to imagine an AP, as shown in Figure 5-5. If you draw in the H-plane and E-plane, you can relate the signal to each plane.

Now that you have a better understanding of how to determine the propagation patterns of an antenna, let's look at some antennas.

2.2-dBi Dipole

The 2.2-dBi *dipole*, or rubber duck, shown in Figure 5-6, is most often seen indoors because it is a very weak antenna. In fact, it's actually designed for a client or AP that doesn't cover a large area. Its radiation pattern resembles a doughnut, because vertically it doesn't propagate much. Instead, it's designed to propagate on the H-plane. The term *dipole* may be new to you. The dipole antenna was developed by Heinrich Rudolph Hertz and is considered the simplest type of antenna. Dipoles have a doughnut-shaped *radiation pattern*. Many times, an antenna is compared to an isotropic radiator. An *isotropic radiator* assumes that the signal is propagated evenly in all directions. This would be a perfect 360-degree sphere in all directions, on the H and E planes. The 2.2-dBi dipole antenna doesn't work this way; rather, it has a doughnut shape.

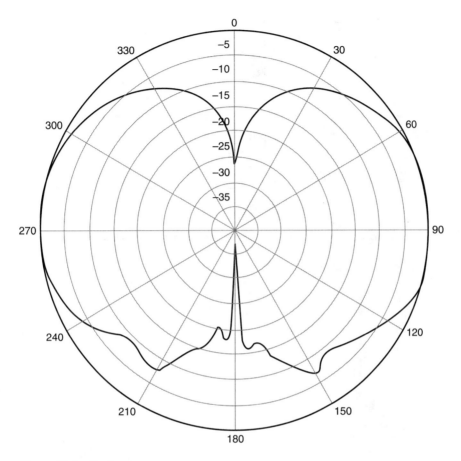

Figure 5-4   *E-plane*

AIR-ANT1728

The AIR-ANT1728, shown in Figure 5-7, is a ceiling-mounted omnidirectional antenna operating at 5.2 dBi.

You would use this when a 2.14-dBi dipole doesn't provide adequate coverage for an area. This antenna has more gain, thus increasing the H-plane, as shown in Figure 5-8.

The easiest way to express the effect of adding gain—in this case, 5.2 dBi versus 2.2 dBi— is to imagine squeezing a balloon from the top and the bottom, as shown in Figure 5-9.

The squeezing represents the addition of gain. The H-plane widens and the E-plane shortens, as shown in Figure 5-10.

Table 5-2 details the statistics of the AIR-ANT1728.

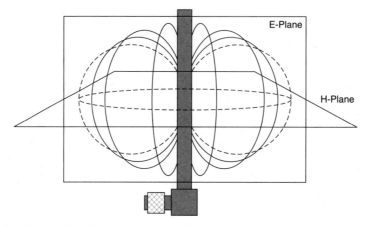

*This figure is based on an original image from the Wikipedia entry: http://en.wikipedia.org/wiki/E-plane_and_H-plane

Figure 5-5   *H-plane and E-plane*

Figure 5-6   *2.14-dBi Dipole Antenna (Rubber Duck)*

Table 5-2   *AIR-ANT1728 Statistics*

Gain	5.2 dBi
Polarization	5.2 dBi
H-plane	Vertical
E-plane	Omnidirectional 360 degrees
Antenna connector type	RP-TNC
Mounting	Drop ceiling cross-member indoor only

*This connector type is covered later, in the section "Antenna Connectors and Hardware."

Key
Topic

Figure 5-7   *AIR-ANT1728*

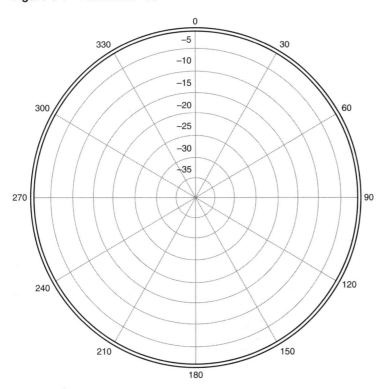

Figure 5-8   *H-plane of the AIR-ANT1728*

Key
Topic

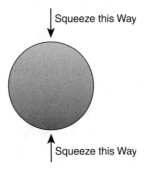

Figure 5-9   *Effect of Adding Gain*

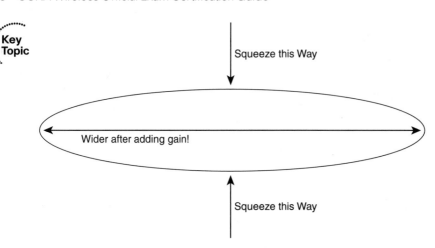

Figure 5-10   *H-plane and E-plane After Gain Is Added*

AIR-ANT2506

The AIR-ANT2506, shown in Figure 5-11, is a mast-mount indoor/outdoor antenna that you mount on a round mast. It is a 5.2-dBi antenna and is omnidirectional.

Table 5-3 gives details on the antenna.

Table 5-3   *AIR-ANT2506*

Gain	5.2 dBi
Polarization	Vertical
H-plane	Omnidirectional 360 degrees
E-plane	RP-TNC
Antenna connector type	Mast-mount indoor/outdoor
Mounting	

*This connector type is covered later, in the section "Antenna Connectors and Hardware."

AIR-ANT24120

The AIR-ANT24120, shown in Figure 5-12, is an omnidirectional antenna that is designed to offer higher gain at 12 dBi. Like the 2506, it is a mast-mount antenna.

Table 5-4 provides more details on the AIR-ANT24120.

Table 5-4   *AIR-ANT24120*

Gain	12 dBi
Polarization	Linear Vertical
H-plane	Omnidirectional 360 degrees
E-plane	7 degrees
Antenna connector type	RP-TNC
Mounting	Mast-mount

*This connector type is covered later, in the section "Antenna Connectors and Hardware."

Figure 5-11   *AIR-ANT2506*

Directional Antennas

Directional antennas are usually mounted on walls and have their radiation patterns focused in a certain direction. This is similar to the earlier example of a flashlight (see the section "Common Antenna Types"). The goal is to provide coverage for areas such as long hallways, a warehouse, or anywhere you need a more directed signal. When used in an indoor environment, this kind of antenna usually is placed on walls and pillars. In an outdoor environment it can be seen on rooftops in the form of a parabolic dish.

This kind of antenna provides more gain than an omnidirectional, but again, the shape or radiation pattern is focused. They employ the "one floor" logic discussed earlier (see the section "Omnidirectional Antennas"). This means that they do not have much of a range vertically.

8.5-dBi Patch, Wall Mount

The 8.5-dBi patch is a wall-mounted directional antenna that provides more gain than a basic omnidirectional rubber duck. This results in 8.5 dBi for directional instead of 2.14 omnidirectional. Figure 5-13 shows the Cisco AIR-ANT2485P-R 8.5-dBi wall-mounted patch antenna.

Notice that this is a flat antenna. It is designed to radiate directionally, as illustrated in Figure 5-14. You place this antenna on a wall. By its form factor, it is very discreet.

Figures 5-15 and 5-16 show the H-plane and E-plane. Notice that the radiation pattern is not 360 degrees, even on the H-plane. However, a bit of signal is seen behind the antenna. This is normal and usually is absorbed by the wall that the antenna is mounted to. When

Figure 5-12   *AIR-ANT24120*

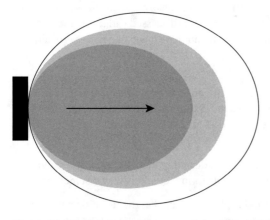

Figure 5-13   *AIR-ANT2485P-R Wall-Mounted Patch Antenna*

Figure 5-14   *Radiation Pattern of the AIR-ANT2485P-R*

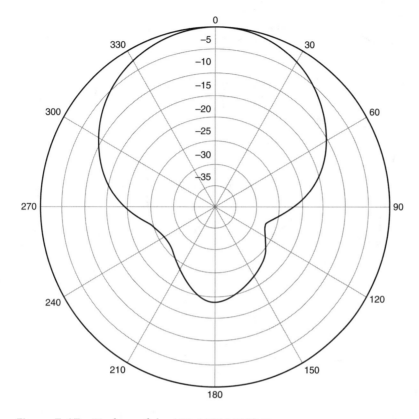

Figure 5-15   *H-plane of the AIR-ANT-2485P-R*

the antenna is mounted above a doorway, the back signal lets a client get the signal from the antenna just as he or she gets to the doorway.

Table 5-5 provides the details of the AIR-ANT2485P-R.

Table 5-5   *AIR-ANT2485P-R*

Gain	8.5 dBi
Polarization	Vertical
H-plane	66 degrees
E-plane	56 degrees
Antenna connector type	RP-TNC
Mounting	Wall mount

*This connector type is covered later, in the section "Antenna Connectors and Hardware."

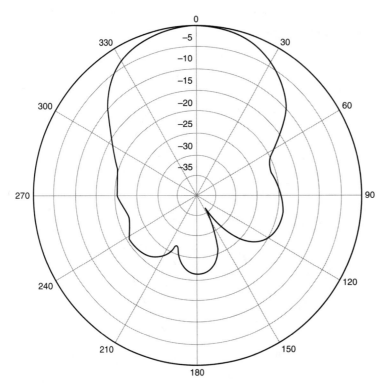

Figure 5-16   *E-plane of the AIR-ANT-2485P-R*

13.5 Yagi Antenna

The 13.5 yagi antenna is a directional antenna that offers a very direct radiation pattern. Sometimes you see these mounted above doorways to cover a long hallway. You can also put a number of them side by side on a wall to cover a large open space such as a warehouse or convention center.

Yagi antennas are sometimes called Yagi-Uda antennas, after their two creators.

Note: For more information on the history of the Yagi-Uda antenna, see http://en. wikipedia.org/wiki/Yagi_antenna#History.

Yagi antennas have a butterfly effect that is an effect of their polarization, as illustrated in Figure 5-17.

You can clearly see the butterfly-type pattern in the figure. Notice that there is also some coverage on the back side of the antenna, even though it is designed as a directional antenna. This fact can be useful if you want to test under the antenna.

Figure 5-18 shows the 10-dBi yagi, one of the yagi antennas offered by Cisco.

Although it is enclosed in an aesthetically pleasing cylinder, the antenna inside is a "comb" that resembles old UHF television antennas that you used to see on the roofs of houses.

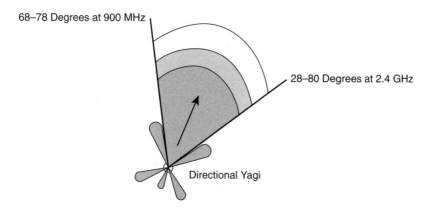

68–78 Degrees at 900 MHz

28–80 Degrees at 2.4 GHz

Directional Yagi

Figure 5-17   *Radiation Pattern of a Yagi Antenna*

Figure 5-18   *AIR-ANT2410Y-R*

Figure 5-19 shows the AIR-ANT1949, another yagi antenna offered by Cisco.

This yagi is a high-gain antenna at 13.5 dBi. Its H-plane and E-plane are shown in Figures 5-20 and 5-21, respectively.

Table 5-6 shows the details of the AIR-ANT1949 yagi.

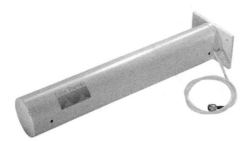

Figure 5-19   *AIR-ANT1949 Yagi*

Table 5-6   *AIR-ANT1949 Yagi*

Frequency range	2.4 to 2.83 GHz
Gain	13.5 dBi
Polarization	Vertical
H-plane	30 degrees
E-plane	25 degrees
Antenna connector type	RP-TNC
Mounting	Mast/wall mount

*This connector type is covered later, in the section "Antenna Connectors and Hardware."

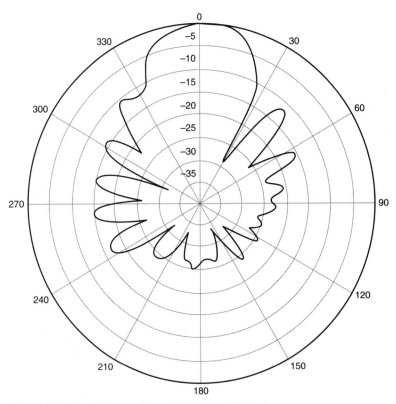

Figure 5-20   *H-plane of the AIR-ANT1949 Yagi*

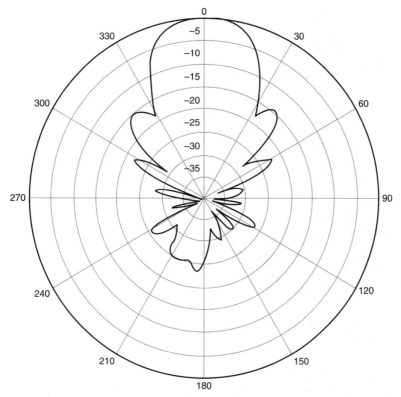

Figure 5-21 *E-plane of the AIR-ANT1949 Yagi*

When you mount a yagi, the polarity is important to consider. Because the antenna is enclosed in a protective casing, you might not be able to look at it and know the radiation pattern. Read the manufacturer documentation or look for manufacturer markings that indicate how to mount the antenna. On a Cisco yagi, the bottom usually is indicated by a black dot. Remember that if you mount it incorrectly, you will degrade the signal.

21-dBi Parabolic Dish

The 21-dBi *parabolic dish* antenna, shown in Figure 5-22, is almost 100 times more powerful than the rubber duck (discussed in the section "2.2-dBi Dipole").

Parabolic dish antennas have a very narrow path. Their radiation pattern is very focused. When you install these, you have to be very accurate in the direction you point them. You would use a parabolic dish in point-to-point scenarios. Distances of up to 25 miles at 2.4 GHz and 12 miles at 5 GHz can be reached using parabolic dish antennas. Parabolic dish antennas have a butterfly effect similar to yagi antennas. Also, some parabolic dish antennas allow polarity to be changed. This is important, because they can be mounted at different angles, and polarity changes how the RF is propagated. Table 5-7 shows the details of the Cisco AIR-ANT3338.

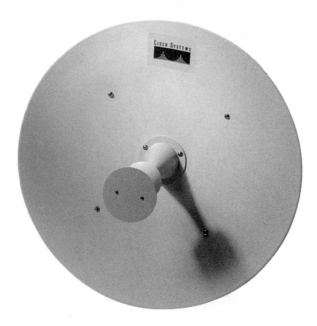

Figure 5-22   *Parabolic Dish Antenna*

Table 5-7   *AIR-ANT3338 Parabolic Dish Antenna*

Power	5 Watts
Gain	21 dBi
Polarization	Vertical
H-plane	12 degrees
E-plane	12 degrees
Antenna connector type	RP-TNC
Mounting	Mast mount

*This connector type is covered later, in the section "Antenna Connectors and Hardware."

Dual-Patch "Omnidirectional" 5.2 dBi, Pillar Mount

Another special type of antenna to consider is the dual-patch 5.2-dBi pillar-mount omni-directional, shown in Figure 5-23.

It is considered "special" because it has two patch directional antennas placed back to back, making it "omnidirectional." Because there are actually two antennas, you can use diversity with this antenna.

Figure 5-23   *AIR-ANT3213 Dual-Patch 5.2-dBi Pillar-Mount Omnidirectional*

You would use this type of antenna to provide access to a hall, because it's usually mounted to a pillar in the middle of the hall. Figures 5-24 and 5-25 show this antenna's radiation patterns.

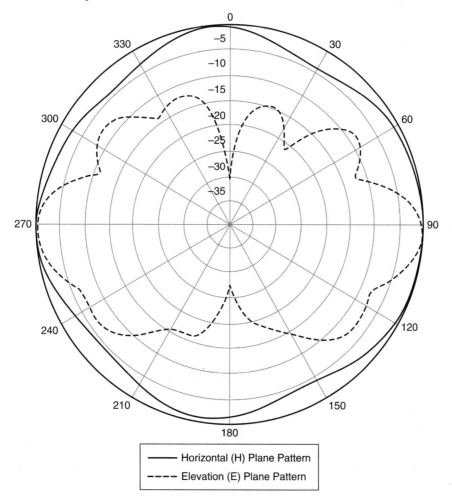

Figure 5-24   *AIR-ANT3213 Left Antenna Radiation Pattern*

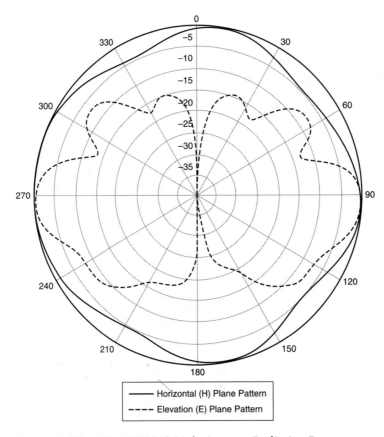

Figure 5-25   *AIR-ANT3213 Right Antenna Radiation Pattern*

In these two figures, the outer line is the H-plane, and the inner, dashed line is the E-plane.

Table 5-8 shows the details of the AIR-ANT3213.

Table 5-8   *AIR-ANT3213 Antenna*

Frequency range	2.4 to 2.83 GHz
Gain	5.2 dBi
Polarization	Vertical
H-plane	Omnidirectional
E-plane	25 degrees
Antenna connector type	RP-TNC

*This connector type is covered in the next section.

Antenna Connectors and Hardware

Cisco uses a connector called the *RP-TNC*, which stands for *Reverse-Polarity Threaded Neill-Concelman*, named for its inventor. Another type that Cisco uses is the *N connector*, invented in the 1940s by Paul Neill at Bell Labs. Different connecters are required because of government regulations. The vendor has to ensure that you use the right antenna with the right product. This doesn't mean that people can't make an antenna, but by using vendor-designed antennas, you can be sure that you are within government guidelines for EIRP.

Other vendors use connectors such as the Subminiature version A (SMA) and its variants, the RP-SMA and SMA-RS. You also find MC and MMCX connectors on PCMCIA cards. There are a number of others; these are only a few. The important thing, though, is that both sides need to match the type.

If the antenna isn't a direct connect, you need to get a cable from the vendor. When you add a cable between the radio and the antenna, you also add loss. The specific vendor documentation should tell you how much loss.

Attenuators

If custom cabling is used, you can end up with too much signal, thus causing bleedover into other networks. You can use an *attenuator* to reduce the signal. You would place an attenuator between the radio and the antenna.

Amplifiers

If you add a cable between an antenna and its radio, you add loss. To make up for this loss, you add gain. However, you may not be able to add enough gain to compensate. In this scenario, you add an *amplifier* between the AP and antenna to strengthen the signal. This method is called an active amplifier because it strengthens the antenna.

Lightning Arrestors

One of the types of antennas discussed in this chapter is a parabolic dish. These antennas offer point-to-point capability between two networks that are far away. This calls for mounting the antenna outdoors, usually on a roof. The antenna cables back to a radio on a bridge or AP and from there makes its way back to the common distribution. In other words, the parabolic dish provides a path back to your wired LAN. So, logically, if a lightning bolt were to hit the antenna or an access point, it could transfer its energy back along the copper cable. This would result in damage to your entire wired LAN as well.

The good news is that you can protect against this by using a *lightning arrestor*. The Cisco Aironet Lightning Arrestor, illustrated in Figure 5-26, prevents surges from reaching the RF equipment by its shunting effect.

Surges are limited to less than 50 volts in about 100 nanoseconds. Because a typical lightning surge is 2 microseconds, this should provide adequate protection from indirect strikes. Lightning arrestors do not try to stop direct strikes. They also require a ground, as shown in Figure 5-26.

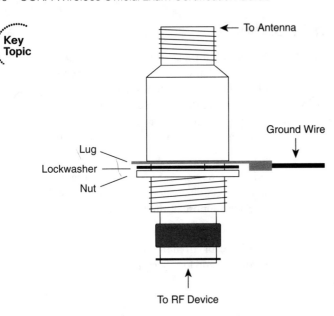

Figure 5-26 *Lightning Arrestor*

Splitters

The final topic of this chapter is installing a *splitter*. Splitters are used mainly in outdoor wireless deployments to split in two a signal coming from a cable and to send it in two directions. You could also use it to receive a signal coming from one direction and forward it through another antenna, connected to the same access point, toward another direction. Although this technique can be useful, the drawback is that it greatly reduces the range and throughput by about 50 percent.

Exam Preparation Tasks

Review All the Key Topics

Review the most important topics from this chapter, denoted with the Key Topic icon. Table 5-9 lists these key topics and the page number where each one can be found.

Table 5-9   *Key Topics for Chapter 5*

Key Topic Item	Description	Page Number
Figure 5-5	H-plane and E-plane	76
Figure 5-6	2.14-dBi dipole	76
Figure 5-9	effect of adding gain	77
Figure 5-10	H-plane and E-plane after adding gain	78
Table 5-2	AIR-ANT1728 statistics	76
Table 5-3	AIR-ANT2506	78
Table 5-4	AIR-ANT24120	79
Table 5-5	AIR-ANT2485P-R	81
Figure 5-17	Radiation pattern of a yagi	83
Table 5-6	AIR-ANT1949 yagi	84
Table 5-7	AIR-ANT3338 parabolic dish antenna	86
Table 5-8	AIR-ANT3213 antenna	88
Figure 5-26	Lightning arrestor	90

Complete the Tables and Lists from Memory

Print a copy of Appendix B, "Memory Tables," (found on the CD) or at least the section for this chapter, and complete the tables and lists from memory. Appendix C, "Memory Tables Answer Key," also on the CD, includes completed tables and lists so that you can check your work.

Definition of Key Terms

Define the following key terms from this chapter, and check your answers in the Glossary:

polarity, diversity vertical polarization, horizontal polarization, circular polarization, omnidirectional antenna, horizontal (H) plane, azimuth, elevation (E) plane, one-floor concept, dipole, radiation pattern, isotropic radiator, directional antenna, rubber duck, Yagi-Uda, parabolic dish, dual-patch "omnidirectional," Reverse-Polarity Threaded Neill-Concelman (RP-TNC), N connector, attenuator, amplifier, lightning arrestor, splitter

References in This Chapter

Cisco Systems, "Cisco Aironet Antennas and Accessories Reference Guide," http://tinyurl.com/2v2dp2

This chapter covers the following subjects:

The 802.11 Protocol Family Overview: A brief overview of the 802.11 family of WLAN protocols.

The Original 802.11 Protocol: A look at the original 802.11 protocol.

The 802.11b Protocol: A look at the 802.11b protocol.

The 802.11g Protocol: A look at the 802.11g protocol and how it operates with 802.11b clients.

The 802.11a Protocol: A look at the 802.11a protocol.

The 802.11n Protocol: A look at the 802.11n draft standard.

CHAPTER 6

Overview of the 802.11 WLAN Protocols

The wireless space consists of numerous protocols. Specifically in the WLAN area, the Institute of Engineers Electrical and Electronic Engineers (IEEE) has created several protocols within the 802.11 category to facilitate the networking process. These protocols define the data rates, the modulation techniques, and more. An understanding of these protocols is essential for any administrator of wireless networks.

In this chapter, you will learn about the 802.11 family of protocols, including 802.11, 802.11a, b, and g. In addition, you will gain an introduction to the 802.11n draft standard.

You should do the "Do I Know This Already?" quiz first. If you score 80 percent or higher, you might want to skip to the section "Exam Preparation Tasks." If you score below 80 percent, you should spend the time reviewing the chapter. Refer to Appendix A, "Answers to the 'Do I Know This Already?' Quizzes" to confirm your answers.

"Do I Know This Already?" Quiz

The "Do I Know This Already?" quiz helps you determine your level of knowledge of this chapter's topics before you begin. Table 6-1 details the major topics discussed in this chapter and their corresponding quiz questions.

Table 6-1 *"Do I Know This Already?" Section-to-Question Mapping*

Foundation Topics Section	Questions
The 802.11 Protocol Family Overview	1
The Original 802.11	2–5
The 802.11b Protocol	6–10
The 802.11g Protocol	11–14
The 802.11a Protocol	16–20
The 802.11n Protocol	21–25

1. What organization standardizes the 802.11 set of protocols?

   a. IANA

   b. IEEE

   c. FCC

   d. ETSI

2. What is the maximum data rate that the original 802.11 protocol supports?

   a. 1 Mbps

   b. 5 Mbps

   c. 2 Mbps

   d. 3 Mbps

3. The original 802.11 protocol supported which two RF technologies? (Choose two.)

   a. FHSS

   b. CDMA

   c. IETF

   d. DSSS

4. The original 802.11 protocol operates in which frequency range?

   a. 2.0 GHz

   b. 900 MHz

   c. 5.0 GHz

   d. 2.4 GHz

5. The original 802.11 protocol operates in the ISM bands. True or false?

   a. True

   b. False

6. 802.11b operates on which frequency range?

   a. 2.0 GHz

   b. 900 MHz

   c. 5.0 GHz

   d. 2.4 GHz

7. 802.11b has how many nonoverlapping channels?

   a. 2

   b. 3

   c. 4

   d. 8

8. Which of the following modulation techniques are used by 802.11b? (Choose all that apply.)

    a. DBPSK

    b. 16-QAM

    c. DQPSK

    d. 64-QAM

9. What coding method is used by 802.11b? (Choose all that apply.)

    a. Barker 11

    b. CCK

    c. Barker 8

    d. QAM-CCK

10. Which 802.11b channels do not overlap? (Choose all that apply.)

    a. 1

    b. 3

    c. 6

    d. 11

11. What modulation technique is used by the 802.11g protocol? (Choose all that apply.)

    a. DBPSK

    b. DQPSK

    c. QAM

    d. Barker

12. What is the maximum data rate that the 802.11g protocol supports?

    a. 22 Mbps

    b. 48 Mbps

    c. 54 Mbps

    d. 90 Mbps

13. When no 802.11b clients are in an 802.11b/g cell, what information will be in the AP beacon?

    a. NON_ERP present: yes; Use Protection: no

    b. NON_ERP present: no; Use Protection: yes

    c. NON_ERP present: yes; Use Protection: yes

    d. NON_ERP present: no; Use Protection: no

14. What are two protection methods used by 802.11g clients when an 802.11b client is in the cell? (Choose two.)

    a. RTS/CTS

    b. LMI

    c. CTS to self

    d. RTS to self

15. The 802.11a protocol is backward compatible only with 802.11g because they support the same maximum data rates. True or false?

    a. True

    b. False

16. An 802.11a client must support which data rates?

    a. 6, 12, 24 Mbps

    b. 11, 24, 54 Mbps

    c. 6, 9, 12, 18, 24, 36, 48, 54 Mbps

    d. 6, 11, 24, 48 Mbps

17. The 802.11a protocol operates in which frequency spectrum?

    a. 2.0 GHz

    b. 900 MHz

    c. 5.0 GHz

    d. 2.4 GHz

18. Which is not a valid modulation technique for 802.11a?

    a. BPSK

    b. QPSK

    c. Barker 11

    d. QAM

19. 802.11a uses the UNII-1, UNII-2, and UNII-3 bands. Which bands are usable without a license in Europe? (Choose all that apply.)

    a. UNII-1

    b. UNII-2

    c. UNII-3

    d. UNII-4.1

20. The FCC and ETSI have imposed what requirements for use in the UNII-2 and UNII-3 bands? (Choose all that apply.)

   a. DFC

   b. TPC

   c. CSMA/CA

   d. MIMO

21. 802.11n supports multiple antennas using what technology?

   a. MIMO

   b. MAO

   c. Multi-scan antenna output

   d. Spatial coding

22. What type of multiplexing does 802.11n use?

   a. Spatial

   b. OFDM

   c. DSSS

   d. FHSS

23. What task does TxBF accomplish in 802.11n networks?

   a. The signal is sent over multiple transmit antennas, improving performance at the receiver.

   b. The signal increases in gain to accomplish greater distances.

   c. The signal is spread across multiple channels and then re-created at the receiver to negate interference issues on sidebands.

   d. The signal is bonded on a 40-MHz channel, giving you more bandwidth.

24. How does 802.11n improve the throughput with acknowledgments?

   a. It uses a 1-for-1 acknowledgment option; 1 sent = 1 acknowledged.

   b. It does not use acknowledgments.

   c. It uses block acknowledgments.

   d. It uses a 2-to-1 ratio of sent frames to acknowledgments.

25. A device that has two transmit antennas and two receive antennas is referred to as which of the following?

   a. Dual TxRx

   b. 2X2

   c. 2x

   d. A double

Foundation Topics

The 802.11 Protocol Family Overview

The IEEE helps to standardize wireless protocols. Those that you must be familiar with for the CCNA Wireless Exam are the 802.11 a/b/g and n protocols. These four IEEE standards define the wireless family that is used in almost all wireless LANS today. The standardization of wireless networking started with the original 802.11 protocol in 1997, and each protocol thereafter has simply added to the benefit of wireless technologies. This chapter looks at the 802.11 protocol families, their history, and how they operate. The 802.11 protocols encompass the 2.4-GHz and 5-GHz range.

The Original 802.11 Protocol

The original 802.11 protocol was where wireless LANs find there beginnings. It is rare to find this original protocol in new hardware today, probably because it only operates at 1 and 2 Mbps. The 802.11 standard describes frequency-hopping spread spectrum (FHSS), which operates only at 1 and 2 Mbps. The standard also describes direct sequence spread spectrum (DSSS), which operates only at 1 and 2 Mbps. If a client operates at any other data rate, it is considered non-802.11 compliant, even if it can use the 1- and 2-Mbps rates.

Table 6-2 highlights the characteristics of the original 802.11 protocol.

Table 6-2   *The 802.11 Protocol*

Ratified	1997
RF Technology	FHSS and DSSS
Frequency Spectrum	2.4-GHz

The original 802.11 protocol falls within the industry, scientific, and medical (ISM) bands and operates only in the 2.4-GHz range. The 2.4-GHz range has up to 14 channels depending on the country you are in. In the United States, the FCC allows channels 1 through 11 to be used. This gives you 3 nonoverlapping channels: 1, 6, and 11. This is important because you do not want to have APs and clients operating on the same channel placed near each other for interference reasons.

The 802.11b Protocol

802.11b is a supplement to the 802.11 protocol. To get an better feel for how the 802.11 protocols progressed, understand that technology moves faster than the standards do. 802.11 was quickly outgrown because wired networks offered 10 Mbps versus the 1 and 2 Mbps of 802.11. Vendors developed methods of achieving higher data rates. The danger in vendor-designed protocols, of course, is *interoperability*. The job of the IEEE was simply to define a standard that all vendors could follow based on the proprietary implementations that they were using.

802.11b offers higher data rates—up to 11 Mbps—with backward compatibility at 1 and 2 Mbps. At 1 and 2 Mbps, the same coding and modulation as 802.11 is used. When operating at the new speeds—5.5 Mbps and 11 Mbps—a different modulation and coding is used. 802.11 uses Barker 11 coding, as covered in Chapter 1, "Introduction to Wireless Networking Concepts," and 802.11b uses complementary code keying (CCK) for coding. For modulation, 802.11 uses differential binary phase-shift keying (DBPSK), whereas 802.11b uses differential quadrature phase-shift keying (DQPSK). The result is more data sent in the same period.

802.11b was ratified in September 1999. The United States has 11 channels, the same as 802.11. In Europe, the ETSI defines 13 channels, and Japan has 14. 802.11b allows dynamic rate shifting (DRS) to enable clients to shift rates to lower rates as they travel farther away from an AP and higher rates as they get closer to an AP. Today, 802.11b is the most popular and most widely deployed wireless standard. Table 6-3 gives some basic information on the 802.11b standard.

Table 6-3   *The 802.11b Protocol*

Ratified	1999
RF Technology	DSSS
Frequency Spectrum	2.4-GHz
Coding	Barker 11 and CCK
Modulation	DBPSK and DQPSK
Data Rates	1, 2, 5.5, 11 Mbps
Nonoverlapping Channels	1, 6, 11

The 802.11g Protocol

The IEEE ratified 802.11g in June 2003. In addition to the four data rates of 802.11b, it added eight more. The maximum data rate of 54 Mbps places 802.11g in the same speed range as 802.11a; however, it remains in the 2.4-Ghz frequency range. On the lower end, 802.11g is still compatible with 802.11b, using the same modulation and coding as 802.11b for the 1-, 2-, 5.5-, and 11-Mbps rates. To achieve the higher data rates, 802.11g uses orthogonal frequency division multiplexing (OFDM) for modulation. OFDM is the same modulation that 802.11a uses.

There are still only three nonoverlapping channels. With OFDM, you must be careful about power outputs; the power needs to be reduced to handle the peaks in the modulation technique and still fall within governmental regulations. Table 6-4 shows some details about 802.11g.

Key Topic

Table 6-4 *The 802.11g Protocol*

Ratified	June 2003
RF Technology	DSSS and OFDM
Frequency Spectrum	2.4 GHz
Coding	Barker 11 and CCK
Modulation	DBPSK and DQPSK
Data Rates	1, 2, 5.5, 11 Mbps with DSSS 6, 9, 12, 18, 24, 36, 48, 54 Mbps with OFDM
Nonoverlapping Channels	1, 6, 11

How 802.11g Interacts with 802.11b

One interesting point about 802.11g is that, although it is backward compatible with 802.11b clients, you probably do not want it to be because if you must support 802.11b clients, the entire cell suffers. In fact, if the average bandwidth is 22 Mbps in an 802.11g cell and an 802.11b client shows up, the cell performance could degrade. This degradation in performance is because 802.11b clients do not understand OFDM. If an 802.11b client sends when an 802.11g client is sending, a collision will occur, and both clients will have to resend.

However, protection mechanisms are built in. To understand how this protection works, examine Figure 6-1.

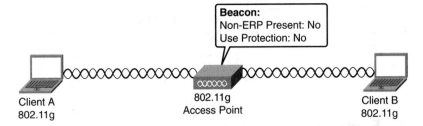

Beacon:
Non-ERP Present: No
Use Protection: No

Client A
802.11g

802.11g
Access Point

Client B
802.11g

Figure 6-1 *802.11g Cell with No 802.11b Clients*

Assume that initially 802.11b clients do not exist. The default behavior of an AP is to send beacons that include information about the AP and the wireless cell. Without 802.11b clients, the AP sends the following information in a beacon:

NON_ERP present: no

Use Protection: no

ERP is Extended Rate Physical. These are devices that have extended data rates. In other words, NON_ERP is talking about 802.11b clients. If they were ERP, that would support the higher data rates, making them 802.11g clients.

Now, going back to Figure 6-1 with no 802.11b clients, the AP tells everyone that 802.11b clients are unavailable and that they do not need to use protection mechanisms.

After an 802.11b client associates with the AP, things change. In Figure 6-2, the AP alerts the rest of the network about the NON_ERP client. This is done in the beacon that the AP sends.

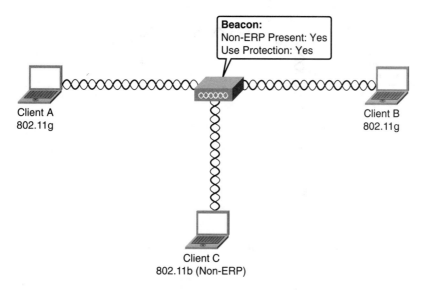

Beacon:
Non-ERP Present: Yes
Use Protection: Yes

Client A
802.11g

Client B
802.11g

Client C
802.11b (Non-ERP)

Figure 6-2   *802.11g Cell with an 802.11b Client*

Now that the cell knows about the 802.11b clients, the way that data is sent within the cell changes. When an 802.11g client sends a frame, it first must warn the 802.11b clients by sending a request to send (RTS) message at 802.11b speed so the 802.11b clients can hear and understand it. The RTS is not a broadcast as you might think, but rather a unicast that is sent to the recipient of the frame that the 802.11g client wants to send to. The recipient then responds with a clear to send (CTS) at 802.11b speed. Figure 6-3 illustrates this process.

In Step 1, the client knows that the 802.11b client is present; therefore, before sending, it issues an RTS at 802.11b speeds.

In Figure 6-4, the 802.11b client hears the RTS (Step 2), which includes the duration, and it waits until the duration is over before sending its data even though it cannot hear the 802.11g data that will be sent during the duration. Client B also hears the RTS and decides to send a CTS (Step 3).

In Step 4, shown in Figure 6-5, Client B sends a CTS back to Client A. Client C hears the CTS in Step 5.

In Step 6, Figure 6-6, Client A sends data to Client B at 802.11g speeds. The 802.11b client (Client C) cannot hear the data that it perceived as noise, but it still waits the duration seen in the RTS/CTS before sending data.

This protection mechanism works well because the 802.11b client can hear the RTS and the CTS no matter which client he is closest to. Another protection mechanism exists,

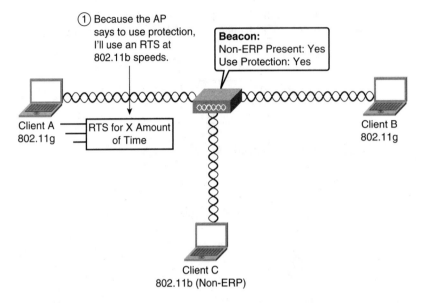

Figure 6-3   *802.11g Cell Using Protection: Part 1*

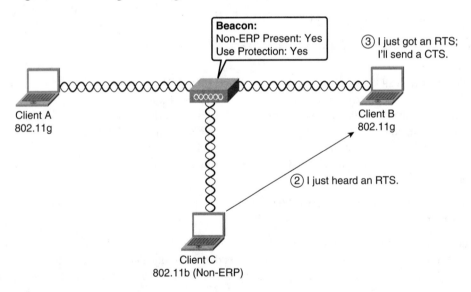

Figure 6-4   *802.11g Cell Using Protection: Part 2*

clear to send to self (CTS to self), but this is not a preferred method because a client that is not close to the sender might not hear the CTS to self.

Another bad side effect of 802.11b clients in an 802.11g cell is sort of a domino effect. As one AP advertises:

NON_ERP present: yes

Use Protection: yes

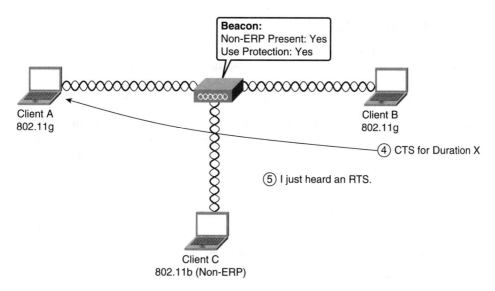

Figure 6-5   *802.11g Cell Using Protection: Part 3*

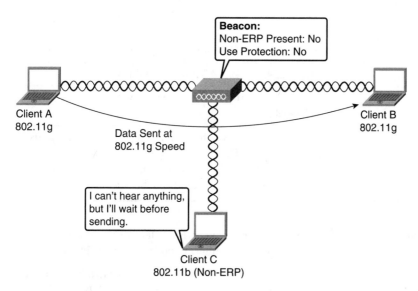

Figure 6-6   *802.11g Cell Using Protection: Part 4*

Nearby APs that hear this beacon start to advertise:

NON_ERP present: no

Use Protection: yes

The nearby cell advertises NON_ERP present to indicate that it did not hear NON_ERP devices, yet it advertises "Use Protection: yes" to be safe. This in effect forces the cell to use protection even without 802.11b clients in that particular cell, thus degrading performance for everyone in the cell. This is why APs have the option to use 802.11g only.

The 802.11a Protocol

802.11a was ratified in 1999 and operates in the 5-GHz frequency range. This makes it incompatible with 802.11, 802.11b, and 802.11g, while avoiding interference from these devices in addition to microwaves, Bluetooth devices, and cordless phones. 802.11a had late-market adoption, so it is not as widely deployed as the 802.11b and g protocols.

Another difference is that 802.11a supports anywhere from 12 to 23 nonoverlapping channels as opposed to the 3 nonoverlapping channels in 802.11b/g. Because OFDM is used, subchannels can overlap. 802.11a requires that the data rates of 6, 12, and 24 Mbps be supported but allows for data rates up to 54 Mbps.

Table 6-5 shows some details on the 802.11a standard.

Key Topic

Table 6-5 *The 802.11a Protocol*

Ratified	1999
RF Technology	OFDM
Frequency Spectrum	5.0 GHz
Coding	Convolution Coding
Modulation	BPSK, QPSK, 16-QAM, 64-QAM depending on the subcarrier.
Data Rates	6, 9, 12, 18, 24, 36, 48, 54 Mbps with OFDM
Nonoverlapping Channels	Each band has a 4; the middle 8 are used with 52 subcarriers on each channel.

*Convolution coding is a form of error correction in which redundant information analogous to a parity bit in a file system is added to the data. The error correction is calculated across all the subcarriers, so if narrowband interference corrupts data on one subcarrier, the receiver can reconstruct that data using the convolution coding on another subcarrier.[1]

The rules under ETSI specifications are a little different. ETSI allows 19 channels and requires that dynamic frequency control (DFC) and transmit power control (TPC) be used.

What makes 802.11a unique is the way the 5-GHz frequency band is divided into multiple parts. These parts, the Unlicensed National Information Infrastructure (UNII), were designed for different uses. UNII-1 was designed for indoor use with a permanent antenna. UNII-2 was designed for indoor or outdoor use with an external antenna, and UNII-3 was designed for outdoor bridges and external antennas.

The FCC revised the use of the frequency in 2004 by adding channels and requiring compliance of DFC and TPC to avoid radar. The revision also allows all three parts of the UNII to be used indoors. This is not the case with ETSI, however, because it does not allow unlicensed use of UNII-3.

Table 6-6 shows the frequency ranges of each of the UNII bands.

Table 6-6   *The UNII Frequency Bands*

Key
Topic

Band	Frequency	Use
UNII-1	5.15–5.25 GHz (UNII Indoor)	FCC allows indoor and outdoor use.
UNII-2	5.25–5.35 GHz (UNII Low)	Outdoor/indoor with DFC and TPC
UNII-3	5.725–5.825 GHz (U-NII/ISM)	FCC allows indoor and outdoor use.
		ETSI does not allow unlicensed use.

In the 802.11a spectrum, the higher-band channels are 30 MHz apart. This includes UNII-2 and above. The lower bands are 20 MHz apart.

802.11a Power Requirements

Table 6-7 details the rules for power as stated by the FCC in the United States. The "Output Power Not to Exceed" column in the table reflects the output power when using an omnidirectional antenna with 6-dBi gain.

Table 6-7   *FCC Regulations on Output and EIRP for UNII*

Band	Output Power Not to Exceed	EIRP Maximum
UNII-1	50 mW	22 dBm
UNII-2	250 mW	29 dBm
UNII-2 Extended	1 W	36 dBm
UNII-3	1W	36 dBm

As you can see from the table, UNII-1 is not to exceed 50 mW of output power or 22 dBm EIRP. UNII-2 is not to exceed 250 mW of output power and 29 dBm EIRP, whereas the extended UNII-2 and UNII-3 should be no more than 1 Watt of output power and 36 dBm EIRP. The FCC states that the responsibility of staying within output power regulations for wireless networks falls on the operator. For this reason, understanding the EIRP maximum values will help keep you within the guidelines.

The ETSI, of course, has its own rules, as seen in Table 6-8.

Table 6-8   *ETSI Regulations on Output and EIRP for UNII*   *(continued)*

Band	Output Power Not to Exceed	EIRP Maximum
UNII-1	200 mW	23 dBm
UNII-2	200 mW	23 dBm

continues

Table 6-8   *ETSI Regulations on Output and EIRP for UNII*   *(continued)*

Band	Output Power Not to Exceed	EIRP Maximum
UNII-2 Extended	1 W	30 dBm
UNII-3	Licensed use only	—

The IEEE rules are a bit more strict but should keep you within the federal regulations.

The 802.11n Protocol

802.11n is currently a draft standard. Again, technology has progressed more rapidly than the standards, because vendors are already shipping 802.11n APs and clients. What makes 802.11n special is that in a pure 802.11n environment, you can get speeds up to 300 Mbps, but most documentation says it will provide 100 Mbps. This is probably because the expectation is that other 802.11 clients will be present. 802.11n is, in fact, backward compatible with 802.11b/g and a.

The backward compatibility and speed capability of 802.11n come from its use of multiple antennas and a technology called Multiple-Input, Multiple-Output (MIMO). MIMO, pronounced Mee-Moh, uses different antennas to send and receive, thus increasing throughput and accomplishing more of a full duplex operation.

MIMO comes in three types:

- Precoding
- Spatial multiplexing
- Diversity coding

Precoding is a function that takes advantage of multiple antennas and the multipath issue that was discussed in Chapter 3, "WLAN RF Principles." 802.11n uses transmit beam-forming (TxBF), which is a technique that is used when more than one transmit antenna exists where the signal is coordinated and sent from each antenna so that the signal at the receiver is dramatically improved, even if it is far from the sender. This technique is something that you would use when the receiver has only a single antenna and is not moving. If the receiver is moving, then the reflection characteristics change, and the beamforming can no longer be coordinated. This coordination is called channel state information (CSI).

Spatial multiplexing takes a signal, splits it into several lower rate streams, and then sends each one out of different antennas. Each one of the lower rate streams are sent on the same frequency. The number of streams is limited to the lowest number of antennas on either the transmitter or the receiver. If an AP has four antennas and a client has two, you are limited to two.

Currently, the Wi-Fi Alliance is certifying 802.11n devices even though they are still in draft status. The Wi-FI Alliance is doing this using the interim IEEE 802.11n draft 2.0.

802.11n and the other 802.11 protocol standards are different in other ways, too. For example, at the physical layer, the way a signal is sent considers reflections and interferences an advantage instead of a problem. Another way that throughput is increased is by aggregation of channels. In 802.11n, two channels are aggregated to increase throughput. 802.11n uses 20-MHz and 40-MHz channels. The 40-MHz channels in 802.11n are actually two 20-MHz channels that are adjacent to each other and bonded.

Clients in 802.11n environments are pretty complex, so 802.11n is combined with OFDM. This enables the use of more subcarriers that range from 48 to 52.

With 802.11n, you can get up to 32 data rates.

Sending Frames

For the allocated time to send frames, only CTS to self is used with 802.11n; the RTS/CTS that was discussed earlier in this chapter is not used.

Another feature of 802.11n that makes it much more efficient is the way it uses block acknowledgments as opposed to acknowledging each unicast packet like the other 802.11 protocols do. A block acknowledgment works by sending a number of frames before having them acknowledged. This is similar to the way TCP works.

Another aspect of sending requires knowledge of how frames are sent in a normal 802.11 a/b/g world. You will learn more about this in Chapter 7, "Wireless Traffic Flow and AP Discovery," but the following is a quick look:

> Each sending station must wait until a frame is sent before sending the next frame; this is called distributed interframe space (DIFS).

This DIFS can cause more overhead than necessary. 802.11n improves on this DIFS mechanism by using a smaller interframe space called reduced interframe space (RIFS). This reduces delay and overhead.

Antenna Considerations

The number of antennas that the sender and the receiver have can differ. Here is how they work.

If a transmitter can emit over three antennas, it has three data streams. If it can receive over three antennas, it has three receive chains. In documentation, this is called a 3×3. Two receive chains and two data streams is called a 2×2.

This is important because the Cisco 1250 AP is a 2×3 device. If you have a laptop that is a 2×2, you can start to see how this takes on meaning. When using special multiplexing, you are limited to the same number of streams as the lowest number of antennas. In this scenario, you would have two streams.

Finally, note that even if you do not have 802.11n clients, you can expect to see about a 30 percent improvement, based on these features.

Exam Preparation Tasks

Review All Key Concepts

Review the most important topics from this chapter, noted with the Key Topics icon in the outer margin of the page. Table 6-9 lists a reference of these key topics and the page number where you can find each one.

Table 6-9   *Key Topics for Chapter 6*

Key Topic Item	Description	Page Number
Table 6-2	The 802.11 protocol	100
Table 6-3	The 802.11b protocol	101
Table 6-4	The 802.11g protocol	102
Table 6-5	The 802.11a protocol	106
Table 6-6	The UNII frequency bands	107

Complete the Tables and Lists from Memory

Print a copy of Appendix B, "Memory Tables" (found on the CD) or at least the section for this chapter, and complete the tables and lists from memory. Appendix C, "Memory Tables Answer Key," also on the CD, includes completed tables and lists to check your work.

Definition of Key Terms

Define the following key terms from this chapter, and check your answers in the Glossary:

FHSS, DSSS, ISM, OFDM, beacons, ERP, RTS/CTS, CTS to self, DFC, TPC, MIMO, precoding, transmit beamforming, spatial multiplexing, channel state information, block acknowledgments, DIFS, RIFS

End Notes

[1]CWNA Certified Wireless Network Administrator; Official Study Guide, Planet 3 Wireless, McGraw Hill/Osborne 2005

This chapter covers the following subjects:

Wireless Frame Transmission: A discussion of how frames are transmitted on a wireless LAN.

Wireless Frame Headers: A look at the headers used in wireless transmissions.

Frame Types: Putting together how the frame types are used in managing and connecting to a network.

A Wireless Connection: A look at a wireless connection.

CHAPTER 7

Wireless Traffic Flow and AP Discovery

It is not likely that in your everyday activity you will be following the flow of traffic. At least the hope is that you will not have to. On occasion, however, you will need to analyze the flow of traffic in troubleshooting network issues. For this reason and just so that you have a complete understanding of what is involved in wireless transmissions, you need to understand wireless traffic flow and the process of discovering an AP. In this chapter, you will learn how a client finds an AP, associates, and sends traffic.

You should do the "Do I Know This Already?" quiz first. If you score 80 percent or higher, you may want to skip to the section "Exam Preparation Tasks." If you score below 80 percent, you should spend the time reviewing the entire chapter. Refer to Appendix A, "Answers to the 'Do I Know This Already?' Quizzes" to confirm your answers.

"Do I Know This Already?" Quiz

The "Do I Know This Already?" quiz helps you determine your level of knowledge of this chapter's topics before you begin. Table 7-1 details the major topics discussed in this chapter and their corresponding quiz questions.

Table 7-1 *"Do I Know This Already?" Section-to-Question Mapping*

Foundation Topics Section	Questions
Wireless Frame Transmission	1–5
Wireless Frame Headers	6–7
Frame Types	8–12

1. What are the three frame types seen in a wireless LAN? (Choose three.)

   a. Management

   b. Control

   c. Data

   d. Contention

2. What type of frame is used for acknowledging receipt of data?

   a. Control

   b. Reply

   c. Null

   d. Management

3. What frame type is used to send beacons?

   a. Control

   b. Management

   c. Informational

   d. Data

4. To determine if the medium is in use, which of the following are used? (Choose all that apply.)

   a. CCA

   b. CAS

   c. VCA

   d. VCS

5. Which interframe space is used for quickly sending a frame?

   a. UIFS

   b. DIFS

   c. SIFS

   d. PIFS

6. How many MAC addresses can be present in a wireless header?

   a. 1

   b. 2

   c. 3

   d. 4

7. Which of the following is a management frame type?

   a. Probe response

   b. ACK

   c. RTS

   d. Null function

8. Beacons contain information to assist clients in accessing the network. Which of the following is *not* in a beacon?

   a. Beacon interval

   b. Capability information

   c. A reference time for the cell

   d. The WEP passphrase

9. A client that connects by hearing a beacon is said to use what type of scanning?

   a. Passive

   b. Classic

   c. Active

   d. Fast

10. A client that sends a probe request is said to use what type of scanning?

   a. Preemptive

   b. Dynamic

   c. Passive

   d. Active

11. A client that sends a deauthentication message must reauthenticate when it returns to the cell. True or false?

   a. True

   b. False

12. A client that sends a disassociation message must reauthenticate when it returns to the cell. True or false?

   a. True

   b. False

Foundation Topics

Wireless Frame Transmission

When people talk about wireless networks, they often say that they are just like wired 802.3 LANs. This is actually incorrect, aside from the fact that they use MAC addresses. Wireless LANs use the 802.11 frame structure, and you can encounter multiple types of frames. To get a better understanding, you can begin by learning the three types of wireless frames. Once you are familiar with the three types of wireless frames, you can further your knowledge by taking a deeper look at interframe spacing (IFS) and why it is necessary.

Wireless Frame Types

Wireless LANs come in three frame types:

- **Management frames:** Used for joining and leaving a wireless cell. Management frame types include association request, association response, and reassociation request, just to name a few. (See Table 7-2 for a complete list.)

- **Control frames:** Used to acknowledge when data frames are received.

- **Data frames:** Frames that contain data.

Now that you have an idea of what frames are used, it is helpful to see how these frames are sent. For this, you need to understand a few more terms that might be new to you. Because all the terms meld together to some degree, they are explained in context throughout the next section.

Sending a Frame

Recall that wireless networks are half-duplex networks. If more than one device were to send at the same time, a collision would result. If a collision occurs, the data from both senders would be unreadable and would need to be resent. This is a waste of time and resources. To overcome this issue, wireless networks use multiple steps to access the network. Wireless LANs use carrier sense multiple access collision avoidance (CSMA/CA), which is similar to the way 802.3 LANs work. The *carrier sense* part means that a station has to determine if anyone else is sending. This is done with clear channel assessment (CCA), and what it means is that you listen. You can, however, run into an issue where two devices cannot hear each other. This is called the hidden node problem. This issue is overcome using virtual carrier sense (VCS). The medium is not considered available until both the physical and virtual carrier report that it is clear.

Each station must also observe IFS. IFS is a period that a station has to wait before it can send. Not only does IFS ensure that the medium is clear, but it ensures that frames are not sent so close together that they are misinterpreted. The types of IFS periods are as follows:

- **Short interframe space (SIFS):** For higher priority and used for ACKs, among other things

- **Point-coordination interframe space (PIFS):** Used when an AP is going to control the network

- **Distributed-coordination interframe space (DIFS):** Used for data frames and is the normal spacing between frames

Each of these has a specific purpose as defined by the IEEE.

SIFS is used when you must send a frame quickly. For example, when a data frame is sent and must be acknowledged (ACK), the ACK should be sent before another station sends other data. Data frames use DIFS. The time value of DIFS is longer than SIFS, so the SIFS would preempt DIFS because it has a higher priority.

Figure 7-1 illustrates the transmission of a frame. In the figure, Station A wants to send a frame. As the process goes, both the physical and virtual carrier need to be free. This means the client has to listen. To listen, the client chooses a random number and begins a countdown process, called a *backoff timer*. The speed at which the countdown occurs is called a *slottime* and is different for 802.11a, b, and g.

Key Topic

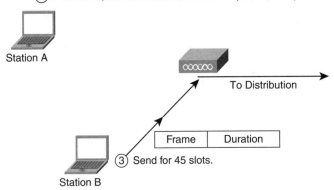

① Select a random timer (29), 28, 27, 26....

② Listen during countdown.

④ I was at 18; add 45 to that and continue (63, 62, 61...).

Station A

To Distribution

| Frame | Duration |

③ Send for 45 slots.

Station B

Figure 7-1 *Sending a Frame: Part 1*

It works like this:

1. Station A selects the random timer value of 29.

2. Station A starts counting at 29, 28, 27, 26, and so on. While Station A is counting down, it is also listening for whether anyone else is sending a frame.

3. When the timer is at 18, Station B sends a frame, having a duration value in the header of 45.

4. The duration of 45 that is in the header of the frame sent by Station B is called a *network allocation vector (NAV)* and is a reservation of the medium that includes the amount of time to send its frame, wait for the SIFS, and then receive an ACK from the AP.

5. Station A adds 45 to the 18 that is left and continues counting down, 63, 62, 61, and so on. The total time that Station A waits before sending is called the *contention window*.

6. After the timer on Station A reaches 0, it can send its frame as illustrated in Figure 7-2. At this point, the medium should be clear.

If Station A sends but fails, it resets the backoff timer to a new random number and counts down again. The backoff timer gets larger as the frames fail in transmission. For example, the initial timer can be any number between 0 and 31. After the first failure, it jumps to any number between 0 and 127. It doubles for the next failure, then again, then again.

This entire process is known as the *distributed coordination function* (DCF). This simply means that each station is responsible for coordinating the sending of its data. The alternative to DCF is *point coordination function (PCF)*, which means the AP is responsible for coordination of data transmission.

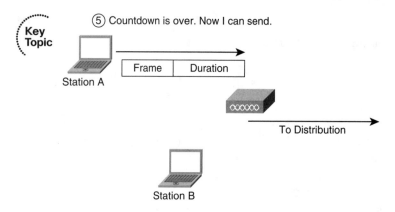

Figure 7-2   *Sending a Frame: Part 2*

If the frame is successful, an ACK must be sent. The ACK uses the SIFS timer value to make sure it is sent quickly. Some amount of silence between frames is natural. The SIFS is the shortest period of silence. The NAV reserves this time. A normal silence time is the DIFS. Again, the ACK uses SIFS because you want it to be sent immediately. The station that sends the ACK waits for the SIFS and then ACKs with the duration of 0. This is how the end of the transmission is indicated.

Wireless Frame Headers

Figure 7-3 shows a wireless frame. Each of the fields has been expanded so you can see it more clearly. It is beneficial to understand these fields and how they play a part in the sending and receiving of wireless frames.

```
▶ Frame 217 (66 bytes on wire, 66 bytes captured)
▼ IEEE 802.11 Data, Flags: ....R.F.
    Type/Subtype: Data (0x20)
  ▽ Frame Control: 0x0A08 (Normal)
      Version: 0
      Type: Data frame (2)
      Subtype: 0
    ▽ Flags: 0xA
        DS status: Frame from DS to a STA via AP(To DS: 0 From DS: 1) (0x02)
        .... .0.. = More Fragments: This is the last fragment
        .... 1... = Retry: Frame is being retransmitted
        ...0 .... = PWR MGT: STA will stay up
        ..0. .... = More Data: No data buffered
        .0.. .... = Protected flag: Data is not protected
        0... .... = Order flag: Not strictly ordered
    Duration: 44
    Destination address: Apple_ab:14:26 (00:1e:c2:ab:14:26)
    BSS Id: Cisco-Li_0d:21:3d (00:12:17:0d:21:3d)
    Source address: Cisco-Li_0d:21:3b (00:12:17:0d:21:3b)
    Fragment number: 0
    Sequence number: 1419
```

Figure 7-3   *Wireless Frame Capture 1*

As you can see from the capture, a preamble is present, denoted with the Type/Subtype label, followed by a Frame Control field. The preamble can be anywhere from 76 to 156 bytes. The Frame Control field is 2 bytes. It tells what type of frame it is, represented with 2 bytes. In this case, it is a data frame.

The Flags field indicates that the frame is traveling *from* the DS, not toward the DS. This is represented with a single byte. In the figure, this is a frame that is coming back to the client.

Following the Flags field is a Duration field. The Duration field indicates how long the medium is reserved while this frame is being sent and includes time for an ACK to be sent in reply. The idea behind this process is to prevent collisions.

A wireless frame can have up to three MAC addresses following the Duration field. This is a total of 18 bytes. In the figure, you can see the following:

- Destination MAC address

- BSS ID, which is also a MAC address

- Source MAC address

The source address (SA) is the station that sent the frame. The transmitter address (TA) is the address of the station that is emitting the frame; in Figure 7-3, a TA is not shown. In some scenarios, a TA might vary from an SA. For example, if a wireless frame is relayed through a repeater, the TA would be the radio of the repeater, and the SA would be the sending device. The destination address (DA) is the final destination of the frame; in this case, it is the wireless client.

The Sequence Control field (2 bytes) indicates whether the frame is a fragment. Again, in Figure 7-3, the Sequence Control field is indicated with *Fragment Number* and shows that this is number 0, or the last fragment. This leads to an interesting topic—fragmentation. When and why would you fragment on a wireless network? The answer is that a wireless frame is, by default, 2346 bytes long. Considering that the frame is going to move to or from an Ethernet distribution that has a maximum transmission unit (MTU) of 1500 bytes and can see frames as big as 1518 bytes or slightly larger (depending on the trunking used), the frames on the wireless side are too big and need to be chopped up.

Optionally, you can see a fourth MAC address, a receiving address (RA), which is the address of the *direct* station that this frame is sent to; however, this is not seen in the figure. The frame could be relayed through a wireless bridge or repeater. This additional address adds six more bytes.

Finally, the frame body follows (not seen in the figure). It can be up to 2306 bytes and references only two MAC addresses, just like any other L2 frame. The frame body is encapsulated inside the last header shown in the figure.

In addition, you might see a 4-byte frame check sequence (FCS) following the L2 frame. This is common but not required.

Frame Types

For the most part, all frames are going to have the same type of header. The difference is in the body of the frame. The body is more specific and indicates what the frame is all about. Table 7-2 shows some frame types.

Table 7-2 *Frame Types Table*

Management	Control	Data
Beacon	Request to Send (RTS)	Simple data
Probe Request	Clear to Send (CTS)	Null function
Probe Response	Acknowledgment	Data+CF-ACK
Association Request	Power-Save-Poll (PS-Poll)	Data+CF-Poll
Association Response	Contention Free End (CF-End)	Data+CF-Ack
Authentication Request	Contention Free End + Acknowledgment (CF-End +ACK)	ACK+CF-Poll
Authentication Response	CF-ACK	
Deauthentication	CF-ACK+CF-Poll	
Reassociation request		
Reassociation response		
Announcement traffic indication message (ATIM)		
Each frame type merits its own discussion to follow.		

Management Frames

Management frames, as their name indicates, are used to manage the connection. In looking at a frame capture, the Type field indicates Management, and the subtype tells what
kind of management frame it is. As Table 7-2 listed, there are 11 Management frame types.
There are some more-often seen frames that you should be familiar with. These frame
types are discussed in the following sections.

Beacons and Probes

Figure 7-4 shows a management frame with a subtype of 8. This indicates that it is a beacon frame, which is used to help clients find the network.

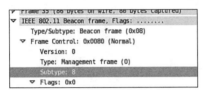

Key
Topic

Figure 7-4 *Management Frame Capture*

Figure 7-5 shows a sample network where the AP is sending a beacon frame.

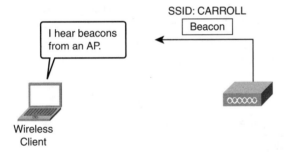

Figure 7-5 *Sample Network Using Beacon Frames*

When the client hears the beacon frame, it can learn a great deal of information about the
cell. In Figure 7-6, you can see that the beacon frame includes a timestamp that gives a reference time for the cell, the beacon interval, and a field called Capability Information,
which provides specifics for this cell. The Capability Information field includes information regarding power save mode, authentication, and preamble information.

A beacon frame also includes the SSIDs that the AP supports, the rates that are supported,
and six fields called Parameter Set that indicate modulation methods and such.

Another field you will find is Traffic Indication Map (TIM), which indicates whether the
AP is buffering traffic for clients in power-save mode.

When a client sees a beacon frame, it should be able to use that information to determine
if it is able to connect to the wireless Cell. Chapter 16, "Wireless Clients," covers the

Key Topic

```
▽ IEEE 802.11 wireless LAN management frame
  ▽ Fixed parameters (12 bytes)
       Timestamp: 0x0000000A7341A18A
       Beacon Interval: 0.102400 [Seconds]
  ▽ Capability Information: 0x0401
       .... .... .... ...1 = ESS capabilities: Transmitter is an AP
       .... .... .... ..0. = IBSS status: Transmitter belongs to a BSS
       .... ..0. 00.. = CFP participation capabilities: No point coordinator at AP (0x0000)
       .... .... ...0 .... = Privacy: AP/STA cannot support WEP
       .... .... ..0. .... = Short Preamble: Short preamble not allowed
       .... .... .0.. .... = PBCC: PBCC modulation not allowed
       .... .... 0... .... = Channel Agility: Channel agility not in use
       .... ...0 .... .... = Spectrum Management: dot11SpectrumManagementRequired FALSE
       .... .1.. .... .... = Short Slot Time: Short slot time in use
       .... 0... .... .... = Automatic Power Save Delivery: apsd not implemented
       ..0. .... .... .... = DSSS-OFDM: DSSS-OFDM modulation not allowed
       .0.. .... .... .... = Delayed Block Ack: delayed block ack not implemented
       0... .... .... .... = Immediate Block Ack: immediate block ack not implemented
  ▽ Tagged parameters (52 bytes)
    ▷ SSID parameter set: "carroll"
    ▷ Supported Rates: 1.0(B) 2.0(B) 5.5(B) 11.0(B) 18.0 24.0(B) 36.0 54.0
    ▷ DS Parameter set: Current Channel: 6
    ▷ Traffic Indication Map (TIM): DTIM 0 of 1 bitmap empty
```

Figure 7-6 *Beacon Frame Details*

process of how a client searches channels and displays connection capability information. For now, just understand that the beacon frame allows a client to passively scan a network.

Sometimes, however, you do not want to passively scan a network. Perhaps you know exactly what cell you want to connect to. In this situation, you can actively scan a network to determine if the cell you are looking for is accessible. When a client actively scans a network, it uses probe request and probe response messages. Figure 7-7 shows a client actively scanning.

Figure 7-7 *Active Scanning*

As you can tell in the figure, the client is looking for a wireless cell with the SSID of "Carroll." This client sends a probe request and the AP, upon receiving the probe request, issues a probe response. The probe response is similar to the beacon frame, including capability information, authentication information, and so on. The difference is that a beacon frame is sent frequently and a probe response is sent only in response to a probe request.

Connecting After a Probe or Beacon

After a client has located an AP and understands the capabilities, it tries to connect using an authentication frame. This frame has information about the algorithm used to authenticate, a number for the authentication transaction, and information on whether authentication has succeeded or failed.

One thing to note is that authentication can be *Open*, meaning that no authentication algorithm such as WEP is being used. The only reason an authentication message is used is to indicate that the client has the capability to connect. In Figure 7-8, the client is sending an authentication request, and the AP is sending an authentication response. Upon authentication, the client sends an association request, and the AP responds with an association response.

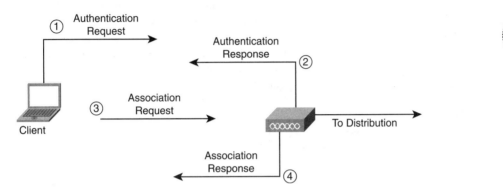

Key
Topic

Figure 7-8 *Authentications and Association*

Leaving and Returning

When a client is connected to a wireless cell, either the client or the AP can leave the connection by sending a deauthentication message. The deauthentication message has information in the body as to why it is leaving. In addition, a client can send a disassociation message, which disassociates the client from the cell but keeps the client authenticated. The next time a client comes back to the wireless cell, it can simply send a reassociation message, and the AP would send a reassociation response—eliminating the need for authentication to reconnect to the cell.

Note: Cisco Unified Wireless networks use deauthentication and disassociation messages to contain rogue APs. This concept is a little outside of this discussion but will be covered in Chapter 10, "Cisco Wireless Networks Architecture."

Control Frames

One of the most common control frames is the ACK, which helps the connection by acknowledging receipt of frames. Other control frames include the request to send (RTS) and clear to send (CTS), which were discussed in Chapter 6, "Overview of the 802.11 WLAN Protocols." The ACK, RTS, and CTS frames are used in DCF mode.

The control frames that are used in PCF mode are as follows:

■ Contention Free End (CF+End)

■ Contention Free End Ack (CF +end_ack_)

- CF-Ack

- CF Ack+CF Poll

- CF-Poll

These frames are also discussed in the paragraphs to follow.

When an AP takes control of a network and shifts from DCF mode (every station for it-self) to PCF mode (the AP is responsible for everyone sending), the AP lets all stations know that they should stop sending by issuing a beacon frame with a duration of 32768. When this happens and everyone stops sending, there is no longer a contention for the medium, because the AP is managing it. This is called a *contention free window (CFW)*. The AP then sends poll messages to each client asking if they have anything to send. This is called a CF-Poll, as illustrated in Figure 7-9.

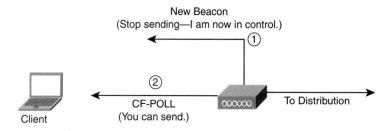

Figure 7-9   *CF-Poll in PCF Mode*

Figure 7-10 illustrates how the AP might control communication. Here, the AP has data to deliver to the client (DATA). It allows the client to send data (CF-Poll) and acknowledges receipt of the client data (CF-ACK).

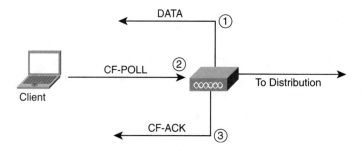

Figure 7-10   *Data + CF-Poll + CF-ACK*

Other variations exist, but from these examples you should have a decent understanding of PCF operation.

Power Save Mode and Frame Types

Another mode of operation mostly seen on laptops is called power save mode. Looking back at Table 7-2, you can see that a control frame is related to a power save (PS-Poll). In a power save, a client notifies an AP that it is falling asleep by using a null function frame. The client wakes up after a certain period of time, during which the AP buffers any traffic for it. When the client wakes up and sees a beacon frame with the TIM listing that it has frames buffered, the client sends a PS-Poll requesting the data.

Frame Speeds

One final item to discuss before putting it together is frame speed. The AP advertises mandatory speeds at which a client must be able to operate. You can use other speeds, but they are not mandatory. For example, 24 Mbps might be mandatory, but an AP might also be capable of 54 Mbps. A client *must* support 24 Mbps but is allowed to use the best rate possible, in this example 54 Mbps. When data is sent at one rate, the ACK is always sent at 1 data rate lower.

A Wireless Connection

Using Figures 7-11 through 7-18, you can step through a simple discovery and association process.

1. The AP sends beacons every 2 seconds, as shown in Figure 7-11.

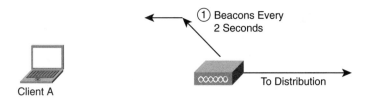

Figure 7-11   *AP Beacons*

2. Client A is passively scanning and hears the beacon. This enables the client to determine whether it can connect. You can see this in Figure 7-12.

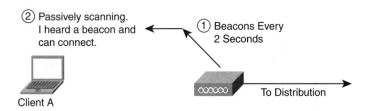

Figure 7-12   *Passive Scanning*

3. A new client (Client B) arrives. Client B is already configured to look for the AP, so instead of passive scanning, it sends a probe request for the specific AP (see Figure 7-13).

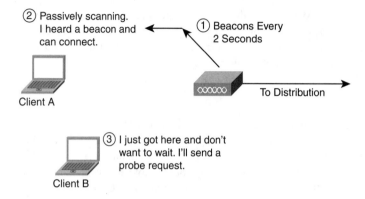

Figure 7-13 *Active Scanning Probe Request*

   4. The AP sends a probe response, seen in Figure 7-14, which is similar to a beacon. This lets Client B determine if it can connect.

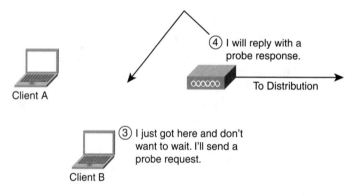

Figure 7-14 *Probe Response*

   5. From this point on, the process would be the same for Client A and Client B. In Figure 7-15, Client B sends an authentication request.

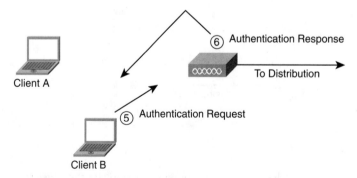

Figure 7-15 *Association Request and Response*

6. Also seen in Figure 7-15, the AP returns an authentication response to the client.

7. The client then sends an association request, as seen in Figure 7-16.

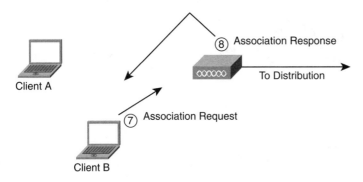

Figure 7-16 *Association Request and Response*

8. Now the AP sends an association response, also seen in Figure 7-16.

9. When the client wants to send, it uses an RTS, assuming this is a mixed b/g cell. The RTS includes the duration, as you can see in Figure 7-17.

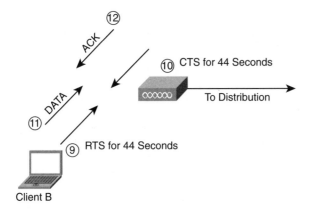

Figure 7-17 *RTS/CTS*

10. Also seen in Figure 7-17, the AP returns a CTS.

11. The client sends the data (see Figure 7-17).

12. The AP sends an ACK after each frame is received (Figure 7-17).

13. In Figure 7-18, the client sends a disassociation message.

14. The AP replies with a disassociation response (Figure 7-18).

15. The client returns and sends a reassociation message (Figure 7-18).

16. The AP responds with a reassociation response (Figure 7-18).

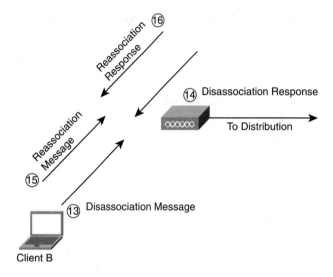

Figure 7-18   *Reassociation*

Again, this process has other variations, but this should give you a pretty good understanding of how to manage a connection.

Exam Preparation Tasks

Review All the Key Concepts

Review the most important topics from this chapter, noted with the Key Topics icon in the outer margin of the page. Table 7-3 lists a reference of these key topics and the page number where you can find each one.

Table 7-3 *Key Topics for Chapter 7*

Key Topic Item	Description	Page Number
Figure 7-1	Sending a frame: part 1	117
Figure 7-2	Sending a frame: part 2	118
Figure 7-3	Wireless frame capture	119
Table 7-2	Frame types table	120
Figure 7-4	Management frame capture	121
Figure 7-6	Beacon frame details	122
Figure 7-8	Authentication and association	123

Complete the Tables and Lists from Memory

Print a copy of Appendix B, "Memory Tables," (found on the CD) or at least the section for this chapter, and complete the tables and lists from memory. Appendix C, "Memory Tables Answer Key," also on the CD, includes completed tables and lists to check your work.

Definition of Key Terms

Define the following key terms from this chapter, and check your answers in the Glossary:

management frames, control frames, data frames, CSMA/CA, CCA, hidden node problem, virtual carrier sense, IFS, SIFS, DIFS, ACK, backoff timer, NAV, slottime, contention window, DCF, PCF, SA, RA, TA, DA, MTU, beacon, probe request, probe response, authentication request, authentication response, association request, association response, TIM, ATIM, passive scan, active scan, deauthentication message, deauthentication response, disassociation message, disassociation response, null function frame, PS-Poll

This chapter covers the following subjects:

Cordless Phones: Briefly looks at cordless phone technology and why it interferes with WLANs.

Bluetooth: Discusses Bluetooth and its standardization progression.

ZigBee: Shows how ZigBee is used and how it interferes with WLANs.

WiMax: Describes WiMax technology as it compares to Wi-Fi.

Other Types of Interference: Covers additional sources of wireless interference.

CHAPTER 8

Additional Wireless Technologies

Although the 802.11 wireless spectrum is the best-known technology, others are in use and, believe it or not, are very popular. The purpose of this chapter is to discuss some, not all, of the other wireless technologies and how they might interfere or interact with the 802.11 WLAN standards. These technologies include cordless phone technology, Bluetooth, ZigBee, WiMax, and some other odds and ends.

You should take the "Do I Know This Already?" quiz first. If you score 80 percent or higher, you might want to skip to the section "Exam Preparation Tasks." If you score below 80 percent, you should review the entire chapter.

"Do I Know This Already?" Quiz

The "Do I Know This Already?" quiz helps you determine your level of knowledge of this chapter's topics before you begin. Table 8-1 details the major topics discussed in this chapter and their corresponding quiz questions.

Table 8-1 *"Do I Know This Already?" Section-to-Question Mapping*

Foundation Topics Section	Questions
Cordless Phones	1–2
Bluetooth	3–7
ZigBee	8–9
WiMax	10–14
Other Types of Interference	15

1. Who developed the DECT standard?

   a. FCC

   b. IEEE

   c. ITUT

   d. ETSI

2. DECT devices in the U.S. use what designation to differentiate them from European DECT devices?

   a.   DECT 1.0

   b.   DECT 2.0

   c.   DECT 6.0

   d.   US-DECT

3. Bluetooth is designed to cover what type of area?

   a.   Metropolitan

   b.   Wide area

   c.   Local area

   d.   Personal area

4. How many Bluetooth devices can be paired?

   a.   Two

   b.   Four

   c.   Six

   d.   Eight

5. Bluetooth operates in which frequency band?

   a.   2.4 GHz

   b.   5.0 GHz

   c.   900 MHz

   d.   10 GHz

6. What is the current Bluetooth standard?

   a.   Bluetooth 2008

   b.   Bluetooth 2.1 + EDR

   c.   Bluetooth 2.0

   d.   Bluetooth 1.1

7. Which group is responsible for Bluetooth development?

   a.   IEEE

   b.   Bluetooth SIG

   c.   Bluetooth Forum

   d.   Bluetooth Inc.

8. ZigBee is used for what common deployments? (Choose all that apply.)

   a.   Home automation

   b.   Monitoring

   c.   GPS location

   d.   Control systems

9. ZigBee operates in which frequency band?

   a.   2.4 GHz

   b.   5.0 GHz

   c.   900 MHz

   d.   10 GHz

10. True or false: WiMax interferes with 802.11 LANs because it operates on the same frequency band.

   a.   True

   b.   False

11. WiMax is designed for what type of connections?

   a.   Last-mile access

   b.   Wireless mesh LANs

   c.   Point-to-multipoint WANs

   d.   Single-cell

12. WiMax is defined in which IEEE specification?

   a.   802.15.1

   b.   802.16e

   c.   802.1

   d.   802.3

13. Fixed line of sight (LOS) offers which data rate?

   a.   40 Mbps

   b.   100 Mbps

   c.   1 Gbps

   d.   10 Mbps

14. NLOS advertises which data rate?

   a.   30 to 40 Mbps

   b.   100 Mbps

   c.   70 Mbps

   d.   1 Gbps

15. Which of the following are potential sources of interference for WLANs? (Choose all that apply.)

   a.   Microwave

   b.   Fluorescent light

   c.   Magnet

   d.   Microphone

Foundation Topics

Cordless Phones

Cordless phones have been around as long as I can remember—or at least since I was in junior high. Cordless phones sometimes operate in the wireless spectrum as WLANs, which can cause interference issues. Visit an electronics store, and you'll find some phones that operate at 2.4 GHz and others that operate at 5.8 GHz. This should be a consideration when you purchase cordless phones. If you have 802.11a deployed, a 2.4-GHz phone should suffice. If you have 802.11b/g, you should avoid a phone that operates in the 2.4-GHz range and go with a 5.8-GHz phone. With that said, let's look at cordless phone technology in more detail.

To begin with, cordless phones can use *Time Division Multiple Access (TDMA)* or *Frequency Division Multiple Access (FDMA)*. The Multiple Access technology is used to allow more than one handset to access the frequency band at the same time, as shown in Figure 8-1. As you can see, a cordless phone communicates with the base station. Multiple cordless phones can use the same base station at the same time by using TDMA or FDMA.

Figure 8-1 *Standard Cordless Phone Usage*

It's common for cordless phones to use the *Digital Enhanced Cordless Telecommunications (DECT)* standard. DECT is an ETSI standard for digital portable phones and is found in cordless technology that is deployed in homes and businesses. Currently, the DECT standard is a good alternative for avoiding interference issues with any 802.11 technologies. The original DECT frequency band was 1880 to 1900 MHz. It's used in all European countries. It is also used in most of Asia, Australia, and South America.

In 2005, the FCC changed channelization and licensing costs in the 1920 to 1930 MHz, or 1.9 GHz, band. This band is known as Unlicensed Personal Communications Services (UPCS). This change by the FCC allowed the use of DECT devices in the U.S. with few changes. The modified DECT devices are called DECT 6.0. This allows a distinction to be made between DECT devices used overseas and other cordless devices that operate at 900 MHz, 2.4 GHz, and 5.8 GHz.

Bluetooth

Bluetooth is a personal-area technology that was named after a king of Denmark, Harald "Bluetooth" Gormson. It is said that the use of his name is based on his role in unifying Denmark and Norway. Bluetooth technology was intended to unify the telecom and computing industries. Today, Bluetooth can be found integrated into cell phones, PDAs, laptops, desktops, printers, headsets, cameras, and video game consoles. Bluetooth has low power consumption, making it a good choice for mobile, battery-powered devices.

The Bluetooth Special Interest Group (SIG) was formed in 1998, and the name "Bluetooth" was officially adopted. In 1999, Bluetooth 1.0 and 1.0b were released, although they were pretty much unusable. Bluetooth 1.1 followed and was much more functional. Eventually, based on Bluetooth 1.1, the 802.15.1 specification was approved by the IEEE to conform with Bluetooth technology.

Bluetooth 1.2 was then adopted in 2003 with faster connections and discovery of devices as well as the use of adaptive Frequency Hopping Spread Spectrum technology. In 2004, Bluetooth 2.0 + *Enhanced Data Rate (EDR)*, supporting speeds up to 2 Mbps, was adopted by the Bluetooth SIG. The IEEE followed with 802.15.1-2005, which is the specification that relates to Bluetooth 1.2. After the 802.15-2005 standard, the IEEE severed ties to the Bluetooth SIG because the Bluetooth SIG wanted to pursue functionality with other standards.

As of July 26, 2007, the adopted standard according to the Bluetooth SIG is Bluetooth 2.1 + EDR. One of the key features of the 2.1 standard is an improved quick-pairing process, in which you simply hold two devices close together to start the quick-pairing process. Also, a new technology called "sniff subrating" increases battery life up to five times. Bluetooth 2.1 + EDR is backward-compatible with Bluetooth 1.1.

Bluetooth technology might interfere with 802.11 LANs, because it operates in the 2.4-GHz range. However, because it is designed for a proximity of about 35 feet, has low transmit power, and uses Frequency Hopping Spread Spectrum, it is unlikely that Bluetooth will interfere.

Bluetooth is considered a piconet; it allows eight devices (one master and seven slaves) to be paired, as shown in Figure 8-2. Although the figure is a little extreme, it shows you just how many devices can be paired with a laptop or desktop. You can download photos you've taken, while listening to music with your headphones, synchronizing your cell phone's contacts and PDA calendar with Outlook, and using your mouse to print that new white paper on Cisco.com, all while playing a video game. Imagine the wire mess you would have without Bluetooth.

ZigBee

Many people have never heard of ZigBee, but it's a technology that is well-designed and very useful. ZigBee was developed by the ZigBee Alliance. It consists of small, low-power digital radios based on the IEEE 802.15.4 standard for *wireless personal-area networks (WPAN)*, such as wireless headphones connecting to cell phones via short-range radio. If you look at the ZigBee Alliance home page at http://www.zigbee.org, you'll likely notice

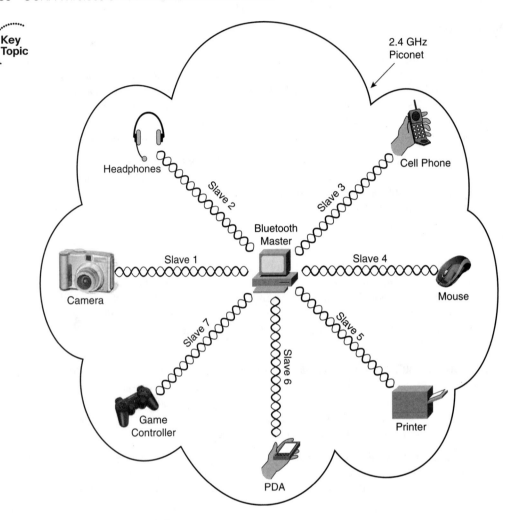

Key Topic

2.4 GHz Piconet

Headphones
Slave 2
Cell Phone
Slave 3
Bluetooth Master
Slave 1
Camera
Slave 4
Mouse
Slave 7
Slave 6
Slave 5
Game Controller
PDA
Printer

Figure 8-2 *Bluetooth Piconet*

that ZigBee relates much of its use to control and monitoring. In fact, ZigBee is often used for monitoring, building automation, control devices, personal healthcare devices, and computer peripherals.

The ZigBee website says:

> "ZigBee was created to address the market need for a cost-effective, standards-based wireless networking solution that supports low data-rates, low-power consumption, security, and reliability.
>
> "ZigBee is the only standards-based technology that addresses the unique needs of most remote monitoring and control and sensory network applications.
>
> "The initial markets for the ZigBee Alliance include Energy Management and Efficiency, Home Automation, Building Automation and Industrial Automation."[1]

You might be wondering how this technology relates to WLANs and how it might interfere. The answer is that ZigBee operates in the ISM bands: 868 MHz in Europe, 915 MHz in countries such as the U.S. and Australia, and 2.4 GHz pretty much everywhere. The 2.4 GHz operation range is where the issue lies, because that is the range in which 802.11b/g WLANs operate.

Figures 8-3, 8-4, and 8-5 show some common ZigBee topologies. Figure 8-3 shows the star topology, in which the center device is a network coordinator (NC). Every network has an NC. Other devices can be full-function devices, and still others can be reduced-function devices. Full-function devices can send, receive, and so on. A reduced-function device doesn't have as much capability and could do something like report the temperature of a system back to a controller.

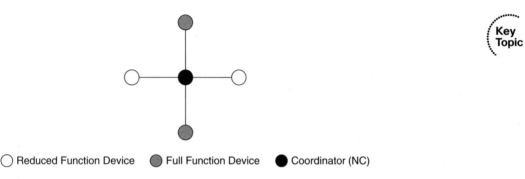

Key Topic

Figure 8-3   *ZigBee Star Topology*

The cluster topology shown in Figure 8-4 also has an NC, as well as some full-function devices and reduced-function devices. This cluster topology resembles an extended star in LAN terms.

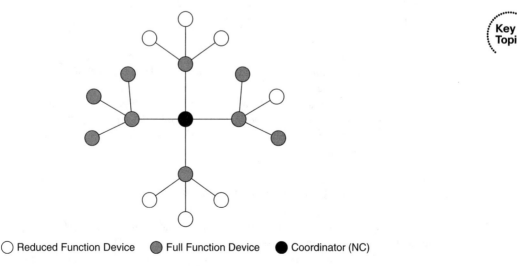

Key Topic

Figure 8-4   *ZigBee Cluster Topology*

Certain scenarios call for all devices to communicate with each other in a coordinated effort to provide some sort of information. This is where you find a mesh topology, as shown in Figure 8-5.

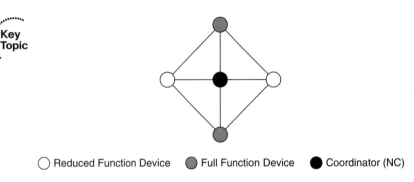

○ Reduced Function Device   ◉ Full Function Device   ● Coordinator (NC)

Figure 8-5   *ZigBee Mesh Topology*

WiMax

Worldwide Interoperability for Microwave Access (WiMax) is defined by the WiMax forum and standardized by the IEEE 802.16 suite. The most current standard is 802.16e.

According to the WiMax Forum:

> "WiMAX is a standards-based technology enabling the delivery of last mile wireless broadband access as an alternative to wired broadband like cable and DSL. WiMAX provides fixed, nomadic, portable and, soon, mobile wireless broadband connectivity without the need for direct line-of-sight with a base station. In a typical cell radius deployment of three to ten kilometers, WiMAX Forum Certified systems can be expected to deliver capacity of up to 40 Mbps per channel, for fixed and portable access applications.

> "This is enough bandwidth to simultaneously support hundreds of businesses with T-1 speed connectivity and thousands of residences with DSL speed connectivity. Mobile network deployments are expected to provide up to 15 Mbps of capacity within a typical cell radius deployment of up to three kilometers. It is expected that WiMAX technology will be incorporated in notebook computers and PDAs by 2007, allowing for urban areas and cities to become 'metro zones' for portable outdoor broadband wireless access."[2]

You must understand a few aspects of WiMax; the first is the concept of being fixed line of sight (LOS) or non-LOS (mobile). In non-LOS, *mobile* doesn't mean mobile in the sense that most of us think. WiMax mobility is more like the ability to travel and then set up shop temporarily. When you are done, you pack up and move on. A few service providers use this technology to provide end-user access as an alternative to DSL or cable modem. Your signal range in this Non-LOS scenario is about 3 to 4 miles, and data rates are advertised at around 30 Mbps, but you can expect less—closer to 15 Mbps.

Other service providers are targeting business customers in a fixed LOS WiMax deployment in which the topology most closely resembles that of a traditional T1, being a point-to-point type of topology and providing backhaul or backbone services. This fixed LOS advertises 30 to 70 Mbps throughput, but you can expect around 40 Mbps.

Note   I know of a company in the Seattle area that advertises a 100-Mbps connection point-to-point with 10 Gbps of bandwidth per month at no additional charge. If you go over the 10 Gbps limit, you are charged additional fees.

As the IEEE standardizes WiMax technology, it has progressed from the original 802.16 to 802.16a, c, d, and finally 802.16e.

As mentioned, the WiMax defines last-mile access. Figure 8-6 shows a sample topology in which subscribers have a point-to-point connection back to a service provider and from there have access to the public Internet.

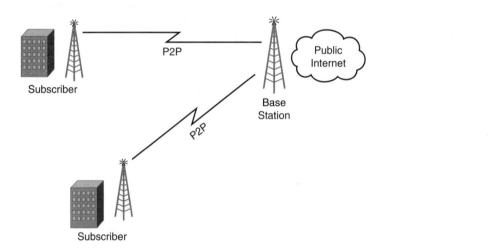

Figure 8-6   *WiMax Deployment*

WiMax operates on the 10- to 66-GHz frequency band, so it doesn't interfere with 802.11 LANs. So why is it discussed in this section? The school of thought here is that, with some planning, a device acting as a gateway can be deployed offering 802.11 LAN access with 802.16 last-mile access or upstream access to a service provider, thus removing the need for wires. The question of how feasible this is lies in the hands of the vendors developing the products and the standards committees ensuring interoperability. Some vendors, however, have tested this technology in lab environments with much success.

Other Types of Interference

Other types of interference can occur in the same frequency ranges. These devices might not be the most obvious, but they should be considered. They can include the following:

- Microwaves (operate at 1 to 40 GHz)

- Wireless X11 cameras (operate at 2.4 GHz)

- Radar systems (operate at 2 to 4 GHz for moderate-range surveillance, terminal traffic control, and long-range weather and at 4 to 8 GHz for long-range tracking and airborne weather systems)

- Motion sensors (operate at 2.4 GHz)

- Fluorescent lighting (operates at 20000 Hz or higher)

- Game controllers and adapters (usually operate at 2.5 GHz)

When dealing with wireless deployments, you can use tools to determine signal strength and coverage, but just knowing about these additional sources of interference will save you some time in determining where to place APs and clients.

Exam Preparation Tasks

Review All the Key Topics

Review the most important topics from this chapter, denoted with the Key Topic icon. Table 8-2 lists these key topics and the page number where each one can be found.

Table 8-2 *Key Topics for Chapter 8*

Key Topic Item	Description	Page Number
Figure 8-1	Standard cordless phone usage	134
Figure 8-2	A Bluetooth piconet	136
Figure 8-3	ZigBee star topology	137
Figure 8-4	ZigBee cluster topology	137
Figure 8-5	ZigBee mesh topology	138
Figure 8-6	A WiMax deployment	139

Definition of Key Terms

Define the following key terms from this chapter, and check your answers in the Glossary:

Bluetooth, ZigBee, WiMax, Time Division Multiple Access (TDMA), Frequency Division Multiple Access (FDMA), Digital Enhanced Cordless Telecommunications (DECT), Special Interest Group (SIG), adaptive Frequency Hopping Spread Spectrum technology, Enhanced Data Rate (EDR), 802.15.1, 802.15.1-2005, sniff subrating, wireless personal-area network (WPAN), 802.16e, WiMax

Endnotes

[1]About ZigBee, http://www.zigbee.org/en/markets/index.asp

[2]About WiMax, http://www.wimaxforum.org/technology/

References in This Chapter

Digital Enhanced Cordless Telecommunications, Wikipedia.org, http://en.wikipedia.org/wiki/Digital_Enhanced_Cordless_Telecommunications, December 2006

Bluetooth, Wikipedia.org, http://en.wikipedia.org/wiki/Bluetooth

ZigBee, Wikipedia.org, http://en.wikipedia.org/wiki/Zigbee, February 2008

This chapter covers the following subjects:

The Wireless Network Road Trip: A look at the packet delivery process on a wireless-to-wired network.

Using VLANs to Add Control: How VLANs are used in wireless networks to separate subnets.

Configuring VLANs and Trunks: How to apply a configuration of VLANs and trunks on a Cisco switch.

CHAPTER 9

Delivering Packets from the Wireless to Wired Network

Much coordination is involved with the delivery of wireless packets to and from the wireless networks. This chapter focuses on delivery of packets to the wired network and the path that traffic will traverse. It is intended to give you a good understanding of what devices are involved and how they manipulate packets as they are transmitted.

You should do the "Do I Know This Already?" quiz first. If you score 80 percent or higher, you may way to skip to the section "Exam Preparation Tasks." If you score below 80 percent, you should spend the time reviewing the entire chapter.

"Do I Know This Already?" Quiz

The "Do I Know This Already?" quiz helps you determine your level of knowledge of this chapter's topics before you begin. Table 9-1 details the major topics discussed in this chapter and their corresponding quiz questions.

Table 9-1 *"Do I Know This Already?" Section-to-Question Mapping*

Foundation Topics Section	Questions
The Wireless Network Road Trip	1–4
Using VLANs to Add Control	5–8
Configuring VLANs and Trunks	9–12

1. When a client wants to send traffic to another device, it must use what protocol to resolve the MAC addresses?

   a. ARP

   b. CDP

   c. NPR

   d. OFDM

2. If a client wants to communicate with a device on another subnet, what device handles the communication?

    a. WLC

    b. Switch

    c. AP

    d. Gateway router

3. How many MAC addresses can be seen in an 802.11 frame?

    a. 1

    b. 2

    c. 3

    d. 4

4. What protocol is the 802.11 frame encapsulated in when it is sent from the AP to the WLC?

    a. LDAP

    b. CDP

    c. 802.3

    d. LWAPP

5. A VLAN is used to define a _____ and isolate a _____ . (Choose two.)

    a. Logical broadcast domain

    b. Transparent network

    c. Virtual trunk

    d. Subnet

6. Clients see VLANs. True or False?

    a. True

    b. False

7. How many VLANs typically are assigned to an access port on a switch?

    a. 2

    b. 4

    c. 256

    d. 1

8. What are trunks normally used for?

   a. Connections between APs

   b. Connections between switches and clients

   c. Connections between switches

   d. Switches do not support trunks

9. Which of the following configurations is used to create a Layer 2 (nonrouted) VLAN on a Cisco IOS–based switch?

   a.
```
config t
interface fa0/1
vlan enable
vlan 5
```

   b.
```
config t
vlan database
vlan
vlan enable 7
```

   c.
```
config t
vlan 7
end
```

   d.
```
config t
interface vlan 1
no shut
end
```

10. Which of the following commands is used to create a trunk?

   a. `switchport mode trunk`

   b. `switchport trunk enable`

   c. `switchport trunk`

   d. `trunk enable`

11. Which of the following commands defines the native VLAN?

   a. `native vlan 1`

   b. `switchport native vlan 1`

   c. `switchport mode native 1`

   d. `switchport trunk native vlan 1`

12. Which of the following configurations applies VLAN 25 to FastEthernet interface 0/3?

a.
```
conf t
interface f0/1
switchport mode trunk
vlan 25
```

b.
```
conf t
interface f0/3
switchport mode access
vlan 25
```

c.
```
conf t
interface f0/3
switchport mode access
switchport access vlan 25
```

d.
```
conf t
interface f0/4
switchport mode trunk
vlan 25
```

Foundation Topics

The Wireless Network Road Trip

At this point, you already have an understanding of how frames are sent on a wireless network. In the Cisco Unified Wireless Network, frames do not stay on the wireless network; rather, they travel from a lightweight AP to a wireless LAN controller (WLC). The WLC and lightweight APs are discussed in Chapter 10, "Cisco Wireless Networks Architecture." The purpose of this chapter is to familiarize you with how traffic is kept separate as it travels from the AP to the WLC and then to the wired network. To better understand this process, you must understand how a network typically looks and the process that each device uses to send and receive data.

The Association Process

To begin, you need a network. This chapter uses the common logical topology seen in Figure 9-1. As you can see, multiple wireless clients are in range of an AP that is advertising multiple service set identifiers (SSID). One SSID puts users on a network that is offered to guest users called Guest. The other SSID is called UserNet and is designed for authenticated users of the corporate network. Naturally, more security is going to be applied to users of UserNet, such as authentication and encryption, as opposed to the network Guest. The Guest network places users on the 172.30.1.0/24 subnet. The UserNet places users on the 10.99.99.0/24 network. Although these two networks are on different subnets and users associate with different SSIDs, recall that an AP can advertise multiple SSIDs but actually uses the same wireless radio. In the wireless space, the SSID and IP subnet keep the networks logically separated.

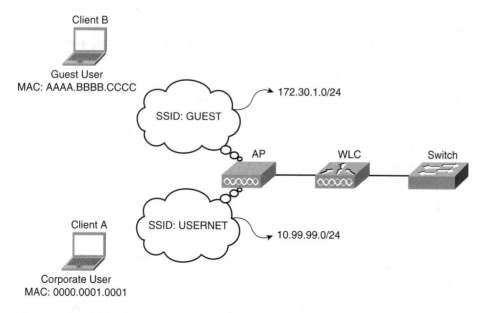

Figure 9-1 *A Simple Wireless Network*

Clients have more than one way to find an AP and associate with it. A client can passively scan the network and listen on each frequency for beacons being sent by an AP, or it can use an active scan process and send a probe request in search of a specific AP. Users of the UserNet would likely actively scan the network, whereas a guest would passively scan. The detailed method of client interaction is covered in Chapter 16, "Wireless Clients."

Getting back to the association process, a client scans the channels hoping to hear a beacon from an AP or actively sends a probe request. If a probe response is received or a beacon is heard, the client can attempt to associate with the SSID received in that probe response or beacon.

The next step is to authenticate and associate with the AP. When the client chooses an SSID, it sends an authentication request. The AP should reply with an authentication response. After this occurs and a "Success" message is received, an association request is sent, including the data rates and capabilities of the client, followed by an association response from the AP. The association response from the AP includes the data rates that the AP is capable of, other capabilities, and an identification number for the association.

Next, the client must determine the speed. It does this by determining the Received Signal Strength Indicator (RSSI) and signal-to-noise ratio (SNR), and it chooses the best speed to send at based on these determinations. All management frames are sent at the lowest rate, whereas the data headers can be sent faster than management frames, and the actual data frames at the fastest possible rate. Just as the client determines its rates to send, the AP, in turn, does the same. Now that the client is associated, it can attempt to send data to other devices on the network.

Sending to a Host on Another Subnet

When a client is associated with an AP, the general idea is to send data to other devices. To illustrate this, first try to send data between Client A in Figure 9-2, which is on the User-Net network, and Client B, which is on the Guest network. Although a typical network would not allow guest users to send traffic to internal WLAN users for security purposes, this will provide an example of how the connection works.

The two clients are clearly on two different subnets, so the rules of how IP works are still in play. The clients cannot send traffic directly to each other. Based on normal IP rules, they would first determine that the other is *not* on the same subnet and then decide to use a default gateway to relay the information. If a client has never communicated with the default gateway, it uses Address Resolution Protocol (ARP) to resolve its MAC address. The process would appear as follows:

Step 1.   Client A wants to send traffic to Client B.

Step 2.   Client A determines that the IP address of Client B is not on the same subnet.

Step 3.   Client A decides to send the traffic to the default gateway of 10.99.99.5.

Step 4.   Client A looks in its ARP table for a mapping to the gateway, but it is not there.

Step 5.   Client A creates an ARP request and sends to the AP, as seen in Figure 9-3.

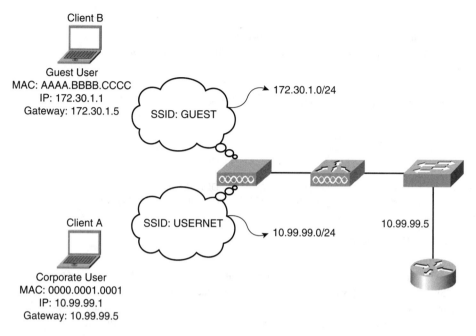

Figure 9-2   *Client A Communicating with Client B*

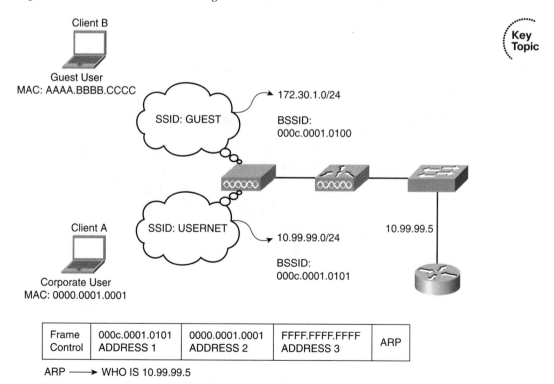

Figure 9-3   *ARPing for the Gateway*

When the ARP request is sent to the AP, it is an interesting process and actually works a little bit differently than on a wired network. Remember that on a wired network, the header has only two MAC addresses: the source address and the destination address. An 802.11 frame can have four addresses: the source address (SA), destination address (DA), transmitter address (TA), and receiving address (RA). In this situation, the SA is the MAC of the client sending the ARP request, the DA is broadcast (for the ARP), and the RA is the AP. No TA is present in this example.

Figure 9-4 shows the ARP request.

Frame Control	ADDRESS 1 000c.0001.0101	ADDRESS 2 0000.0001.0001	ADDRESS 3 FFFF.FFFF.FFFF	ARP REQUEST

Figure 9-4 *ARP Request*

The AP receives the ARP and sees its MAC address. It verifies the frame check sequence (FCS) in the frame and waits the short interframe space (SIFS) time. When the SIFS time expires, it sends an ACK back to the wireless client that sent the ARP request. This ACK is not an ARP response; rather, it is an ACK for the wireless frame transmission.

The AP then forwards the frame to the WLC using the Lightweight Access Point Protocol (LWAPP), as illustrated in Figure 9-5.

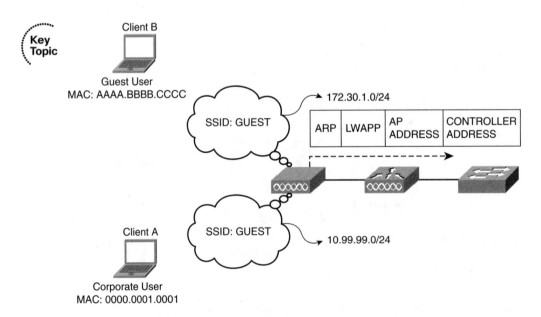

Figure 9-5 *ARP Forwarded in LWAPP Frame*

The LWAPP frame that travels from the AP to the WLC is traveling on a wired network. This brings forth the question, "What happened to the 802.11 frame format?" LWAPP simply encapsulates the frame inside a 6-byte header. The new 6-byte header has the AP IP and MAC address as the source and the WLC IP and MAC address as the destination. Encapsulated inside of that header is the original 802.11 frame with the three MAC addresses, including the broadcast MAC address for the ARP process. When the WLC receives the LWAPP frame, it opens the frame revealing the ARP request and rewrites the ARP request in an 802.3 frame that can be sent across the wired network. The first address from the 802.11 frame is dropped, the second address is placed as the source address in the new 802.3 frame, and the third address, the broadcast address, is placed as the destination address. The WLC then forwards the ARP request, in 802.3 format, across the wired network, as seen in Figure 9-6. Here you can see how the frame appears between the wireless Client A and the AP, how the AP encapsulates the frame and sends it to the WLC, and how the WLC rewrites the frame and sends it to the wired network.

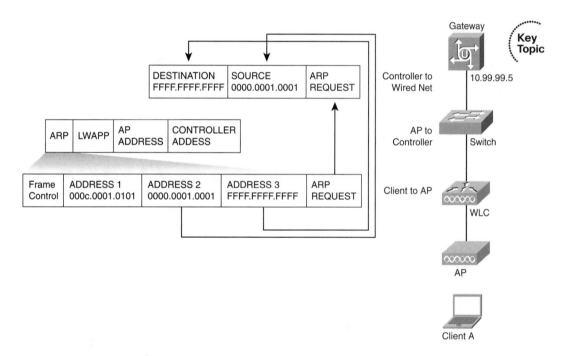

Figure 9-6 *WLC Forwarding the ARP Toward the Gateway*

As switches receive the ARP request, they read the destination MAC address, which is a broadcast, and flood the frame out all ports except the one it came in on. The exception to this rule is if VLANs are in use, in which case the frame would be flooded to all ports that are members of the same VLAN. Assuming that VLANs are not in use, the frame, as stated, is flooded out all ports except the one it came in on.

At some point, the frame will be received by a Layer 3 device, hopefully the default gateway. In Figure 9-7, the router has received the ARP request and will respond to it with its MAC address.

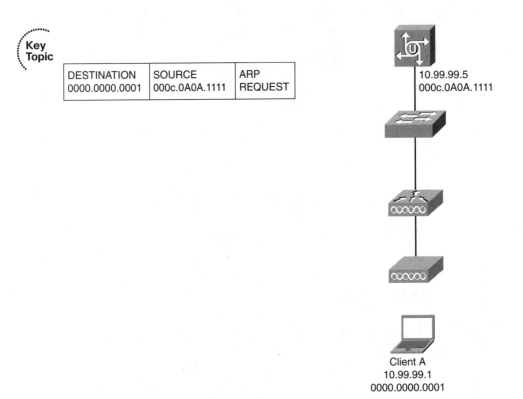

DESTINATION	SOURCE	ARP
0000.0000.0001	000c.0A0A.1111	REQUEST

10.99.99.5
000c.0A0A.1111

Client A
10.99.99.1
0000.0000.0001

Figure 9-7   *Gateway Responds to ARP*

That ARP response is sent back as a unicast message, so the switches in the path are going to forward it directly to the port that leads back to the wireless client, rather than flooding the frame out all ports. Eventually the frame is received by the WLC, and it must be rebuilt as an 802.11 frame. When the WLC rewrites the frame, it places the DA as address 1, the SA as address 3, and the TA as address 2, which is the SSID of the AP. Figure 9-8 illustrates this process.

As illustrated in Figure 9-9, the newly formed 802.11 frame is placed inside an LWAPP header where the AP IP and MAC is the destination and the WLC IP and MAC is the source. The LWAPP frame is forwarded to the AP.

Next, the AP must remove the LWAPP header, exposing the 802.11 frame. The 802.11 frame is buffered, and the process of sending a frame on the wireless network begins. The AP starts a backoff timer and begins counting down. If a wireless frame is heard during the countdown, the reservation in the heard frame is added to the countdown and the AP continues. Eventually, the timer expires, and the frame can be sent an 802.11 frame.

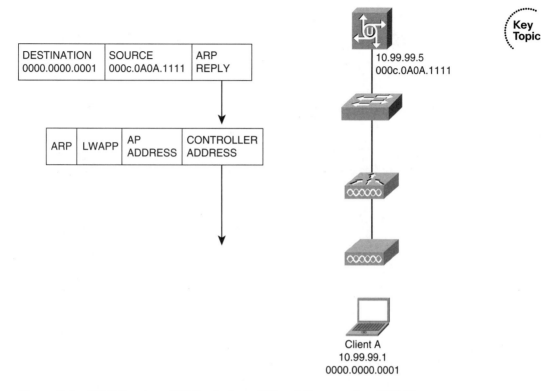

Figure 9-8 *WLC Receives ARP Reply from GW and Converts It to LWAPP*

The client, upon receiving the frame, sends an ACK after waiting the SIFS value.

The ARP process of the client now has a mapping to the GW MAC address and can dispatch the awaiting frame. Remember that it still must follow the rules, a backoff timer, and a contention window and eventually transmit the frame following the ARP response.

Using VLANs to Add Control

Here is where things get a little tricky, which brings out the real purpose for this section. According to the topology that this example is using, the client is trying to communicate with another device that is connected to the same AP, but it just associates with a different SSID and on a different subnet. The question is, "How do the AP and WLC keep the two subnets separate when they are on the wired network?" The answer is VLANs. A *VLAN* is a concept in switched networks that allows segmentation of users at a logical level. By using VLANs on the wired side of the AP and WLC, the client subnet can be logically segmented, just as it is on the wireless space. The results look like this:

SSID = Logical Subnet = Logical VLAN or Logical Broadcast Domain

After the wireless frames move from the AP to the wired network, they must share a single physical wire. You may think this is hard because having multiple BSSIDs means there is more than one network, but it is not hard. The way this is accomplished is by using the 802.1Q protocol. 802.1Q places a 4-byte tag in each 802.3 frame to indicate which VLAN

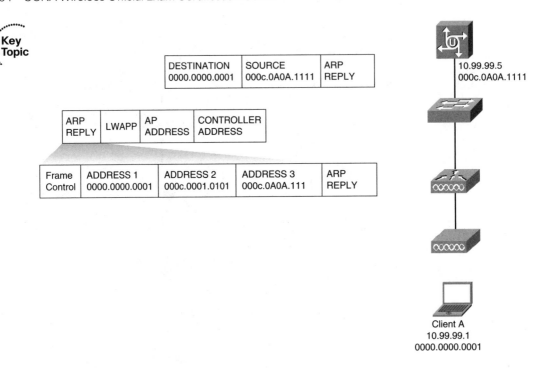

Figure 9-9 *WLC Forwards LWAPP Frame to AP*

the frame is a member of. If the frames from the Guest network are on VLAN 10, the tag indicates VLAN 10; in turn, the frames from the UserNet network would be tagged with VLAN 20. Although they ride the same wire, they are logically segmented by their VLAN membership. The switches on either end of the "trunk link" know which VLAN frames belong to based on their 802.1Q tag.

VLAN Membership Modes

Ports on switches are either going to be access ports that are associated with one VLAN or trunk ports that allow traffic for more than one VLAN to traverse them provided they are tagged by 802.1Q. The only exception to the rule is when frames are on the native VLAN, which is discussed in the next section.

When in access mode, no VLAN tag exists; rather, the port is assigned the VLAN membership. When traffic comes off that port and is destined for another port that connects to another switch, the 802.1Q protocol uses the VLAN membership information to create the tag. Therefore, all traffic that is sent on a trunk link includes a tag, with the exception of the native VLAN. But what is a native VLAN?

The native VLAN is an IEEE stipulation to the 802.1Q protocol that states that frames on the native VLAN are not modified when they are sent over trunk links. In Cisco switches, the default native VLAN is VLAN 1. An administrator can change this, however. Because you can modify it, it is important to ensure that the native VLAN is the same VLAN on both ends of the link. Because the traffic for the native VLAN is not tagged, the switches assume that the frames are on the native VLAN. If the native VLAN is different on either side, traffic can hop from one VLAN to another, as seen in Figure 9-10.

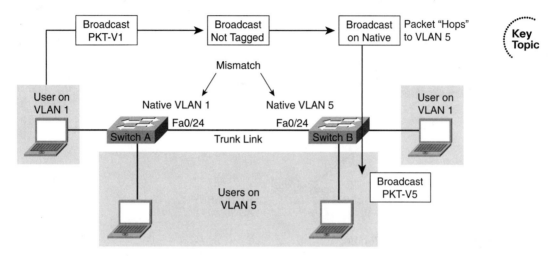

Figure 9-10 *Native VLAN Mismatch*

Because the native VLAN on Switch A port Fa0/24 is sent to VLAN 1, all traffic on VLAN 1 will not be tagged. On Switch B, port Fa0/24, the native VLAN is 5. This means that all traffic coming across the link from Switch A, without a tag, is assumed to be in VLAN 5. When the user attached to a VLAN 1 interface on Switch A sends a broadcast, it is forwarded across the trunk link without a tag. Switch B believes the broadcast to be for VLAN 5 users because that is the native VLAN on that interface, and it forwards the frame to users of VLAN 5. Again, this is to be avoided because it can be a security concern in one aspect, and it can break overall connectivity in another. In the end, the easiest way to avoid this is to ensure that both interfaces between switches are configured for the same native VLAN.

Configuring VLANs and Trunks

To configure VLANs and trunks to support your wireless topology, first understand your topology. By understanding your topology, you will see where to use access ports, where to use trunk ports, and how the configuration will come together. Figure 9-11 shows a sample topology that is used for the remainder of the configuration examples given in this chapter.

Although a switched network has additional design aspects, do not concern yourself with them for the CCNA wireless certification. Understand that you simply need to be proficient in configuring the ports. To do so, you need to perform the following tasks:

Step 1.   Create a VLAN on the switch.

Step 2.   Assign ports to the VLAN that you create.

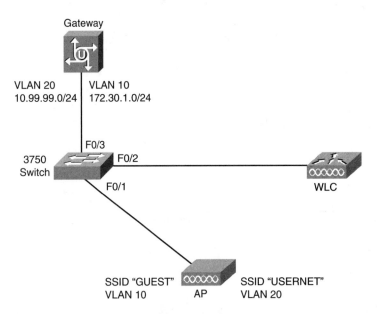

Figure 9-11   *VLAN Topology*

Step 3.   Save the configuration.

Step 4.   Configure trunk ports where necessary.

Using the standard topology in Figure 9-11, the first step is to create the VLANs that you will use. In the figure, VLANs 10 and 20 are in use. You will then assign a VLAN to an interface on the switch or configure the proper interface as a trunk. You should begin with the VLAN configuration.

Creating VLANs

VLANs are identified by a number ranging from 1 to 4094 on most switch platforms. VLANs ranging from 1 to 1001 are stored in a VLAN database. VLANs 1002 through 1005 are reserved for Token Ring and FDDI VLANs and are created by default. You cannot remove them. VLANs greater than 1005 are considered extended-range VLANs and are not stored in the VLAN database.

Follow these guidelines when defining VLANs:

■   The switch supports 1005 VLANs in VTP client, server, and transparent modes.

Note: VTP is the VLAN Trunk Protocol, designed to maintain consistency of VLANs in a network. This topic is beyond the scope of this book and will not be discussed. For more information on VLANs, see *Interconnecting Cisco Network Devices, Part 2 (ICND2): (CCNA Exam 640-802 and ICND Exam 640-816)*, 3rd Edition, published by Cisco Press.

■   Normal-range VLANs are identified with a number between 1 and 1001. VLAN numbers 1002 through 1005 are reserved for Token Ring and FDDI VLANs.[1]

- VLAN configuration for VLANs 1 to 1005 is always saved in the VLAN database. If the VTP mode is transparent, VTP and VLAN configuration are also saved in the switch running configuration file.[1]

- The switch also supports VLAN IDs 1006 through 4094 in VTP transparent mode (VTP disabled). These are extended-range VLANs, and configuration options are limited. Extended-range VLANs are not saved in the VLAN database.

- Before you can create a VLAN, the switch must be in VTP server mode or VTP transparent mode. If the switch is a VTP server, you must define a VTP domain, or VTP will not function.[1]

Cisco switches have default VLAN values. VLAN 1 is assigned to each interface, and the port is configured to dynamically determine if trunking is being used.

To add a VLAN to a switch, use the command **vlan** *vlan-id*. You can see this in Table 9-2.

Table 9-2 *VLAN Creation Commands*

Command	Action
vlan *vlan-id*	Enter a VLAN ID, and enter config-vlan mode. Enter a new VLAN ID to create a VLAN, or enter an existing VLAN ID to modify that VLAN.
name *vlan-name*	(Optional) Enter a name for the VLAN. If no name is entered for the VLAN, the default is to append the VLAN ID with leading zeros to the word *VLAN*.

The steps to create a VLAN are as follows:

Step 1. Access global configuration mode using the **configure terminal** command.

Step 2. Create the VLAN using the **vlan** command.

Step 3. Optionally give the VLAN a name using the **name** command.

Step 4. Exit to privileged EXEC mode using the **end** command.

You can verify your work using the **show vlan** command.

In Example 9-1, VLANs 10 and 20 are created on the 3750 switch seen in Figure 9-11. These VLANs are used for the trunk interfaces between the AP and switch, switch and controller, and switch and GW router.

Example 9-1 *Creating the VLANs*

```
Switch#configure terminal
Enter configuration commands, one per line. End with CNTL/Z.

Switch(config)#vlan 10
Switch(config-vlan)#exit

Switch(config)#vlan 20
Switch(config-vlan)#exit
```

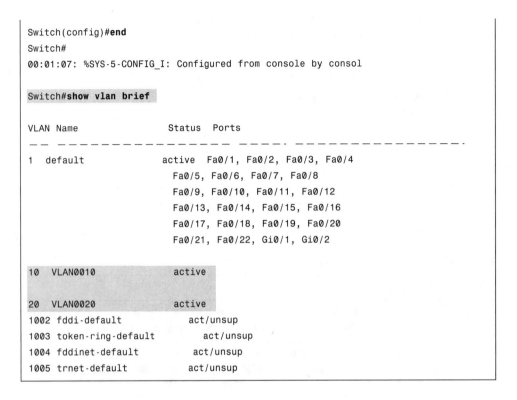

```
Switch(config)#end
Switch#
00:01:07: %SYS-5-CONFIG_I: Configured from console by consol

Switch#show vlan brief

VLAN Name                      Status  Ports
---- ------------------------- ------  ------------------------------

1    default                   active  Fa0/1, Fa0/2, Fa0/3, Fa0/4
                                       Fa0/5, Fa0/6, Fa0/7, Fa0/8
                                       Fa0/9, Fa0/10, Fa0/11, Fa0/12
                                       Fa0/13, Fa0/14, Fa0/15, Fa0/16
                                       Fa0/17, Fa0/18, Fa0/19, Fa0/20
                                       Fa0/21, Fa0/22, Gi0/1, Gi0/2

10   VLAN0010                  active

20   VLAN0020                  active
1002 fddi-default              act/unsup
1003 token-ring-default        act/unsup
1004 fddinet-default           act/unsup
1005 trnet-default             act/unsup
```

The next step is to assign ports to a VLAN.

Assigning Ports to a VLAN

After you have created the VLANs you plan to use, you need to manually assign them to a port and place the port in access mode. To do this, use the **switchport access** and **switchport mode** commands, as seen in Table 9-3.

Key Topic

Table 9-3   *Port Assignment Commands*

Command	Action
switchport mode access	Defines the VLAN membership mode for the port
switchport access vlan *vlan-id*	Assigns the port to a VLAN

The steps to assign a port to a VLAN are as follows:

Step 1.   Access global configuration mode using the **configure terminal** command.

Step 2.   Access the interface using the **interface** command.

Step 3.   Set the membership mode to access using the **switchport mode access** command.

Step 4.   Assign a VLAN to the port using the **switchport access vlan** *vlan-id* command.

Step 5.   Exit to privileged EXEC mode using the **end** command.

Step 6.   You can verify your work using the **show interface status** and **show interface** *interface* **switchoprt** commands.

In Figure 9-11, no ports will be made access ports, but if you needed to do this, your configuration would resemble Example 9-2. Notice that you can use the **show interface status** command to verify the VLAN assignment.

Example 9-2   *Assigning a Port to a VLAN*

Key
Topic

```
Switch#conf t
Enter configuration commands, one per line. End with CNTL/Z.
Switch(config)#int f0/5

Switch(config-if)#switchport mode access

Switch(config-if)#switchport access vlan 10
Switch(config-if)#

Switch#show interface status
00:13:00: %SYS-5-CONFIG_I: Configured from console by consoleerface status


Port    Name          Status     Vlan    Duplex Speed Type
Fa0/1                 connected  1       a-full a-100 10/100BaseTX
Fa0/2                 connected  1       a-full a-100 10/100BaseTX
Fa0/3                 connected  1       a-full a-100 10/100BaseTX
Fa0/4                 connected  1       a-full a-100 10/100BaseTX

Fa0/5                 connected  10      a-full a-100 10/100BaseTX
Fa0/6                 connected  1       a-full a-100 10/100BaseTX
Fa0/7                 connected  1       a-full a-100 10/100BaseTX
Fa0/8                 connected  1       a-full a-100 10/100BaseTX
<text omitted>
```

After you save the configuration, the next step is to create the trunks.

Creating Trunk Ports

The next task to accomplish is the trunk configuration. You normally perform this configuration on interfaces that connect between switches, on AP-to-controller interfaces where an AP is supporting more than on SSID, and on controller-to-switch interfaces, where the controller is supporting multiple SSIDs mapped to multiple dynamic interfaces.

To enable trunking in the interface, use the **switchport mode** command. Next, use the **switchport trunk** command to set the native VLAN and the encapsulation type. Most switches default to use 802.1Q trunking, but on some switches, you might have other options. Table 9-4 lists the commands that you use to enable trunking.

Table 9-4 *Enable Trunking Commands*

Command	Action
switchport mode trunk	Defines the interface as a trunk
switchport trunk encapsulation dot1q	Defines the trunking protocol as 802.1Q
switchport trunk native *vlan#*	Configures the native VLAN is using something other than VLAN 1
switchport nonegotiate	Tells the switch that either side of the link must be hard coded to trunk and no type of dynamic negotiation is taking place

The steps to create a trunk port are as follows:

Step 1. Access global configuration mode using the **configure terminal** command.

Step 2. Access the interface using the **interface** command.

Step 3. Set the interface to use 802.1Q encapsulation using the **switchport trunk encapsulation dot1q** command.

Step 4. Set the interface to trunk using the **switchport mode trunk** command.

Step 5. (Optional) Set the trunk's native VLAN using the **switchport trunk native** *vlan#* command.

Step 6. Tell the switch not to negotiate using the **switchport nonegotiate** command.

Step 7. Exit to privileged EXEC mode using the **end** command.

Step 8. You can verify your work using the **show interface status** and **show interface** *interface* **switchport** and **show interface** *interface* **trunk** commands.

With these configuration items in place, you can successfully control the flow of traffic and keep subnets segmented in your switches. For Figure 9-11, the trunk configuration takes place on interface Fa0/1, Fa0/2, and Fa0/3, as seen in Example 9-3.

Example 9-3 *Trunk Configuration*

```
Switch#enable
! To simplify configuration, you can set the parameters on a range of interfaces
rather than one at a time

Switch(config)#interface range f0/1 - 3

Switch(config-if-range)#switchport trunk encapsulation dot1q
```

```
Switch(config-if-range)#switchport mode trunk
Switch(config-if-range)#
00:15:42: %LINEPROTO-5-UPDOWN: Line protocol on Interface FastEthernet0/1, changed
   state to down
00:15:42: %LINEPROTO-5-UPDOWN: Line protocol on Interface FastEthernet0/2, changed
   state to down
00:15:42: %LINEPROTO-5-UPDOWN: Line protocol on Interface FastEthernet0/3, changed
   state to downswitchpoer
00:15:45: %LINEPROTO-5-UPDOWN: Line protocol on Interface FastEthernet0/1, changed
   state to up
00:15:46: %LINEPROTO-5-UPDOWN: Line protocol on Interface FastEthernet0/2, changed
   state to up
00:15:46: %LINEPROTO-5-UPDOWN: Line protocol on Interface FastEthernet0/3, changed
   state to up

Switch(config-if-range)#switchport nonegotiate

Switch(config-if-range)#switchport trunk native vlan 1
Switch(config-if-range)#
! Exit Back to Priviledge EXEC to verify

Switch(config-if-range)#end
!Use the following command to verify what interfaces are enabled for trunking
Switch#show interface trunk
00:19:55: %SYS-5-CONFIG_I: Configured from console by consoleow interface trunk

Port    Mode     Encapsulation Status    Native vlan

Fa0/1    on       802.1q      trunking    1

Fa0/2    on       802.1q      trunking    1

Fa0/3    on       802.1q      trunking    1
Fa0/23   desirable 802.1q      trunking    1
Fa0/24   desirable 802.1q      trunking    1
! Output omitted for brevity
```

With this minimal switch configuration, the APs, controllers, and gateway should all be able to communicate.

Note: The **native vlan** statement is only required to switch configurations on controllers when the value is left to "0" in the controller.

Exam Preparation Tasks

Review All the Key Concepts

Review the most important topics from this chapter, noted with the Key Topics icon in the outer margin of the page. Table 9-5 lists a reference of these key topics and the page number where you can find each one.

Table 9-5   *Key Topics for Chapter 9*

Key Topic Item	Description	Page Number
Figure 9-3	ARPing for the gateway	149
Figure 9-4	ARP request	150
Figure 9-5	ARP forwarded in LWAPP frame	150
Figure 9-6	WLC forwarding the ARP toward the gateway	151
Figure 9-7	Gateway responds to ARP	152
Figure 9-8	WLC receives ARP reply from GW and converts it to LWAPP	153
Figure 9-9	WLC forwards LWAPP frame to AP	154
Figure 9-10	Native VLAN mismatch	155
Table 9-2	VLAN creation commands	157
Example 9-2	Creating VLANs	159
Table 9-3	Port assignment commands	158
Example 9-3	Assigning a port to a VLAN	160
Table 9-4	Enable trunking commands	160

Complete the Tables and Lists from Memory

Print a copy of Appendix B, "Memory Tables," (found on the CD) or at least the section for this chapter, and complete the tables and lists from memory. Appendix C, "Memory Tables Answer Key," also on the CD, includes completed tables and lists to check your work.

Definition of Key Terms

Define the following key terms from this chapter, and check your answers in the Glossary:

lightweight AP, WLC, ARP, SA, TA, RA, DA, LWAPP, VLAN, access port, trunk port, 802.1Q, native VLAN

Command Reference to Check Your Memory

This section includes the most important configuration and EXEC commands covered in this chapter. To check to see how well you have memorized the commands as a side effect of your other studies, cover the left side of Table 9-6 with a piece of paper, read the descriptions on the right side, and see whether you remember the command.

Table 9-6   *Chapter 9 Command Reference*

Command	Description
vlan *vlan-id*	Creates a VLAN
switchport mode access	Configures a port as an access port
switchport access vlan *vlan-id*	Assigns a VLAN to a port
switchport mode trunk	Enables a port to act as a trunk port
switchport trunk native vlan *vlan-id*	Sets the native VLAN on a trunk
show interface status	Verifies VLAN assignments
show interface trunk	Verifies trunk configurations

End Notes

[1]Configuring VLANs, http://tinyurl.com/588kw9

Cisco Published 640-721 IUWNE Exam Topics Covered in This Part

Install a basic Cisco wireless LAN

- Describe the basics of the Cisco Unified Wireless Network architecture (Split MAC, LWAPP, stand-alone AP versus controller-based AP, specific hardware examples)

- Describe the Cisco Mobility Express Wireless architecture (Smart Business Communication System — SBCS, Cisco Config Agent — CCA, 526WLC, 521AP - stand-alone and controller-based)

- Describe the modes of controller-based AP deployment (local, monitor, HREAP, sniffer, rogue detector, bridge)

- Describe controller-based AP discovery and association (OTAP, DHCP, DNS, Master-Controller, Primary-Secondary-Tertiary, n+1 redundancy)

- Describe roaming (Layer 2 and Layer 3, intra-controller and inter-controller, mobility groups)

- Configure a WLAN controller and access points WLC: ports, interfaces, WLANs, NTP, CLI and Web UI, CLI wizard, LAG AP: Channel, Power

- Configure the basics of a stand-alone access point (no lab) (Express setup, basic security)

- Describe RRM

Install Wireless Clients

- Describe client OS WLAN configuration (Windows, Apple, and Linux.)

- Install Cisco ADU

- Describe basic CSSC

- Describe CCX versions 1 through 5

Part II: Cisco Wireless LANs

This chapter covers the following subjects:

The Need for Centralized Control: Briefly discusses the need for centralized control in a wireless deployment.

The Cisco Solution: Looks at the Cisco Unified Wireless Network.

The CUWN Architecture: Covers the devices in a Cisco Unified Wireless Network.

CHAPTER 10

Cisco Wireless Networks Architecture

In the past, wireless networks were deployed on an AP-by-AP basis, and the configuration for each AP was stored on the AP itself. Management solutions existed, but all in all this is not a scalable solution. The Cisco Unified Wireless Solution involves an AP that is managed by a controller device. The controller devices can manage multiple APs. The AP configuration is performed on the controller, and each AP added to the network gets its configuration from a controller. This makes it a more viable solution for large enterprise networks.

You should do the "Do I Know This Already?" quiz first. If you score 80 percent or higher, you might want to skip to the section "Exam Preparation Tasks." If you score below 80 percent, you should review the entire chapter. Refer to Appendix A, "Answers to the 'Do I Know This Already?' Quizzes," to confirm your answers.

"Do I Know This Already?" Quiz

The "Do I Know This Already?" quiz helps you determine your level of knowledge of this chapter's topics before you begin. Table 10-1 details the major topics discussed in this chapter and their corresponding quiz questions.

Table 10-1 *"Do I Know This Already?" Section-to-Question Mapping*

Foundation Topics Section	Questions
The Need for Centralized Control	1
The Cisco Solution	2–7
The CUWN Architecture	8–17

1. What kind of AP does a controller manage?

   a. Lightweight AP

   b. Managed AP

   c. LDAP AP

   d. Autonomous AP

2. Which of the following is not a functional area of the Cisco Unified Wireless Network?

   a. AP

   b. Controller

   c. Client

   d. ACS

3. Of all the Cisco Wireless LAN Controllers, what is the greatest number of APs you can support?

   a. Up to 50

   b. Up to 150

   c. Up to 300

   d. Up to 30,000

4. What protocol is used for communication between an AP and a WLC?

   a. STP

   b. LWAPP

   c. LDAP

   d. TCP

5. Which of the following functions does the controller handle? (Choose all that apply.)

   a. Association

   b. Reassociation when you have clients that are roaming

   c. The authentication process

   d. Frame exchange and the handshake between the clients

6. Which of the following functions does the AP handle? (Choose all that apply.)

   a. Buffer and transmit the frames for clients that are in power-save mode

   b. Frame bridging

   c. Send responses to probe requests from different clients on the network

   d. Forward notifications of received probe requests to the controller

7. How many VLANs does an AP typically handle?

   a. 13

   b. 15

   c. 16

   d. 512

8. How many elements comprise the CUWN architecture?

    a. 5

    b. 10

    c. 15

    d. 20

9. Which of the following APs support 802.11a/b and g? (Choose all that apply.)

    a. 1130AG

    b. 1240AG

    c. 1300 series

    d. 1400 series

10. Which AP supports the 802.11n draft version 2.0?

    a. 1250 series AP

    b. 1240 AG

    c. 1300 series

    d. 1130 AG

11. When an AP operates in H-REAP mode, where would it be seen?

    a. In a campus

    b. At the remote edge of a WAN

    c. In the data center

    d. Bridging site-to-site

12. The 4400 series WLC, model AIR-WLC4404-100-K9, can support up to how many APs?

    a. 50

    b. 100

    c. 300

    d. 600

13. True or false: An AP must run the same version of code as the controller.

    a. True

    b. False

14. What type of device is the 3750G series Wireless LAN Controller integrated into?

    a. A router as a module

    b. A router as part of the code

    c. A 3750 series switch

    d. It's a blade for the 6500 series.

15. How many APs can the Cisco WiSM manage?

   a.   100

   b.   150

   c.   300

   d.   600

16. How many lightweight APs can you have in a mobility domain?

   a.   512

   b.   1024

   c.   3068

   d.   7200

17. With wireless network management, what device is used to track more than one device at a time?

   a.   WCS

   b.   WCS navigator

   c.   Location appliance

   d.   Rogue AP detector

Foundation Topics

The Need for Centralized Control

There is certainly a need for centralized control in wireless deployments today. Initial wireless deployments were based on standalone access points called *autonomous access or fat APs*. An autonomous AP is one that does not rely on a central control device. Although this is a great start, the problem lies in scalability. Eventually, you will have problems keeping your configurations consistent, monitoring the state of each AP, and actually taking action when a change occurs. You end up with holes in your coverage area, and there is no real dynamic method to recover from that. There is certainly a need for centralized control, and the Cisco Unified Wireless Network (CUWN) is based on centralized control.

Eventually you will want or need to convert those standalone APs, if possible, to lightweight APs. A lightweight AP is managed with a controller.

Traditionally after a site survey, you would deploy your wireless network based on the information you gathered. As time passes, the environment you did the original site survey in will change. These changes, although sometimes subtle, will affect the wireless coverage. The CUWN addresses these issues.

An AP operating in lightweight mode gets its configuration from the controller. This means that you will perform most of your configuration directly on the controller. It dynamically updates the AP as the environment changes. This also allows all the APs to share a common configuration, increasing the uniformity of your wireless network and eliminating inconsistencies in your AP configurations.

The Cisco Solution

The CUWN solution is based on a centralized control model. Figure 10-1 illustrates the numerous components of the CUWN.

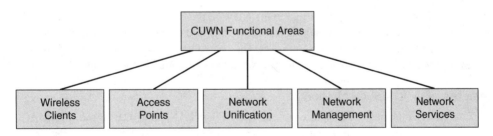

Figure 10-1 *Quick Look at the CUWN*

As you can see, five functional areas exist:

■   Wireless clients

- Access points

- Network unification

- Network management

- Network services

APs in the CUWN

Another type of device in a CUWN is a lightweight access point (AP). The lightweight AP is controlled and monitored by the Cisco Wireless LAN Controller (WLC). The AP communicates using a special protocol called the *Lightweight AP Protocol (LWAPP)* to relay information to the WLC about the coverage, the interference that the AP is experiencing, and client data about associations, among other pieces of information. This is a management type of communication, and via LWAPP it is encrypted. Client data is also sent inside these LWAPP frame headers. Client data travels from the wireless space to an AP, and then through a WLC and off to the rest of the network. When client data is encapsulated into an LWAPP header, you have not only the data, but also information about the Received Signal Strength Indicator (RSSI) and signal-to-noise ratio (SNR). The WLC uses this information to make decisions that can improve coverage areas.

WLCs in the CUWN

A single WLC can manage from six to 300 access points. You can create groupings of controllers for more scalability. This type of network could easily get out of hand if you had more than 300, 600, or 900 APs. In cases such as this, a WCS application can manage a number of controllers as well as a location appliance that can help track where devices are in the network.

> **Note:** There is obviously more to the solution that what has been discussed in this section. For more information on the Unified Wireless Solution, visit http://www.cisco.com/go/wireless. This is the home page for the Cisco Unified Wireless Network. Here you can dig into the white papers, configuration guides, and much more.

The major point to understand is that in the CUWN, the AP uses LWAPP to exchange control message information with the controller. Client data is also encapsulated into LWAPP between the AP and the controller. The controller then forwards the data frames from those wireless clients to the wired network to get that traffic back and forth.

Features of the Cisco Controllers

One of the implemented designs of the Cisco Wireless LAN Controllers is the *split MAC* design. This means that you split 802 protocols between the controller and the APs. On one side, the APs handle the real-time portion and time-sensitive packets. On the other side, the controller handles the packets that are not time-sensitive.

The AP handles the following operations:

Key Topic

- Frame exchange and the handshake between clients

- Transmits beacons

- Buffers and transmits the frames for clients that are in power-save mode

- Sends responses to probe requests from different clients on the network

- Forwards notifications of received probe requests to the controller

- Provides real-time quality information to the controller

- Monitors all channels for noise and interference

The controller handles pretty much everything else. Remember that the controller handles packets that are not considered time-sensitive. This includes the following:

- Association

- Reassociation when you have clients that are roaming

- The authentication process

- Frame translation

- Frame bridging

Part of the control traffic that is sent back and forth via LWAPP is information that provides radio resource management (RRM). This RRM engine monitors the radio resources, performs dynamic channel assignments, provides detection and avoidance of interference, and provides the dynamic transmit power control (TPC) that was discussed in Chapter 1, "Introduction to Wireless Networking Concepts." Also, whenever coverage holes (such as when one AP goes down) are detected by another access point, the controller can actually adjust power settings on other APs in the area to correct the coverage hole.

LWAPP can operate in two modes:

- **Layer 2 LWAPP mode:** This mode deals only with MAC addresses. This makes sense, because this is the only type of addressing at Layer 2. In Layer 2 mode, the AP needs to be in the same subnet as the controller and hence does not provide much flexibility for large customer installations.

- **Layer 3 LWAPP mode:** When operating in Layer 3 mode, the LWAPP can see and use Layer 2 addresses (MAC addresses) and Layer 3 addresses (IP addresses). Layer 3 mode LWAPP allows the network administrator to place APs in different subnet boundaries, and the protocol traverses those boundaries.

Supporting Multiple Networks

Previous chapters discussed that an AP can actually advertise multiple SSIDs, which lets the AP offer guest access as well as corporate user access and maybe even access for wireless IP phones. Each Wireless LAN Controller actually can support 512 different VLAN instances. Remember that on the connection between the AP and the Wireless LAN Controller, all your wireless client data is passed via the LWAPP tunnel as it travels toward the wired domain.

To review, recall that an SSID exists only in the wireless space. An SSID is then tied to a VLAN within the controller. Each lightweight AP can support 512 different VLANs, but you don't very often see that many on one AP.

On the other hand, your Wireless LAN Controller can have up to 16 wireless LANs (WLAN) tied to each AP. Each WLAN is assigned a wireless LAN identification (WLANID) by the controller. This is a number between 1 and 16, and you don't get to choose which one to use.

So, now you have a WLAN that brings together the concept of an SSID on the wireless space and a VLAN on the wired space. By having separate WLANs, you can assign different quality-of-service (QoS) policies to the type of traffic encountered on each of them. An example of this would be to have a WLAN for IP Phones and a different WLAN for regular network users.

Each AP supports up to 16 SSIDs; generally, one SSID is mapped to one VLAN. With that said, even though a Wireless LAN Controller can support up to 512 VLANs per AP, you see a maximum of only 16 VLANs in most situations.

The CUWN Architecture

The Cisco Unified Wireless Network defines a total of five functional areas or interconnected elements, as shown in Figure 10-2.

The five elements or components all work together. It's no longer about point products, where you can buy a standalone AP and deploy it and then later get management software to handle it. Today it is all about everything working together to create a smarter, more functional network. To illustrate how it all comes together, consider a Cisco wireless network. This type of network includes the following wireless clients (the first component of the CUWN):

■ Cisco Aironet client devices

■ Cisco-compatible client devices (not necessarily Cisco products, but still compatible)

■ Cisco Secure Services Client (SSC)

The client devices get a user connected.

The second component, the access point, is dynamically managed by your controllers, and they use LWAPP to communicate. The AP bridges the client device to the wired network. A number of APs that could be discussed here are as follows:

■ The 1130AG

■ The 1240AG

■ The 1250AG

■ The 1300 series bridge

■ The 1400 series bridge

■ The 1500 series outdoor mesh

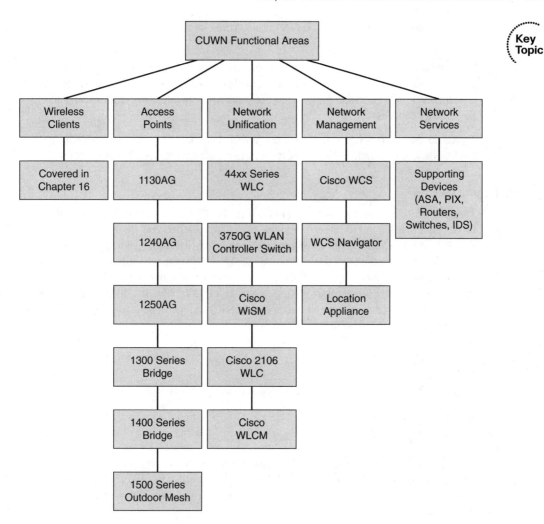

Figure 10-2 *CUWN Architecture*

Each of these access points is discussed in further detail in the section "Access Points."

The next functional area of the CUWN architecture—network unification—is the module that includes your controllers, including the following:

■ The 6500 series Catalyst switch Wireless Services Module (WiSM)

■ Cisco Wireless LAN Controller module (WLCM)

■ Cisco Catalyst 3750 series integrated WLC

■ Cisco 4400 series WLC

■ Cisco 2000 series WLC

The next functional area of the CUWN architecture—network management—is provided by the Cisco wireless control module.

The final functional area of the CUWN architecture—network services—includes everything else: the self-defending network, enhanced network support, such as location services, intrusion detection and prevention, firewalls, network admission control, and all those other services.

Those are the five functional areas of the CUWN. The following sections highlight the topics that you will want to be the most familiar with for the CCNA Wireless exam.

Client Devices

The Cisco wireless clients are covered in Chapter 16, "Wireless Clients," in greater detail. However, it is still good to understand what is available. When you are on a Cisco wireless network, you can actually use most vendors' wireless clients. Cisco provides wireless software called the Aironet Desktop Utility (ADU). The ADU is specifically used to manage and configure the Cisco wireless cards. Those wireless cards are discussed in more detail in Chapter 16. There is a cardbus version as well as a PCI version. In addition to the ADU, another client called the Secure Services Client (SSC) can help you configure security profiles for wired and wireless use on a Cisco network.

Access Points

As previously mentioned, there are two types of access points:

■ Autonomous APs

■ Lightweight APs

Some APs are built into modules and deployed in ISR routers at branch sites; other APs are deployed as just standalone devices. Cisco APs are known to offer the best range and throughput in the industry, as well as a number of security features that you do not find with other vendors.

Cisco APs offer multiple configuration options. Some of them support external antennas, some support internal antennas, and some are to be deployed outdoors. Still others are designed to be deployed indoors. Some APs are designed to be implemented for wide-area networking and bridging purposes and, while operating as a bridge, may also allow client connections. The point is that Cisco APs can serve a number of purposes.

The benefit of the CUWN APs is that they are zero-touch management, assuming that Layer 2 connectivity is already in place. As soon as they are plugged in and powered on, you don't have to do anything else at the AP level. The models that you need to be familiar with for the CCNA Wireless exam include the 1130AG, 1240AG, 1250AG, 1300, and 1400 series wireless bridges.

Note: Currently, the 1400 series bridge cannot be managed by the controller and is not considered an AP.

The 1130, 1240, and 1250 can be both autonomous and lightweight APs. Whereas the 1300 and 1400 series are designed to operate as bridges, the 1300 series can also support wireless clients. In turn, the 1400 series supports bridging only. Another model is the outdoor mesh 1500 series, which supports only LWAPP, so that would be designed for a lightweight scenario only.

Cisco is known for being ahead of the curve. That's where the special functionality of the 1250AG comes in. The 1250AG is one of the first access points to support the 802.11n draft version 2.0 standard and is the basis for all 802.11 Wi-Fi interoperability testing. For a client vendor to get the v2.0 stamp of approval, it must be validated against the 1250, and the 1250 is the only AP used during this validation.

The 1130AG

The 1130AG, shown in Figure 10-3, is a dual-band 802.11 a/b or g AP that has integrated antennas.

Figure 10-3 *Cisco 1130AG Series AP*

The 1130AG can operate as a standalone device or in lightweight AP mode. It also can operate as a Hybrid Remote Edge AP (H-REAP) device. An H-REAP device operates on the far side of a WAN, and its controller is back at the core site.

The 1130AG is 802.11i/WPA2-compliant, and it has 32 MB of RAM and 16 MB of flash memory. The 1130 AP typically is deployed in office or hospital environments. Naturally, the internal antennas do not offer the same coverage and distance as APs that are designed for external antennas. Consider the 1130s. They have 3 dB gain and 4.5 dB gain for the 2.4- and 5-GHz frequencies, respectively. If you were to compare the 1131 to the 1242 with the 2.2 dipole antennas, you would see a larger coverage area than with the 1242.

The 1240AG

The 1240AG series AP, shown in Figure 10-4, is also a dual-band 802.11 a/b or g device, similar to the 1130AG; however, it supports only external antennas.

Figure 10-4   *Cisco 1240AG Series AP*

Those external antennas would connect using the RP-TNC connectors. The 1240AG can operate as an autonomous AP and in lightweight AP mode. Like the 1130AG, it also can operate in H-REAP mode. It too is 802.11i/WPA2-compliant.

The 1250 Series AP

Shown in Figure 10-5, the 1250 series AP is one of the first enterprise APs to support the 802.11n draft version 2.0.

Because it supports the 802.11n draft standard, you can get data rates of about 300 Mbps on each radio and the 2-by-3 multiple input and multiple output technology. The 2-by-3 is discussed in Chapter 6, "Overview of the 802.11 WLAN Protocols." Also, because the 1250 is modular, it can easily be upgraded in the field. It operates in controller-based and standalone mode and is also 802.11i/WPA2-compliant.

The 1250 is designed for a more rugged type of indoor environment. You might see this at more hazardous locations such as packaging plants, or in situations where you might need

Figure 10-5 *Cisco 1250 Series AP*

to place an antenna in a hazardous location and the AP elsewhere. You might see this type of AP in factories and hospitals. It has 64 MB of DRAM and 32 MB of flash memory. It has 2.4-GHz and 5-GHz radios.

The 1300 Series AP/Bridge

The Cisco Aironet 1300 series outdoor access point/bridge, shown in Figure 10-6, is designed to act as an AP for clients as well as act as a bridge.

The 1300 operates in only 802.11b or g modes because it does not have a 5-GHz radio. It has a NEMA-4-compliant enclosure, so you can deploy it in an outdoor environment and it can withstand the elements.

The 1300 series is available in two versions—one with integrated antennas and one with antenna connectors so that you can add your own antennas to it. The connectors would be 2.4-GHz antennas, because the 1300 series does not support 802.11a.

You would expect to find the 1300 series on a college campus in a quad-type area with outdoor users or mobile clients. You might also see it in public settings, such as a park, or as a temporary type of network access for a trade show. The 1300 requires a special power supply, provided and shipped by Cisco when the product is purchased. The power supply provides power to the 1300 via coaxial. You should place it indoors or at least in an enclosure to protect it, because it is *not* NEM-4-compliant. The 1300 is a very good point-to-point and point-to-multipoint bridge that can be used to interconnect buildings and to connect buildings that do not have a wired infrastructure in place.

Figure 10-6   *Cisco 1300 Series AP*

The 1400 Series Wireless Bridge

The Cisco Aironet 1400 series wireless bridge, shown in Figure 10-7, is designed for outdoor environments.

It has a rugged enclosure that can withstand the elements. It is designed for point-to-point or point-to-multipoint networks. It can be mounted on poles, walls, or even roofs. You can also change the polarization, which, depending on how the wireless bridge is mounted, could be a very important aspect of deploying this wireless bridge. As far as the antennas go, it has a high-gain internal radio, and you can also get a version of this hardware that allows you to do a professional installation of radios with N-type connectors. This means that you can actually connect a high-gain dish. The 1400 series does not support LWAPP and operates only in standalone mode.

Note: Currently the 1400 series bridge cannot be managed by the controller and is not considered an AP.

Cisco Access Point Summary

Table 10-2 summarizes the Cisco APs.

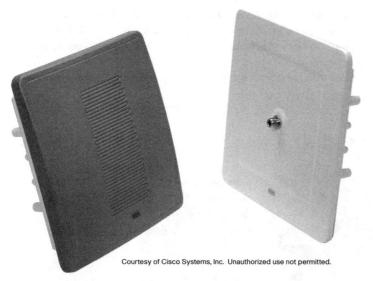

Courtesy of Cisco Systems, Inc. Unauthorized use not permitted.

Figure 10-7   *Cisco 1400 Series AP*

Table 10-2   *Summary of Cisco APs*

AP	Modes Supported	Environment	Antennas Supported	802.11 Protocols Supported	Max Data Rates Supported
1130AG	Autonomous/ lightweight AP.HREAP	Indoor	Integrated	a/b/g	54 Mbps
1240AG	Autonomous/ lightweight AP.HREAP	Rugged Indoor	External	a/b/g	54 Mbps
1250 AP	Autonomous/ lightweight AP	Rugged Indoor	External	a/b/g/n	300 Mbps
1300 AP/bridge	Autonomous/ lightweight AP, bridge	Outdoor	Internal or External	b/g	54 Mbps
1400	Bridge only (not an AP)	Outdoor	Internal or External	a/b/g	N/A

Wireless LAN Controllers

The entire design of the Wireless LAN Controllers is for scalability. The communication between a lightweight AP can happen over any type of Layer 2 or Layer 3 infrastructure using LWAPP. There are integrated controller platforms designed for installation in switches. The 3750-G actually comes as an integrated 2RU switch with either a 25 or 50 AP controller, as well as the WiSM and the WLCM. These are both modular controllers that can be installed in 6500 series switches or in Integrated Services Routers (ISR). There are also appliance-based controllers, which include the 44xx series WLC as well as the 2100 series WLC. Which controller you require depends on how many APs you need deployed. This can be anywhere from six to 300 access points per controller. This is a fixed value and can't be upgraded via licensing. If you need to support more APs, you need another controller or a controller that supports more APs.

The Cisco 44xx Series WLC

Key Topic

The Cisco 44xx series Wireless LAN Controller, shown in Figure 10-8, is a standalone appliance.

Courtesy of Cisco Systems, Inc. Unauthorized use not permitted.

Figure 10-8 *Cisco 4400 Series Wireless LAN Controller*

It is designed to take up one rack unit. It has either two or four Gigabit Ethernet uplinks, and they use mini-GBIC FSG slots. It can support 12, 25, 50, or 100 APs, depending on the model. And it can support up to 5000 MAC addresses in its database.

The 4400 series has a 10/100 interface called a service port; it is used for SSH and SSL connections for management purposes. The service port can be used for out-of-band management, but it is not required to manage the device. You can manage the device via the controller's logical management interface. There is also a console port that you can use to connect via HyperTerminal or Teraterm Pro.

Depending on the country you are in, power requirements vary, but the chassis has two power supply slots.

The controller code version used for the CCNA Wireless exam is version 5.x, and the AP runs the same version. It's actually a requirement that they run the same version, so when an AP joins with a controller, the controller upgrades or downgrades the AP. The controller upgrades four APs at a time. The 4400 series can support up to 100 access points. So, a 4400 would upgrade ten APs at a time until they are all upgraded.

The 3750-G WLC

The 3750-G Wireless LAN Controller, shown in Figure 10-9, is integrated into a switch.

There are two assemblies—the WS-C3750G-24PS-E and the AIR-WLC4402-*-K9. The two assemblies are connected to the SEPAPCB assembly, which has two Gigabit Ethernet links connecting through SFP cables and two GPIO control cables. The major benefits of this integration into the switching platform include the following:

■ Conservation of space

Courtesy of Cisco Systems, Inc. Unauthorized use not permitted.

Figure 10-9   *Cisco 3750-G Series Wireless LAN Controller*

■   Integration of the backplane of the controller and switch

■   It saves ports

The 3750G is stackable with the 3750G switches, so you can stack it with other 3750s that do not have the controller in them. The features it supports are the same as with the 4402 controllers; the only difference is the physical ports.

The Cisco WiSM

The Cisco WiSM, shown in Figure 10-10, is a services module that installs in the 6500 series switch or 7600 series router with the Cisco Supervisor Engine 720.

Courtesy of Cisco Systems, Inc. Unauthorized use not permitted.

Figure 10-10   *Cisco WiSM*

It has the same functionality as the 4400 series standalone controllers; the difference is that it supports up to 300 APs. The WiSM supports 150 access points per controller, with each blade having two controllers. Thus, you can have a total of 300 access points. You can also cluster 12 of them into a mobility domain. This allows up to 7200 lightweight APs in a mobility domain.

The Cisco 2106 WLC

The Cisco 2106 Wireless LAN Controller, shown in Figure 10-11, is also a single-rack unit design with eight 10/100 Ethernet ports.

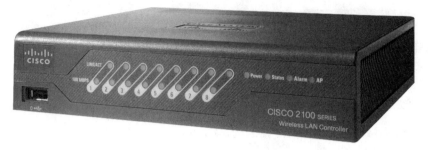

Courtesy of Cisco Systems, Inc. Unauthorized use not permitted.

Figure 10-11   *Cisco 2106 Series Wireless LAN Controller*

It can support up to six primary access points. It has an RJ-45 console port and two RJ-45 ports that support PoE. It has nearly all the same features as the 4400 series controllers but has eight built-in switch ports. You can expect to see this controller in a small branch environment.

The Cisco WLCM

The Wireless LAN Controller Module (WLCM), shown in Figure 10-12, is designed for the ISR routers. You would see this controller in a small office.

Courtesy of Cisco Systems, Inc. Unauthorized use not permitted.

Figure 10-12   *Cisco WLCM*

It has the same functionality as the 2106, but it does not have the directly connected AP and console port. It supports six APs. The WLCM-Enhanced (WLCM-E) supports eight or 12 APs, depending on which module you get.

Of course, some limitations apply. Most of the features are similar to the 4000 series:

- LWAPP

- RF control

- The ability to be a DHCP server

- Layer 2 security

The differences are things such as the following:

- Lack of PoE ports

- The number of APs supported

- The LWAPP modes supported

For these reasons, you see the WLCM deployed in smaller branches.

Wireless LAN Controller Summary

Table 10-3 summarizes the Cisco Wireless LAN Controller models.

Table 10-3 *Controller Summary*

Controller Mode	Number of APs Supported	Environment Deployed In
4400	Up to 100	Enterprise
3750G	—	Enterprise
WiSM	300 per WiSM, up to 3600	Enterprise (service module)
2106	6	Branch
WLCM	6	Branch

Wireless Network Management

In very large networks, a single wireless controller isn't enough to manage all your APs. This type of scenario might call for the Cisco Wireless Control System (WCS). The WCS is a single point of management for up to 3000 lightweight APs and 1250 autonomous APs. The WCS runs on a Windows or Red Hat Linux server. To scale beyond 3000 APs, you would need the WCS Navigator. The WCS Navigator enables you to navigate between different wireless control systems. It is a manager of managers, so to speak. You can use the WCS Navigator to navigate between different WCS servers. You can then scale it up to 30,000 APs in a single deployment and support up to 20 WCS deployments, all within the WCS Navigator. There is also an additional appliance you can use, called the Cisco Wireless Location Appliance, as shown in Figure 10-13.

Courtesy of Cisco Systems, Inc. Unauthorized use not permitted.

Figure 10-13   *Cisco Location Appliance*

This is designed to do location tracking for Wi-Fi devices and RFID tags. It helps track thousands of devices.

Exam Preparation Tasks

Review All the Key Topics

Review the most important topics from this chapter, denoted with the Key Topic icon. Table 10-4 lists these key topics and the page number where each one can be found.

Table 10-4 *Key Topics for Chapter 10*

Key Topic Item	Description	Page Number
Paragraph from the section "Features of the Cisco Controllers"	Lists detailing access point and Cisco controller responsibilities	172
Figure 10-2	The CUWN architecture	175
List from the section "Access Points"	Description of the two types of access points	176
Paragraphs from the section "The Cisco 44xx Series WLC"	Description of the specifications and capabilities of the Cisco 44xx series WLC	182

Complete the Tables and Lists from Memory

Print a copy of Appendix B, "Memory Tables" (found on the CD) or at least the section for this chapter, and complete the tables and lists from memory. Appendix C, "Memory Tables Answer Key," also on the CD, includes completed tables and lists to check your work.

Definition of Key Terms

Define the following key terms from this chapter, and check your answers in the glossary:

Lightweight AP, Autonomous AP, WLCM, WLCS

References

Cisco Wireless Services Module (WiSM): http://tinyurl.com/6mngkj

Migrate to the Cisco Unified Wireless Network: http://tinyurl.com/5uo78w

Cisco Unified Wireless Network: Secure Wireless Access for Business-Critical Mobility: http://tinyurl.com/687nff

This chapter covers the following subjects:

Understanding the Different LWAPP Modes: A discussion of Layer 2 and Layer 3 LWAPP.

How an LWAPP AP Discovers a Controller: A discussion regarding the process that an AP goes through when finding a controller.

How an LWAPP AP Chooses a Controller and Joins It: The process an AP takes when it chooses a controller to join.

How an LWAPP AP Receives Its Configuration: The process an AP takes when it retrieves its configuration.

Redundancy for APs and Controllers: How to provide redundancy for your APs.

The AP Is Joined, Now What?: A discussion on the different functions an AP can perform.

CHAPTER 11

Controller Discovery and Association

When a lightweight AP boots up, it cannot function without a controller. In this chapter, you will learn about the Lightweight Access Point Protocol (LWAPP) and the modes in which it can operate. You will also learn about how an AP finds controllers on the network, chooses one to join with, and then retrieves its configuration. In addition, you will look at the ways to provide redundancy for your AP in the event that a controller goes down. Finally, when an AP is joined with a controller, it can operate in certain modes that can be used for different reasons. You will learn these operational modes and when they are used.

You should do the "Do I Know This Already?" quiz first. If you score 80 percent or higher, you may want to skip to the section "Exam Preparation Tasks." If you score below 80 percent, you should spend the time reviewing the entire chapter. Refer to Appendix A, "Answers to the 'Do I Know This Already?' Quizzes," to confirm your answers.

"Do I Know This Already?" Quiz

The "Do I Know This Already?" quiz helps you determine your level of knowledge of this chapter's topics before you begin. Table 11-1 details the major topics discussed in this chapter and their corresponding quiz questions.

Table 11-1 *"Do I Know This Already?" Section-to-Question Mapping*

Foundation Topics Section	Questions
Understanding the Different LWAPP Modes	1–3
How an LWAPP AP Discovers a Controller	4–5
How an LWAPP AP Chooses a Controller and Joins It	6–8
How an LWAPP AP Receives Its Configuration	9
Redundancy for APs and Controllers	10–11
The AP Is Joined, Now What?	12–14

1. What two modes can LWAPP operate in? (Choose two.)

    a. Layer 2 LWAPP mode

      b. Joint LWAPP mode

      c. Autonomous LWAPP mode

      d. Layer 3 LWAPP mode

2. When LWAPP communication between the access point and the wireless LAN controller happens in native, Layer 2 Ethernet frames, what is this known as?

      a. EtherWAPP

      b. Hybrid mode

      c. Native mode LWAPP

      d. Layer 2 LWAPP mode

3. What is the only requirement for Layer 3 LWAPP mode?

      a. IP connectivity must be established between the access points and the WLC.

      b. You must know the IP addressing on the AP.

      c. Client devices must be in the same VLAN.

      d. Each device in the Layer 3 domain must be on the same subnet.

4. Which state is not a valid state of an AP that is discovering and joining a controller?

      a. Discover

      b. Join

      c. Image Data

      d. Hybrid-REAP

5. What is the first step in a Layer 3 LWAPP discovery?

      a. Priming

      b. AP Join Request

      c. Subnet broadcast of Layer 3 LWAPP discovery message

      d. OATAP

6. AP-Priming is used for which of the following?

      a. Prime an AP prior to bootup with complex algorithms

      b. Deliver a list of controllers to the AP using a hunting process and discovery algorithm

      c. Perform basic setup of controller configurations delivered to the AP

      d. Provision an AP over the air

7. Which of the following is not contained in a join response message?

      a. Type of controller

      b. Interfaces in the controller

      c. Number and type of radios

      d. AP name

8. The join request message is sent to the primary controller only under what condition?

   a.   The controller is reachable.

   b.   The AP has an IP address.

   c.   The primary controller has low load.

   d.   The AP is primed.

9. If no primed information is available, what does the AP look for next when trying to join a controller?

   a.   A master controller

   b.   A primer controller

   c.   A new controller

   d.   A new subnet

10. When an AP retrieves its configuration file, where is it applied?

   a.   RAM

   b.   ROM

   c.   NVRAM

   d.   Flash

11. How many backup controllers are in an N + 1 design?

   a.   1

   b.   2

   c.   3

   d.   4

12. Which method is considered the most redundant?

   a.   N + 1

   b.   N + N

   c.   N + N + 1

   d.   N * N + 1

13. Which AP mode can you use for site surveys?

   a.   Local mode

   b.   H-REAP mode

   c.   Bridge mode

   d.   Rogue Detection mode

14. In Monitor mode, which command can you use to change the value of the channels monitored?

   a.   `config advanced channel-list`

   b.   `config advanced 802.11b channel-list monitor`

   c.   `config advanced 802.11b monitor channel-list`

   d.   `config advanced monitor channel-list`

Foundation Topics

Understanding the Different LWAPP Modes

LWAPP can operate in either Layer 2 LWAPP mode or Layer 3 LWAPP mode. The Layer 2 mode is considered out of date, and Cisco prefers and recommends Layer 3 mode. Layer 3 mode is the default LWAPP mode on most Cisco devices.

At a high level, and after the AP has an IP address, the phases of LWAPP operation include these:

Step 1.   An AP sends an LWAPP discovery request message. This is a broadcast that is sent at Layer 2.

Step 2.   Assuming that a controller is operating in Layer 2 LWAPP mode, the wireless LAN controller (WLC) receives the LWAPP discovery request and responds with an LWAPP discovery response message.

Note: Only Cisco 1000 Series LAPs support Layer 2 LWAPP mode. Also, Layer 2 LWAPP mode is not supported on Cisco 2000 Series WLCs. These WLCs support only Layer 3 LWAPP mode.

Step 3.   The AP chooses a controller based on the response received and sends a join request.

Step 4.   The WLC receiving the LWAPP join request responds to the AP join request with an LWAPP join response. This process is going to include a mutual authentication. An encryption key is created to secure the rest of the join process and any future LWAPP control messages.

Step 5.   After the AP has joined the WLC, LWAPP messages are exchanged, and the AP initiates a firmware download from the WLC (if the AP and WLC have a version mismatch). If the onboard firmware of the AP is not the same as that of the WLC, the AP downloads firmware to stay in sync with the WLC. The firmware download mechanism utilizes LWAPP.

Step 6.   After the WLC and AP match firmware revisions, the WLC provisions the AP with the appropriate settings. These settings might include service set identifiers (SSID), security parameters, 802.11 parameters such as data rates and supported PHY types, radio channels, and power levels.

Step 7.   After the provisioning phase is completed, the AP and WLC enter the LWAPP runtime state and begin servicing data traffic.

Step 8.   During runtime operations, the WLC might issue various commands to the AP through LWAPP control messages. These commands might be provisioning commands or requests for statistical information that the AP collects and maintains.

Step 9.   During runtime operations, LWAPP keepalive messages are exchanged between the AP and WLC to preserve the LWAPP communication channel. When an AP misses a sufficient number of keepalive message exchanges, it attempts to discover a new WLC.

LWAPP Layer 2 Transport Mode

When operating in Layer 2 mode, LWAPP has the following characteristics and requirements:

- LWAPP communication between the AP and the WLC is in native, Layer 2 Ethernet frames. This is known as Layer 2 LWAPP mode.

- In Layer 2 LWAPP mode, although the APs might get an IP address via DHCP, all LWAPP communications between the AP and WLC are in Ethernet encapsulated frames, not IP packets.

- The APs must be on the same Ethernet network as the WLC. This means that Layer 2 mode is not very scalable.

The source and destination MAC addresses depend on the direction of the frame:

- An LWAPP control frame sent from the AP to the WLC uses the AP Ethernet MAC address as the source address and the WLC MAC address as the destination address.

- An LWAPP control frame sent from the WLC to the AP uses the WLC MAC address as the source address and the AP MAC address as the destination address.

Data packets between wireless LAN clients and other hosts are typically IP packets. Figure 11-1 illustrates the process of clients sending frames in a logical topology. Do not be concerned with the underlying network here, but rather the process between devices that will occur.

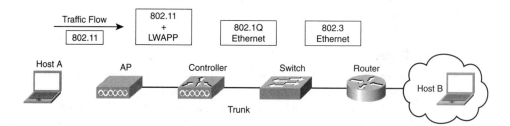

Figure 11-1   *Host A Sending to Host B*

In this figure, a host, Host A, is seen sending a packet to Host B. The following sequence occurs:

Step 1.   Host A transmits an IP packet over the 802.11 RF interface after it is encapsulated in an 802.11 frame with the Host A MAC address as the source address and the access point radio interface MAC address as the destination address.

Step 2. At the AP, the AP adds an LWAPP header to the frame with the C-bit set to 0 and then encapsulates the LWAPP header and 802.11 frame into an Ethernet frame. This Ethernet frame uses the AP Ethernet MAC address as the source MAC address and the WLC MAC address as the destination MAC address.

Step 3. At the WLC, the Ethernet and LWAPP headers are removed, and the original 802.11 frame is processed.

Step 4. After processing the 802.11 MAC header, the WLC extracts the payload (the IP packet), encapsulates it into an Ethernet frame, and then forwards the frame onto the appropriate wired network, typically adding an 802.1Q VLAN tag.

Step 5. The packet then travels through the wired switching and routing infrastructure to Host B.

After receiving the frame, Host B will likely reply. When Host B returns an IP packet to Host A, the following sequence occurs:

Step 1. The packet is carried from Host B over the wired switching and routing network to the WLC, where an Ethernet frame arrives with the Host A MAC address as the destination MAC address. The IP packet from Host B is encapsulated inside this Ethernet frame.

Step 2. The WLC takes the entire Ethernet frame, adds the LWAPP header with the C-bit set to 0, and then encapsulates the combined frame inside an LWAPP Ethernet frame. This LWAPP Ethernet frame uses the WLC MAC address as the source MAC address and the access point Ethernet MAC address as the destination MAC address. This frame is sent out over the switched network to the AP.

Step 3. At the AP, the Ethernet and LWAPP headers are removed and processed.

Step 4. The payload (the IP packet) is then encapsulated in an 802.11 MAC frame and transmitted over the air by the AP to Host A.

LWAPP Layer 3 Transport Mode

As previously mentioned, Cisco prefers Layer 3 LWAPP mode. This is because it is more scalable than Layer 2 LWAPP. Layer 3 LWAPP control and data messages are transported over the IP network in User Datagram Protocol (UDP) packets. Layer 3 LWAPP is supported on all Cisco WLC platforms and lightweight APs.

The only requirement is established IP connectivity between the APs and the WLC. The LWAPP tunnel uses the IP address of the AP and the AP-Manager interface IP address of the WLC as endpoints. On the AP side, both LWAPP control and data messages use an ephemeral port that is derived from a hash of the AP MAC address as the UDP port. On the WLC side, LWAPP data messages always use UDP port 12222, and LWAPP control messages always use UDP port 12223. The process of clients sending frames in Layer 3

LWAPP mode is similar to that of Layer 2 mode; however, the frames are now encapsulated in UDP. The process is as follows:

Step 1.   Host A transmits the packet over the 802.11 RF interface. This packet is encapsulated in an 802.11 frame with the MAC address of Host A as the source address and the radio interface MAC address of the AP as the destination address.

Step 2.   At the AP, the AP adds an LWAPP header to the frame with the C-bit set to 0 and then encapsulates the LWAPP header and 802.11 frame into a UDP packet that is transmitted over IP. The source IP address is the IP address of the AP, and the destination IP address is the AP Manager Address of the WLC. The source UDP port is the ephemeral port based on a hash of the access point MAC address. The destination UDP port is 12222.

Step 3.   The IP packet is encapsulated in Ethernet as it leaves the AP and is transported by the switching and routed network to the WLC.

Step 4.   At the WLC, the Ethernet, IP, UDP, and LWAPP headers are removed from the original 802.11 frame.

Step 5.   After processing the 802.11 MAC header, the WLC extracts the payload (the IP packet from Host A), encapsulates it into an Ethernet frame, and then forwards the frame onto the appropriate wired network, typically adding an 802.1Q VLAN tag.

Step 6.   The packet is then transmitted by the wired switching and routing infrastructure to Host B.

When Host B receives the packet, it is likely to respond, so the reverse process is as follows:

Step 1.   The packet is delivered by the wired switching and routing network to the WLC, where an Ethernet frame arrives with the MAC address of Host A as the destination MAC address.

Step 2.   The WLC removes the Ethernet header and extracts the payload (the IP packet destined for Host A).

Step 3.   The original IP packet from Host A is encapsulated with an LWAPP header, with the C-bit set to 0, and then transported in a UDP packet to the AP over the IP network. The packet uses the WLC AP Manager IP address as the source IP address and the AP IP address as the destination address. The source UDP port is 12222, and the destination UDP port is the ephemeral port derived from the AP MAC address hash.

Step 4.   This packet is carried over the switching and routing network to the AP.

Step 5.   The AP removes the Ethernet, IP, UDP, and LWAPP headers, and it extracts the payload, which is then encapsulated in an 802.11 frame and delivered to Host A over the RF network.

For Layer 3 LWAPP, a 1500-byte maximum transmission unit (MTU) is assumed. You can change this, but 1500 is the default.

How an LWAPP AP Discovers a Controller

When an AP discovers and joins a controller, the AP proceeds through several states. In Figure 11-2, you can see these states and when they happen.

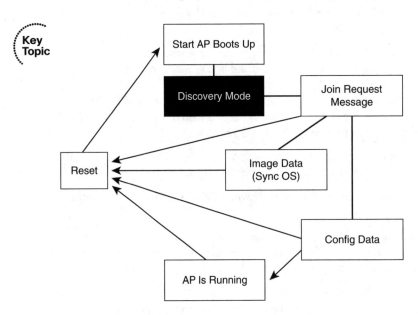

Figure 11-2 *AP States*

The process begins with the discovery of a controller. Because the lightweight APs are by definition "zero-touch" when deployed, you should only need to plug them in and let them do the rest. On the back end, the part you do not see is a little more complex. The steps in this process, beginning with discovery, are as follows:

Step 1.   The APs send LWAPP discovery request messages to WLCs. This is broadcast at Layer 2. Because Layer 3 mode is what you want to use, this should fail.

Step 2.   Upon failing, the AP proceeds to Layer 3 by checking its configuration for an IP address. If no IP address exists, the client uses DHCP to obtain one.

Step 3.   The AP uses information obtained in the DHCP response to contact a controller.

Step 4.   Any WLC receiving the LWAPP discovery request message responds with an LWAPP discovery response message. If no controller responds, the AP reverts to Layer 2 broadcasts and starts the process again.

The Cisco implementation uses the hunting process and discovery algorithm to find as many controllers as possible. The AP builds a list of WLCs using the search and discovery process, and then it selects a controller to join from the list.

The controller search process repeats continuously until at least one WLC is found and joined. IOS-based APs only do a Layer 3 discovery.

The Layer 3 discovery process follows a certain order:

Step 1.   The AP does a subnet broadcast to see if a controller is operating in Layer 3 mode on the local subnet.

Step 2.   The AP does an over-the-air provisioning (OTAP).

Note: Although OTAP is not fully covered here, you can find a detailed document at http://tinyurl.com/5hah9q.

Step 3.   When other APs exist and are in a joined state with a controller, they send messages that are used for resource management. These messages have the IP address of the controller in it. The AP can listen to these messages and get the controller IP address. The AP can then send a directed discovery message to the controller.

Step 4.   The next process is called *AP priming*.

AP priming is something that happens after an AP is associated with at least one controller. The AP then gets a list of other controllers that it can associate with from the one it is already associated with. These other controllers are part of a *mobility group*. This information then gets stored in NVRAM and can be used if the AP reboots. To contact these controllers, the AP sends a broadcast to the primary controller and all the other controllers in the group.

Another method of discovering a controller is via DHCP using Vendor Option mode. This simply uses DHCP option 43 to learn the IP address of the management interface of a controller.

The final method of discovering a controller is using Domain Name System (DNS). You use DHCP to get IP information, including a DNS server entry. Then the AP looks for a DNS entry for CISCO-LWAPP-CONTROLLER. This should return the IP address of a controller management interface. The AP can use this address to send a unicast query. This process results in an AP finding a controller, all of which happens during the Discovery mode indicated in Figure 11-2.

Note: With APs running 12.3.11-JX1 and later, you can manually prime the APs with a console cable to aid in the join process.

How an LWAPP AP Chooses a Controller and Joins It

Now that the AP potentially has numerous controllers to join, it must choose one and send it a join request message. Figure 11-3 illustrates this portion of communication.

A join request message contains the following information:

■ Type of controller

■ MAC of controller

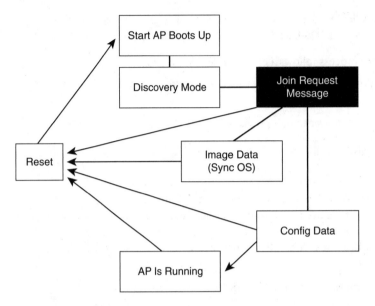

Figure 11-3 *AP Join State*

- AP hardware version

- AP software version

- AP name

- Number and type of radios

- Certificate payload (x.509)

- Session payload to set up the session values

- Test payload to see if jumbo frames can be used

This join request message is sent using a predefined method consisting of the following steps:

Step 1.   An AP chooses the primary controller (if primed).

   This can be defined in each AP and stored in flash to survive a reboot. Using the controller GUI, go to **WIRELESS > Access Points > All APs >** *SelectedAp* **> Details**, as seen in Figure 11-4.

Step 2.   Choose the secondary controller, tertiary (if primed).

Step 3.   If no primed information is available, then look for a master controller.

   The definition of a controller as master is configured in the GUI under **CONTROLLER > Advanced > Master Controller Mode**, as shown in Figure 11-5.

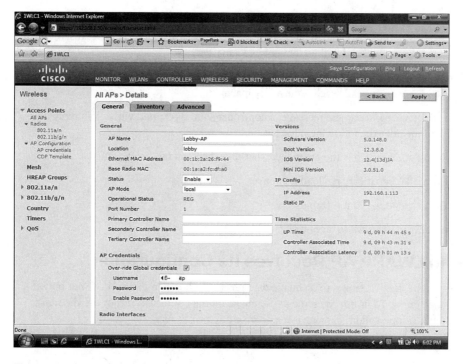

Figure 11-4 *Define Primary Controller*

Figure 11-5 *Enable Master Controller Mode*

A mobility group should have only one master controller. Turn this feature off after you have added all new APs. After you have added the new APs, they will be primed and will no longer need a master.

Step 4.   When all else fails, look for the least loaded AP-Manager interface based on how many APs each is currently managing.

Upon receiving a join request message, a controller should respond with a join reply message. This includes the following information:

■   Result code, which is the green light that says they can talk

■   Controller certificate payload response

■   Test payload for jumbo frames

This process joins an AP to a controller.

How an LWAPP AP Receives Its Configuration

After joining, the AP moves to an image data phase, as shown in Figure 11-6, but only if the image on the AP is not the same as the image on the controller. If they are the same, this step is skipped and the image is used.

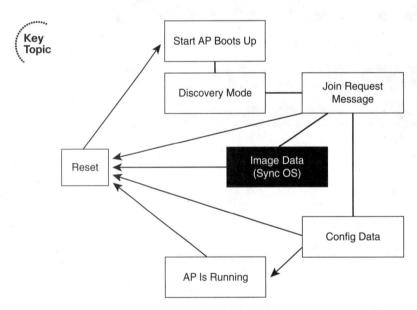

Figure 11-6   *The Image Data State*

The controller upgrades or downgrades the AP at this point, and then it resets the AP. After a reset, the process begins again. The code is downloaded in LWAPP messages.

After the process of discovery and join happen and the image is the same on the controller and the AP, the AP gets its configuration from the controller. This happens during the config data stage, as illustrated in Figure 11-7.

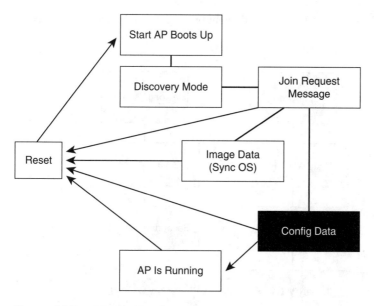

Figure 11-7   *AP Gets Config*

The AP then prompts the controller for a config by sending an LWAPP configure request message that contains parameters that can be configured as well as any values that are currently set; however, most of these values are empty.

When the controller gets the request, it sends a configure response message, which has the configuration values.

The AP then applies the configuration values in RAM. It is important to understand that these values are not stored in flash. If the AP reboots, the process begins again.

After applying the configuration, the AP is up and running.

Redundancy for APs and Controllers

Networks today involve a mix of critical forms of data, be it voice traffic or business transactions. Redundancy is a part life. You need to be familiar with two forms of redundancy for the CCNA Wireless exam:

- AP redundancy

- Controller redundancy

AP redundancy is seen when APs exist in the same RF domain. They are designed to self-heal when poor coverage exists. This involves increasing power levels by stepping up one or two levels or even changing the channel on which they operate.

Controller redundancy is seen in multiple forms. One form of controller redundancy is having a primary, secondary, and tertiary controller, as shown in Figure 11-8. As you can see in the figure, Controller A is the primary controller for WLAN A. Controller C is acting as the secondary controller for WLAN A, and Controller B is acting as the tertiary controller for WLAN A. Each WLAN has a different primary, secondary, and tertiary controller.

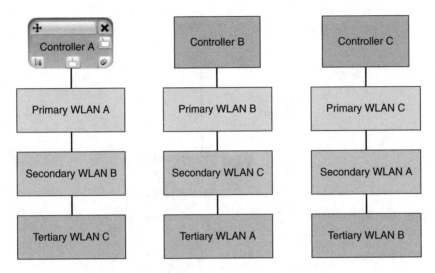

Figure 11-8   *Controller Redundancy*

Another form of controller redundancy is using link aggregation (LAG) or multiple AP managers.

You can also have a primary and backup port on a controller. If the primary goes down, you can use the backup.

Common designs for controller redundancy include the following:

- **N + 1:** This design has a single backup for multiple controllers. If you have five controllers with one backup for all of them to share, the backup can easily become overwhelmed if more than one controller is down at a time.

- **N + N:** This design allows each controller to back up the other. For example, AP-1 points to WLC1 as its primary and WLC2 as its secondary. AP-2 points to WLC2 as its primary and WLC1 as its secondary. Load balancing is desired between APs and controllers. Also, if one controller is maxed out with APs, the design is no good.

- **N + N + 1:** This is the most redundant design. Each controller backs up the other, and an extra is designed as a backup. Take the same example as N + N but add a third controller, WLC-BACKUP, that every AP points to as the tertiary.

The AP Is Joined, Now What?

You can change the mode by navigating to **Wireless > APs > All APs > Detail**.

Now that you have an AP joined with a controller, what can it do? Most people expect it to get them to the Internet. Your AP can actually serve numerous roles based on the mode it is in. Different APs support different modes. An AP can operate in each of the following modes:

- Local

- Monitor

- Sniffer

- Rogue Detector

- Hybrid REAP

- Bridge

The sections that follow describe each of these modes in greater detail.

Local Mode

This is business as usual for an AP. In this mode, the AP scans all channels over a 180-second period for monitoring services, and it inspects management packets for intrusion detection system (IDS) signature matches.

You can also use this mode for site surveys.

When the AP scans channels, it jumps to each unassigned channel for 60 ms and then goes back to its assigned channel for 13 seconds. The purpose of scanning channels is to monitor traffic.

Monitor Mode

Monitor mode is passive. When in this mode, the AP does not send traffic out of its radios, and it does not allow client connections. This mode is used for finding rogue APs or IDS matches, troubleshooting, or site surveys. Monitor mode APs can be used with the location appliance to increase accuracy. Scanning is based on the country, and the command **config advanced 802.11b monitor channel-list** can change the value of the channels monitored.

Sniffer Mode

This mode operates with an OmniPeak, Airmagnet, or Wireshark server to capture data. The encapsulation of the captured data is specific to the product with which it is used. The AP sends the data to the specified device for review. This mode is used to gather time stamps, signal strength, packet size, and other relevant information. You can use this mode as a troubleshooting tool for forensics.

Rogue Detection Mode

This special role communicates rogue AP information between WLCs. In this mode, the radios on the AP are turned off, and it listens for ARP messages on the wired network. It compares the MAC information to a rogue AP and client MAC list that it receives from the controller. The AP forwards this to other controllers. If an ARP is heard on the wired LAN, the controller generates an alarm.

H-REAP Mode

H-REAP mode is designed to be used when you have APs across a WAN and you want to use the controller at a central site. The big issue is that the controller is connected via a WAN link, so you must follow certain guidelines:

■ The link cannot be any slower than 128 kbps.

■ Roundtrip latency cannot be more than 100 ms roundtrip.

■ The AP needs to get a 4-MB code update across the WAN link.

The AP needs to communicate with the controller for only a short time during the initial phase, and then it can function without it but with reduced functionality. The two modes of operation are as follows:

■ **Connected mode:** In Connected mode, the AP can communicate with the controller.

■ **Standalone mode:** In Standalone mode, the AP is disconnected and is unable to reach the controller. All client requests are based on a configuration that is local to the AP. This mode is supported on the AP 1130, AP 1240, and AP 1250.

Bridge Mode

In Bridge mode, the AP can act as a bridge and allow client access. APs can use point-to-point or point-to-multipoint links. To determine the best path, the APs use a protocol called Adaptive Wireless Path Protocol (AWPP). Cisco calls this an iMesh for indoor APs and a mesh for outdoor APs.

Exam Preparation Tasks

Review All the Key Concepts

Review the most important topics from this chapter, noted with the Key Topics icon in the outer margin of the page. Table 11-2 lists a reference of these key topics and the page number where you can find each one.

Table 11-2   *Key Topics for Chapter 11*

Key Topic Item	Description	Page Number
List in the section "Understanding the Different LWAPP Modes"	Steps of LWAPP	193
Figure 11-2	AP states	196
List in the section "How an LWAPP AP Discovers a Controller"	AP states process	200
Figure 11-4	How the AP gets its image	199

Definition of Key Terms

Define the following key terms from this chapter, and check your answers in the Glossary:

Lightweight Access Point Protocol (LWAPP), Layer 3 LWAPP mode, LWAPP discovery request, LWAPP discovery response, AP priming, join request message, master controller, N + 1, N + N, N + N + 1, Local mode, Monitor mode, Sniffer mode, Rogue Detection mode, Hybrid REAP mode, Bridge mode, over-the-air provisioning (OTAP)

This chapter covers the following subjects:

Understanding Roaming: Looks at the concept of roaming and how it should work.

Types of Roaming: Discusses Layer 2 and Layer 3 roaming as well as mobility anchor configurations.

CHAPTER 12

Adding Mobility with Roaming

More and more frequently, end users are expecting the ability to begin a transfer and then change locations seamlessly. This is where roaming functionality comes into play. Roaming is a big part of wireless networks. To facilitate this process, you need to be aware of some terms and options. This chapter introduces you to those terms and how the roaming process is configured.

You should take the "Do I Know This Already?" quiz first. If you score 80 percent or higher, you might want to skip to the section "Exam Preparation Tasks." If you score below 80 percent, you should review the entire chapter.

"Do I Know This Already?" Quiz

The "Do I Know This Already?" quiz helps you determine your level of knowledge of this chapter's topics before you begin. Table 12-1 details the major topics discussed in this chapter and their corresponding quiz questions.

Table 12-1 *"Do I Know This Already?" Section-to-Question Mapping*

Foundation Topics Section	Questions
Understanding Roaming	1–5
Types of Roaming	6–11

1. Which of the following describes a mobility group?

    a. A set of users with rights to roam

    b. A group of controllers configured with the same hostname

    c. A group of controllers configured in the same mobility group

    d. A set of controllers that roam

2. Controllers that are aware of each other but that are in different mobility groups are said to be in what?

   a. Mobility chain

   b. Mobility mode

   c. Mobility-aware mode

   d. Mobility domain

3. How many mobility domains can a controller be a member of?

   a. One

   b. Two

   c. Three

   d. Four

4. True or false: A client can roam from one mobility group to another in the same mobility domain.

   a. True

   b. False

5. True or false: A client can roam between two controllers in different mobility domains.

   a. True

   b. False

6. Which of the following are valid roaming types? (Choose two.)

   a. Layer 2 roaming

   b. Seamless AP roaming

   c. Layer 3 roaming

   d. Layer 4 roaming

7. Which of the following statements is not true?

   a. For roaming to work, the controllers need to be in the same mobility domain.

   b. For roaming to work, the controllers need to run the same code version.

   c. For roaming to work, the controllers need to operate in the same LWAPP mode.

   d. For roaming to work, the SSID (WLAN) does not necessarily need to be the same.

8. What is the term for roaming from one AP to another AP managed by the same controller?

   a. Same-controller roaming

   b. Intercontroller roaming

   c. Intracontroller roaming

   d. This is not roaming.

9. What is the term for roaming from one AP to another AP managed by a different controller?

   a. Same-controller roaming

   b. Intercontroller roaming

   c. Intracontroller roaming

   d. This is not roaming.

10. What is it called when client traffic is tunneled back to the anchor controller before being sent to its destination?

   a. Symmetric tunneling

   b. Asymmetric tunneling

   c. Anchor roaming

   d. Layer 2 roaming

11. What is it called when client traffic is sent directly to a destination and return traffic goes to an anchor controller before being sent back to the client on a foreign controller?

   a. Symmetric tunneling

   b. Asymmetric tunneling

   c. Anchor roaming

   d. Layer 3 roaming

Foundation Topics

Understanding Roaming

It's probably safe to say that most people understand the concept of roaming at a high level. You want to move from your desk to the conference room. The conference room is on the other side of the building, but you are in the middle of a large upload. You don't sweat it because you are on a wireless network and wireless is..."everywhere"!

That sounds nice, and that's what wireless networks have to offer, but how does wireless get "everywhere"? From what you have learned so far, you know that a wireless signal can't travel "everywhere" because of absorption, refraction, scattering, and more. You've also learned a little about roaming and how an AP needs some overlap to facilitate the process. But there is still more to it. If you step back and look at the big picture, you start to see that the controller has to be involved in this lightweight AP deployment. How is the controller involved? To understand that, you need to understand mobility groups.

Understanding Mobility Groups

In simple terms, a *mobility group* is a setting on a controller that defines the controller as a member of a group. Other controllers would also be members of that group. These controllers share information about the clients that are roaming. In Figure 12-1, two controllers are in the same mobility group. They can exchange information about the client that is roaming. Figure 12-2 shows a network with three controllers. Controller1 and Controller2 are in the same mobility group, and Controller3 is in a different one. When this scenario occurs, the three controllers are considered to be in the same *mobility domain*. A controller can be aware of another controller in a different mobility group as long as they are in the same mobility domain. This allows them to exchange information regarding their clients. This allows clients in different mobility groups to roam between the different mobility domains. If the controllers were in different mobility groups and did not have knowledge of each other, roaming could not occur. To provide this knowledge, you as an administrator need to enter the MAC address and management IP address of the other controller in the first controller, and vice versa. In other words, Controller2 needs to be configured with Controller3's MAC and management IP addresses, and Controller3 needs to be configured with Controller2's MAC and IP addresses.

To set this up in the controller, first you need to configure the controller's mobility domain. Remember that multiple controllers share the same mobility group, and controllers in different mobility groups can communicate with each other if they are part of the same mobility domain. To configure the mobility *domain* using the controller web interface, choose **CONTROLLER > General**.

A controller can be in only one mobility group and one mobility domain. To configure the mobility group, choose **CONTROLLER > Mobility Management**. Controllers that are in the same mobility group have the same virtual gateway IP address. You can add these controllers by clicking **New** and then adding the IP address, MAC address, and mobility group of the other controller, as shown in Figure 12-3. In Figure 12-3, Controller2 is added to Controller1. If you have more than one controller to add, you can do it all at once. First you create a text file that includes the controller MAC address and IP address for each

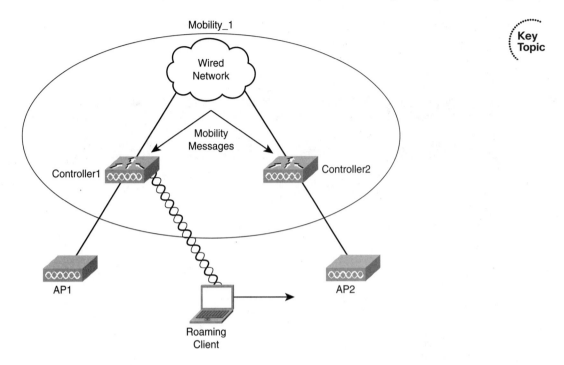

Figure 12-1 *Mobility Group*

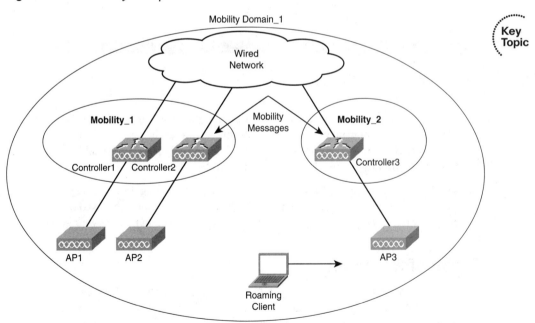

Figure 12-2 *Mobility Domain*

controller you want to add. Then you paste the contents of the text file into the Edit All page. In Figure 12-3, two controllers are listed on the Edit All page. You can have up to 24 controllers in a mobility group.

Figure 12-3   *Edit All Page*

So what happens if a user moves to another mobility domain? Because a controller in a different mobility domain does not have information about the client, the client must reassociate. When the client reassociates, it will most likely get a new IP address, and any sessions it currently has will need to be restarted.

So now you understand the part that controllers play in roaming. In truth, they play an even bigger part, depending on the type of roaming that is happening. Cisco controllers can support a Layer 2 or Layer 3 roaming process, as detailed in the following sections.

Types of Roaming

Before we dive into roaming as a Layer 2 or 3 process, let's define it. Roaming is the movement of a client from one AP to another while still transmitting. Roaming can be done across different mobility groups, but must remain inside the same mobility domain. Consider the following examples.

Figure 12-4 shows a client transmitting data and moving from AP1 to AP2. These two APs are in the same mobility domain. This is roaming.

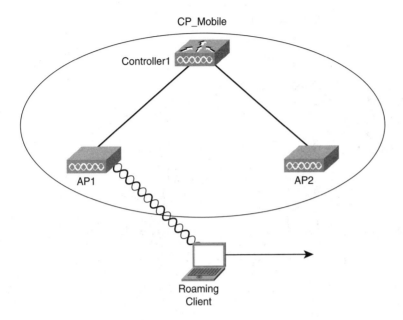

Figure 12-4   *Client Roaming in the Same Mobility Group*

Figure 12-5 shows a client transmitting data and moving from AP2 to AP3. These two APs
are in different mobility groups but are in the same mobility domain. This too is roaming.

Now here is where roaming breaks. In Figure 12-6, a user is transmitting data and decides
to go work at a local coffee shop that offers wireless network access. After buying a $5
cup of coffee and settling down into a cushy sofa, he fires up his laptop and continues
surfing the net. This is *not* roaming. In this case, the user has a new IP address, and any
sessions that were active before need to be restarted.

The following must occur for your controllers to support roaming:

■   The controllers need to be in the same mobility domain.

■   The controllers need to run the same code version.

■   The controllers need to operate in the same LWAPP mode.

■   Access control lists (ACL) in the network need to be the same.

■   The SSID (WLAN) needs to be the same.

Let's return to Layer 2 versus Layer 3 roaming. Here is the simple explanation. Layer 2
roaming happens when the user roams to a different AP and keeps his existing IP address.
Layer 3 roaming occurs when a client leaves an AP on one subnet and associates with another AP on a different subnet, but using the same SSID.

The following section takes a closer look at the Layer 2 roaming process.

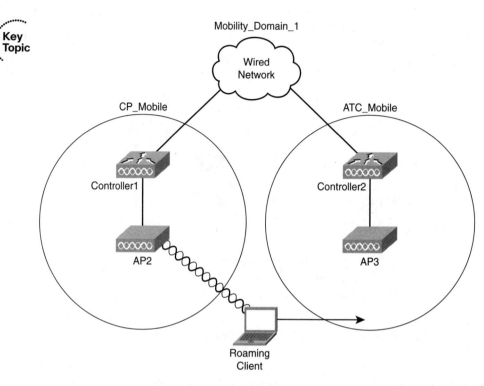

Figure 12-5 *Client Roaming in the Same Mobility Domain*

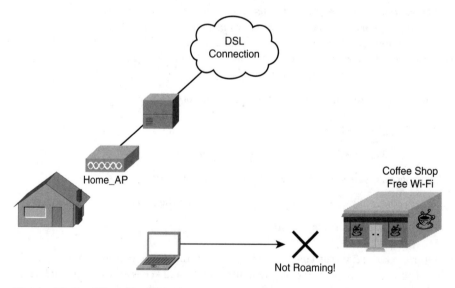

Figure 12-6 *Client Not Roaming*

The Layer 2 Roaming Process

As previously discussed, Layer 2 roaming happens when a user moves to another AP but stays on the same VLAN and the same IP subnet. As far as the user is concerned, nothing special has happened. The client isn't notified that he is roaming. He also keeps his IP address, and all active transmissions stay active. This process is handled within a single controller. This process is called *intracontroller roaming* and takes less than 10 ms. Behind the scenes, the client, when roaming to a new AP, sends a query to request authentication. The query is sent from the AP to the controller, where the controller realizes that the client is already authenticated, just via another AP. The client is then registered as roaming in the controller, although you do not see this in the controller or in the WCS, and life goes on. Figure 12-7 depicts this scenario.

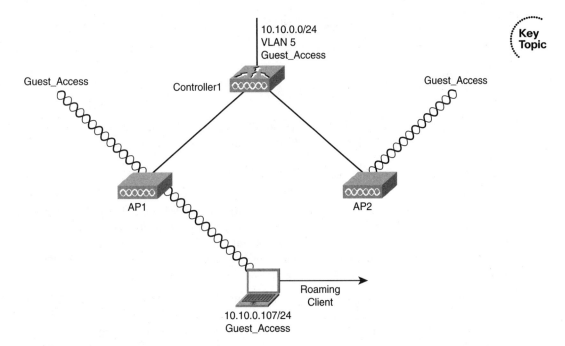

Figure 12-7 *Intracontroller Roaming*

Now take that same scenario and add another controller, as shown in Figure 12-8. Here, the client associated with Controller1 is on VLAN10. Upon roaming to AP3, which is managed by Controller2, the connection stays active. What happened? In this situation, *intercontroller roaming* happened. This occurs when a user roams from one controller to another but remains on the same VLAN and does not have to perform a DHCP process again, which would force the session to break. The two controllers are configured with the same mobility group. The two controllers then exchange mobility messages. Using mobility messages, the client database entry on Controller1 is moved to Controller2. This happens in less than 20 ms. Again, the process is transparent to the user. He roams, data keeps flowing, sessions stay active, and life is good.

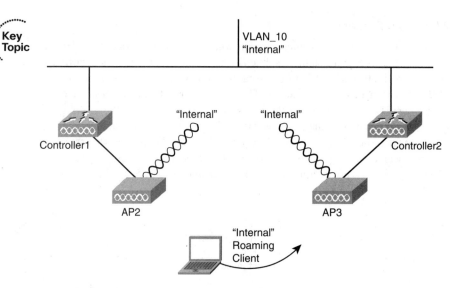

Figure 12-8 *Intercontroller Roaming*

Both intracontroller roaming and intercontroller roaming allow the user to roam and remain on the same IP subnet. This is Layer 2 roaming. Now let's explore Layer 3 roaming.

The Layer 3 Roaming Process

As with Layer 2 roaming, the goal of Layer 3 roaming is for a client to roam transparently. The difference is that you are working with multiple controllers on different subnets. The catch is that although the controllers are on different subnets, the user does not change IP addresses. Instead, the controllers tunnel the traffic back to the original controller. So it's a smoke-and-mirrors configuration. You are literally making the network believe that the user hasn't roamed. The two tunneling methods are as follows:

- **Asymmetric tunneling:** In asymmetric tunneling, traffic from the client is routed to the destination, regardless of its source address, and the return traffic is sent to its original controller, called an *anchor*, and is tunneled to the new controller.

- **Symmetric tunneling:** In symmetric tunneling, all traffic is tunneled from the client to the anchor controller, sent to the destination, returned to the anchor controller, and then tunneled back to the client via the foreign controller.

The following sections discuss these two types of tunneling in more detail.

Asymmetric Tunneling

When a client roams in an intercontroller roam, the database entry moves to the new controller. That's not the case with Layer 3 roaming. In the case of Layer 3 roaming, the client's entry in the original controller is marked as an anchor entry. Then the database entry is not moved; instead, it is copied to the foreign controller. On the foreign controller, the entry is marked "Foreign." The client is then reauthenticated, the entry is updated in the new AP, and the client is good to go. The client's IP address doesn't change. All this is transparent to the user. Figure 12-9 depicts this process.

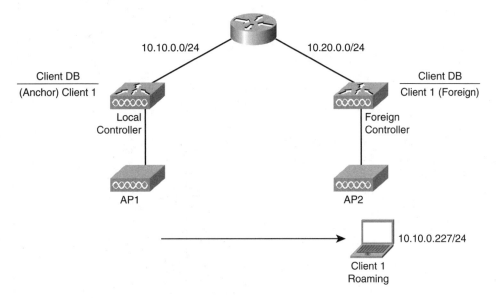

Figure 12-9 *Layer 3 Roaming*

Normally when a client sends traffic, it is sent to a default gateway, assuming that it is leaving the subnet, and then on to the destination. The traffic makes its way back to the client, taking the reverse path that it traveled to get there. This means that if Controller1 sends traffic to Router1 and then to Server1, Server1 returns the traffic via Router1 and then Controller1, as shown in Figure 12-10.

After the client roams to a new controller and a new AP, the return traffic is not delivered to the correct controller. So the anchor controller sees that the return traffic is for a client with an entry marked anchor and knows that it needs to tunnel it to the foreign controller. The foreign controller, upon receiving the packet, forwards it to the client, and all is well. This is how asymmetric tunneling works.

However, this configuration has some problems. Today's networks are taking more and more security precautions; one of these precautions is Reverse Path Filtering (RPF), a function used by routers. The router examines all packets received as input on that interface to make sure that the source address and source interface appear in the routing table and match the interface on which the packet was received. Also, following RFC 3837 and some other antispoofing ACL recommendations, the source address would not match what is expected to be seen, and it would be dropped. So what do you do when this happens? The answer is symmetric tunneling.

Symmetric Tunneling

In general, when a client sends a packet for Server1, much like what is shown in Figure 12-10, the following occurs:

The foreign controller tunnels the packet to the anchor controller rather than forwarding it. Then the anchor controller forwards the packet to Server1. Server1 replies, sending the traffic back to the anchor controller. The anchor controller tunnels it back to the foreign

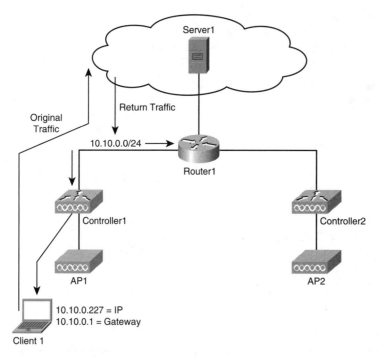

Figure 12-10   *Original Traffic Flow*

controller. The foreign controller delivers the packet back to the client. If the client roams to another foreign controller, the database is moved to the new foreign controller, but the anchor controller does not change.

Configuring Tunneling

To begin the tunneling configuration, first you must decide which type of tunneling you will do. The default mode is asymmetric, and the controllers must match in their configuration. Select **CONTROLLER > Mobility Management > Mobility Anchor Config**. Figure 12-11 shows the resulting configuration page.

This configuration page enables you to configure a Keep Alive Count and Keep Alive Interval. There also is a checkbox for symmetric mobility tunneling mode, which is not enabled by default. The Keep Alive Count is the number of times a ping request is sent to an anchor controller before the anchor is considered unreachable. The default value is 3. The Keep Alive Interval is the amount of time (in seconds—the default is 10) between each ping request sent to an anchor controller.

Mobility Anchors

With mobility anchors, also called guest tunneling or auto anchor mobility, all the client traffic that belongs to a WLAN (especially the Guest WLAN) is tunneled to a predefined WLC or set of controllers that are configured as an anchor for that specific WLAN. This feature helps restrict clients to a specific subnet and have more control over the user

Figure 12-11   *Mobility Anchor Configuration*

traffic. Normally what happens is that a client anchors to the first controller it associates through. But what if you want clients anchored to a controller on a DMZ interface of a firewall? Using a mobility anchor forces clients to be anchored to a controller other than the one they first associate with. This forces their traffic to be tunneled to the DMZ. Then it must pass through the firewall and its associated policies before getting anywhere. This is done on a per-WLAN basis.

Note: The protocol used for tunneling is known as EoIP. It's beyond the scope of the CCNA Wireless exam, but you can find more information in RFC 3439.

You should configure the same mobility anchors for a WLAN. If a client associates with a WLAN in which the local controller is the mobility anchor, the client is anchored locally.

The whole mobility anchor concept might seem strange at first, but think of it as roaming ahead of time. That's basically what it is. As soon as the client associates to a WLAN, it is known to be anchored somewhere else, and a tunnel is set up. This means that the foreign controller sets up the tunnel before the client has an IP address. So the foreign controller doesn't have any knowledge of the client's IP address. This tunnel is the same type of tunnel that is created when Layer 3 roaming occurs between controllers.

To configure a controller to act as mobility anchor, follow these steps:

Step 1.   Click **WLANs** to open the WLANs page.

Step 2.   Click the blue down arrow for the desired WLAN or wired guest LAN, and choose **Mobility Anchors,** as shown in Figure 12-12.

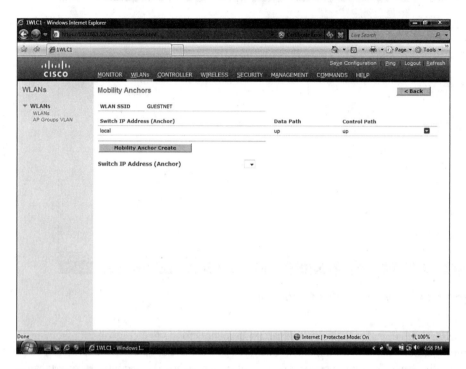

Figure 12-12   *Selecting a Mobility Anchor*

Note: On a WiSM running controller code 4.1.185.0, you do not click the blue down arrow; you just hover the mouse pointer over it.

Step 3.   Select the IP address of the controller to be designated a mobility anchor in the Switch IP Address (Anchor) drop-down box.

Step 4.   Click **Mobility Anchor Create.** The selected controller becomes an anchor for this WLAN or wired guest LAN.

Step 5.   Click **Save Configuration** to save your changes.

Step 6.   Repeat this process for any other mobility anchors you want to designate for this WLAN.

Step 7.   Repeat this process on *every* controller where this WLAN exists.

Exam Preparation Tasks

Review All the Key Topics

Review the most important topics from this chapter, denoted with the Key Topic icon. Table 12-2 lists these key topics and the page number where each one can be found.

Table 12-2 *Key Topics for Chapter 12*

Key Topic Item	Description	Page Number
Figure 12-1	A mobility group	211
Figure 12-2	A mobility domain	211
Figure 12-4	A client roaming in the same mobility group	213
Figure 12-5	A client roaming in the same mobility domain	214
List from the section "Types of Roaming"	Requirements for controllers to support roaming	213
Figure 12-7	Intracontroller roaming	215
Figure 12-8	Intercontroller roaming	216

Definition of Key Terms

Define the following key terms from this chapter, and check your answers in the glossary:

mobility group, mobility domain, roaming, intracontroller roaming, intercontroller roaming, asymmetric tunneling, symmetric tunneling, anchor, mobility anchor

This chapter covers the following subjects:

Controller Terminology: A discussion of the terminology used with Cisco controllers.

Connecting to the Controller: How to connect to a Cisco controller via the CLI and web interfaces.

Configuring the Controller Using the Web Interface: How to build a simple guest network, allow connections, and control where access is permitted.

Monitoring with the Controller: A look at the Monitor interface and how to perform various monitoring tasks.

CHAPTER 13

Simple Network Configuration and Monitoring with the Cisco Controller

One essential task of a CCNA Wireless certification candidate is being able to create a basic configuration. This involves tasks such as accessing the controller interface, creating a WLAN, and making sure that the WLAN is active on the access points (AP). The ultimate goal is to be able to send traffic from a client on that WLAN to some destination on the wired side of the network. To do this, you need to understand some terminology used with the controllers, how to connect to a controller, how to configure the WLAN from the GUI utility of the controller, and how to perform basic monitoring of the controller. These topics are discussed in this chapter.

You should do the "Do I Know This Already?" quiz first. If you score 80 percent or higher, you might want to skip to the section "Exam Preparation Tasks." If you score below 80 percent, you should spend the time reviewing the entire chapter. Refer to Appendix A, "Answers to the 'Do I Know This Already?' Quizzes," to confirm your answers.

"Do I Know This Already?" Quiz

The "Do I Know This Already?" quiz helps you determine your level of knowledge of this chapter's topics before you begin. Table 13-1 details the major topics discussed in this chapter and their corresponding quiz questions.

Table 13-1 *"Do I Know This Already?" Section-to-Question Mapping*

Foundation Topics Section	Questions
Controller Terminology	1–4
Connecting to the Controller	5–9
Configuring the Controller Using the Web Interface	10–13
Monitoring with the Controller	14–19

1. Which of the following describes a port as related to the controller terminology?

    a. It is a logical interface.

    b. It is a physical interface.

    c. It is not an interface; it is a slot.

    d. A port is a connection to an application; for example, port 23 would connect to Telnet.

2. What command configures a static route on the controller?

    a. route add

    b. ip route

    c. default route

    d. config route

3. Which port is active during the boot process?

    a. Service

    b. Management

    c. AP-Manager

    d. Virtual

4. Which of the following best defines a mobility group?

    a. A group of APs that allow roaming

    b. A group of controllers that communicate

    c. A group of traveling clients

    d. A group of mobile AP configurations

5. How was the following menu accessed?

    ```
    Please choose an option from below:
    1. Run primary image (version 4.1.192.17) (active)

    2. Run backup image (version 4.2.99.0)

    3. Manually update images

    4. Change active boot image

    5. Clear Configuration

    Please enter your choice:
    ```

    a. During bootup, this menu automatically shows.

    b. A break sequence was entered from the CLI.

    c. The Controllers menu command was used.

    d. The Esc key was pressed during bootup.

6. What is the default password for the Cisco controller CLI?

    a. Cisco

    b. cisco

    c. admin

    d. San-Fran

7. Which command is used to save the configuration from the Cisco controller CLI?

    a. wr em

    b. copy run start

    c. save config

    d. save

8. What is the default IP address of the Cisco controller?

    a. 10.1.1.1

    b. 10.1.209.1

    c. 172.16.1.1

    d. 192.168.1.1

9. Which is not a top-level menu of the Cisco controller?

    a. MONITOR

    b. COMMANDS

    c. SECURITY

    d. PING

10. Which is the correct path to create an interface?

    a. CONTROLLER > Interfaces > New

    b. CONTROLLER > Inventory > New Interface

    c. INTERFACES > New

    d. CONTROLLER > Ports > New

11. When creating the WLAN profile, what two pieces of information do you need? (Choose two.)

    a. Name

    b. SSID

    c. Port

    d. Interface

12. What does it mean if the Radio Policy is set to **All** in the Configuration tab of the WLAN?

   a. All WLANs are on.

   b. The WLAN supports all radio types.

   c. The WLAN has all radios in it.

   d. Users must have all radios.

13. You have selected **WIRELESS > Access Points > Radios > 802.11a/n**. From there, you select the **Configure** option for one of the listed APs. What does the WLAN Override drop-down control?

   a. The WLAN mode of the radio

   b. Whether the WLAN SSID is broadcast via the radio

   c. Whether a WLAN is accessible via the radio

   d. Whether you can change the settings on this radio

14. Which management area provides information about APs that are not authorized in your network?

   a. Access Point Summary

   b. Client Summary

   c. Top WLANs

   d. Rogue Summary

15. Which three pieces of information can you find on the controller Summary page? (Choose all that apply.)

   a. Software version

   b. Internal temperature

   c. Port speeds

   d. System name

16. A radio power level of 3 indicates what?

   a. Three times the power

   b. The third level of power

   c. 25% of the maximum power

   d. 1/3 power

17. What criteria defined a wireless client, thus adding it to the Clients list?

   a. A probe is seen.

   b. It is associated.

   c. It is authenticated.

   d. It is statically defined.

18. How many rogue APs can one AP contain?

    a. 1

    b. 2

    c. 3

    d. 4

19. What would cause a client to be excluded?

    a. The client has passed 802.11 authentication five times.

    b. The client has passed 802.11 association five times.

    c. The client has failed 802.11 authentication five times.

    d. The client has attempted 802.11 association five times.

Foundation Topics

Controller Terminology

Now that you have some understanding about the different types of controllers that are available, it is helpful to understand some of the terminology that goes along with them. The term *interface*, when related to a Cisco controller, is not the same as you would experience on a router. With Cisco routers, an interface can be a physical or logical (loopback) entity. With Cisco controllers, an interface is logical. It can include VLANs, which in turn have a port association. Some interfaces are static, because your controller must always have them.

Key Topic

The next term to understand is port. A *port* is a physical interface on your controller. It is something that you can touch.

The second term that you need to understand is interface. An *interface* can be logical and dynamic.

Another term to understand is WLAN. A *WLAN* consists of a service set identifier (SSID) and all the parameters that go along with it. A WLAN ties to a port.

A port ties together a VLAN and SSIDs. A 4404 has four ports, and a 4402 has two. The Cisco Wireless Service Manager (WiSM) has eight virtual ports. Some interfaces are static, and others are virtual. Some static interfaces cannot be removed because they serve a specific purpose. The static interfaces include these:

- Management interface

- AP-Manager

- Service port

- Virtual

The dynamic interfaces include a user-defined list. These interfaces are similar to subinterfaces and use 802.1 Q headers.

If you allow users to roam, you are going to have a mobility group. A *mobility group* is numerous APs configured with common interfaces. These interfaces must be defined on all the controllers within the mobility group. If one controller does not have an interface configured, a user cannot roam to that controller.

So far, you seen that both static and dynamic interfaces exist. Further discussion of these interfaces might help to clarify how to use them.

Dynamic Interfaces

Administrators define dynamic interfaces, and the system defines static interfaces. Static interfaces have specific system roles and are required.

Static Interfaces

The *management interface* is one that controls communications in your network for all the physical ports. It can be untagged, which means that the VLAN identifier is set to 0. By leaving the VLAN identifier set to 0, the controller does not include an 802.1Q tag with the frame; rather, the frame is sent untagged. This means that if the traffic for the management interface travels across a trunk port on the switch where the controller is connected, the traffic is on the native VLAN of that trunk. Your APs use the management interfaces to discover the controller. Mobility groups also exchange information using the management interface.

The AP manager interface is another static interface. The address that is assigned to this interface is used as the source for communications between the wireless controller and the Cisco access point. That means that this address has to be unique, but it can be in the same subnet as the management interfaces.

Another static interface is what is known as a *virtual interface*. The virtual interface controls the Layer 3 security and mobility manager communications for all of the physical ports of the controller. The virtual interface also has the DNS gateway hostname used by the Layer 3 security and mobility managers so they can verify the source of the certificates. When Layer 3 web authorization is enabled, the virtual interface will be used on the wireless side to force an authorization. For example, a user associates to an AP that is configured for web authorization. Next, the user opens a web browser, which attempts to access the default home page. With web authorization enabled, the web browser is redirected to the virtual interface IP address, which is commonly set to 1.1.1.1.

At this point, the user needs to enter credentials for the web authorization. After the user is authorized, he is redirected to his home page. Alternatively, he could be redirected to a Terms of Use page instead of his home page.

Another static interface is the service port. The service port of the 4400 series controller is a 10/100 copper Ethernet interface. This service port is designed for out-of-band management and can also be used for system recovery and maintenance purposes. This is the only port that will be active when the controller is in its boot mode. Note that the service port is not autosensing—you must use the right type of cable with it. Therefore, if you were going to plug in between a switch and a service port, you would have to use the right cable, because it does not autosense. Also, no VLAN tag is assigned to the port, so the port should not be a configured as a trunk port on the switch.

Another interesting feature of the service port is that you cannot configure a default gateway for the port via the web interface, but you can go into the CLI and define a static route. To define a static route, use the **config route** command.

This new terminology might seem a little overwhelming at first, but after you get into the controller interface and start to create wireless LANs, much of your understanding will fall into place.

Connecting to the Controller

To begin configuring the controller, you need a connection to it. You can access the controller in more than one way; however, this section focuses on creating a command-line interface (CLI) connection. After you have CLI access, you can observe the boot sequence and run though a basic configuration. Doing so provides an IP address that you can use later to browse to the HTML interface.

You will be connecting to the serial interface, so you will use a DB9 serial cable. You will also need a laptop with a serial connection. Many new laptops do not have serial connections, although you can purchase an adapter that connects to a USB port.

After you set up the connection from the laptop to the serial port, you need to use a terminal emulation application such as HyperTerminal, SecureCRT, or ZTerm (for Mac OSX). Using the terminal emulation application, you can boot the controller to view the boot process.

Controller Boot Sequence

As you boot the controller, you are given an option to press Esc for boot options, along with other information regarding the device, as seen in Example 13-1.

Example 13-1 *Controller Bootup Sequence as Seen from the CLI*

```
Bootloader 4.1.171.0 (Apr 27 2007 - 05:19:36)
Motorola PowerPC ProcessorID=00000000 Rev. PVR=80200020
CPU: 833 MHz
CCB: 333 MHz
DDR: 166 MHz
LBC: 41 MHz
L1 D-cache 32KB, L1 I-cache 32KB enabled.
I2C: ready
DTT: 1 is 20 C
DRAM: DDR module detected, total size:512MB.
512 MB
8540 in PCI Host Mode.
8540 is the PCI Arbiter.
Memory Test PASS
FLASH:
Flash Bank 0: portsize = 2, size = 8 MB in 142 Sectors
8 MB
L2 cache enabled: 256KB
Card Id: 1540
Card Revision Id: 1
Card CPU Id: 1287
Number of MAC Addresses: 32
Number of Slots Supported: 4
Serial Number: FOC1206F03A
Unknown command Id: 0xa5
```

```
Unknown command Id: 0xa4
Unknown command Id: 0xa3
Manufacturers ID: 30464
Board Maintenance Level: 00
Number of supported APs: 12
In: serial
Out: serial
Err: serial


.o88b. d888888b .d8888. .o88b. .d88b.
d8P Y8 `88' 88' YP d8P Y8 .8P Y8.
8P 88 `8bo. 8P 88 88
8b 88 `Y8b. 8b 88 88
Y8b d8 .88. db 8D Y8b d8 `8b d8'
`Y88P' Y888888P `8888Y' `Y88P' `Y88P'
Model AIR-WLC4402-12-K9 S/N: FOC1206F03A
Net:
PHY DEVICE : Found Intel LXT971A PHY at 0x01
FEC ETHERNET
IDE: Bus 0: OK
Device 0: Model: STI Flash 8.0.0 Firm: 01/17/07 Ser#: STI1M75607342054704
Type: Removable Hard Disk
Capacity: 245.0 MB = 0.2 GB (501760 x 512)
Device 1: not available
Booting Primary Image...
Press <ESC> now for additional boot options...
***** External Console Active *****
Boot Options
Please choose an option from below:
1. Run primary image (version 4.1.192.17) (active)
2. Run backup image (version 4.2.99.0)
3. Manually update images
4. Change active boot image
5. Clear Configuration
Please enter your choice:
```

The Esc key was issued in Example 13-1. From the highlighted output, you can do the following:

Step 1.   Run the primary image.

Step 2.   Run the backup image.

Step 3.   Manually update images.

Step 4.   Change the active boot image.

Step 5.   Clear the configuration.

The correct choice at this point is to run the primary image. When the HTML interface is accessible, you can upgrade the code on the controller. Because this is covered in Chapter 19, "Maintaining Wireless Networks," it will not be covered now. Of course, you can also manually update the image, as seen in Step 3. Alternatively, you can change the active boot image or clear the configuration file.

Performing Initial CLI Configurations

Initially, the controller looks for a configuration file. If the controller finds such a file, it loads it and then prompts you for a username and password. If no configuration exists, you see a prompt to run through a dialog and a message stating that the certificate was not found, as in Example 13-2.

Example 13-2   *Certificate Not Found Message*

```
Starting LOCP: ok
Starting CIDS Services: ok
Starting Ethernet-over-IP: ok
Starting Management Services:
Web Server: ok
CLI: ok


Secure Web: Web Authentication Certificate not found (error).
(Cisco Controller)



Welcome to the Cisco Wizard Configuration Tool
Use the '-' character to backup
System Name [Cisco_32:af:43]:
```

For the CCNA Wireless exam, you should be familiar with the CLI Wizard Configuration tool. This tool is designed for quick setup of the controller. Example 13-3 shows a CLI Wizard configuration.

> **Note**   During the startup script, any time that you make a mistake after pressing the **Enter** key, you can move back a step to fix the error by pressing the (-) key.

Key Topic

Example 13-3   *CLI Wizard Configuration*

```
Welcome to the Cisco Wizard Configuration Tool
Use the '-' character to backup
System Name [Cisco_32:af:43]: WLC_1
Enter Administrative User Name (24 characters max): admin
```

```
Enter Administrative Password (24 characters max): *****
Re-enter Administrative Password : *****
Service Interface IP Address Configuration [none][DHCP]: 10.1.1.1
Invalid response

Service Interface IP Address Configuration [none][DHCP]: none
Service Interface IP Address: 10.1.1.1
Service Interface Netmask: 255.255.255.0
Enable Link Aggregation (LAG) [yes][NO]:
Management Interface IP Address: 192.168.1.75
Management Interface Netmask: 255.255.255.0
Management Interface Default Router: 192.168.1.1
Management Interface VLAN Identifier (0 = untagged):
Management Interface Port Num [1 to 2]: 1
Management Interface DHCP Server IP Address: 192.168.1.1
AP Transport Mode [layer2][LAYER3]:
AP Manager Interface IP Address: 192.168.1.80
AP-Manager is on Management subnet, using same values
AP Manager Interface DHCP Server (192.168.1.1):
Virtual Gateway IP Address: 1.1.1.1
Mobility/RF Group Name: CP_Mobile1
Enable Symmetric Mobility Tunneling [yes][NO]: no
Network Name (SSID): OpenAccess
Allow Static IP Addresses [YES][no]:
Configure a RADIUS Server now? [YES][no]:
Enter the RADIUS Server's Address: -
Configure a RADIUS Server now? [YES][no]: no
Warning! The default WLAN security policy requires a RADIUS server.
Please see documentation for more details.
Enter Country Code list (enter 'help' for a list of countries) [US]:
Enable 802.11b Network [YES][no]:
Enable 802.11a Network [YES][no]:
Enable 802.11g Network [YES][no]:
Enable Auto-RF [YES][no]:
Configuration saved!
Resetting system with new configuration...

Configuration saved!
Resetting system with new configuration...
Bootloader 4.1.171.0 (Apr 27 2007 - 05:19:36)
Motorola PowerPC ProcessorID=00000000 Rev. PVR=80200020
CPU: 833 MHz
CCB: 333 MHz
DDR: 166 MHz
LBC: 41 MHz
```

continues

```
L1 D-cache 32KB, L1 I-cache 32KB enabled.
I2C: ready`
DTT: 1 is 31 C
DRAM: DDR module detected, total size:512MB.
512 MB
8540 in PCI Host Mode.
8540 is the PCI Arbiter.
Memory Test PASS
```

After the controller reboots, you are prompted for a username. This, of course, is the username that you created in the CLI Wizard:

```
Enter User Name (or 'Recover-Config' this one-time only to reset configura-
tion to factory defaults)

User: admin

Password:*****

(Cisco Controller) >
```

After you are authenticated, you can become familiar with some of the commands available to you in the CLI. Press the question mark key (**?**) to get a list of commands. Similar to the Cisco routers and security appliances, the **?** can follow a letter to give you a list of commands that begin with that letter. For example, issuing the **p?** command shows that **ping** is available. Use the space key to complete the command if it is unique. Ping is a common utility that helps to verify connectivity. Another common command is the command to save your work. Unlike Cisco routers, **copy run start** does not work here. Instead, you use the **save config** command. In Example 13-4, you can see the process of saving the configuration. After you issue the command, you are asked to verify. You need not press **Enter** after making your selection. Simply press the letter **y** for yes and press **n** for no.

Example 13-4 *Saving Your Configuration from the CLI*

```
(Cisco Controller) >save config
Are you sure you want to save? (y/n) y

Configuration Saved!
(Cisco Controller) >
```

Just as routers have a global configuration mode, so does the controller. Accessing the configuration mode of the controller is a little different from what you might expect. You use the **config** command followed by what it is you want to configure. For example, if you want to configure 802.11a parameters, you type **config 802.11a ?**. You need to type the **?** because you have to enter the complete string, and the question mark helps you find the syntax, as demonstrated in Example 13-5.

Example 13-5   *Using the ? Help Facility*

```
(Cisco Controller) >config 802.11a ?
11nSupport Configure 802.11n-5Ghz parameters.
antenna Configures the 802.11a antenna
beaconperiod Configures the 802.11a beacon interval (20..1000)
cac Configure Call Admission Control parameters for 802.11a radios.
channel Configures the 802.11a channel
chan_width Configure 802.11a channel width
disable Disables 802.11a.
dtim Configures the 802.11a DTIM Period
enable Enables 802.11a.
fragmentation Configures the 802.11a Fragmentation Threshold
l2roam Configures 802.11a l2roam information.
pico-cell Configures the 802.11a pico-cell mode
picocell-V2 Configures the 802.11a picocell-V2 mode
rate Configures 802.11a operational rates.
txPower Configures the 802.11a Tx Power Level
dtpc Configures the 802.11a DTPC Setting
tsm Configures the 802.11a Traffic stream Metrics option
exp-bwreq Configures the 802.11a Expedited BW Request option
(Cisco Controller) >config 802.11a
```

You can also perform **debug** commands from the CLI interface. This is important because these commands are not available from the web interface.

Note: **debug** commands, although useful, can be dangerous. They take up a lot of resources, so use them sparingly. Also, they turn off when your session times out.

Performing Initial Web Configurations

You can connect to the web interface without ever running though the CLI by browsing to the default IP address on the controller, which is 192.168.1.1. Assume, for the purposes of demonstration, that the controller IP address is 192.168.1.50. This is the IP address that has been assigned to the management interface. When you browse to the controller after using the Setup dialog, you use HTTPS, as seen in Figure 13-1.

After you have accessed the Controller Login page, click the **Login** button. You then see the controller Summary page, shown in Figure 13-2.

Navigating the Web Interface of the Controller

It is beneficial to take time to understand the controller interface. The main menus along the top of the interface are as follows:

- MONITOR
- WLANs

Figure 13-1   *Browsing to the Controller*

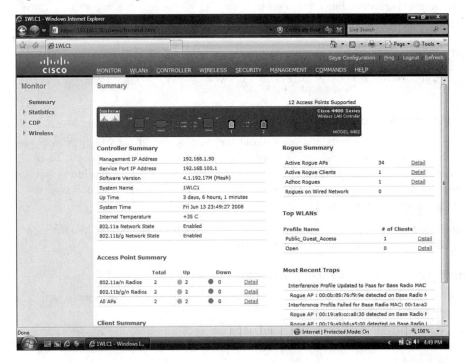

Figure 13-2   *Controller Summary*

- CONTROLLER

- WIRELESS

- SECURITY

- MANAGEMENT

- COMMANDS

- HELP

Also, along the top right you have access to links that save your configuration, access a ping utility, log out, and refresh the page.

When you select one of the top-level configuration tabs, the menu in the left margin of the screen changes. The change enables configuration and monitoring options that pertain to the main level with which you are working. For example, if you are working in the WIRELESS tab, the left menus include the following configuration areas, as seen in Figure 13-3:

- Access Points

- Mesh

- HREAP Groups

- 802.11a/n

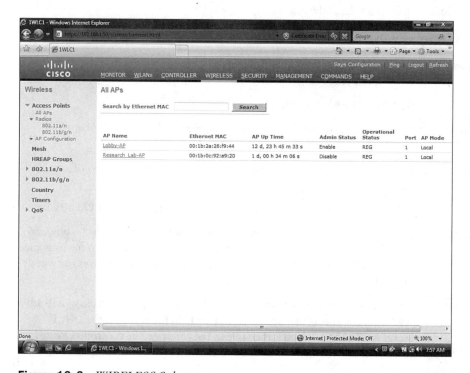

Figure 13-3   *WIRELESS Submenus*

- 802.11b/g/n

- QoS

Each top-level heading you change results in a new side menu.

Configuring the Controller Using the Web Interface

For this example, you build basic wireless connectivity. The process is as follows:

- Build the controller interface.

- Create the WLAN and tie it to the interface.

- Modify security settings.

Building the controller interface is required because, as you might recall from the beginning of this chapter, the interface is a logical entity. It is not a physical port that you can touch, although the interface you create will end up having access to the network via one of the physical ports. After you have created the interface, you need to create the WLAN. The WLAN defines the wireless side, whereas the interface creates the wired side of the configuration. You then need to bind these two to each other so that users on the wireless side can access the wired side of the network.

The default settings for a WLAN apply certain security settings that prohibit a user from connecting without additional configuration. The last step in creating a functional WLAN allowing anyone access with no security is to modify the security settings of the WLAN. The following sections detail the process.

Building the Controller Interface

Step 1.   Create an interface in the controller that ties to the VLAN that you want the GUESTNET users on.

CONTROLLER > Interfaces > New

Step 2.   Populate the fields with the appropriate values for the Interface Name and VLAN Id fields, as shown in Figure 13-4. Click **Apply**.

Step 3.   Define the IP address for this interface. This should be an address that resides on the same subnet as the GUEST_LAN network.

In Figure 13-5, the IP address is 172.30.1.50, and the gateway is 172.30.1.1.

Step 4.   Next, on the same configuration page shown in Figure 13-5, select a physical port for this GUEST_LAN to use to access the wired network. In the example, port 1 is used because it is a trunk back to the switch that accesses the wired network.

Step 5.   The next step involves defining the DHCP servers. These servers assign IP addresses to the clients that access the network. In the example, the DHCP server is 172.30.1.1, which is the same as the gateway. The controller queries this DHCP server when clients need IP addresses.

Step 6.   Click **Apply**.

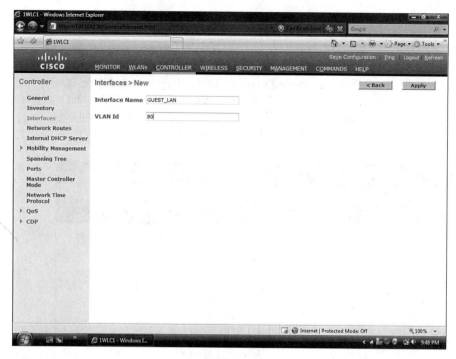

Figure 13-4 *Creating the GUEST_LAN Interface*

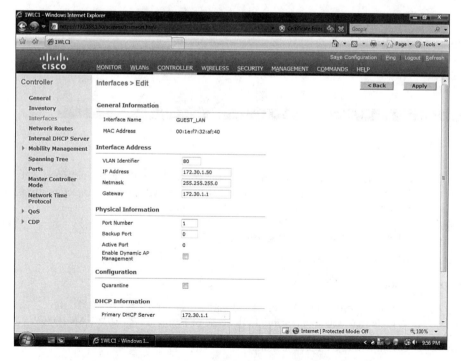

Figure 13-5 *Adding an IP Address to the GUEST_LAN Interface*

Note   You will receive a message indicating that WLANS are disabled temporarily when you click Apply. This is normal.

After you click Apply, you are returned to the list of interfaces seen in Figure 13-6. Notice that physical interfaces are listed here, such as the service-port, ap-manager, and management. These interfaces are tied to VLANs that you can access via the physical connection—port 1. Port 1 is connected to a switch and is operating as an 802.1Q trunk.

Figure 13-6   *Interface Listing*

The GUEST_LAN interface that you created ties the controller to the wired network over port 1 on VLAN 80. No WLAN is associated with it, and no AP is sending beacons advertising GUEST_LAN access. That part has yet to be configured.

Creating the WLAN and Tying It to the Interface

The next piece of the configuration is creating the wireless side.

Step 1.   Choose **WLANs > New.**

You see a configuration page that assigns an arbitrary WLAN ID to the WLAN that you are creating. In the case of Figure 13-7, the WLAN ID is 2.

Step 2.   Give the WLAN a profile name.

Step 3.   Give the WLAN an SSID. In this case, the SSID chosen is GUESTNET.

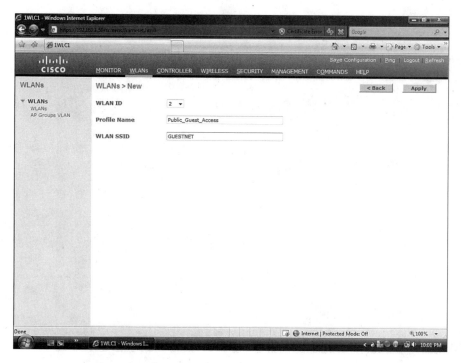

Figure 13-7   *Creating the WLAN Profile Name*

Step 4.   Click **Apply.**

The next page that you arrive at has four tabs, seen in Figure 13-8. These tabs allow you to configure the General, Security, QoS, and Advanced settings for the WLAN.

Step 5.   On the General tab, make sure of the following:

- The WLAN Status is **Enabled.** If it is not, the WLAN settings are not sent to all APs.

Note: Skip the Security Policies field. You will change this in the Security tab.

- For the Radio Policy, if **All** is left selected, all radios are available for the GUESTNET network. It is common to allow 802.11b/g for guests and then use 802.11a for private WLANs, because 802.11b/g usually experience more interference than 802.11a. For guests, quality of service is probably not the highest concern; however, it is for internal users. For now, just leave Radio Policy at the default value of **All.**

Step 6.   Next is the important step of choosing the interface in the Interface dropdown that ties this GUESTNET WLAN to the **guest_lan** physical interface on VLAN 80. If you choose the wrong interface here, people can end up on the wrong network.

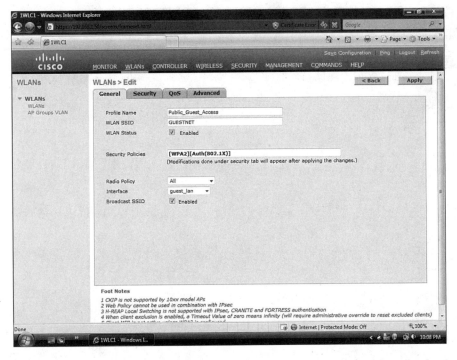

Figure 13-8   *WLAN Configuration Tabs*

Step 7.   Choose not to broadcast the SSID by deselecting the Broadcast SSID check box. This adds a little security, but, as you will learn in Chapter 17, "Securing the Wireless Network," it is not a high degree of security. The default value is to broadcast the SSID.

Step 8.   Do not click **Apply** yet.

Modifying the Security Settings

Before you apply the configuration, you need to modify the security settings. Follow these steps:

Step 1.   Click the Security tab within the WLAN configuration window.

You are presented with three additional tabs:

- Layer 2

- Layer 3

- AAA Servers

For now, you should only be concerned with the Layer 2 policy, because the Layer 3 policy defaults to None.

Step 2.   Choose **None** as the Layer 2 security method.

Step 3.   Click **Apply**.

Success! You now have a functional WLAN, as Figure 13-9 illustrates. That is, it is functional as long as the wired network behind it is good to go.

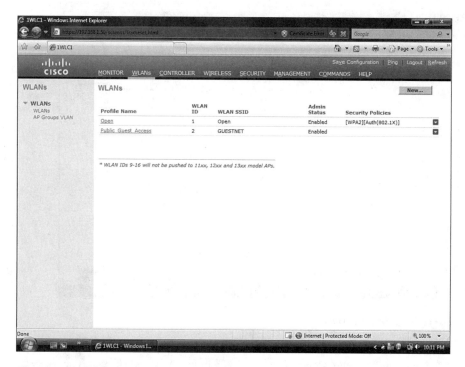

Figure 13-9 *Listing WLAN Profiles*

Naming Access Points

Still, you might want to do some tweaks to the network. For example, suppose that you have two APs. One AP is in the lobby, and the other is in the research lab. You do not want anyone to access the AP in the research lab using the GUESTNET. What do you do? You just control the APs that allow GUESTNET access. To begin, though, you should identify which AP is in the lobby and which is in the research lab. Figure 13-10 shows that the two APs are identified by a MAC address as the AP name.

This can be confusing. I recommend changing the name of the AP to something that makes sense. Here is how to do it:

Step 1.   Find the MAC address of the AP in the lobby. It is printed on the bottom of the AP.

Step 2.   After you have the MAC of the lobby AP, go to the WLC interface and browse to **WIRELESS > Access Points > All APs.**

Step 3.   Select the AP that matches the MAC address. The AP name begins with "AP" followed by the MAC address.

Step 4.   Change the Name in the General tab to **Lobby-AP.**

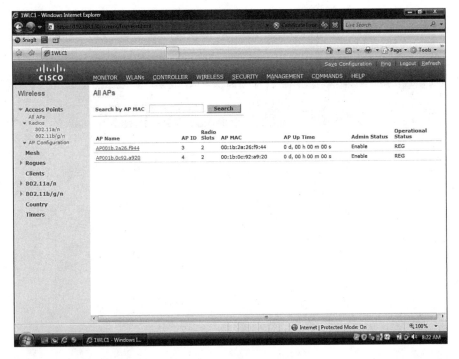

Figure 13-10 *Listing All APs*

Note: This name follows the AP when you move it within your network, so it is important to update the name on the controller if you ever move the AP or swap it out. Also, it is good practice to label the Cisco PoE switch port with the same name. This helps when you are troubleshooting any issues and might need to remotely power cycle the AP by shutting its switch port.

Step 5.   Optionally add a location. These steps are seen in Figure 13-11.

Step 6.   Click **Apply**.

Step 7.   Next, select the other AP.

Note: You might have more than two APs in your own deployment. The term *other AP* in this case simply refers to the only other AP used in the example.

Step 8.   Repeat Steps 5 through 7 to assign a different name and location for the Research_Lab AP.

When completed, you should see two APs that are easy to identify based on their name.

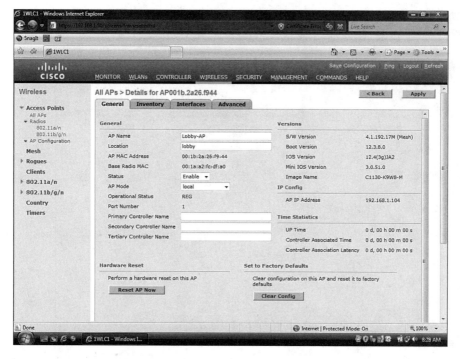

Figure 13-11   *Naming the AP*

Restricting Access to Access Points

Now is where the control part comes in. Remember that you do not want the GUESTNET access going through the Research_Lab-AP. Following is how to prevent it:

Step 1.   Start by selecting **WIRELESS > Access Points > Radios > 802.11a/n.**

Step 2.   Find the Research_Lab-AP seen in Figure 13-12.

Step 3.   To the right of the entry, hover your mouse over the arrow seen in Figure 13-13, and select **Configure.**

Step 4.   Select the WLAN Override by selecting **enable**, as seen in Figure 13-14. A new list of WLANS appears.

Step 5.   Select the WLAN that you want this AP to support.

In this case, leaving the GUESTNET WLAN unchecked removes that access through this AP.

Step 6.   Click **Apply.**

Step 7.   Repeat these steps for the 802.11b/g/n radio.

After you have done this for the Research_Lab-AP, you probably want to do the same for the Lobby_AP, but only allow GUESTNET access though it, removing any other networks.

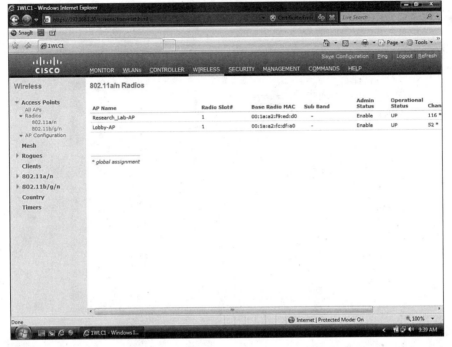

Figure 13-12 *802.11a/n Radios*

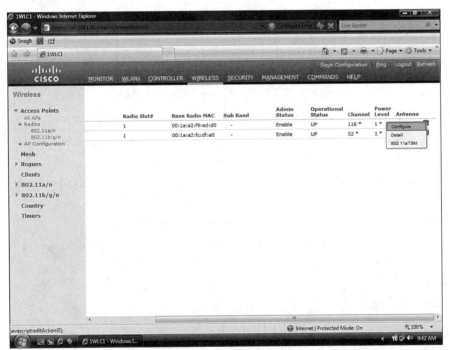

Figure 13-13 *802.11a/n Radio Options Menu*

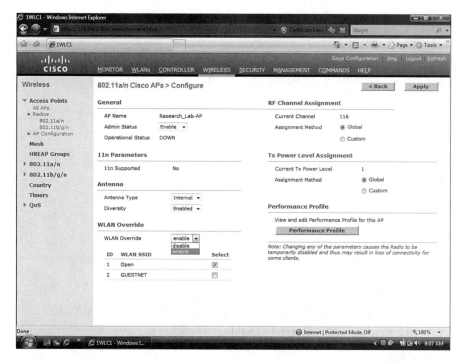

Figure 13-14   *Enabling WLAN Override*

Summary of Controller Configuration Using the Web Interface

At this point you have accomplished much by way of your controller. Through one interface, you can see how much power in configuration you have. What did you do? Here is the list:

- You set up multiple APs at the same time.

- You easily configured a WLAN connection to provide GUESTNET access.

- You controlled which APs allows GUESTNET access.

Of course, more options are available that you might want to understand, and many relate to security. First, however, it is beneficial to understand how to monitor the network from the interface of the controller, view your APs, and simply get a better picture of what is going on in the network. The following sections discuss these aspects.

Monitoring with the Controller

As far as the management and monitoring of the network go, you have much power by way of the controller. The controller is a central point of intelligence that can give you valuable information regarding the network overall as well as specifics related to APs, clients, rogues, and more. The main login page of the controller provides an excellent starting point.

General Monitoring

The Controller Summary page is the first thing you see when you log in. At first glance, it might seem like a simple overview, but it has much more than that. Examine Figure 13-15, where you will notice the following functional areas of the Summary page:

■ Controller Summary

■ Access Point Summary

■ Client Summary

■ Rogue Summary

■ Top WLANs

■ Most Recent Traps

Each area provides a wealth of information, as described in the sections that follow.

Controller Summary

Controller Summary provides the management IP address and the service port address. You can also see the software version. In Figure 13-15, you can see that the version is 4.1.192.17M (Mesh). Eventually you will learn to upgrade it to version 5.x. For now, this version is acceptable.

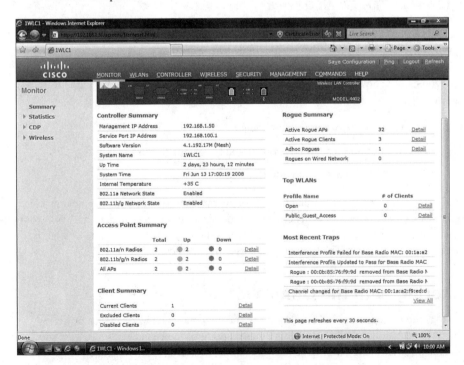

Figure 13-15 *Monitor Summary*

You can also gather the name of the controller and its uptime. Next, you can see the up time and system time on the controller, as well as the internal temperature. In addition, you can see that the 802.11a and 802.11b/g networks are enabled.

Access Point Summary

The next functional area is Access Point Summary, which shows the total number of 802.11a.n and 802.11b/g/n radios that are present, how many are up, and how many are down. You can click **Detail** for more information. 802.11b/g/n Radios details have been selected, and you are presented with a list of APs, as seen in Figure 13-16.

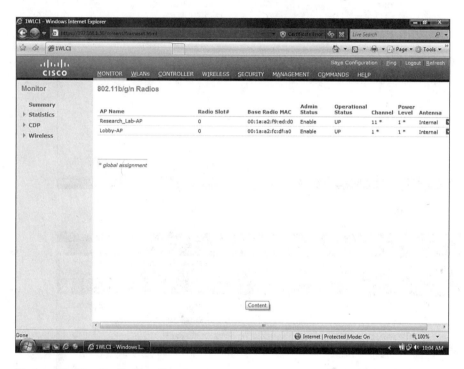

Figure 13-16   *Radio Details*

This list provides valuable information regarding the administrative status of the APs as well as the channel they are operating on and their power level. A power level of 1 indicates the highest level of power legal in the country you are in. You can change these levels by hovering your mouse over the blue arrow on the right and selecting the **Configure** link, as seen in Figure 13-17.

After you select **Configure**, you are taken to the page shown in Figure 13-18 that allows you to set General parameters, including enabling and disabling the radios, 11n parameters if available, and antenna type and diversity.

You can also gather information about management frame protection and perform a WLAN override. A WLAN override lets you control which SSIDs are made available by this AP. You saw this in the section "Configuring the Controller Using the Web Interface."

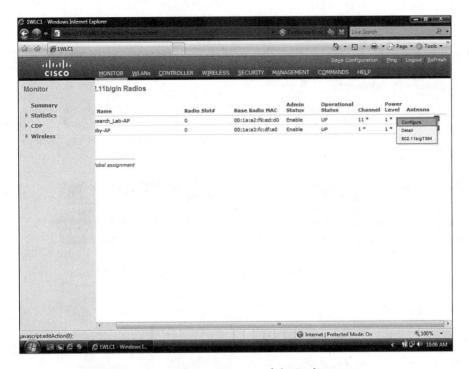

Figure 13-17   *Access the Configure Options of the Radios*

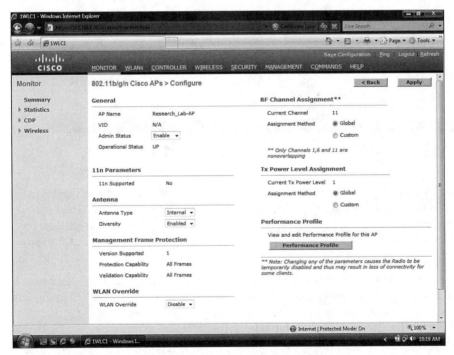

Figure 13-18   *802.11b/g/n Cisco APs > Configure Screen*

On the right side of the page, you can change the RF channel assignment and the TX (transmit) power level assignment. The higher the number of the power setting, the lower the power level is. For example, changing the level from 1 to 2 decreases the power by 50 percent. Changing it to 3 decreases it by 25 percent, and 4 decreases it by 12.5 percent. Each level halves the one before it.

You can also change and edit a performance profile. The Performance Profile link takes you to a page that lets you define RF values and thresholds. Additionally, from the Monitor page, you can select the Wireless link on the left side of the page, as shown in Figure 13-19.

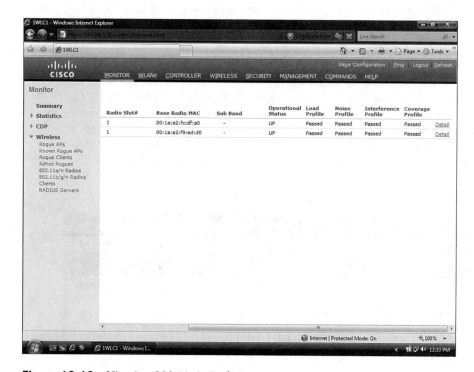

Key Topic

Figure 13-19   *Viewing 802.11a/n Radios*

In the figure, you can see a list containing the following links:

- **Rogue APs:** Selecting **Rogue APs** takes you to a page that lists the rogue APs.

- **Known Rogue APs:** Selecting **Known Rogue APs** takes you to a page of known rogue APs.

- **Rogue Clients:** The **Rogue Clients** link takes you to a list of rogue clients.

- **Adhoc Rogues:** **Adhoc Rogues** takes you to a list of clients that are creating ad-hoc networks. This can pose a serious security risk, because it can enable access to the wired infrastructure.

- **802.11a/n Radios / 802.11b/g/n Radios:** The 802 Radios links provide a list of APs with that specific type of radio.

- **Clients:** This link ties you to a page that provides a list of clients and lets you search by MAC address for clients.

- **RADIUS Servers:** This link provides a list of RADUIS Authentication and Accounting servers.

Looking further into the 802.11a/n Radios and 802.11b/g/n Radios options, you can gain even more information by selecting the **Details** link for a radio from the Monitor Summary page. Here is what you get. You see the slot that the radio is in and the base radio MAC address. Looking more closely at Figure 13-19, you can see that Operational Status is UP. You can gain information regarding a load profile, noise profile, interference profile, and coverage profile.

Load Profile is set to 80% by default. If the load of this particular AP goes over that threshold, Load Profile shows a warning rather than the status Passed. Likewise, if the SNR is too low, Load Profile indicates a warning. Should too much interference be on the same channel that this AP is operating on, the Interference Profile shows a warning. If clients roam away and are not able to relay off another AP, the Coverage Profile shows a warning. To see the details of these profiles, from the screen in Figure 13-18, select the **Details** link at the right side of the page. This causes a page similar to Figure 13-20 to be displayed.

Figure 13-20 *Radio Statistics*

The resulting page is Radio Statistics. Numerous items are of interest here that are not seen in the figure:

Note: To see the content discussed in the previous bulleted list, you need to scroll down in the web interface of the controller, because the page is long for this output and is not shown completely in Figure 13-20.

- The Noise vs. Channel chart shows each channel of the AP and the level of non-802.11 noise interference on that particular channel.

- The Interference by Channel shows statistics for other 802.11 interference.

- The Load Statistics section provides information about transmit and receive utilization, channel utilization, and attached clients.

- Two charts exist: % Client Count vs. RSSI and % Client Count vs. SNR.

- The next section covers the Rx Neighbors Information. This section displays neighboring APs along with their IP address and Received Signal Strength Indicator (RSSI). The controller uses this to allocate channels and ensure adequate coverage by shaping the coverage area.

As far as the CCNA Wireless exam is concerned, you should be familiar with the overall concept, but you do not need to understand each area in great detail. Still, with all this information for monitoring the APs that this controller manages and their radios, you must contend with those rogue devices. Rogue devices include *any* wireless device that can interfere with the managed APs. The following section discusses how to manage them.

Managing Rogue APs

You can manage rogue APs from the controller interface. Recall that on the Monitor page, the second column has information on rogue devices. This is a good place to start. Reviewing the Monitor page, seen in Figure 13-21, notice that the first line below Rogue Summary is Active Rogue APs.

A rogue AP is an AP that is unknown to the controller. You want to avoid jumping to conclusions here. It might simply be an AP in a neighboring business. It does not necessarily represent the bad guys. This takes a little work to figure out, however.

The next line is Active Rogue Clients. This is a wireless device that sends an unexpected frame. This is usually from a default configuration on client devices.

Next is Adhoc Rogues, which is, as previously mentioned, any device setting up an Adhoc network.

Finally, you have the Rogues on a Wired Network field. This is a count of rogues that a Rogue Detector AP has discovered. It works by the AP detecting ARP requests on the wired network for APs marked as rogue.

You can gather more information by selecting the **Detail** link on the right. Selecting this for the Active Rogue APs presents a list of the designated rogue APs. The key on this page is the number of detecting radios. Examine Figure 13-22. Notice that 20 of 32 rogues are

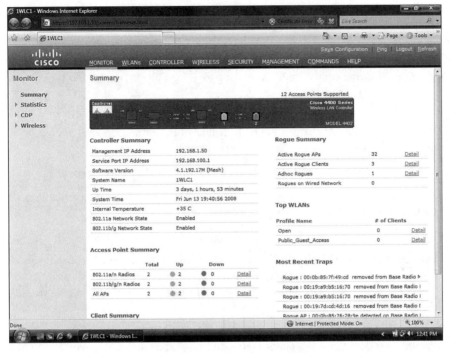

Figure 13-21 *Review Rogues from the Monitor Page*

listed. Also key in on the number of detecting radios. The fewer radios, the better. That is because if only one or two detect the rogue, the rogue is probably on the edge of the network, most likely coming from a neighboring business, as is the case with this figure.

If the number of detecting radios is high, the rogue is being seen by a number of APs and most likely is within your network, probably sitting under a desk exactly where it should not be.

You can click on the rogue that you are concerned with and select **Contain Rogue**, as seen in Figure 13-23.

When you contain the rogue, your AP spoofs its MAC address and sends deauthentication frames that appear to come from the contained AP. When clients see this, they are unable to stay associated with the contained AP. This should stress the importance of ensuring that it is not the AP of your neighbor.

Another note related to containment relates to the number of devices you can contain. You cannot contain more than three rogues per AP because the AP that is performing containment takes a CPU hit of up to 10 percent per contained AP. The system cap is 30 percent. This means that if an AP contains two rogues, it takes a 20 percent CPU hit. With the system cap of 30 percent, it can contain only one more rogue.

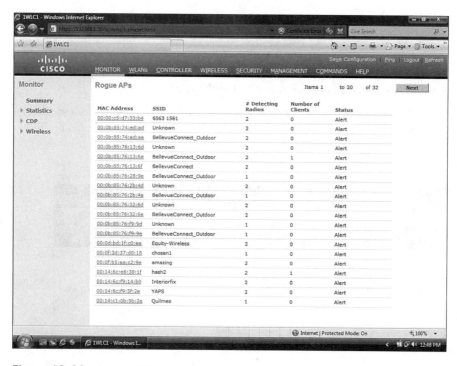

Figure 13-22   *Rogue APs*

Key Topic

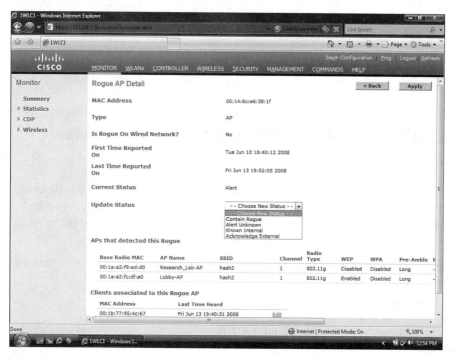

Figure 13-23   *Contain the Rogue AP*

Managing Clients

Managing clients is another important aspect to master. From the Monitor page, you can see the client summary. This gives a total of current clients, excluded clients, and disabled clients. Any device that sends a probe is considered a current client, so this number might be inflated even if the client does not associate with the AP.

Clicking on **details** provides a list of clients, as shown in Figure 13-24. You can see the MAC address of the clients, the AP with which they are associated, the WLAN profile they are using, and the protocol they are using.

Figure 13-24   *Clients*

In the case of Figure 13-24, the client with MAC address 00:1e:c2:ab:14:26 is associated with the Public_Guest_Access profile. Next you have the status, in this case Associated. Also, the client is authenticated, and port 1 on the controller is the means to the wired network. This client is not a workgroup bridge.

As seen in other examples, you can hover your mouse over the blue arrow to the right for a list of options, including these:

- LinkTest
- Disable
- Remove

- 802.11aTSM

- 802.11b/gTSM

The LinkTest provides a way to test the link of the client by reporting the number of sent and received packets, the signal strength, and the signal-to-noise ratio (SNR).

Disabling the client puts it into a Disabled Client list and bans it until it is manually removed. To view this list, select **Security > Disabled Clients**. To manually add clients, click **New**.

The **Remove** link disassociates the client. However, this does not prevent it from attempting association again, like disabling would.

For more details, click the client MAC address. This presents the Detail page, as seen in Figure 13-25. The five sections are as follows:

- Client Properties

- Security Information

- Quality of Service Properties

- Client Statistics

- AP Properties

Finally, there are excluded clients. Clients can be excluded for the following reasons:

- The client has failed 802.11 authentication five times.

- The client has failed 802.11 association five times.

- The client has failed 802.1x authentication three times.

- The client has failed the policy on an external server.

- The client has an IP that is already in use.

- The client has failed three web authentication attempts.

By default, these clients are excluded for 60 seconds. Think of it as a waiting period. If a client retries after that 60 seconds and does not fail any of the criteria in the preceding list, the client is no longer excluded.

Using Internal DHCP

One reason for exclusion is that the client might be trying to use an IP that is in use already. You can solve this issue using DHCP. If your network does not have a DHCP server, the controller can act as one for you. To configure the controller as a DHCP server, go to **CONTROLLER > Internal DHCP Server > New**. The rest of the DHCP server configuration is pretty self-explanatory.

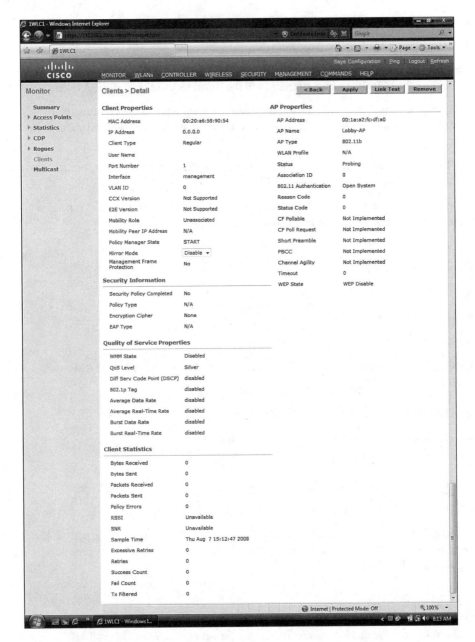

Figure 13-25   *Clients > Detail*

Exam Preparation Tasks

Review All the Key Concepts

Review the most important topics from this chapter, noted with the Key Topics icon in the outer margin of the page. Table 13-2 lists a reference of these key topics and the page number where you can find each one.

Table 13-2   *Key Topics for Chapter 13*

Key Topic Item	Description	Page Number
Controller Terminology	Section defining controller terms	228
Example 13-3	Setup Wizard	232
Configuring the Controller Using the Web Interface	Creating an interface and creating a WLAN	238
Figure 13-12	802.11a/n radios	246
Figure 13-13	802.11a/n Radio Options menu	246
Figure 13-19	Viewing 802.11a/n radios	251
Figure 13-21	Review rogues from the Monitor page	254

Definition of Key Terms

Define the following key terms from this chapter, and check your answers in the Glossary:

port, interface, WLAN, static interface, dynamic interface, roaming, mobility group

This chapter covers the following subjects:

Connecting to a Standalone AP: A brief discussion on how to gain access to a standalone AP using various methods.

Using the Express Setup and Express Security for Basic Configuration: How to set up the standalone AP for wireless access using the Express Setup and Express Security configurations.

Converting to LWAPP: How to convert a standalone AP to lightweight mode using the Upgrade tool.

CHAPTER 14

Migrating Standalone APs to LWAPP

Many Cisco APs are capable of operating in both autonomous mode and lightweight mode. APs that can do both usually ship in standalone mode. Some may choose to use these APs in standalone mode. Others might immediately convert them to Lightweight Access Point Protocol (LWAPP)–capable APs and integrate them into a network designed after the Cisco Unified Wireless Network (CUWN). In this chapter, you will learn how to access a standalone AP, how to configure it in standalone mode, and how to convert it to lightweight mode.

You should do the "Do I Know This Already?" quiz first. If you score 80 percent or higher, you might want to skip to the section "Exam Preparation Tasks." If you score below 80 percent, you should spend the time reviewing the entire chapter. Refer to Appendix A, "Answers to the 'Do I Know This Already?' Quizzes," to confirm your answers.

"Do I Know This Already?" Quiz

The "Do I Know This Already?" quiz helps you determine your level of knowledge of this chapter's topics before you begin. Table 14-1 details the major topics discussed in this chapter and their corresponding quiz questions.

Table 14-1 *"Do I Know This Already?" Section-to-Question Mapping*

Foundation Topics Section	Questions
Connecting to a Standalone AP	1–4
Using the Express Setup and Express Security for Basic Configuration	5–6
Converting to LWAPP	7–10

1. A standalone AP has a console port. True or False?

   a. True

   b. False

2. Which methods can be used to assign an IP address to a standalone AP? (Choose all that apply.)

    a. DHCP

    b. Static through the CLI

    c. TFTP

    d. DNS

3. What are three methods that require an IP address? (Choose all that apply.)

    a. Console to it using a console cable and the console port.

    b. Telnet into it if it has an IP address.

    c. Web browse to it if it has an IP address.

    d. SSH into it if it has an IP address.

4. Which of the following methods can be used to obtain the IP address of the AP? (Choose all that apply.)

    a. DHCP server logs

    b. CDP

    c. NTP server statistics

    d. IP Setup Utility

5. You can apply a separate SSID to different radios. True or False?

    a. True

    b. False

6. More than one authentication server can be configured. True or False?

    a. True

    b. False

7. What is required if you are converting from standalone to lightweight mode? (Choose all that apply.)

    a. An upgrade image

    b. A DHCP server

    c. An upgrade tool

    d. A WLC

8. If you are using the Autonomous to Lightweight Mode Upgrade tool, what else must you obtain from Cisco?

    a.   A TFTP server

    b.   A WCS

    c.   The correct LWAPP software (version 12.3(JA) or better)

    d.   Autonomous to Lightweight Mode Upgrade image

9. What protocol is used for the upgrade from autonomous to lightweight?

    a.   FTP

    b.   TFTP

    c.   SCP

    d.   SSH

10. A controller must be reachable after the AP is upgraded for the AP to function. True or False?

    a.   True

    b.   False

Foundation Topics

Connecting to a Standalone AP

Almost any AP that is capable of operating in both autonomous and lightweight mode ships in autonomous mode. You need to convert the device to lightweight mode if you plan to use it in that mode. Luckily, you can accomplish this conversion in two ways. You can get a Windows application called the Upgrade tool to do it, and you can get it done using the Cisco Wireless Control System (WCS). Either method accomplishes the same task; it is simply a matter of what you prefer and what you have access to. After the device is in lightweight mode, you can manage it through the Cisco wireless LAN controllers (WLC). Understand, however, that Cisco provides customers with the flexibility of running either IOS or LWAPP, and an AP can be purchased in whatever form as needed.

Accessing the AP in Autonomous Mode

You can access an autonomous AP in four ways:

- Console to it using a console cable and the console port.

- Telnet into it if it has an IP address.

- Browse to it with a web browser if it has an IP address.

- SSH into it if configured (preferred over Telnet).

You might be wondering how to get an IP address for an autonomous AP. The answer is simple: use DHCP. You just plug in the autonomous AP, and it grabs an address on its own. Note, however, that the device does not have a service set identifier (SSID) configured by default, and the radio is disabled by default; this is true for any IOS release later than 12.3(4)JA. In fact, the autonomous AP has a yellow sticker right on the outside of the box that indicates this. When you consider why, you begin to realize that it is a good security mechanism. You do not have to worry about people associating with the AP while you are scrambling to set it up.

If you are wondering how you are going the find the AP when it has a dynamic address, you can try to get the IP from the DHCP server, which you might or might not have access to. You can also use Cisco Discovery Protocol (CDP) on the switch that the AP is connected to, and you can sometimes use the command **show arp | include** *mac-address* (assuming that the IP address is in the CAM table), or you can use a tool created by Cisco called the IP Setup Utility, seen in Figure 14-1. The IP Setup Utility takes the MAC address of the AP and resolves the IP address associated with it. You can get the MAC address from a sticker on the AP.

After you obtain the IP address, you can access the AP via a web browser. Figure 14-2 shows the initial page when you log in to the AP.

To quickly configure the settings of the AP, you can use the Express Setup and Express Security Pages.

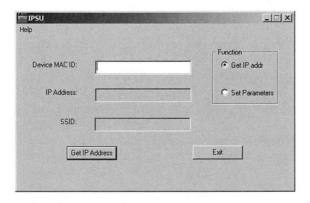

Figure 14-1 *IP Setup Utility*

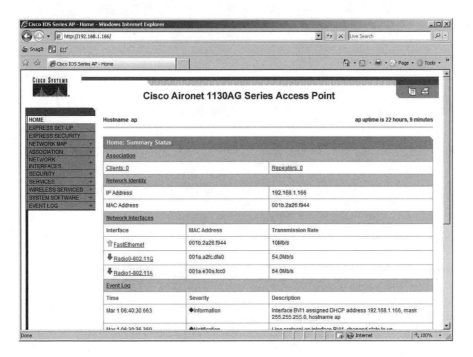

Figure 14-2 *Initial Login to the AP*

Using the Express Setup and Express Security for Basic Configuration

From the initial login screen, you quickly can gain valuable information about clients, repeaters, interfaces, and events.

To quickly set up the AP, use the EXPRESS SET-UP and EXPRESS SECURITY links in the left menu. You are prompted for the following:

■ Hostname of the device

- Method of IP address assignment

- IP address

- Subnet mask

- Default gateway

- SNMP community

- Radio properties, as seen in Figure 14-3

- 802.11G properties, including its role

- 802.11A properties, including its role

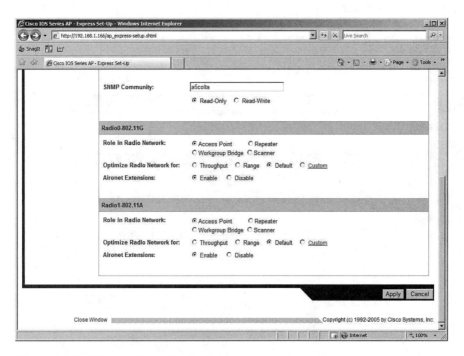

Figure 14-3   *Express Setup Radio Properties*

It is that easy. Simply click **Apply** for the settings in the Express Setup page to take effect.

As for the Express Security configuration, this is where you assign an SSID, determine whether it will be broadcast, apply VLANs, and define the security settings such as Wired Equivalent Privacy (WEP), Wi-Fi Protected Access (WPA), and WPA2. If you enable VLAN IDs, you can have more than one SSID and apply the security settings differently to each VLAN. Again, you need to apply the changes with the **Apply** button. Figure 14-4 shows a sample of the Express Security page.

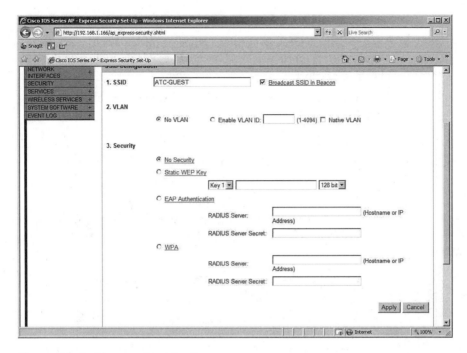

Figure 14-4 *Express Security Setup*

Following are some other important facts related to the configuration of SSIDS and security:

■ You cannot tie an SSID to a particular radio; the SSID configured applies to both radios.

■ You cannot set up more than one authentication server.

■ You cannot combine authentication types.

After applying the Express Setup and Express Security configuration, you can use the web interface for additional configuration.

Working with the Web Interface

At this point, assuming you have followed along through the section, "Using the Express Setup and Express Security for Basic Configuration," you do not necessarily have a functional AP. As mentioned previously, the radios are now disabled by default. You can see this from the home page:

Step 1.   Click **HOME** from the left menu.

Step 2.   View the status of the radios under the Network Interfaces section.

You can use two different methods to enable the radios:

- Select the **NETWORK INTERFACES** link on the left menu, select the radio, and then select the Settings button and enable the radio with the **Enable** radio button.

- Click on the radio link on the home page, as seen in Figure 14-5 (in this case, Radio0-802.11G or Radio1-802-802.11A).

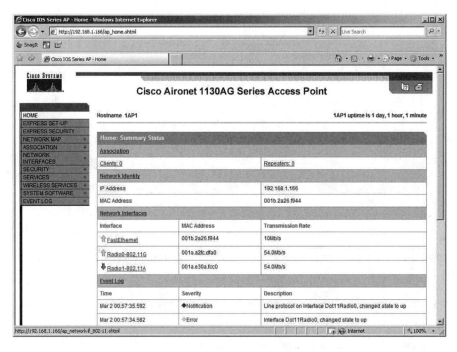

Figure 14-5   *Radio Configuration*

After you have accessed the Settings page, you can enable the radio following the same process as the first method described. When the radio is enabled, you have a working AP.

Note: You might want to spend some time getting familiar with the options in the web interface; however, for the CCNA wireless exam, it is not as significant of a topic as the lightweight configurations.

That being said, with a functional AP, you can allow users access to the network. Recall, however, that the goal is to use this AP with a controller. This means you need to convert this autonomous AP to a lightweight AP.

Converting to LWAPP

Three methods you can use to convert the AP to lightweight mode are as follows:

■ Use the IOS to LWAPP conversion utility. This is an installable application that you can download from Cisco.com.

■ Use the WCS. If you have a WCS, this method is probably preferred; however, it is not covered as part of the CCNA wireless certification.

■ As of July 2005, simply archive the image to the AP to convert it to LWAPP.

The section that follows examines the IOS-to-LWAPP conversion.

Converting to LWAPP Using the IOS-to-LWAPP Conversion Utility

Before you can use the IOS-to-LWAPP conversion utility, you need to obtain the software. To do so, you need to access the AP download page at Cisco.com. To do so, follow these steps:

Step 1.   Go to www.cisco.com/go/wireless.

Step 2.   Click the AP you are working with. The list of APs is at the bottom of the page.

Step 3.   On the AP page, from the right side of the page in a box labeled **Support**, click the **Download Software** link.

Step 4.   Using the menu tree, find the AP you are looking for, and expand the folder.

Step 5.   Select the link to the AP inside that folder.

Step 6.   Enter your Cisco username and password.

When you have authenticated to Cisco, you will see a page similar to the one in Figure 14-6. Notice that this page offers four links:

■ Autonomous to Lightweight Mode Upgrade Image

■ Autonomous to Lightweight Mode Upgrade Tool

■ IOS Software

■ IP Setup Utility (IPSU)

The first link is to the Autonomous to Lightweight Mode Upgrade Image. You need this image to perform the upgrade. It is not the same image that runs on the controller. Recall that the controller and AP need to be on the same version; however, any mismatch is corrected when an AP finds a controller. If the code versions are different, the controller either upgrades or downgrades the AP. This Autonomous to Lightweight Mode Upgrade image simply gets LWAPP functionality on the AP. From there, the controller can handle the rest.

Figure 14-6 *Download Area of Cisco.com*

The second link on the Downloads page is to the Autonomous to Lightweight Mode Upgrade Tool. This is the software application you need to perform the upgrade. This software installs on a Windows computer.

The third link on the Downloads page is to IOS Software, and the fourth link is for the IP Setup Utility. Select the link to download the software you need. Because you want the IP Setup Utility for this task, click that link.

After you have the Autonomous to Lightweight Mode Upgrade Tool software and the Autonomous to Lightweight Mode Upgrade image, you are ready to install it on a Windows PC. After it is installed, you can perform the upgrade.

Before performing the upgrade, however, you must meet the following requirements:

■ IOS on the AP must be version 12.3(7)JA or above. If it is not, upgrade it first by selecting the IOS Software link on the Downloads page.

■ The WLC must be running version 3.1 or later. Keep in mind that after you do the upgrade from autonomous to lightweight, the AP cannot function without the controller, and the console port is no longer useful. Also, the upgrade supports only Layer 3 LWAPP mode.

To begin the upgrade, first check to see if you are running a code version on the AP that is capable of being upgraded. In Figure 14-7, the code version is 12.3(7)JA4. This indicates that the version is compatible.

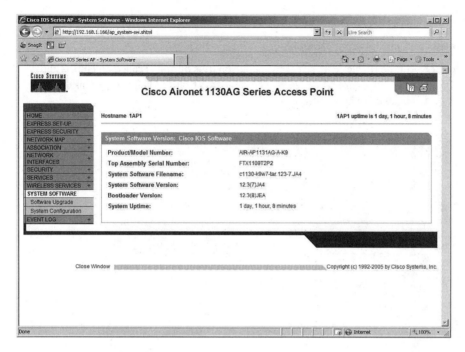

Figure 14-7 *Verify the IOS Version*

Note: You can order new LWAPP-capable APs with the lightweight code already installed if desired.

After you have verified the IOS version, you need to make sure that the controller and the AP are on the same subnet or that the controller is reachable after the upgrade. You can do this via DHCP option 43 or DNS.

The next step is to prepare a text file of APs that you want to upgrade. I recommend using Notepad so that you can save it as a .txt file. In the text file, the format should resemble the following:

> *ap-ip-address, telnet-username, telnet-Password, enable-password*

Create a new line for each AP that you want to convert. When you are finished with the text file, save it somewhere that you can find it, and name it something like **APList.txt**. You are going to browse to this file in the Upgrade tool interface.

As a final preparation step, you need to make sure that the upgrade code is on the local machine. The steps described in the preceding paragraphs detailed where you can obtain this, so make sure you have it.

You will be using the TFTP protocol to upgrade the AP, so you can use Tftpd32, which you can download for free from http://tftpd32.jounin.net, or you can use the TFTP service that is integrated in the Upgrade tool.

Key Topic

The overall upgrade process is as follows:

Step 1.   Open the Upgrade tool.

Step 2.   In the IP File field, select the ... button (this button is called an ellipsis and looks like three dots), select the **APList.txt** file, and click **Open**, as demonstrated in Figure 14-8.

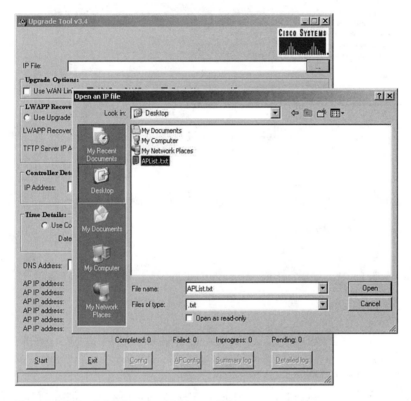

Figure 14-8   *Selecting the APList.txt File*

Step 3.   In the Upgrade Options field, choose any options that apply. These pertain to how to handle the upgrade. Are the APs being upgraded over a WAN link? Should the AP be converted to DHCP after the upgrade? Should they keep their existing hostname after the upgrade? Select the check box to indicate your choice based on your preferences and network situation. In Figure 14-9, the APs are going to retain their hostnames.

Step 4.   In the LWAPP Recovery Image section shown in Figure 14-9, select the method of TFTP you want to use, whether it is internal to the Upgrade tool or using an external application such as Tftpd32. Then select the LWAPP Recovery image. Choose how many APs can upgrade at once in the Max. AP at run field.

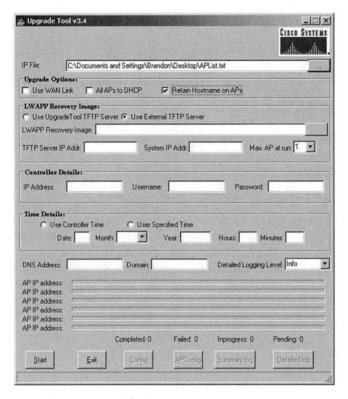

Figure 14-9 *Upgrade Options*

Step 5.   In the Controller Details section, define the controllers management IP address, username, and password.

Step 6.   In the Time Details section, select the User Controller Time radio button.

Step 7.   If resolving by DNS, enter the DNS address and domain name. Optionally, change the logging level if you want to see more verbose information.

Step 8.   Click the **Start** button to begin the process.

The upgrade process verifies each parameter you have entered and errors out if inconsistencies are noted. After the conversion, the AP reboots. After the reboot, the AP behaves like any lightweight AP and tries to find a controller.

Note: During the upgrade process to the lightweight code, a self-signed certificate is generated for each AP and sent to the WLC if the AP is an older AP without a Cisco signed certificate. It is important that all the controllers that the AP may associate with have this certificate. In this case, if the CUWN has a WCS server, you would import the self-signed certificate to WCS from the controller the AP is currently associated with. You would do this by refreshing the controller config to WCS from the controller the AP is associated to and then push it to all other controllers.

This is an important note for those who are upgrading from older APs that support the upgrade path from autonomous APs to the lightweight code for the CUWN, but it is not so important for those looking to take the CCNA Wireless Exam.

You can read more about it in the article "Self-Signed Certificate Manual Addition to the Controller for LWAPP-Converted APs" at http://tinyurl.com/4l3p3c.

If you want to convert an AP from lightweight to standalone, you can do so via the command-line interface (CLI) or by resetting the AP to factory defaults. If you do it from the CLI, you use the following command:

```
config ap tftp-downgrade tftp-server-ip-address filename apname
```

If you are resetting to factory defaults, use the **mode** button by holding it down until the LED turns red. This causes the AP to reboot, ignoring its lightweight code, apply an IP address of 10.0.0.1, and broadcast for an IOS file. This means you need a TFTP server on that subnet and a default file on there with the naming convention **cplatform_name-k9w7-tar.default**. This is what the AP looks for. If the file can be found, the downgrade will take place. You probably will not be doing this unless you plan to move a lightweight AP out of the lightweight deployment and place it somewhere else as a standalone AP.

Exam Preparation Tasks

Review All the Key Concepts

Review the most important topics from this chapter, noted with the Key Topics icon in the outer margin of the page. Table 14-2 lists a reference of these key topics and the page number where you can find each one.

Table 14-2 *Key Topics for Chapter 14*

Key Topic Item	Description	Page Number
Paragraph/list in the section "Accessing the AP in Autonomous Mode"	List of methods used to access the AP	264
Paragraph/list in the section "Using the Express Setup and Express Security for Basic Configuration"	List of requirements for Express Setup	265
Paragraph/list in the section "Converting to LWAPP	List of requirements to meet before upgrading to light-weight mode	269
List in the section "Converting to LWAPP	Steps to perform the upgrade using the Upgrade tool	272

Definition of Key Terms

Define the following key terms from this chapter, and check your answers in the Glossary:

Upgrade tool, IP Setup Utility

This chapter covers the following subjects:

Overview of the Small Business Communication System: An introduction to the Small Business Communication System, its components, and how mobility fits in.

Configuring the 521 AP and 526 Controller: A look at three methods used to configure the Cisco Mobility Express solution.

CHAPTER 15

Cisco Mobility Express

Cisco Mobility Express was designed to offer wireless services to small businesses in a form factor similar to the lightweight architecture. It is not the full Lightweight Access Point Protocol (LWAPP) but rather a subset of LWAPP functionality. This means that although the 521 AP runs the subset of LWAPP, it cannot communicate with enterprise controllers. The Cisco Mobility Express solution delivers best-in-class wireless capabilities that until recently had been reserved for enterprises. The solution is sold at a premium accessible to small to medium-sized business (SMB) customers who are seeking to gain a competitive edge without having to compromise between price and sophistication. SMBs now have an alternative to consumer-grade products and can benefit from the latest enterprise-class services available over Wi-Fi. Also of noteworthiness is that Linksys offers an upgrade program for businesses that want to get enterprise-class devices into the network. This is a key type of business to see this in.

You should do the "Do I Know This Already?" quiz" first. If you score 80 percent or higher, you might want to skip to the section "Exam Preparation Tasks." If you score below 80 percent, you should spend the time reviewing the entire chapter. Refer to Appendix A, "Answers to the 'Do I Know This Already?' Quizzes," to confirm your answers.

"Do I Know This Already?" Quiz

The "Do I Know This Already?" quiz helps you determine your level of knowledge of this chapter's topics before you begin. Table 15-1 details the major topics discussed in this chapter and their corresponding quiz questions.

Table 15-1 *"Do I Know This Already?" Section-to-Question Mapping*

Foundation Topics Section	Questions
Overview of the Small Business Communication System	1–5
Configuring the 521 AP and 526 Controller	6–10

1. The Cisco Mobility Express solution is part of what system?

   a. ACCID

   b. SBCS

   c. SAFE

   d. IOS

2. Which of the following devices is *not* part of the Cisco Smart Business Communication System?

   a. Cisco Unified Communications 500 Series for Small Businesses

   b. Cisco Unified IP Phones

   c. The Cisco 4402 Wireless LAN controller

   d. The Cisco 521 Wireless Express Access Point

3. What protocol manages the Cisco 521 AP when operating in lightweight mode?

   a. LWAPP

   b. CDP

   c. IP Discovery

   d. A subset of LWAPP

4. The Cisco 521 AP supports which of the following protocols? (Choose all that apply.)

   a. 802.11a

   b. 802.11b

   c. 802.11g

   d. WPA2

5. The Cisco 526 Express Controller supports RRM. True or False?

   a. True

   b. False

6. The Cisco Mobility Express solution can be managed by which of the following? (Choose all that apply.)

   a. Cisco Security Manager

   b. Command-line interface

   c. Web interface

   d. CCA

7. From the CLI, which is not a valid boot option?

   a. Run the primary image (Version 4.2.61.8) (active).

   b. Run the backup image (Version 4.1.154.22).

   c. Manually upgrade the primary image.

   d. Manually downgrade the primary image.

    e. Change the active boot image.

    f. Clear the configuration.

8. The Cisco 526 Express Controller supports NTP. True or False?

    a. True

    b. False

9. Which of the following is the correct way to access the web interface of a Cisco 526 Express Controller if you have never performed CLI setup?

    a. http://10.1.1.1

    b. https://10.1.1.1

    c. http://192.168.1.1

    d. https://192.168.1.1

10. What is the PC application that manages the Cisco Mobility Express solution?

    a. CCA

    b. CSA

    c. ACS

    d. AAA

Foundation Topics

Overview of the Small Business Communication System

The Cisco Mobility Express solution, seen in Figure 15-1, is either a standalone or a controller-based access point (AP) and a controller-based solution.

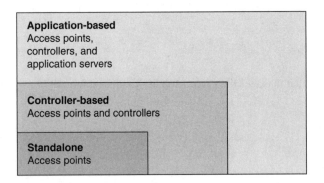

Figure 15-1 *Cisco Mobility Express Solution*

You manage the solution through a configuration assistant software application. The Cisco Mobility Express solution is only a portion, however, of the Cisco Smart Business Communication System (SBCS). This SBCS includes the following:

Key Topic

■   Cisco Unified Communications 500 Series for Small Businesses

This device can support up to 48 users and acts as a DHCP server. This DHCP functionality is important because it is a requirement of the AP, and the controller does not act as a DHCP server. Only the Cisco UC 500 series and the Cisco 870W router support DHCP.

■   Cisco Unified IP Phones

■   Cisco Monitor Director

■   The Cisco Mobility Solution, including the following:

The Cisco 526 Wireless Express Controller

The Cisco 521 Wireless Express Access Point

The design of this solution is perfect for small businesses that want a controller-based AP deployment but do not plan to grow to more than 12 APs, because the architecture allows one controller to support six APs, with two controllers able to communicate with each other. The devices are managed by a central application called the Cisco Configuration Assistant (CCA), which is a Windows application that you can download from

Cisco.com and install locally. Along with the Cisco Configuration Assistant and the Radio Resource Management (RRM) capabilities of the Cisco Mobility Solution, this network is self-configuring, self-optimizing, and self-healing in the event of interference.

521 AP

The Cisco 521 AP has a form factor that is similar to the 1130 series AP. The Cisco 521 AP, seen in Figure 15-2, has internal 802.11 b/g antennas.

Figure 15-2   *The Cisco 521 AP*

When managed by the Cisco 526 controller, the Cisco 521 AP uses a protocol subset of LWAPP. The Cisco 521 AP cannot communicate with the CUWN controllers because a hardware check during the AP bootup process does not allow it to join any other controller besides the 526.

Features of the Cisco 521 AP include the following:

- 802.11g radio

- Industry-leading radio design

- Variable transmit power settings

- Integrated antennas

- Hardware-assisted Advanced Encryption Standard (AES) encryption

- IEEE 802.11i-compliant; WPA2 and WPA certified

- Low-profile design

- Multipurpose and lockable mounting bracket

- Power over Ethernet (IEEE 802.3af and Cisco Inline Power)

- Field-upgradeable from standalone to controller mode

- Inclusion of Cisco Configuration Assistant management software

526 Wireless Express Controller

The Cisco 526 Wireless Express Mobility controller harnesses the power of Cisco LWAPP technology, best-in-class automatic radio optimization, mobility performance, and multiaccess point management. On top of the basic transport layer, the controller supports Cisco Secure Guest Access and Voice-over-WLAN advanced mobility services. As part of the Smart Business Communications System, this controller is managed by the Cisco Configuration Assistant, easing deployment and decreasing the cost of ongoing maintenance. A single Cisco 526 controller supports up to six Cisco 521 access points, and up to two controllers can be deployed per network, delivering the capacity, simplicity, and price point that is appropriate for the SMB.[1]

The Cisco 526 Wireless Express controller supports the following features:

- Secure network access for guest users

- Support for Cisco voice-over-WLAN optimization

- Easy management with CCA

- Support for Cisco LWAPP

- Support for up to six access points per controller and up to 2 controllers per network, for a total of 12 access points

- Multiaccess point RRM

- Support for a wide range of authentication mechanisms to enable scalable security architectures and minimize security interoperability issues (WEP, MAC filtering, WPA, WPA2, WebAuth, 802.1X, and EAP)

- Wired/wireless network virtualization

Comparing the Cisco Mobility Express Architecture to the CUWN

When you compare the Cisco Mobility Express Architecture to the Cisco Unified Wireless Network, you will find that the model is similar; however, the protocols are different. The Mobility Express solution does not use the full enterprise class version of LWAPP; rather, it uses a subset of LWAPP. In addition, the Cisco 521 AP cannot communicate with CUWN wireless LAN controllers. Likewise, the Cisco 526 cannot communicate with APs from the 1100 series or higher. The 526 supports control of up to 12 APs in a small network.

Configuring the 521 AP and 526 Controller

In general, you can configure the Mobility Express solution in three ways, none of which are performed on the AP. You do not even need to directly access the AP. Instead, on the controller itself, use either the CLI, which is normally used for basic setup and initialization, or the web interface. After a basic setup on the controller, you can use the Configuration Assistant management tool. Each of these methods is discussed in the following sections.

Using the CLI to Configure the Controller

To configure the Cisco Mobility Express solution, you need a console connection to the Cisco 526. You do not need to do anything on the AP because the controller takes care of it. After you have a console connection, you can power on the device and view the boot process. In Example 15-1, notice that if you press the **Esc** key, you are presented with multiple boot options. The normal selection is to run the primary image.

Example 15-1   *Booting the Cisco 526 Controller*

```
Booting Primary Image...
Press <ESC> now for additional boot options...


Boot Options


Please choose an option from below:


1. Run primary image (Version 4.2.61.8) (active)
2. Run backup image (Version 4.1.154.22)
3. Manually upgrade primary image
4. Change active boot image
5. Clear Configuration


Please enter your choice:
```

Continuing with the boot process, Example 15-2 shows the tests that are performed as the device initializes.

Example 15-2   *Tests During the Boot Process*

```
CISCO SYSTEMS
Embedded BIOS Version 1.0(12)6 08/21/06 17:26:53.43


Low Memory: 632 KB
High Memory: 251 MB
PCI Device Table.
Bus Dev Func VendID DevID Class Irq
00 01 00 1022 2080 Host Bridge
00 01 02 1022 2082 Chipset En/Decrypt 11
00 0C 00 1148 4320 Ethernet 11
00 0D 00 177D 0003 Network En/Decrypt 10
00 0F 00 1022 2090 ISA Bridge
00 0F 02 1022 2092 IDE Controller
00 0F 03 1022 2093 Audio 10
00 0F 04 1022 2094 Serial Bus 9
00 0F 05 1022 2095 Serial Bus 9


Evaluating BIOS Options ...
Launch BIOS Extension to setup ROMMON


Cisco Systems ROMMON Version (1.0(12)7) #2: Fri Oct 13 10:52:36 MDT 2006
```

continues

```
Platform AIR-WLC526-K9


Launching BootLoader...

Cisco Bootloader (Version 4.0.191.0)



.o88b. d888888b .d8888. .o88b. .d88b.
d8P Y8 `88' 88' YP d8P Y8 .8P Y8.
8P 88 `8bo. 8P 88 88
8b 88 `Y8b. 8b 88 88
Y8b d8 .88. db 8D Y8b d8 `8b d8'
`Y88P' Y888888P `8888Y' `Y88P' `Y88P'


Booting Primary Image...
Press <ESC> now for additional boot options...
Detecting hardware . . . .

Generating Secure Shell DSA Host Key ...
Generating Secure Shell RSA Host Key ...
Generating Secure Shell version 1.5 RSA Host Key ...
XML config selected
Cisco is a trademark of Cisco Systems, Inc.
Software Copyright Cisco Systems, Inc. All rights reserved.


Cisco AireOS Version 4.2.61.8
Initializing OS Services: ok
Initializing Serial Services: ok
Initializing Network Services: ok
Starting ARP Services: ok
Starting Trap Manager: ok
Starting Network Interface Management Services: ok
Starting System Services: ok
Starting FIPS Features: Not enabled
Starting Fast Path Hardware Acceleration: ok
Starting Switching Services: ok
Starting QoS Services: ok
Starting Policy Manager: ok
Starting Data Transport Link Layer: ok
Starting Access Control List Services: ok
Starting System Interfaces: ok
Starting Client Troubleshooting Service: ok
```

```
Starting Management Frame Protection: ok
Starting LWAPP: ok
Starting Certificate Database: ok
Starting VPN Services: ok
Starting Security Services: ok
Starting Policy Manager: ok
Starting Authentication Engine: ok
Starting Mobility Management: ok
Starting Virtual AP Services: ok
Starting AireWave Director: ok
Starting Network Time Services: ok
Starting Cisco Discovery Protocol: ok
Starting Broadcast Services: ok
Starting Power Over Ethernet Services: ok
Starting Logging Services: ok
Starting DHCP Server: ok
Starting IDS Signature Manager: ok
Starting RFID Tag Tracking: ok
Starting Mesh Services: ok
Starting TSM: ok
Starting LOCP: ok


Starting CIDS Services: ok
Starting Ethernet-over-IP: ok
Starting Management Services:
Web Server: ok
CLI: ok
Secure Web: Web Authentication Certificate not found (error).
dhcp pool 192.168.1.100(0xc0a80164) — 192.168.1.102(0xc0a80166), network
192.168.1.0(0xc0a80100) netmask 255.255.255.0(0xffffff00), default gateway 0xc0
internal dhcp server is config successfully

(Cisco Controller)
```

Upon completing the boot sequence, a controller with no configuration prompts you to perform the setup using the Cisco Wizard Configuration tool, as demonstrated in Example 15-3. Be prepared to provide the following information:

- Hostname of the device

- Username of the administrator

- Password for the administrator

- Management interface information

- AP-Manager interface information

- Virtual gateway IP address

Example 15-3   *Cisco Wizard Configuration*

```
Welcome to the Cisco Wizard Configuration Tool
Use the '-' character to backup
System Name [Cisco_be:7a:e0]: 526-3
Enter Administrative User Name (24 characters max): admin3
Enter Administrative Password (24 characters max): *****
Re-enter Administrative Password : *****

Management Interface IP Address: 10.30.1.100
Management Interface Netmask: 255.255.255.0
Management Interface Default Router: 10.30.1.254
Management Interface VLAN Identifier (0 = untagged): 0
Management Interface Port Num [1 to 2]: 1
Management Interface DHCP Server IP Address: 10.30.1.253

AP Manager Interface IP Address: 10.30.1.101

AP-Manager is on Management subnet, using same values
AP Manager Interface DHCP Server (10.30.1.253):

Virtual Gateway IP Address: 1.1.1.1

Mobility/RF Group Name: CP-POD3

Enable Symmetric Mobility Tunneling [yes][NO]: NO

Network Name (SSID): IUWNE-301
Allow Static IP Addresses [YES][no]: YES

Configure a RADIUS Server now? [YES][no]: no
Warning! The default WLAN security policy requires a RADIUS server.
Please see documentation for more details.

Enter Country Code list (enter 'help' for a list of countries) [US]: US

Enable 802.11b Network [YES][no]: yes
Enable 802.11g Network [YES][no]: yes
Enable Auto-RF [YES][no]: yes

Configure a NTP server now? [YES][no]: no
Configure the system time now? [YES][no]: no

Warning! No AP will come up unless the time is set.
Please see documentation for more details.

Configuration correct? If yes, system will save it and reset. [yes][NO]: yes
```

After you have completed the configuration from the CLI, you can browse to the IP address of the management interface.

Using the Web Browser to Configure the Controller

To access the controller via a web browser, enter the IP address of the management interface of the controller preceded by **https://**. This is either the IP address you configured in the CLI Wizard or the default address of 192.168.1.1. In Figure 15-3, you can see the login page for the controller that will appear.

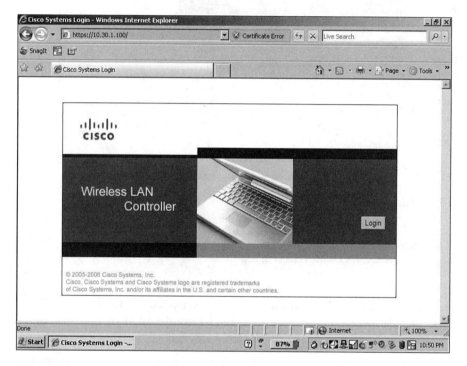

Figure 15-3   *Login Screen to the 526 Controllers*

Notice that the connection is secure via HTTPS. Click the **Login** button and enter a username and password before performing any configuration. After you are logged in, you are presented with a Summary page, as seen in Figure 15-4.

The Summary page gives you a look at the controller status, the AP status, and the top WLANs. Changes are logged as you make them, and you can see them on the Summary page.

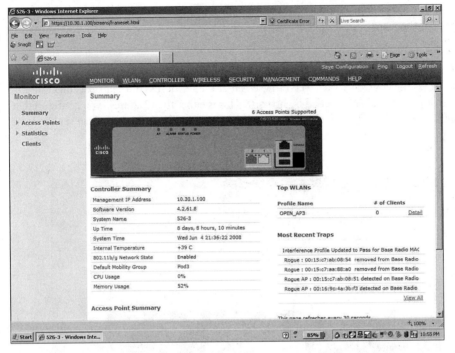

Figure 15-4   *Summary Page*

Note: The Wireless Express controller web interface is quite similar to the WLC web interface used in the CUWN architecture.

When it comes to the controllers, you do not need to do much work. The AP and controllers will find each other. You can see in Figure 15-5 that the All APs option from the WIRELESS menu is showing an AP that has been discovered.

When you select the AP name, you are taken to a page that allows you to enter details specific to that AP, such as its name and its primary controller, as shown in Figure 15-6. You can also enable or disable the AP from this menu. Other options include resetting the AP and clearing the AP configuration.

Using the Cisco Configuration Assistant

With the configuration as is, you can access the Configuration Assistant. The Cisco Configuration Assistant (CCA) is a management tool that installs on a Windows computer and is based on an application called Cisco Network Assistant, which has been modified to support the Cisco Mobility solution. After you have installed the CCA, you can access it via a desktop shortcut. When the application launches, you need to connect to or create a community. When you log in for the first time, you create a community. A *community* is a group name for your Mobility Express network. Figure 15-7 shows the configuration page that you see when creating a community.

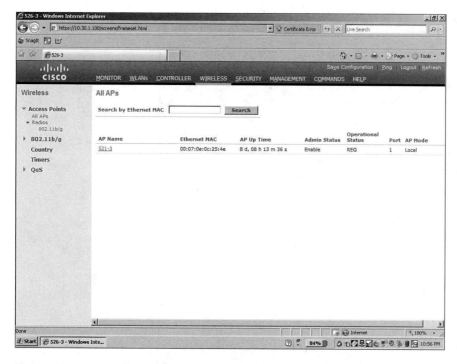

Figure 15-5 *The All APs List*

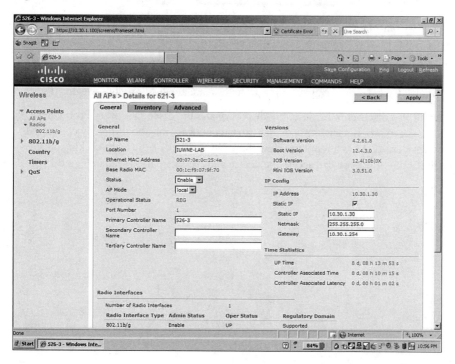

Figure 15-6 *Details Page for AP Configuration*

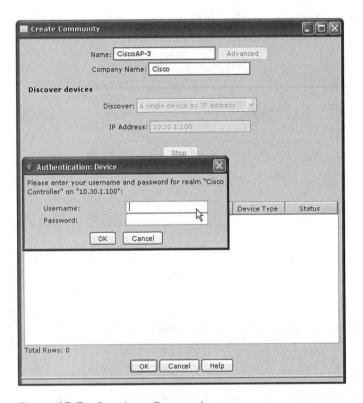

Figure 15-7   *Creating a Community*

CCA will discover the standalone APs. The APs will appear in the CCA interface. If you are running CCA 1.5 or later, you can migrate the standalone APs to lightweight APs.

CCA will also discover WLCs using IP discovery and the Cisco Discovery Protocol (CDP). CDP is a Cisco proprietary protocol that can gain information about directly connected Cisco devices. CCA has a topology view shown in Figure 15-8; by right-clicking on a device in the topology, you can access the device and configure it, as seen in Figure 15-9.

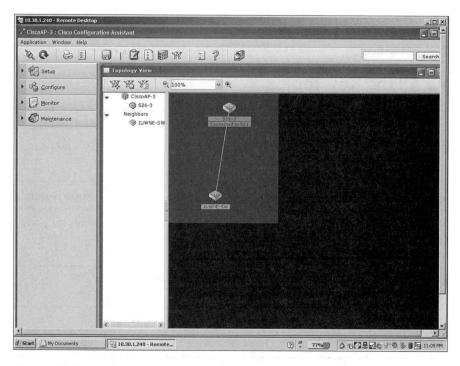

Figure 15-8   *CCA Topology View*

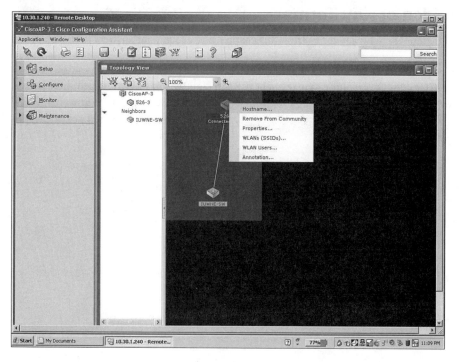

Figure 15-9   *Configuration Menu in Topology View*

Exam Preparation Tasks

Review All the Key Topics

Review the most important topics from this chapter, noted with the Key Topics icon in the outer margin of the page. Table 15-2 lists a reference of these key topics and the page number where you can find each one.

Table 15-2 *Key Topics for Chapter 15*

Key Topic Item	Description	Page Number
Paragraph from the section, "Overview of the Small Business Communication System"	Bullet points detailing the components of the solution	280
Example 15-1	Booting the Cisco 526 controller	283
Example 15-3	Cisco Wizard configuration	286
Figure 15-4	Summary page	288

Definition of Key Terms

Define the following key terms from this chapter, and check your answers in the Glossary:

SMB, Cisco Smart Business Communication System (SBCS), Cisco Configuration Assistant (CCA), Radio Resource Management (RRM), Lightweight Access Point Protocol (LWAPP), Cisco Wizard Configuration tool, community, Cisco Discovery Protocol (CDP)

References

[1]Cisco 526 Wireless Express Mobility Controller: http://tinyurl.com/2rbfxg

Cisco 521 Wireless Express Access Point: http://tinyurl.com/6bxhze

This chapter covers the following subjects:

Using Windows to Connect to a Wireless LAN: Looks at using the Windows Wireless Zero Configuration Utility to connect to a wireless LAN.

Using a Mac to Connect to a Wireless LAN: Shows how to use Mac OSX to connect to a wireless LAN.

Using Linux to Connect to a Wireless LAN: Covers how to use Linux NetworkManager to connect to a wireless LAN.

Using the ADU to Connect to a Wireless LAN: Describes how to install a Cisco wireless card and use the ADU to manage enterprise class profiles.

The ACAU: Covers using the Aironet Client Administration Utility to deploy profiles to the enterprise.

The Cisco Secure Services Client: Shows how to use the Cisco Secure Services Client to manage customer and guest access to Cisco networks.

The Cisco Client Extension Program: Looks at free licensing to Cisco extensions for third-party vendors.

CHAPTER 16

Wireless Clients

Networks today have many different types of clients. Users with PCs and laptops running Linux or the Mac OS are becoming more common. In a mobile environment, these devices must support connectivity to wireless networks. This chapter introduces the network configuration tools found in Windows, Linux, and Mac devices. In addition to these packaged clients, Cisco provides the Aironet Desktop Utility (ADU), discussed in this chapter, along with some of its available utilities.

You should do the "Do I Know This Already?" quiz first. If you score 80 percent or higher, you might want to skip to the section "Exam Preparation Tasks." If you score below 80 percent, you should review the entire chapter. Refer to Appendix A, "Answers to the 'Do I Know This Already?' Quizzes," to confirm your answers.

"Do I Know This Already?" Quiz

The "Do I Know This Already?" quiz helps you determine your level of knowledge of this chapter's topics before you begin. Table 16-1 details the major topics discussed in this chapter and their corresponding quiz questions.

Table 16-1 *"Do I Know This Already?" Section-to-Question Mapping*

Foundation Topics Section	Questions
Using Windows to Connect to a Wireless LAN	1–4
Using a Mac to Connect to a Wireless LAN	5
Using Linux to Connect to a Wireless LAN	6
Using the ADU to Connect to a Wireless LAN	7–9
The ACAU	10
The Cisco Secure Services Client	11
The Cisco Client Extension Program	12

1. What is the name of the Windows utility for configuring wireless profiles?

    a. Zero Day Configuration

    b. Wireless Zero NetworkManager

    c. AirPort Zero Configuration

    d. Wireless Zero Configuration Utility

2. The Windows Wireless Zero Configuration Utility can set up which of the following enterprise class profiles? (Choose all that apply.)

    a. 802.1x

    b. WPA/WPA2/CCKM

    c. WEP static keys

    d. None of these

3. True or false: When the WZC is in use, the ADU can also be used.

    a. True

    b. False

4. True or false: The WZC will choose the most secure network available when starting up.

    a. True

    b. False

5. What configuration tool is used to set up wireless profiles on Mac OSX?

    a. WZC

    b. AirPort

    c. AirWave

    d. Aironet

6. What graphical configuration tool is used in Linux to set up wireless networks?

    a. iwconfig

    b. NetworkManager

    c. WZC

    d. Ubuntu ADU

7. Cisco offers which types of wireless cards? (Choose all that apply.)

    a. Cardbus

    b. PCI

    c. USB

    d. Flash

    e. PCMCIA

8. What does the term CAM refer to in the ADU advanced parameters?

   a. Constant Awake Mode

   b. Content Addressable Memory

   c. Confidential Aironet Module

   d. Constant Airwave Mode

9. When you perform a site survey with the CSSU, what indicates a good SNR?

   a. A higher number in dBm

   b. A lower number in dBm

   c. The CSSU can't determine the SNR.

   d. An equal receive strength

10. What software lets you create profiles for deployment with the ADU?

    a. ACCU

    b. ASSCU

    c. ACAU

    d. SSC

11. What software is designed for both wired and wireless profile management and access to Cisco enterprise networks?

    a. SSC

    b. SSM

    c. ASA

    d. ADU

12. What program is designed for vendors to create compatible hardware?

    a. CCX

    b. Compatibility Program

    c. CCA

    d. Cisco Client Portability Program

Foundation Topics

Using Windows to Connect to a Wireless LAN

The wireless configuration tool for Microsoft Windows is called the Windows Wireless Zero Configuration Utility (WZC). The WZC is designed to provide the basic capabilities necessary to access most WLANs; however, it is not very powerful when it comes to troubleshooting utilities. Many vendors such as IBM/Lenovo install a custom client that can be used to create and manage profiles as an alternative to the WZC. So when you use these vendor-installed clients, you cannot use the Windows WZC.

WZC is a pretty basic client. It's designed to set up the connection for you and take some of the workload off the end user—hence the "Zero Configuration" part of the name. When a computer boots without a WLAN profile preconfigured, the WZC detects any wireless networks that are broadcasting and informs the user that a wireless network is available.

If a profile has already been created, the WZC tries to join it automatically. This WZC behavior can cause confusion when you have a WZC profile configured with the same SSID as another network that is within range. This is why changing default SSIDs such as "linksys" is recommended.

Configuring a Profile

You can set up a profile using Windows Vista in many ways. One method is to follow these steps:

Step 1.   Click **Start** (that's the little round Windows logo if you're running Vista).

Step 2.   Right-click **Network**.

Step 3.   Click **Properties**. You see the Network and Sharing Center window, as shown in Figure 16-1.

Step 4.   Click **Manage wireless networks** in the left panel. The Manage wireless networks window appears. Here you can see all available wireless network connection profiles. If you have yet to create any, this window looks like Figure 16-2.

Step 5.   Double-click an existing profile to view or change its setting. Click the **Add** button to create a new profile.

   If you decide to add a new network, you see a new window that allows you to do so in a wizard-style setup.

Another way to add a wireless profile is to connect to one that is within range of your computer and that Windows has discovered. In Figure 16-3, Windows has detected a wireless network within range.

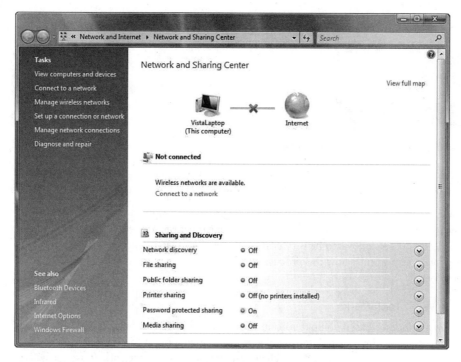

Figure 16-1 *Network and Sharing Center*

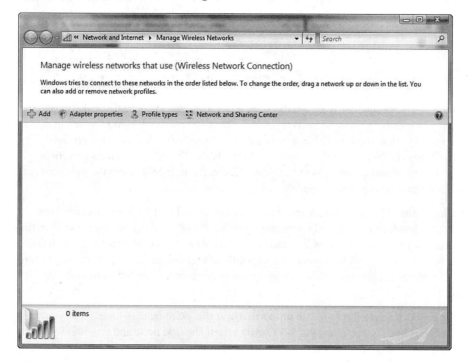

Figure 16-2 *Managing Wireless Networks*

Figure 16-3   *Wireless Networks Detected*

When you click the link, a new window appears, allowing you to connect one of the available networks, as shown in Figure 16-4.

You can select one of the available networks and click the **Connect** button. If there are any security settings, you are prompted for that information. You will probably find the profile setup in Windows to be very easy, especially because it detects networks for you. You might also wonder how this process works. The next section covers the process in more detail.

How the WZC Tool Works

When a Windows-based computer boots up, the Wireless Zero Configuration reports any network that is being broadcast, usually via a balloon window at the bottom right of the screen. This is because when a WZC client attempts to access a network, it uses an active scanning process. This differs from other methods, such as passive scanning, which is used by other clients.

Note: The concept of passive scanning simply involves the client's waiting until it hears a beacon from an access point.

With active scanning, the WZC sends probe requests with a blank SSID field. This is called *active null scanning*. This type of scan causes access points (AP) that are in range to respond with a list of available service set identifiers (SSID). If one of the received SSIDs exists on the preferred networks list in the WZC, the WZC connects to it, or at least tries to. If that connection fails, the WZC tries the next SSID from the preferred networks list that was seen to be available from the scan.

If none of the SSIDs that were learned from the active null scan or in the preferred networks list result in a successful connection, the WZC looks for any ad hoc network in the available networks list. If the WZC finds an ad hoc network, it connects to it, which could be a security issue. This happens in the background without any user intervention. When you set up the profile, you can select an option to connect to only infrastructure networks.

If the connection attempts are still unsuccessful at this point (and assuming that you *are* allowing ad hoc connections), the WZC makes itself the first node and thus allows others

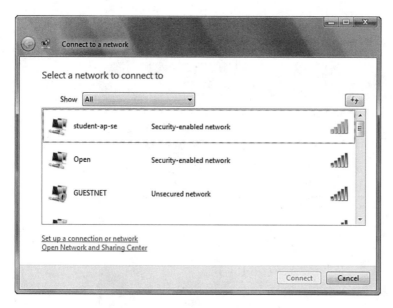

Figure 16-4 *Connecting to a Network*

to connect to it. Then the WZC sends out beacons that others on the network can see, allowing other devices to connect to the WZC sending the beacons.

If the WZC finds no preferred network and no ad hoc network to connect to, it checks the setting **Automatically Connect to non-preferred networks**. This is not enabled by default. If it were enabled, the WZC would try each non-preferred network in the available networks list.

If this setting is left at its default value, the WZC assigns itself a random network name and places the card in infrastructure mode. From this point on, it scans all the channels every 60 seconds, looking for new networks.

Using a Mac to Connect to a Wireless LAN

You can configure WLAN profiles on a Mac using AirPort or AirPort Extreme. This section describes AirPort Extreme, its software interface, and how to configure a profile on a Mac to connect to a WLAN.

AirPort, which really refers to the old version that supported only 802.11b networks, provides a software interface used to configure the WLAN profile, connect to detected networks, and perform advanced configurations and troubleshooting.

Configuring a Profile

To configure a profile in Mac OSX, follow these steps:

Step 1.   Click the **Open Apple** icon in the top-right corner of the screen.

Step 2.   Select **System Preferences**.

Step 3.   Select **Network**. This opens the network configuration page, as shown in Figure 16-5. From here you can select **AirPort**.

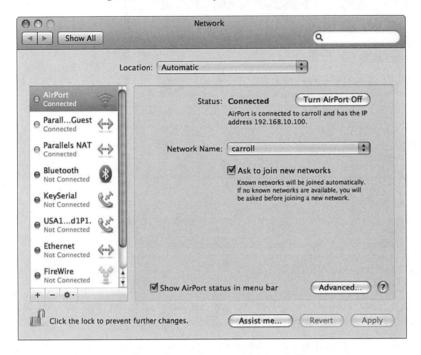

Figure 16-5   *Network Configuration on the Mac OSX*

Step 4.   You can access any already discovered network, create an ad hoc network, or join another network.

How the AirPort Extreme Tool Works

When you access the main AirPort configuration interface in Mac OSX 10.5 and above, you can disable the card, join networks, and even perform advanced configurations. To access the main AirPort interface, click the **Open Apple** icon and select **System Preferences > Network**.

If you want to create a profile, select the **Network Name** drop-down menu. Here you can choose **Join Other Network** or **Create Network**. The **Create Network** option allows you to set up an ad hoc network of computer-to-computer connectivity without using an AP. By selecting the **Join Other Network** option, you can enter an SSID and use the drop-down to select any security settings that may be necessary, as shown in Figure 16-6.

As an alternative, you can join any networks that AirPort has already discovered by selecting the **Network Name** drop-down and choosing one of the networks, as shown in Figure 16-7. If security settings are required, you are prompted.

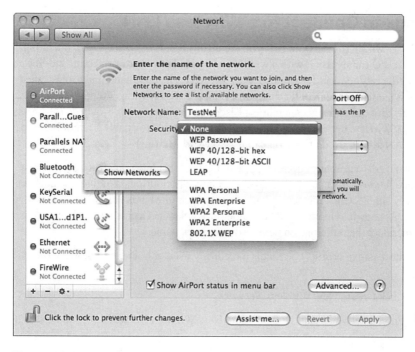

Figure 16-6   *Wireless Security Settings on Mac OSX*

Figure 16-7   *Selecting the Network Name*

Using Linux to Connect to a Wireless LAN

If you or a user within the network that you are involved in is using the Linux operating system, you can certainly use it with a wireless network. Linux has both command-line and GUI interface-type tools for working with WLANs. The command-line tool is called iwconfig. It is similar to the ifconfig that you would use to work with Ethernet interfaces. Although this tool offers many capabilities, Cisco has decided that it is outside the scope of the CCNA Wireless certification. Still, you need to be able to enable a Linux-based device for WLAN access. To do this, you can use NetworkManager.

NetworkManager is a graphical user interface (GUI) tool that lets you create wireless profiles in Linux. It works on a number of different Linux distributions. Finding available networks is fairly simple. Click the network connection icon in what is equivalent to the System Tray. As shown in Figure 16-8, a number of wireless networks are available. To use one of them, select the radio button next to the network name.

You can create a simple profile, one that is most likely used at home, by following these steps:

Step 1.   Click **Create New Wireless Network.**

Step 2.   Enter a network name in the **Create New Wireless Network** pop-up box.

Step 3.   Click **Connect.**

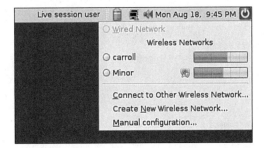

Figure 16-8   *Available Networks in NetworkManager*

Again, this is not the type of profile you would probably see at work, so you should be familiar with creating a more advanced profile.

Note: If you want to try this, I suggest using an Ubuntu Live CD. You can use it to boot your computer to Linux without harming your existing operating system. Best of all, you can download Ubuntu for free at http://www.ubuntu.com.

Configuring a Profile

Don't be alarmed when you see the term "enterprise profile." It just means that the profile contains more options, most likely security options and such. Setting up an advanced profile is not difficult, nor is it too time-consuming. You just have to know the parameters and plug them in. Assuming that you know these parameters, you can select **Connect to Other Wireless Network**, as shown in Figure 16-9, to begin the process of configuring a profile.

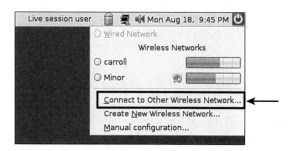

Figure 16-9   *Connecting to Other Wireless Network*

Next you need to enter the network name and use the drop-down menu to select the type of profile. In Figure 16-10, the network MySecureNet is using WPA2 Enterprise. After you make this selection, a number of other options are available to you, such as the EAP method, key type, identity, and password (see Figure 16-11). The values here are the defaults, but they can and usually are changed, depending on the security you have set up in your network.

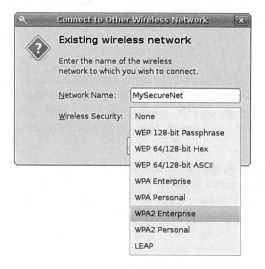

Figure 16-10   *Creating the Profile MySecureNet*

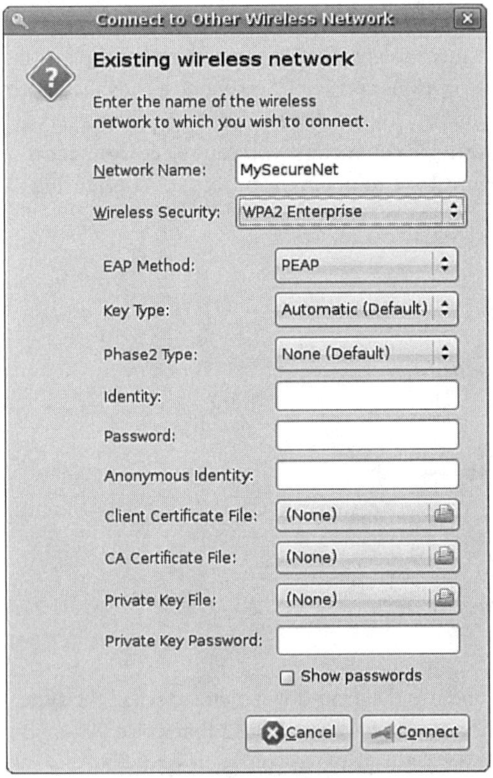

Figure 16-11 *WPA2 Enterprise Options*

Another option you have in the advanced settings is Awake Mode. If you place a card into Constant Awake Mode (CAM), the card is active at all times. This consumes more power.

How the NetworkManager Tool Works

When you click **Connect**, the NetworkManager tool sends discovery messages using the selected profile parameters. If for some reason an invalid parameter is entered in the NetworkManager tool, a message box appears, requesting the correct parameter. A connection does not take place until the parameters in the profile match. When they match, a connection can take place.

When a connection cannot take place due to invalid parameters, it is still added to the list of available networks. However, it indicates a signal power of 0. On the next boot, or if you restart the network daemon, the NetworkManager remembers the parameters.

Using the ADU to Connect to a Wireless LAN

You have a number of ways to connect to a WLAN. Cisco provides software to manage a single a/b/g wireless card called the Aironet Desktop Utility (ADU). As an administrator, you might be called on to use the Aironet Client Administration Utility (ACAU) to deploy across multiple clients. Additionally, you may use the Cisco Aironet Site Survey Utility (CASSU) when performing site surveys. The following sections cover these topics.

Cisco Wireless LAN Adapters

Cisco offers enterprise class wireless LAN adapters in the PCI and cardbus form factors. The AIR-CB21AG-X-K9 is a cardbus model, and the AIR-PI21AG-A-K9 is the PCI model. These adapters support most advanced wireless security configurations when you use Cisco software to manage them. You can, however, use the Windows WZC, but it's better to use the ADU and Aironet System Tray Utility (ASTU) if you want all the features of the cards to be available to you. The ADU has more configuration capability compared to WZC and also includes diagnostic tools, which don't come with the WZC.

With the ADU and a Cisco wireless card, you can

- Scan different channels.

- Determine which APs are on which channels.

- Determine the authentication and security configurations of each detected AP.

- Get Received Signal Strength Indicator (RSSI) information.

- Get signal-to-noise ratio (SNR) information.

Table 16-2 compares the WZC and the ADU.

The Aironet System Tray Utility (ASTU) is a smaller subset of the ADU that lives in your computer's system tray. Right-click it to access more information or even to launch the ADU.

Table 16-2   *Comparing the WZC and the ADU*

Capability	WZC	ADU
Scan different channels	No	Yes
Determine which APs are on which channels	No	Yes
Determine the authentication and security configurations of each detected AP	No	Yes
Get RSSI information	No	Yes
Get SNR information	No	Yes

Installing the ADU

When you install the ADU, you have three options, as shown in Figure 16-12:

■ **Install Client Utilities and Driver:** Installs the drivers for the card and the ADU software.

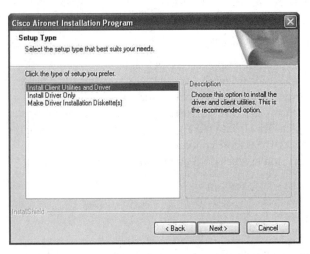

Figure 16-12 *Three Options When Installing the ADU*

■ **Install Driver Only:** Indicates that you will manage profiles and connect to networks with the WZC.

■ **Make Driver Installation Diskette(s):** Indicates that you will export these to a removable device such as a USB drive and take it with you.

In the following example, you will install the drivers and the client utility.

The process is pretty simple. It's best to start by inserting the card. You may see the Windows Found New Hardware Wizard, as shown in Figure 16-13. If you see this, close it. You don't need it.

After you have closed the Found New Hardware Wizard, continue with the installation by selecting the type of install you want to perform. In this case, it's the default option: **Install Client Utilities and Driver**, as shown previously in Figure 16-12.

As the installation progresses (as you click the **Next** button), you are given the option to install the CASSU, as shown in Figure 16-14.

One thing to point out with this site survey utility is that it's by no means a complete site survey tool because it has no mapping capability. It can, however, be used along with other site survey tools that do provide mapping capability. As a free utility that comes with the purchase of a Cisco network adapter, it's a good site survey tool. Some customers might not be able to afford the higher-priced tools provided by Ekahau, Wireless Valley, or AirMagnet, so a free survey tool is better than no survey tool. However, if you can afford the

Figure 16-13 *Found New Hardware Wizard*

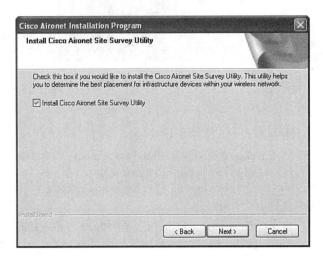

Figure 16-14 *Site Survey Utility Install Option*

higher-priced tools, the CSSU wouldn't provide any additional benefits over the higher-end tools.

The next option you have in the install program is the use of the ADU or third-party tools such as the WZC. This still installs the ADU. Again, you can choose to use the WZC, although it's not recommended. Later you can switch to the ADU by deselecting the **Use Windows to configure my wireless network settings** option in the WZC, as shown in Figure 16-15.

You need to reboot when the install is finished. If there are any open APs, the ADU finds them when the computer is restarted. You will most likely want to create an actual profile with security settings and such. The next section discusses the profile configuration.

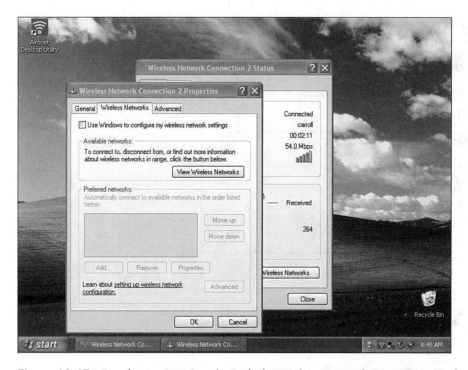

Figure 16-15   *Deselecting WZC as the Default Wireless Network Connection Tool*

Configuring a Profile

In this example, after a reboot, the ADU picked up an open AP and associated with it. The ADU did this because the Windows client was associated with it before the ADU was even installed. To get information on a connection, you can hover the mouse over the ADU icon on the systray, as shown in Figure 16-16.

You can also right-click this icon, which is the ASTU, and choose either **Show Connection Status** or **Open Aironet Desktop Utility**. Figure 16-17 shows these options as well as others available in the ASTU.

As you become more familiar with the ADU, you will see that these options in the ASTU are merely a subset of what is available in the actual ADU interface.

Figure 16-16   *Getting Information About a Connection*

Figure 16-18 shows the ADU interface for a connected profile called Default.

Figure 16-17 *ASTU Options*

If you don't access the ADU from the ASTU, you can start it by choosing **Start > All Programs > Cisco Aironet > Aironet Desktop Utility.** If you use the classic Start menu in Windows XP, choose **Start > Programs > Cisco Aironet > Aironet Desktop Utility.**

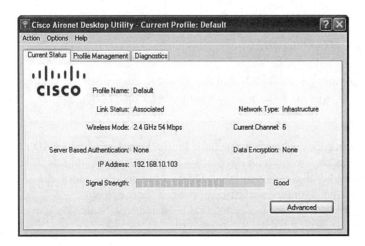

Figure 16-18 *ADU Interface*

Connecting to Preferred Networks

You can connect to preferred networks that the ADU has scanned for and found. In this case, you can enter security information and save it as a profile, or you can create a profile manually. To see what APs are nearby, select the Profile Management tab in ADU (see Figure 16-19), and then click the **Scan** button.

To connect to an AP in the scan list, select it and click **Activate**. A Profile Management window appears. Its three tabs—General, Security, and Advanced—allow any special AP settings to be entered into the profile and saved. The General tab sets up options such as the name of the connection and general parameters. The Security tab is where you

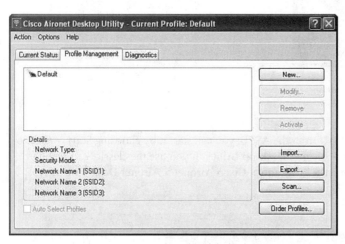

Figure 16-19   *Profile Management in ADU*

configure the security settings for the WLAN, and the Advanced tab is where you configure advanced settings such as power levels and wireless modes for the WLAN.

Manually Creating a Profile

To create a profile, you can click the **New** button on the Profile Management tab of ADU. A Profile Management window appears with three tabs—General, Security, and Advanced. Give the profile a name and enter up to three SSIDs. After you have named the profile, select the Security tab. From the Security tab, you can choose from WPA/WPA2/CCKM, WPA/WPA2 Passphrase, 802.1x, Pre-Shared Key (Static WEP), or None, as shown in Figure 16-20.

Unsecure Profiles

By leaving the default option (None), you would essentially be creating an unsecure profile. This is not a recommended practice.

802.1x Profiles

You can also create an 802.1x profile, but understand that it is authentication only. This means that your data is not encrypted. It does, however, use a central authentication server. To talk to this server, you must choose between Lightweight Extensible Authentication Protocol (LEAP), which is the default, Extensible Authentication Protocol Transport Layer Security (EAP-TLS), Protected Extensible Authentication Protocol (PEAP),

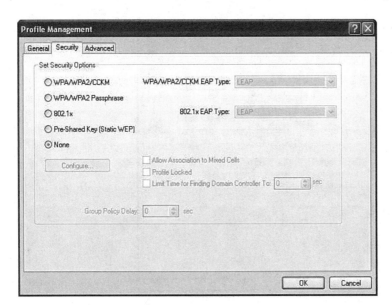

Figure 16-20 *Security Options*

Extensible Authentication Protocol Generic Token Card (EAP-GTC), PEAP with EAP Microsoft Challenge Handshake Authentication Protocol Version 2 (EAP MS-CHAP V2), EAP Flexible Authentication via Secure Tunneling (EAP-FAST), and Host-Based EAP.

Click **Configure** to add a temporary username and password or to use a saved username and password.

WPA/WPA2/CCKM Profiles

WPA/WPA2/CCKM lets you select an EAP type, as shown in Figure 16-21.

This method performs encryption with a rotated encryption key and authentication with 802.1x.

WPA/WPA2 Passphrase Profiles

You can choose to use WPA/WPA2 Passphrase. This method uses encryption with a rotated encryption key and a common authentication key, called a passphrase. To configure the passphrase, click the **Configure** button and enter the ASCII or hexadecimal passphrase, as shown in Figure 16-22.

By following the preceding steps, you can create any of the available profiles. Table 16-3 compares the different security options.

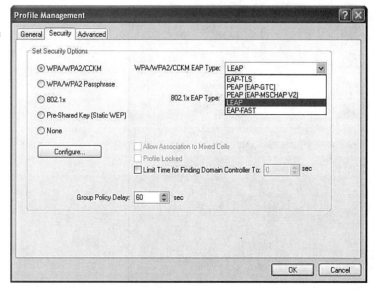

Figure 16-21 *WPA/WPA2/CCKM*

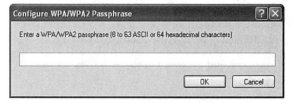

Figure 16-22 *WPA/WPA2 Passphrase*

Table 16-3 *Security Options Comparison*

Security Option	Encryption	Authentication
WPA/WPA2/CCKM	Rotating key	EAP methods (see 802.1x)
WPA/WPA2 Passphrase	Rotating key	8 to 63 ASCII or 64 hexadecimal passphrase
802.1x	None	EAP-TLS, PEAP, LEAP, EAP-FAST, host-based EAP (host-based is not an option for WPA/WPA2/CCKM)
Pre-Shared Key (Static WEP)	Weak	None
None	None	None

Managing Profiles

You can manage profiles from the Profile Management tab in ADU. You can create a new profile, as already discussed. You can also modify existing profiles. You can import existing profiles by clicking the **Import** button and browsing to the location of a .prf file. You can also export profiles and move them to other computers. To do this, simply click the **Export** button, define a name for the profile (if you want to change it), and browse to where you want to save it. This might be an external USB drive or even the desktop. As soon as you have the location where you want it, click **Save**.

As discussed previously in this chapter, you can scan for nearby networks. You also can change the order of your profiles by clicking the **Order Profiles** button and moving them up or down in the order you want.

Using Diagnostic Tools

After you have created a profile and it is in use, there are likely times when you will need to troubleshoot connectivity issues. If this is the case, a number of tools are available in the ADU. The following sections discuss options that you may find helpful in troubleshooting.

Adapter Information

Begin by looking at the adapter information shown in Figure 16-23. You find this information by clicking the **Adapter Information** button on the Diagnostics tab in the ADU interface. Two important pieces of information that you get from this output are the driver version and the card's MAC address. These can be used in troubleshooting. On the controller, you can enable a debug based on the client's MAC address to get specific information for that client. Also, the driver information can be used to look for bug reports in Cisco's support center.

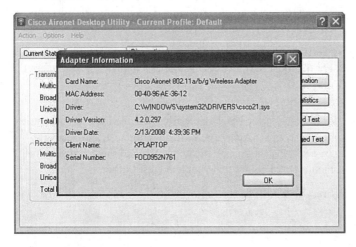

Figure 16-23 *Adapter Information*

Advanced Statistics

The Advanced Statistics button gives information about the frames transmitted and received, as demonstrated in the sample output shown in Figure 16-24.

Advanced Statistics

Transmit			
Frames Transmitted OK:	445	RTS Frames:	49
Frames Retried:	65	CTS Frames:	8
Frames Dropped:	0	No CTS Frames:	41
No ACK Frames:	284	Retried RTS Frames:	41
ACK Frames:	445	Retried Data Frames:	65

Receive			
Beacons Received:	245	Authentication Time-Out:	0
Frames Received OK:	739	Authentication Rejects:	0
Frames Received with Errors:	63	Association Time-Out:	0
CRC Errors:	903	Association Rejects:	0
Encryption Errors:	0	Standard MIC OK:	0
Duplicate Frames:	2	Standard MIC Errors:	0
AP Mismatches:	0	CKIP MIC OK:	0
Data Rate Mismatches:	0	CKIP MIC Errors:	0

OK

Figure 16-24 *Advanced Statistics*

If you note a high count of retries, it is probably due to a high number of collisions. High numbers of RTS/CTS (provided in relation to the total number of frames transmitted) may indicate frame errors and bad link quality. You can use the Advanced Statistics to troubleshoot authentication issues as well as encryption problems. Authentication Rejects indicates that you are in fact talking to a server that is rejecting the authentication attempt. Authentication Time-Outs could indicate a connectivity issue with the AAA server.

Choose **Options > Display Settings** to change how the values appear, selecting either relative or cumulative values. For the most part, the default values (cumulative) are preferred.

Test Utility

An additional set of tools for troubleshooting includes a driver installation test, card insertion test, card enable test, radio test, association test, authentication test, and network test. You access these tests by selecting the **Action** menu in ADU and then choosing the **Client Managed Test** link. Figure 16-25 shows the completed test output.

To begin the test, click the **Start Test** button. The following tests are run sequentially:

1. Driver Installation test
2. Card Insertion test
3. Card Enable test
4. Radio test

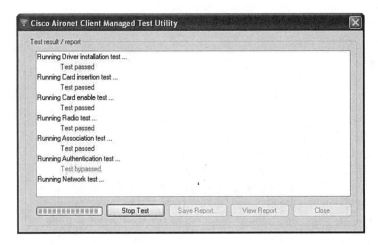

Figure 16-25 *Client Managed Tests*

  5. Association test

  6. Authentication test

  7. Network test

The information gained from each of these tests can quickly point you in the direction of the issue. If the driver is not installed, this could indicate that it was inadvertently removed. If the driver is not installed, the ADU does not work. If the card is not inserted, it does not work. If the card has been disabled, it does not work. Also, if the radio is disabled, it does not function.

The Association test indicates if open association is functioning; the same goes for the Authentication test. These two tests can indicate where the connection is failing.

Finally, the Network test helps determine if the issue lies with the network rather than the wireless connection. Sometimes you get associated but still can't send if the network itself is having issues. Troubleshooting is discussed more in Chapter 20, "Troubleshooting Wireless Networks."

Site Survey Utility

The Site Survey Utility (CSSU) is the optional software set that you select using a checkbox during installation. This can be a handy tool for troubleshooting. As stated earlier in this chapter, it doesn't link to a map; however, it can give you handy information about the signal you are receiving.

To access the CSSU, choose **Start > All Programs > Cisco Aironet > Aironet Site Survey Utility**.

The utility dynamically represents your connection to the wireless network. As shown in Figure 16-26, it displays the AP MAC address, channel, signal strength (RSSI), noise level,

SNR, and speed of the connection. The connection quality is represented with the following colors:

- Green = excellent

- Yellow = good

- Orange = fair

- Red = poor

By default, the output is displayed in dB or dBm, as shown in Figure 16-26. You can change this to display as a percentage, as shown in Figure 16-27. The decibels display unit is recommended because it gives a much more precise view. You can also maximize the window and increase the **Time in seconds** value (up to 60 seconds) to view more information over a greater period of time. Also, Cisco's TAC asks for the information in dB or dBm.

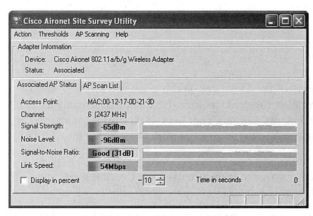

Figure 16-26 *CSSU Display in dBm*

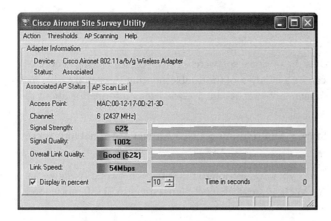

Figure 16-27 *CSSU Display in Percentage*

You can configure the CSSU with thresholds that can trigger an alert or logging. You set thresholds by choosing **Thresholds > Configure Thresholds.**

The AP scan list reports all the APs that your adapter detects. You don't use this information to associate with an AP. Instead, you would use this information to determine the characteristics of the APS around you. Again, this is a troubleshooting utility, so it can help you determine sources of interference.

Another neat feature of the CSSU is the ability to enable a proximity beeper. It beeps more quickly as you get a better signal. To enable it, choose **Action > enable proximity beeper.**

You can change what triggers the proximity beeper under the **Action** drop-down menu by selecting **Options.**

The ACAU

The Aironet Configuration Administration Utility (ACAU) is designed to help automate the process of deploying the ADU and client profiles. The main interface, shown in Figure 16-28, has four configuration families under the Global Settings tab. These configuration families include Setup Settings, User Settings, Profile Settings, and ASTU Settings. If you double-click these, they expand, allowing you to use radio buttons to control the capabilities of the ADU and how it is installed.

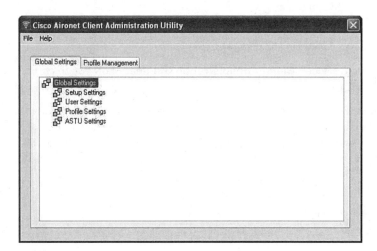

Key
Topic

Figure 16-28 *ACAU Interface*

On the Profile Management tab, you can add up to 16 new profiles, modify them, remove them, import and export them, and reorder them. The profile configuration looks very similar to that of the ADU profile configuration. The difference between the two is that these profiles are not considered local. When you have the Global Settings arranged the way you want them, and then the Profiles set up the way you want them, choose **File >**

Save As. The default name for the file is CiscoAdminConfig.dat. Save this file and then place it in the same directory as the ADU installation executable. When the ADU install executes, it looks for a .dat file and uses it for its setup, automatically bringing in the profiles you configured in the ACAU.

The Cisco Secure Services Client

The Cisco Secure Services Client (SSC) is client software that provides 802.1x (Layer 2) user and device authentication for access to both wired and wireless networks. The SSC does not need a Cisco wireless card to operate the software. It's really an alternative to the WZC, with some major benefits. From the wired network side, it provides 802.1x capabilities for user and device authentication, which is more extensive than the standard wired LAN connection. On the wireless side, it provides all the security capabilities needed for enterprise class connectivity. The interface is very simple, making it easy for customers and guests to connect to a Cisco network.

The CSSC provides a unified wired and wireless supplicant that can provide services across many different vendor network cards as well as provide the ability to centralize management of client adapters. The CSSC also provides a tremendous amount of flexibility for authenticating to the wired and wireless network, not restricted to simply open, WEP, PEAP, and EAP-TLS. One other key advantage is the client's capability to disable the wired interface automatically if the wireless adapter associates to a wireless network. This ensures that IP address space is used efficiently and split tunneling is avoided.

There are three pieces of SSC software:

- **The SSC itself:** Client software that provides 802.1x user and device authentication for access to both wired and wireless networks.

- **The Cisco Secure Services Client Administration Utilities:** Allow you to create complex profiles.

- **The Cisco Secure Services Client Log Packager:** Connects system information for support. An administrator would create profiles using the Cisco Secure Services Client Administration Utilities, which then generate an XML file that can be deployed network-wide to all the client machines.

Licensing

There are three SSC license types:

- 90-day trial

- Nonexpiring wired only

- Nonexpiring wired and wireless

The 90-day trial offers full features for wired and wireless. When the 90 days are up, you must purchase a license, or it will automatically convert to a nonexpiring wired only. This is a limited feature set. If you purchase a license for the wireless features, you will have the full set of capabilities for both wired and wireless enabled.

Installation

The installation process uses a Microsoft Installer (MSI), which you can obtain from
Cisco.com. You must have administrative rights on the computer you are installing on.
Figure 16-29 shows the install wizard of the SSC.

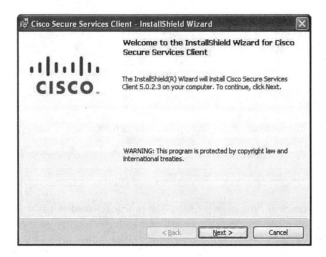

Figure 16-29 *Installing the SSC*

Configuring Profiles

The SSC runs as a service and appears in the systray whether or not it is connected. You
can hover the mouse cursor over the systray icons to find out the status. Right-click to access the menu. Any existing profiles or networks that have been detected appear, as
shown in Figure 16-30.

Figure 16-30 *Right-Click Menu of SSC*

SSC Groups

In the SSC, connections are logically grouped with a name. You can create your own groups, as well as move connections between groups. You can also add basic wireless connections (PSK-based), but not secured or wired connections.

Note: The user interface of SSC talks about profiles. For administrators, the Secure Services Client Administration Utility (SSCAU) talks about networks.

A network can be a wireless connection, a home type like the ones created with the SSC, or an enterprise type, based on individual authentication instead of a common passphrase. A network can also be a wired connection.

The significance of this is that all profiles are networks, but at the same time a network can be more than just an SSC profile.

SSCAU Overview

With the SSCAU, you can create new configuration profiles. The profile is saved as an XML file and then can be deployed to devices in the network. You also can modify existing configuration profiles. Furthermore, you can process existing configuration profiles to verify the profile's policy logic, encrypt the credentials, and sign the file.

There are two ways to deploy the generated profiles:

■ To existing clients

■ Via an MSI that will also install the SSC

The Cisco Client Extension Program

The Cisco Client Extension (CCX) program is no-cost licensing of technology for use in WLAN adapters and devices. This allows for the following:

■ Independent testing to ensure interoperability with the Cisco infrastructure's latest innovation

■ Marketing of compliant products by Cisco and product suppliers under the "Cisco Compatible" brand

CCX for Wi-Fi RFID Tags allows vendors to have a common set of features. More information on the Cisco Compatible Extension Program can be found at http://www.cisco.com/web/partners/pr46/pr147/partners_pgm_concept_home.html.

Exam Preparation Tasks

Review All the Key Topics

Review the most important topics from this chapter, denoted with the Key Topic icon. Table 16-4 lists these key topics and the page number where each one can be found.

Table 16-4 *Key Topics for Chapter 16*

Key Topic Item	Description	Page Number
Table 16-2	Comparison between WZC and ADU	307
Figure 16-12	Three options when installing the ADU	308
Figure 16-19	Profile management in ADU	312
Figure 16-20	Security options	313
Figure 16-21	WPA/WPA2/CCKM	314
Figure 16-22	WPA/WPA2 passphrase	314
Table 16-3	Security options comparison	314
Figure 16-24	Advanced statistics	316
Figure 16-26	CSSU display in dBm	318
Figure 16-28	ACAU interface	319

Complete the Tables and Lists from Memory

Print a copy of Appendix B, "Memory Tables" (found on the CD) or at least the section for this chapter, and complete the tables and lists from memory. Appendix C, "Memory Tables Answer Key," also on the CD, includes completed tables and lists to check your work.

Definition of Key Terms

Define the following key terms from this chapter, and check your answers in the glossary:

WZC, SSID, AirPort Extreme, NetworkManager, iwconfig, WPA, WPA2, ADU, ACAU, 802.1x, CSSU, CSSC, SSCAU, CCX

Cisco Published 640-721 IUWNE Exam Topics Covered in This Part

Describe WLAN fundamentals

- Describe 802.11 authentication and encryption methods (Open, Shared, 802.1X, EAP, TKIP, AES)

Implement basic WLAN Security

- Describe the general framework of wireless security and security components (authentication, encryption, MFP, IPS)

- Describe and configure authentication methods (Guest, PSK, 802.1X, WPA/WPA2 with EAP-TLS, EAP-FAST, PEAP, LEAP)

- Describe and configure encryption methods (WPA/WPA2 with TKIP, AES)

- Describe and configure the different sources of authentication (PSK, EAP-local or -external, Radius)

Operate basic WCS

- Describe key features of WCS and Navigator (versions and licensing)

- Install/upgrade WCS and configure basic administration parameters (ports, O/S version, strong passwords, service vs. application)

- Configure controllers and APs (using the Configuration tab not templates)

- Configure and use maps in the WCS (add campus, building, floor, maps, position AP)

- Use the WCS monitor tab and alarm summary to verify the WLAN operations

Conduct basic WLAN Maintenance and Troubleshooting

- Identify basic WLAN troubleshooting methods for controllers, access points, and clients methodologies

- Describe basic RF deployment considerations related to site survey design of data or VoWLAN applications, Common RF interference sources such as devices, building material, AP location Basic RF site survey design related to channel reuse, signal strength, cell overlap

- Describe the use of WLC show, debug and logging

- Describe the use of the WCS client troubleshooting tool

- Transfer WLC config and O/S using maintenance tools and commands

- Describe and differentiate WLC WLAN management access methods (console port, CLI, telnet, ssh, http, https, wired versus wireless management)

Part III: WLAN Maintenance and Administration

This chapter covers the following subjects:

Threats to Wireless Networks: Discusses threats to wireless networks.

Simple Authentications: Looks at basic wireless security.

Centralized Authentication: Shows how centralized authentication works using various EAP methods.

Authentication and Encryption: Describes WPA and WPA2.

CHAPTER 17

Securing the Wireless Network

It's usually obvious that wireless networks can be less secure than wired networks. This calls for a great deal of thought when you deploy a wireless network. What security do you need? What security measures can you perform? What are the security capabilities of your equipment? Should you authenticate users when they access the network? Should you encrypt traffic over the wireless space? As you can see, there are many options to think about. But let's break this into small parts. First, who are your users? The answer will be different for networks that allow guest access versus those that don't. Second, how hidden do you need to make your users' traffic? Again, this answer will differ depending on the users. If you are offering guest access, encryption probably is not a big concern. If all or even a portion of your users are internal, encryption probably is a concern. In this chapter, you will learn about various methods of securing a wireless network. Some methods provide a way to identify the user. Others offer a way to hide user data. Still other methods do both.

You should take the "Do I Know This Already?" quiz first. If you score 80 percent or higher, you might want to skip to the section "Exam Preparation Tasks." If you score below 80 percent, you should review the entire chapter. Refer to Appendix A, "Answers to the 'Do I Know This Already?' Quizzes," to confirm your answers.

"Do I Know This Already?" Quiz

The "Do I Know This Already?" quiz helps you determine your level of knowledge of this chapter's topics before you begin. Table 17-1 details the major topics discussed in this chapter and their corresponding quiz questions.

Table 17-1 *"Do I Know This Already?" Section-to-Question Mapping*

Foundation Topics Section	Questions
Threats to Wireless Networks	1–4
Simple Authentications	5–7
Centralized Authentication	8–12
Authentication and Encryption	13–14

1. Threats to wireless networks include which of the following? (Choose all that apply.)

    a. Rogue APs

    b. Client misassociation

    c. Unauthorized port access

    d. Stateful inspection

2. Which of the following can be used to prevent misassociation attacks? (Choose all that apply.)

    a. Client MFP

    b. Spoofing

    c. Infrastructure MFP

    d. Rogue-AP containment

3. Client MFP allows clients to perform what function?

    a. Detect invalid clients

    b. Detect invalid APs

    c. Detect invalid controllers

    d. Detect invalid SSIDs

4. To perform Client MFP, what version of CCX is required?

    a. v1.x

    b. v2.x

    c. v5.x

    d. v6.x

5. WEP uses which of the following encryption algorithms?

    a. AES

    b. TKIP

    c. MD5

    d. RC4

6. What key size should be selected to perform 128-bit WEP with a Windows client?

    a. 40-bit

    b. 104-bit

    c. 128-bit

    d. 192-bit

7. How many bits does an IV add to a WEP key?

    a.   24 bits

    b.   48 bits

    c.   188 bits

    d.   8 bits

8. In centralized authentication, a certificate is used based on information from a trusted third party. What information is *not* included in a certificate?

    a.   Username

    b.   Public key

    c.   Validity dates

    d.   Session keys

9. Central authentication uses which IEEE specification?

    a.   802.11a

    b.   802.1q

    c.   802.1d

    d.   802.1x

10. Which protocol is used for the authentication server?

    a.   RADIUS

    b.   Active Directory

    c.   LDAP

    d.   TACACS+

11. Which EAP method uses certificates on both the client and the server?

    a.   EAP-FAST

    b.   EAP-MD5

    c.   EAP-TLS

    d.   PEAP

12. Which EAP method uses a PAC instead of certificates?

    a.   EAP-FAST

    b.   EAP-MD5

    c.   EAP-TLS

    d.   PEAP

13. Which protocol requires the use of TKIP, but can optionally use AES?

    a. WPA2

    b. GTK

    c. MS-CHAPv2

    d. WPA

14. Which protocol mandates that AES must be supported but not TKIP?

    a. WPA2

    b. GTK

    c. MS-CHAPv2

    d. WPA

Foundation Topics

Threats to Wireless Networks

Throughout this book, you have learned about the many threats to wireless networks. If you really wanted to simplify the threats, you could think of it like this: You want legitimate clients to connect to legitimate APs and access corporate resources. Some attacks are formed from the perspective of an AP trying to gain information from clients. Other attacks are from the perspective of getting illegitimate clients onto the network to use corporate resources at no charge or to actually steal data or cause harm to the network.

These threats include the following:

- Ad hoc networks

- Rogue APs

- Client misassociation

- Wireless attacks

Ad Hoc Networks

An ad hoc network is a wireless network formed between two clients. The security risk involves bypassing corporate security policies. An attacker could form an ad hoc network with a trusted client, steal information, and even use it as a means of attacking the corporate network by bridging to the secure wired LAN.

Rogue APs

A rogue AP is not part of the corporate infrastructure. It could be an AP that's been brought in from home or an AP that's in a neighboring network. A rogue AP is not always bad. It could be an AP that's part of the corporate domain yet still operating in autonomous mode. Part of an administrator's job is determining if the AP is supposed to be there. Fortunately, you don't have to do all the work yourself. A few functions of the AP's software can detect rogue APs and even indicate if they are on your network.

Something to consider when looking for rogue APs is what happens to clients that can connect to those rogue APs. If a client connects to a rogue AP, it should be considered a rogue client. The reason is that rogue APs typically are installed with default configurations, meaning that any client that connects bypasses any corporate security policy. So you do not know if the client is a corporate user or an attacker.

Client Misassociation

When a client connects to an AP, operating system utilities normally allow the client to save the SSID. In the future, when that SSID is seen again, the client can create a connection automatically. There is a possibility that clients will be unaware of the connection. If the SSID is being spoofed, the client could connect to a potentially unsafe network. Consider the following scenario. An attacker learns the SSID of your corporate network. Using this information, he sends beacons advertising your SSID. A wireless station in the range of the rogue AP connects to the AP. The AP allows connectivity to the Internet but is not actually on your corporate wired network. Using tools that are easily available on the Internet, another client connected to the same rogue AP attacks the misassociated client and steals valuable corporate data.

This scenario employs multiple attack methods. It uses a method known as *management frame spoofing* as well as an active attack against a misassociated client. So how can this be prevented? The answer begins with a function called Management Frame Protection.

Management Frame Protection

One method of Management Frame Protection (MFP) is *Infrastructure MFP*. With this method, each management frame includes a cryptographic hash called a Message Integrity Check (MIC). The MIC is added to each frame before the Frame Check Sequence (FCS). When this is enabled, each WLAN has a unique key sent to each radio on the AP. Then, the AP sends management frames, and the network knows that this AP is in protection mode. If the frame were altered, or if someone spoofs the SSID of the WLAN and doesn't have the unique key, it invalidates the message. This causes other APs that hear the invalid frames to report them to the controller.

The other method of MFP is called *Client MFP*. If the client is running Cisco Compatible Extensions (CCX) 5 or better, it can talk to the AP and find out what the MIC is. Then it can verify management frames it hears in addition to the APs that provide this function. The major benefit of this mode is the extension of detection. In Figure 17-1, the APs are in the middle of the network, and clients are on the outside. The clients can detect the AP called BAD_AP that is generating invalid frames, even though BAD_AP is out of the range of the APs that are in protection mode.

With MFP version 1, all local mode APs are protectors. They digitally sign all frames they send. Any other AP, or the same local mode AP, for that matter, could be a validator.

With MFP version 2, clients must run the Cisco Secure Services Client (CSSC) or a client that is capable of CCXv5. This enables the client to hear the rogue and report illegitimate frames. You don't have to worry about your client associating with the rogue AP, because it drops invalid frames.

Client MFP has another benefit. Suppose a neighboring AP performed containment as a denial-of-service (DoS) method against your network because it's a deauthentication frame that is used for containment. The client would see that the containment frame doesn't have the MIC and would ignore the deauthentication frame. This would keep people from containing your network as a form of DoS attack.

To enable MFP, choose **SECURITY > Wireless Protection Policies > AP Authentication/MFP**. You view MFP with the Wireless LAN Controller by choosing **SECURITY > Wireless Protection Policies > Management Frame Protection**, as shown in Figure 17-2.

Wireless Attacks

It's not news that networks in general are constantly bombarded with attacks. Some of these attacks are unique to wireless networks, as is the case with management frame spoofing. With management frame spoofing, a rogue AP advertises an SSID known to the

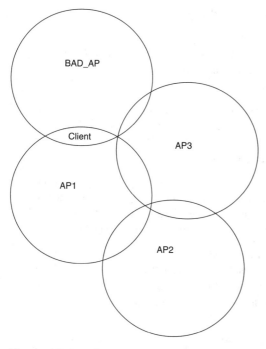

Figure 17-1   *Client MFP in Action*

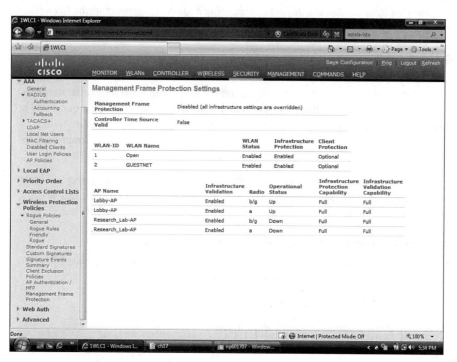

Figure 17-2   *Configuring MFP*

client in an attempt to get the client to connect to the rogue AP. Other attacks apply to both wired and wireless networks:

■ **Reconnaissance attacks:** An attacker attempts to gain information about your network. Initially, the method of mitigating recon attacks involved hiding the SSID by not broadcasting it in beacon frames.

■ **Access attacks:** An attacker tries to gain access to data, devices, and/or the network. Initially the method of preventing access to the network involved MAC-based authentication as well as static Wired Equivalent Privacy (WEP). The problem with WEP today is that the keys can be broken in 4 to 7 minutes.

■ **Denial-of-service (DoS) attacks:** An attacker attempts to keep legitimate users from gaining services they require. Today, the use of intrusion detection system/intrusion prevention system (IDS/IPS) sensors on the wired network can help mitigate these attacks. You also can use MFP to prevent containment DoS attacks.

The mitigation methods used to prevent attacks mentioned here are not very advanced and are considered weak by today's standards. However, you might be wondering how these methods work. What alternatives are there if these mitigation methods are weak? What other options exist? The following sections discuss these aspects.

Simple Authentications

One of the first items to discuss involves users being allowed to connect to the network. Many methods of authenticating users exist, as discussed in the following sections.

Open Authentication

Open authentication is a simple as it gets. The term "authentication" is used loosely here because it's part of the association process, although there really isn't any authentication per se. Figure 17-3 illustrates this process, picking up after the initial probe request and response. The client sends an authentication request to the AP, and the AP replies with a confirmation and registers the client. Then the association request and confirmation take place. WEP is taking place in the figure. Everything is "open."

This type of open authentication is commonly used at hot spots. This is a Layer 2 security method. You choose the **None** option under the **Security** tab while configuring a WLAN, as shown in Figure 17-4.

Preshared Key Authentication with Wired Equivalent Privacy

With static WEP you don't authenticate users; you simply verify that they have a key. You don't know who they are, just that they know your key.

The process of WEP authentication is as follows:

Key Topic

Step 1.   A client sends an authentication request.

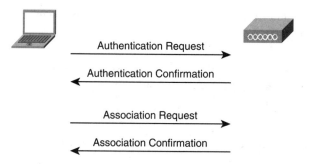

Figure 17-3 *Open Authentication*

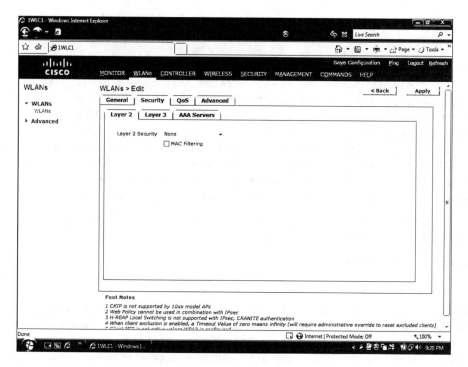

Figure 17-4 *Configuring Open Authentication*

Step 2.   The AP sends an authentication response containing clear-text challenge text.

Step 3.   The client uses the text received to respond with an encrypted authentication packet. The encryption is done using one of the client's static WEP keys.

Step 4.   The AP compares what it received to the AP's own copy of what the response should look like based on the static WEP keys. If they match, the client moves on to association.

This method is actually considered weaker than open authentication, because an attacker could capture the challenge text and then the reply that is encrypted. Because the challenge is clear text, the attacker could easily use it to derive the static WEP key used to create the encrypted packet. They simply use the challenge along with the response to re-create the key. WEP uses the RC4 encryption method.

> **Note:**   It is important to note that although the WEP key is used to encrypt the challenge text, it is used only for authentication purposes. WEP is not used to hide, protect, or encrypt any user data after it is associated with the AP.

Some other interesting caveats about using WEP involve the key size. Three key lengths can be used:

- 40-bit key

- 104-bit key

- 128-bit key

I can't stress enough that these values are not what you think. You see, the key is combined with an *initialization vector (IV)*, which is 24 bits. An IV is a block of bits that is used to produce a unique encryption key. When you add the 24-bit IV to the 40-bit key, the resulting size is 64 bits. When you combine the 24-bit IV with the 104-bit key, the result is 128 bits. When you combine the 24-bit IV with the 128-bit key, the result is 152 bits. This has been a sore spot for Windows users, because the maximum key size supported with the native client is 128 bits. If you choose the key size of 128 bits, when combined with the IV, it yields a 152-bit key, and the authentication fails. Therefore, you should use a 104-bit key for Windows, or it won't work.

After it is authenticated, the client is issued an association identifier and can begin sending data. From this point on, WEP is used to encrypt traffic.

Figure 17-5 shows the configuration of static WEP.

MAC Address Filtering

MAC address filtering is a simple form of authenticating the device that is connecting. MAC address filtering entails defining MAC addresses that are allowed to connect. Although this is an easy way to ensure that people with the defined MAC address are allowed on the network, the danger is that MAC addresses can easily be spoofed. This method is not recommended. To configure MAC address filtering, you simply check a box on the Static WEP configuration page, as shown in Figure 17-6.

Centralized Authentication

Centralized authentication is the act of verifying the user's identity by a means other than the local definitions. In this scenario, a Public Key Infrastructure (PKI) is usually in place. PKI uses digital certificates that are cryptographically signed by a trusted third party. The trusted third party is called a Certificate Authority (CA). If you have ever been pulled over for speeding, you have most likely experienced a PKI infrastructure, so to speak. When the trooper comes to your window, he usually wants to see your driver's license. The trooper did not issue that identification to you; rather, a third party that the trooper trusts did. The concept is the same in the PKI world.

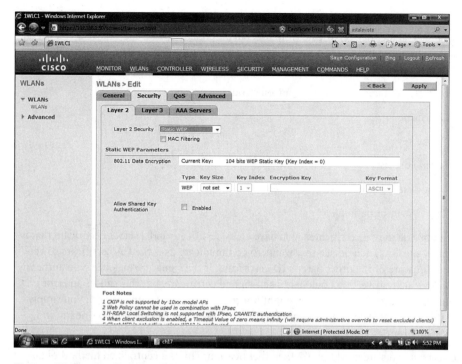

Figure 17-5   *Configuring WEP*

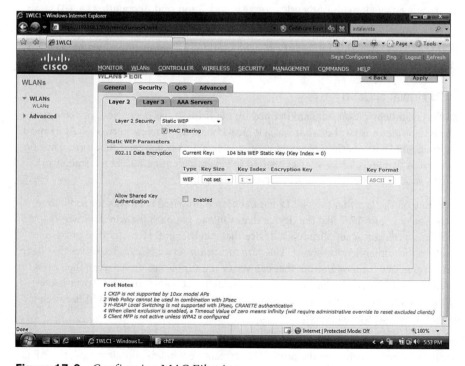

Figure 17-6   *Configuring MAC Filtering*

So to get this to work, the first thing you need is a certificate that identifies who you are. You can get an identity certificate from folks like VeriSign or Entrust. You also can get an identity certificate from a CA server that you have set up. It just so happens that Microsoft Server has a CA that you can manage on your own.

A certificate contains the following information:

■ Username

■ Public key

■ Serial number

■ Valid dates

■ The CA's information

When you use digital certificates, you have a CA certificate and a server certificate that is issued by the CA. Each device that wants to communicate uses the CA certificate to verify the signature of the other party's ID certificate. If the signature matches, you authenticate. As an alternative, you could use a self-signed certificate, but this causes an error on the initial connection, because you might not trust the issuer. It's an easy fix; you simply view the certificate and add it to your certificate store. Then accept the certificate, and you are in business.

These certificates are used for 802.1x authentication. This is a centralized method of authentication that can use various Extensible Authentication Protocol (EAP) methods of authenticating a client to an Authentication, Authorization, and Accounting (AAA) server.

Certificates can also be used for LWAPP control data, but it's not the same certificate that is used for 802.1x. Additionally, certificates are used for web authentication, but again, it's not the same certificate as the one used by 802.1x.

802.1x and How It Is Used

802.1x is an authentication standard defined by the IEEE. It has been used for some time on the wired side of networks, so it was a logical choice for wireless networks. At its most basic level, 802.1x is a method of opening or closing a port based on a condition. The condition here is that an AAA server has verified the client's identity. 802.1x is a framework that uses various EAP methods in its communication.

Elaborating on the fact that the 802.1x has been used on wired networks for some time, you can see in Figure 17-7 that the device that wants to get onto the wired network is called the *supplicant*. A supplicant is a device that can use an EAP method to prove its identity to the authentication server. The *authentication server* is an AAA server that has a list of users in one form or another that can verify the supplicant. In between the two is the *authenticator*, which in this network is the switch. The switch uses EAP over LAN (EAPoL) between the supplicant and itself and then RADIUS (with EAP in it) between itself and the authentication server.

Now swap out that switch with an AP, as shown in Figure 17-8, and you have the same scenario as before, except that the protocol between the wireless supplicant and the AP is EAPoWLAN.

Figure 17-7   *Wired EAP*

Figure 17-8   *Wireless EAP*

Until the user authenticates, no frames can be passed to the wireless network.

The process of authentication involves the following steps:

Step 1.   The client associates with an AP.

Step 2.   The client receives an authentication request.

Step 3.   The client returns an authentication response.

Step 4.   The client receives an association request.

Step 5.   The client sends an association response.

After open authentication takes place, either side can begin the 802.1x process. During this time, the "port" is still blocked for user traffic, and the following happens:

1. The supplicant sends credentials to the authenticator.
2. The AP sends the authentication information to the server via a RADIUS packet.
3. RADIUS traffic returns from the authentication server and is forwarded by the AP back to the client.
4. During the communication, the client and the AP derive unique session keys.
5. The RADIUS server sends an access success message back to the client, along with a session WEP key.
6. The AP keeps the session WEP key to use between the AP and itself.
7. The AP sends the session WEP key, along with a broadcast/multicast WEP key, to the client.
8. The client and AP can use the session WEP keys to encrypt traffic.

The AP keeps the session WEP key so that it can encrypt traffic between the AP and the client protecting the connection. The AP sends a broadcast/multicast WEP key because each session WEP key is unique. So if the client were to use it to encrypt a broadcast or multicast, only the AP would be able to see it.

The EAP Process

Now that you understand the 802.1x process, it's good to remind you at this point that 802.1x is nothing more than a framework. 802.1x does not define how the user credentials are sent, only that they are sent.

EAP controls how the user credentials are sent under the premise that no matter what EAP method you use, they will all use the same process. It involves the following steps:

Step 1. The client requests access.

Step 2. The client is queried for its identity.

Step 3. The client provides the proof.

Step 4. The client gets an answer from the server.

Figure 17-9 illustrates the EAP process.

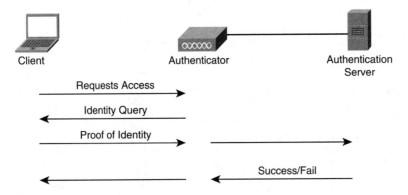

Figure 17-9 *EAP Process*

The Authentication Server

The authentication server can be external and can be a Cisco Secure Access Control Server (ACS) or perhaps a Free RADIUS server. It really doesn't matter what you use as an authentication server, as long as it supports the EAP method configured on the controller and used by the supplicant and AP. You need to define the location of the RADIUS server in the interface of the controller. To do this, choose **SECURITY > RADIUS Authentication Servers > New**, as shown in Figure 17-10.

When you define the RADIUS server, enter the server's IP address and the shared secret (a predefined passphrase that you determine and configure) to be used with the server. Then click **Next**.

You see the server listed on the RADIUS Authentication Servers page, as shown in Figure 17-11.

The next step in enabling the 802.1x authentication is to define the EAP method, as described in the following sections.

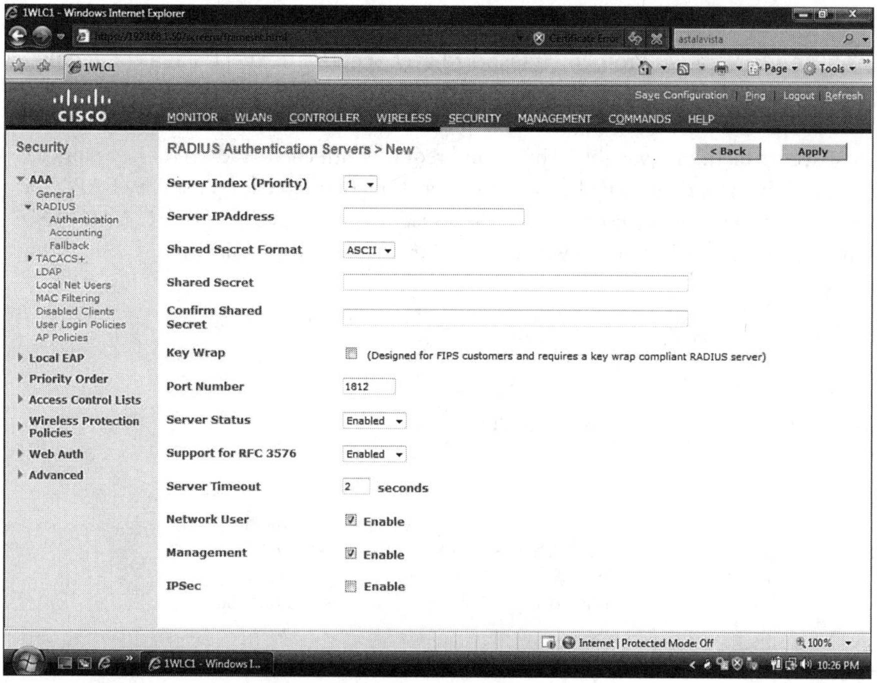

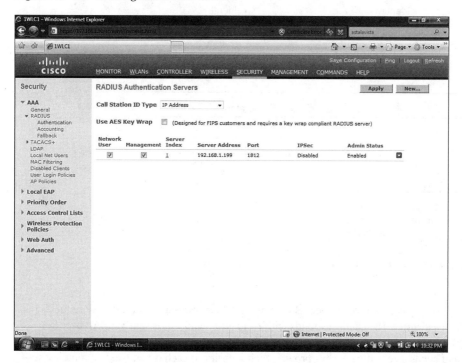

Figure 17-10   *Adding a RADIUS Server*

Figure 17-11   *List of RADIUS Servers*

EAP-TLS

Extensible Authentication Protocol-Transport Layer Security (EAP-TLS) is a commonly used EAP method for wireless networks. In EAP-TLS, a certificate must be installed on both the authentication server and the supplicant. For this reason, it is considered one of the most secure methods available. This would require both client and server key pairs to be generated first and then signed by a CA server. The communication used by EAP-TLS is similar to SSL encryption; however, TLS is considered the successor to SSL. EAP-TLS establishes an encrypted tunnel in which a user certificate is sent inside it.

Note: EAP-TLS is defined in RFC 2716.

Figure 17-12 shows the process of EAP-TLS.

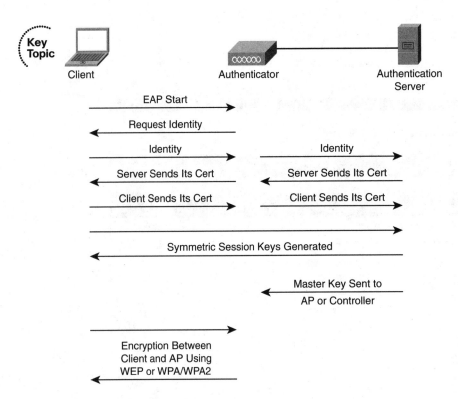

Figure 17-12 *EAP-TLS Process*

As you can see, the process begins with an EAP Start message. Next, the AP requests the client's identity. The client responds with its identity, and this is sent via EAP over RADIUS to the authentication server. The authentication server sends its certificate, and the client sends its certificate, thus proving their identity to each other. Next, symmetric session keys (also called master session keys) are created. The authentication server sends the master session key to the AP or controller to be used for either WEP or WPA/WPA2 encryption between the AP and the client. You configure EAP-TLS in the same location as WEP by selecting 802.1x in the Layer 2 security drop-down (refer to Figure 17-6). The EAP method is between the server and the client, so the AP really doesn't care. You simply select 802.1x.

EAP-FAST

Extensible Authentication Protocol-Flexible Authentication via Secure Tunnel (EAP-FAST) is a protocol that was developed by Cisco Systems. Its purpose was to address weaknesses in Lightweight Extensible Authentication Protocol (LEAP), another Cisco-developed EAP method. The concept of EAP-FAST is similar to EAP-TLS; however, EAP-FAST does not use PKI. Instead, EAP-FAST uses a strong shared secret key called a Protected Access Credential (PAC) that is unique on every client.

EAP-FAST negotiation happens in two phases, phase 1 and phase 2, but it is during phase 0 that the PAC is provisioned. After the PAC has been distributed, phase 1 can happen. In phase 1, the AAA server and the client establish a TLS tunnel after authenticating each other using the PAC. After phase 1 establishes the secure TLS tunnel, phase 2 authenticates the user to the AAA server using another EAP method, with either passwords or generic token cards.

Figure 17-13 shows the details of EAP-FAST negotiation using generic token card authentication for the user.

EAP-FAST negotiation occurs as follows:

1. The client sends an EAPoL start to the AP.
2. The AP, which is the authenticator, sends back an EAP Identity Request Message.
3. The client sends a response to the authenticator. It is forwarded to the authentication server (AAA server) in a RADIUS packet.
4. The authentication server sends an EAP-FAST start message that includes an Authority ID (A-ID).
5. The client sends a PAC based on the received A-ID. The client also sends a *PAC Opaque* reply to the server. The PAC Opaque is a variable-length field that can be interpreted only by the authentication server. The PAC Opaque is used to validate the client's credentials.
6. The authentication server decrypts the PAC Opaque using a master key that was used to derive the PAC key. The authentication server sends an EAP-TLS Server hello along with the *Cipher Trust Protocol Set*.
7. If the keys match, a TLS tunnel is established, with the client sending a confirmation.
8. The server sends an identity request inside the TLS tunnel using a protocol such as Extensible Authentication Protocol-Generic Token Card (EAP-GTC).
9. The client sends an authentication response.
10. The server sends a Pass or Fail message. The Pass message indicates that the client is successfully authenticated.

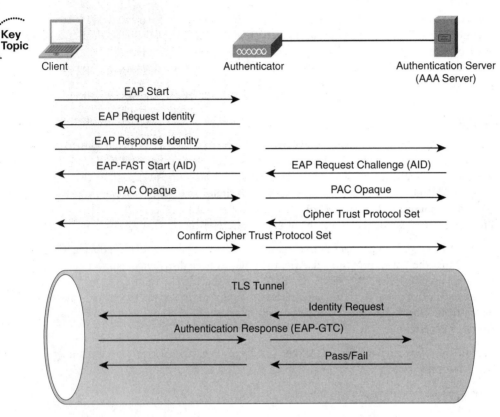

Figure 17-13 *EAP-FAST Negotiation*

PEAP

As you've seen with EAP-TLS, certificates are required on both the client and the server. With EAP-FAST, no certificates are required; rather, the PAC takes care of things. With Protected EAP (PEAP), only a server-side certificate is used. This server-side certificate is used to create a tunnel, and then the real authentication takes place inside. The PEAP method was jointly developed by Cisco Systems, Microsoft, and RSA. PEAP uses Microsoft Challenge Handshake Authentication Protocol version 2 (MS-CHAPv2) or Generic Token Card (GTC) to authenticate the user inside an encrypted tunnel.

To authenticate to Microsoft Windows Active Directory, you would use MS-CHAPv2.

Figure 17-14 shows the PEAP process.

In PEAP, the following occurs:

1. The client sends an EAPoL start, and the authenticator returns a request for identity. This is similar to the other EAP methods.

2. The client returns its identity, and it is forwarded to the AAA server.

3. The AAA server sends a server certificate and begins establishing a TLS tunnel.

4. The client returns a premaster secret.

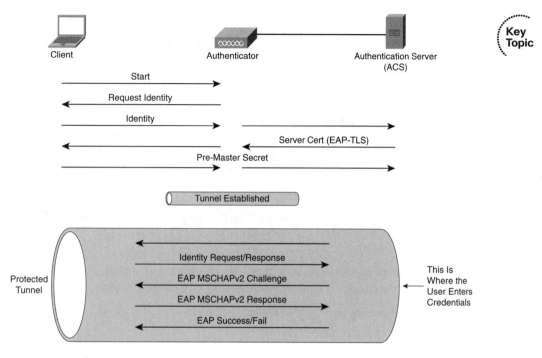

Figure 17-14 *PEAP Process*

5. The tunnel is established.

6. The AAA server sends an identity request to the client.

7. The AAA client sends an identity response.

8. The server sends an EAP-MS-CHAPv2 challenge.

9. The client enters credentials into a popup, and that is sent back as an EAP-MS-CHAPv2 response.

10. The server returns a pass or fail. If it's a pass, the user can send traffic.

LEAP

Lightweight Extensible Authentication Protocol (LEAP) gets honorable mention here mainly because it is a Cisco EAP method that is still seen in 802.11b networks. LEAP is vulnerable to an offline exploit, and you should avoid it if possible. LEAP uses a proprietary algorithm to create the initial session key.

Authentication and Encryption

Now that you understand some of the methods used to authenticate users, it's time to explore some encryption methods. The beginning of this chapter discussed WEP. The problem with WEP is that it can be broken easily. Therefore, other methods have been established in an effort to provide more strength in encryption. In the following sections, you will learn about Wi-Fi Protected Access (WPA) and Wi-Fi Protected Access 2 (WPA2).

WPA Overview

WPA was introduced in 2003 by the Wi-Fi Alliance as a replacement for WEP. WPA uses Temporal Key Integrity Protocol (TKIP) to automatically change the keys. TKIP still uses RC4; it just improves how it's done. This is a major improvement over static WEP. WPA can optionally support Advanced Encryption Standard (AES), but it's not mandatory. WPA is based on 802.11i draft version 3. WEP uses RC4 encryption, which is very weak. The better alternative was to use AES encryption, but that would have required an equipment upgrade. To avoid an equipment upgrade, WPA was developed to use TKIP and a larger IV than WEP. This would make it more difficult to guess the keys while not requiring new hardware. Instead, you could simply perform a firmware upgrade in most cases.

WPA offers two authentication modes:

- **Enterprise mode:** Enterprise mode WPA requires an authentication server. RADIUS is used for authentication and key distribution, and TKIP is used with the option of AES available as well.

- **Personal mode:** Personal mode WPA uses preshared keys, making it the weaker option, but the one that is most likely to be seen in a home environment.

Figure 17-15 shows the process of WPA authentication.

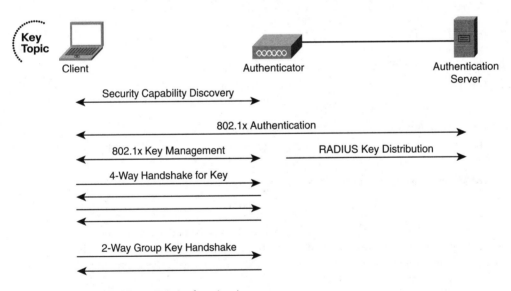

Figure 17-15 *WPA Authentication*

At the beginning of negotiations, the client and AP must agree on security capabilities. After the two agree on the same level of security, the 802.1x process starts. This is the standard 802.1x process, as outlined previously. After successful 802.1x authentication, the authentication server derives a master key and sends it to the AP. The same key is derived from the client. Now the client and the AP have the same *Pairwise Master Key (PMK)*, which will last for the duration of the session.

Next, a four-way handshake occurs (see Figure 17-16), in which the client and authenticator communicate and a new key called a *Pairwise Transient Key (PTK)* is derived. This key confirms the PMK between the two, establishes a temporal key to be used for message encryption, authenticates the negotiated parameters, and creates keying material for the next phase, called the two-way group key handshake.

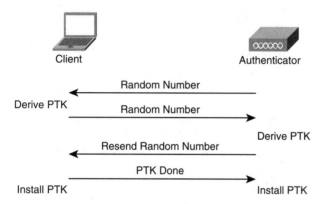

Figure 17-16   *WPA Four-Way Handshake*

When the two-way group key handshake occurs, the client and authenticator negotiate the *Group Transient Key (GTK)*, which is used to decrypt broadcast and multicast transmissions.

In Figure 17-16, you can see that the AP first generates a random number and sends it to the client. The client then uses a common passphrase along with this random number to derive a key that is used to encrypt data to the AP. The client then sends its own random number to the AP, along with a *Message Integrity Code (MIC)*, which is used to ensure that the data is not tampered with. The AP generates a key used to encrypt unicast traffic to the client. To validate, the AP sends the random number again, encrypted using the derived key. A final message is sent, indicating that the temporal key (TK) is in place on both sides.

The two-way handshake that exchanges the group key involves the generation of a *Group Master Key (GMK)*, usually by way of a random number. After the AP generates the GMK, it generates a group random number. This is used to generate a *Group Temporal Key (GTK)*. The GTK provides a group key and a MIC. This key changes when it times out or when a client leaves the network.

To configure WPA, set the Layer 2 security method by choosing **WLANs > Edit**. Then select the Security tab and choose **WPA+WPA2** from the drop-down, as shown in Figure 17-17. To allow WPA, ensure that TKIP is selected. This is automatically done for you when you select the **WPA Policy** check box.

WPA2 Overview

WPA2, as its name implies, is the second attempt at WPA. WPA was not designed to be just a firmware upgrade; instead, you might need new hardware to use it. The reason for

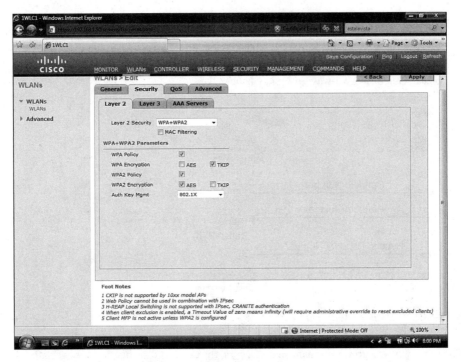

Figure 17-17   *Configuring a WPA Policy*

the more-capable hardware requirement is that WPA2 was designed to use AES encryption. WPA was designed based on the 802.11a draft but was released in 2003, whereas 802.11i was released in 2004. By the time 802.11i was ratified, it had added more support for 802.1x methods and AES/CCMP for encryption. The Wi-Fi Alliance then released WPA2 to be compatible with the 802.11i standard.

It was mentioned that AES is used for encryption. Advanced Encryption Standard-Cipher Block Chaining Message Authentication Code Protocol (AES/CCMP) still uses the IV and MIC, but the IV increases after each block of cipher.

Comparing WPA to WPA2, you can see that

- WPA mandates TKIP, and AES is optional.

- WPA2 mandates AES and doesn't allow TKIP.

- WPA allows AES in its general form.

- WPA2 only allows the AES/CCMP variant.

- With WPA2, key management allows keys to be cached to allow for faster connections.

To configure WPA2, from the **WLANs > Edit** page, select the **WPA2 Policy** option. Then select either **AES** and **TKIP** or just **AES** as the default value, as shown in Figure 17-18. Then select the authentication key management option; the choices are 802.1x, CCKM, PSK, and 802.1X+CCKM.

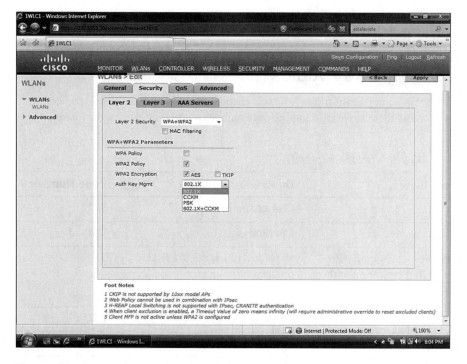

Figure 17-18   *Configuring a WPA2 Policy*

Exam Preparation Tasks

Review All the Key Topics

Review the most important topics from this chapter, denoted with the Key Topic icon. Table 17-2 lists these key topics and the page number where each one can be found.

Table 17-2   *Key Topics for Chapter 17*

Key Topic Item	Description	Page Number
Figure 17-1	Client MFP in action	333
Figure 17-2	Configuring MFP	333
Paragraph from the section "Pre-shared Key Authentication with Wired Equivalent Privacy"	Steps describing the WEP process	334
Figure 17-5	Configuring WEP	337
Figure 17-12	The EAP-TLS process	342
Figure 17-13	The EAP-FAST process	344
Figure 17-14	The PEAP process	345
Figure 17-15	The WPA process	346
Figure 17-18	Configuring WPA2 policy	349

Complete the Tables and Lists from Memory

Print a copy of Appendix B, "Memory Tables" (found on the CD) or at least the section for this chapter, and complete the tables and lists from memory. Appendix C, "Memory Tables Answer Key," also on the CD, includes completed tables and lists to check your work.

Definition of Key Terms

Define the following key terms from this chapter, and check your answers in the glossary:

Management Frame Protection (MFP), Infrastructure MFP, Message Integrity Check (MIC), Frame Check Sequence (FCS), Client MFP, Initialization Vector (IV), supplicant, authentication server, authenticator, Extensible Authentication Protocol (EAP), Extensible Authentication Protocol-Transport Layer Security (EAP-TLS), Extensible Authentication Protocol-Flexible Authentication via Secure Tunnel (EAP-FAST), Protected EAP (PEAP), Microsoft Challenge Handshake Authentication Protocol version 2 (MS-CHAPv2), Generic Token Card (GTC), Lightweight Extensible Authentication Protocol (LEAP), Wi-Fi Protected Access (WPA), Wi-Fi Protected Access 2 (WPA2), Temporal Key Integrity Protocol (TKIP), Advanced Encryption Standard (AES), Pairwise Master Key (PMK), Pairwise Transient Key (PTK), Group Transient Key (GTK), Message Integrity Code (MIC), Group Master Key (GMK), Group Temporal Key (GTK)

References

Infrastructure Management Frame Protection (MFP) with WLC and LAP Configuration Example: http://tinyurl.com/5zbe2o

This chapter covers the following subjects:

Introduction to the WCS: An introduction to the Wireless Control System (WCS).

Installing and Configuring the WCS: An overview of how to install the WCS, log in, and perform basic tasks.

Administration Options in the WCS: A discussion of various options involved in administering the WCS.

Adding Controllers to the WCS: How to add controllers to the WCS and manage them in the WCS.

Maps and APs in the WCS: Viewing and working with maps and APs in the WCS interface.

Monitoring with the WCS: Using WCS to monitor the wireless network.

CHAPTER 18

Enterprise Wireless Management with the WCS and the Location Appliance

In the management scheme of things, the design of the Cisco Unified Wireless Networking (CUWN) enables management of lightweight access points (AP) via a controller. This central form of management allows for consistent policy among all devices from, the controller. However, when a company scales beyond the scope of management with a single controller, the Wireless Control System (WCS) steps in. In addition, the Cisco Wireless Location Appliance can help keep things under control. This chapter is a brief overview of the WCS, how it is installed, how it is managed, how it manages controllers, and how it manages APs.

You should do the "Do I Know This Already?" quiz first. If you score 80 percent or higher, you might want to skip to the section "Exam Preparation Tasks." If you score below 80 percent, you should spend the time reviewing the entire chapter. Refer to Appendix A, "Answers to the 'Do I Know This Already?' Quizzes," to confirm your answers.

"Do I Know This Already?" Quiz

The "Do I Know This Already?" quiz helps you determine your level of knowledge of this chapter's topics before you begin. Table 18-1 details the major topics discussed in this chapter and their corresponding quiz questions.

Table 18-1 *"Do I Know This Already?" Section-to-Question Mapping*

Foundation Topics Section	Questions
Introduction to the WCS	1–3
Installing and Configuring the WCS	4–8
Administration Options in the WCS	9–12
Adding Controllers to the WCS	13–19
Maps and APs in the WCS	20–25
Monitoring with the WCS	26

1. What are three benefits of the WCS?

    a.   Wireless planning

    b.   Wireless design

    c.   Wireless management

    d.   Wireless RF tagging

2. The Cisco Wireless Location Appliance can provide real-time tracking of up to how many clients?

    a.   1500

    b.   2500

    c.   3500

    d.   5000

3. WCS licensing can enable up to how many supported APs?

    a.   5500

    b.   2500

    c.   2000

    d.   5000

4. On which two operating systems can the WCS be installed?

    a.   Windows Server

    b.   Red Hat Linux

    c.   Solaris 9

    d.   Ubuntu Linux

5. Following recommended hardware requirements, you will be able to support how many controllers in a single WCS?

    a.   500

    b.   2500

    c.   5000

    d.   250

6. What type of web server does the WCS run?

    a.   IIS

    b.   Apache

    c.   Sun Java Web Server

    d.   A Proprietary Web Service

7. What action can you take if IIS is running on the server where you are installing the WCS? (Choose all that apply.)

    a. Nothing; they do not conflict.

    b. Just change to the port where you used the WCS.

    c. Disable the IIS Server.

    d. Uninstall IIS.

8. What is the first action when accessing the WCS for the first time?

    a. Enter a license key.

    b. Add a controller.

    c. Save the configuration.

    d. Archive the server.

9. What is the first page you come to upon logging into the WCS?

    a. WCS Start

    b. WCS Home

    c. WCS Summary

    d. WCS Monitor

10. The Client tab provides information about which of the following? (Choose all that apply.)

    a. Top APs by client count

    b. Clients that are associated

    c. Security configuration of the AP

    d. Rogue AP counts

11. Which menu allows you to add users of the WCS system?

    a. Administration > AAA

    b. Configuration > Users

    c. Authentication > AAA

    d. Monitor > AAA

12. Logging options can be changed in which menu?

    a. Administration > SNMP > Logging

    b. Administration > Syslog

    c. Configuration > Logging

    d. Administration > Logging

13. You can add a controller to the WCS through which menu?

   a.   Configure > Controllers

   b.   Controllers > Add

   c.   Administration > Controllers > Add

   d.   Management > Controllers

14. What are the two ways to add a controller to the WCS?

   a.   Use a CSV file

   b.   Use SNMP discovery

   c.   Use Device Info

   d.   Import from CiscoWorks DCR

15. APs are configured from which menu?

   a.   Configure > APs

   b.   Configure > Controllers > APs

   c.   Configure > Access Points

   d.   You do not configure APs, just controllers. APs automatically synch their configuration with that of the controller.

16. How can you verify that the configuration on the controller is consistent with the information in the WCS database?

   a.   Use the Compare tool.

   b.   Use the Sync button.

   c.   Use the Audit Config page.

   d.   You cannot verify this information.

17. You want to configure general settings for a controller once and then apply those settings to all the controllers in your network. This is a perfect opportunity to use what feature of the WCS?

   a.   Copy/Paste

   b.   TFTP

   c.   FTP

   d.   Templates

18. You can use the WCS templates only for controllers. True or False?

   a.   True

   b.   False

19. Auto provisioning relies on which DHCP option?

   a.   66

   b.   53

   c. 20

   d. 150

20. Which of the following WCS menu options enables you to find a list of maps?

   a. **Monitor > Maps**

   b. **Configure > Maps**

   c. **Administration > Maps**

   d. **WCS > Maps**

21. The WCS maps consist of which of the following elements? (Choose all that apply.)

   a. Campus

   b. Building

   c. Floor

   d. Room

22. When you create a map, what important characteristics should you add? (Choose all that apply.)

   a. Obstructions

   b. Walls

   c. Doors

   d. People

23. By adding certain elements to the WCS maps, you aid which process?

   a. RF modeling

   b. RF surveys

   c. Site survey

   d. Imaging

24. Planning mode lets you generate heat maps of theoretical APs placed on your map. The heat map then lets you generate what?

   a. A new map

   b. A summary of equipment used

   c. A proposal of equipment required and deployment locations

   d. Log messages in the WCS

25. Which of the following is a valuable tool accessible from the Monitoring menu?

   a. Site survey

   b. Reset controllers

   c. Client troubleshooting

   d. SNMP traps

Foundation Topics

Introduction to the WCS

The Cisco WCS is a browser-based software application that offers the capability to manage multiple controller deployments through a single interface. Benefits of the WCS include the following:

- Wireless planning

- Wireless design

- Wireless management

The WCS is based on a licensing system. Licensing enables single-server deployments of up to 500 APs to 2500 APs being supported. You can even obtain a 30-day demo license that is fully functional for up to 10 APs.

The Cisco Wireless Location Appliance, accessed via the WCS interface, provides mapping of clients and assistance in enforcing security policies. Using the Location Appliance with the WCS can provide much information to network administrators, including the following:

- Real-time tracking of up to 2500 clients

- Historical information

- RF fingerprinting

- A single point of management

Models include the WCS Base and the WCS Base plus location. You can find detailed product information at http://www.cisco.com/go/wireless.

Installing and Configuring the WCS

The WCS has two deployment possibilities: a Linux-based deployment and a Windows-based deployment. In large deployments, Cisco recommends the Linux-based deployment.

The requirements for the Linux-based deployment are as follows:

- Red Hat Enterprise ES/AS Linux Release 4 (the Cisco WCS can be installed as a service under Linux)

- Intel Xeon Quad 3.15-GHz CPU

- 8-GB RAM, 200-GB HD

Meeting these requirements allows for support of 3000 APs and 250 controllers and really cannot be stressed enough. If you want to be happy with the deployment, make sure you meet the Cisco recommendations on the machine.

In a smaller deployment, you can use the following:

- Windows Server 2003

- Pentium 4/3.06 GHz (minimum) 2-GB RAM, 30-GB hard drive

- Intel dual-core 3.2-GHz CPU 4-GB RAM, 80-GB hard drive

With a deployment using these specifications, you can support up to 2000 APs and 150 controllers.

Other considerations should include the protocol traffic that the WCS uses to manage the controllers. This means you need to consider the transit path and any firewalls, IPS devices, and IOS firewall routers.

In addition to those ports, you need to allow HTTP port 80 and port 443, because the WCS runs an Apache web server, along with port 21 for FTP, port 69 for TFTP, and 162 for Simple Network Management Protocol (SNMP) traps.

The Java portion of the WCS uses ports 1299, 8009, 8456, and 8457. Table 18-2 provides a recap of these ports.

Table 18-2   *WCS Ports*

Port	Use
HTTP: Configurable during install (80 by default)	Web access
HTTPS: Configurable during install (443 by default)	Secure web access
1315	Java
1299	Java
6789	—
8009	Java
8456	Java
8005	—
69	TFTP
21	FTP
162	SNMP traps
8457	—

The easiest way to obtain the WCS software is from Cisco.com, which means you need to log in to the Cisco website with valid credentials (a CCO account) and then download the software. Cisco provides a Quick Install guide for both Linux and Windows versions. The

CCNA Wireless exam focuses primarily on the Windows version, but you should view both versions on the Cisco website to see the entire process.

For a Windows-based installation, you simply launch the executable file and follow the prompts. The install takes you through several pages that relate to the web server, passwords, directories, and so on. The WCS first checks to see if it is already installed. If the WCS is already installed, and depending on the version, you might be able to upgrade rather than do a fresh install. It is always a good idea to back up the WCS prior to an upgrade. If you are performing a fresh install, you need to do the following:

- Accept the license agreement.

- Verify the server ports.

- Enter the passwords.

- Choose the FTP and TFTP root folders.

- Select whether this is a multihomed server (two NIC cards).

- Define the Install folder.

- Verify with a summary page.

- Wait for the installation to complete.

You can access the WCS locally by going to **Start > All Programs >** and then selecting the WCS group. The WCS is installed as a service, and the service should automatically start. You might encounter problems if the WCS and IIS are installed on the same machine, because both would try to secure port 80. To combat this issue, either make sure IIS is not installed prior to installing the WCS or shut down Internet Information Service (IIS). Open a web browser and browse to the IP address of the WCS server. Use the passwords that you defined during the setup process. After you are logged in, you see the main page of the WCS, called WCS Home. As Figure 18-1 illustrates, the WCS home page includes numerous tabs as well as some items that are commonly used for monitoring.

The first thing you want to do after the install and upon the first login is to add a license key to the WCS. The license key should be available in digital format. You need to select **Help > Licensing** and then browse to and upload the key. You cannot add controllers until you do this.

Administration Options in the WCS

In the WCS interface, you have tabs or horizontal menus across the top that access various configuration elements, including these:

- Monitor

- Reports

- Administration

Each of these menus cascade to drop-down submenus that you can access.

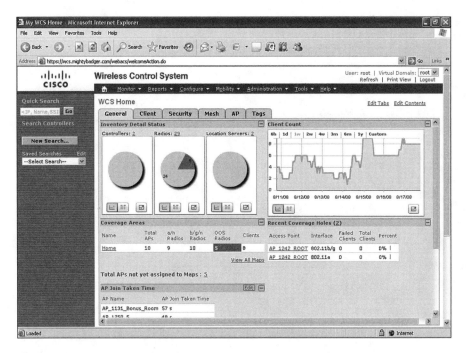

Figure 18-1   *The WCS Interface*

When you log in, the page you see is called the WCS Home, which has four primary tabs that we will discuss out of the six seen in Figure 18-2:

■ **General:** Provides information about the inventory, the coverage, and the client count

■ **Client:** Provides information about the top APs by client count, clients that are associated, and other information related to clients

■ **Security:** Includes information about rogue APs, alarms, and attacks

■ **Mesh:** Provides information about the signal-to-noise ratio (SNR) of the backhaul link and the node hop count

Figure 18-2 shows these tabs on the WCS home page.

The Administration drop-down menu provides access to control over the various background tasks that the WCS performs. This includes the logging settings, the system settings, and user preferences.

The Administration drop-down menu also enables configuration of AAA. To access AAA settings, go to **Administration > AAA**. Add users by going to **Administration > AAA > Users > Add Users**. To configure groups, go to **Administration > AAA > Groups**. To see a list of who is logging into the WCS, go to **Administration > AAA > Users > Audit Trail**. To change the WCS logging options, go to **Administration > Logging**.

Because the WCS tracks wireless networks, the volume of information can get overwhelming, and space can become an issue. To configure aggregation settings, go to

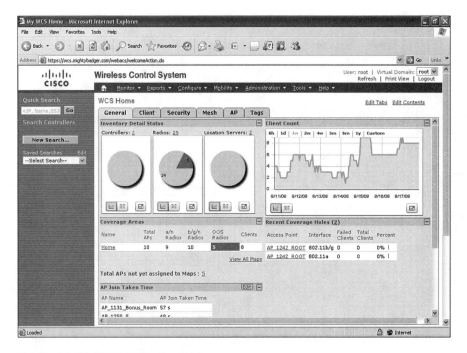

Figure 18-2 *WCS Home Page Tabs*

Administration > Settings > Data Management. You can also configure the WCS to send email to a user when an event is triggered. To configure the email preferences, go to **Administration > Settings > Mail Server.**

Adding Controllers to the WCS

To add controllers to the WCS, use the Configure tab. From there, you cannot only add controllers, but you can configure APs. You can also create templates here that allow the deployment of common configurations among multiple devices. To add controllers, browse to **Configure > Controllers,** as shown in Figure 18-3.

The Configure Controllers page summarizes all the controllers in the WCS and allows you to add controllers. Using the **Select a command** drop-down (seen in Figure 18-3), select **Add Controller,** and then select **GO.** This takes you to the configuration page shown in Figure 18-4.

Notice that the Add Format Type is configured for **Device Info.** The other option is **File.** You use the **File** option if you want to bring in several devices from a CSV file. When you add a controller to the WCS using the **Device Info** option, you use SNMP. You need to enter the IP address of the device as well as the SNMP version, retries, timeout in seconds, and community string. Click **OK** to apply. After you have added the controller, you can configure it on an individual basis. This is good, but the power of using the WCS comes in using templates. This is the second way you can configure the controller. The next section, "Working with Templates," provides more information.

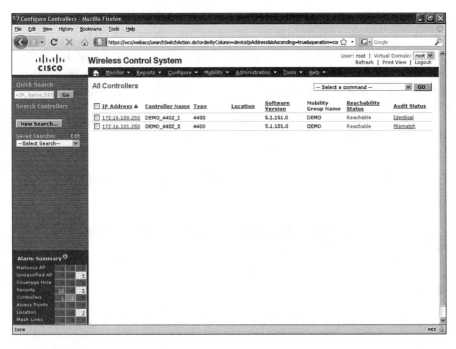

Figure 18-3   *Configuring Controllers in the WCS*

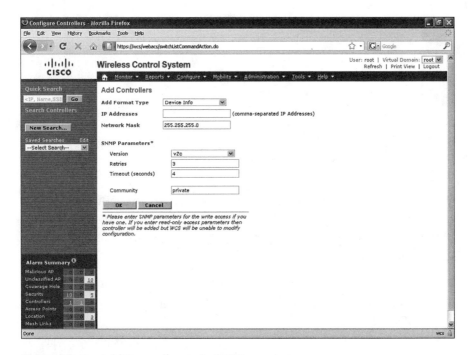

Figure 18-4   *Add Controller to the WCS*

You can also configure APs from the Configure menu by selecting **Configure > Access Points**. As with controllers, you can configure the APs using templates.

You now have the WCS, designed to manage many devices. It is important for the configuration on the controller to be the same as the configuration in the WCS database. To make sure all the configurations are consistent, you should run an audit regularly. You run an audit by going to **Configure > Controllers**. Select a controller and then, using the drop-down, choose **Audit Now** and click **Go**. Figure 18-5 shows the resulting Audit Report page.

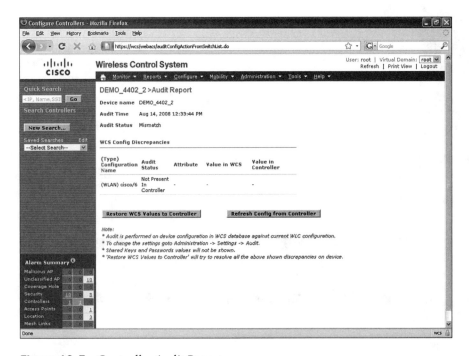

Figure 18-5 *Controller Audit Report*

Working with Templates

Everyone likes to save time, and templates can help with that. WCS templates allow administrators to save time by configuring them once and then applying them to more than one device.

To add templates, follow these steps:

Step 1. Choose **Configure > Controller Templates**.

Step 2. Choose **Add Template** from the **Select a command** drop-down menu and click **GO**.

Step 3.   Enter the template name.

Step 4.   Provide a description of the template.

Step 5.   Click **Save**.

You have several templates available. Some of the common ones include the following:

■ Configure WLAN Templates

■ Configure a RADIUS Authentication Template

■ Configure a Local EAP General Template

■ Configure a Local EAP Profile Template

■ Configure an EAP-FAST Template

■ Configure Access Control List Templates

■ Configure a TFTP Server Template

■ Configure a Telnet SSH Template

■ Configure a Local Management User Template

■ Configure Radio Templates

Again, the benefit is that you can save the template and apply it to multiple controllers.

You can apply a controller template to a controller by following these steps:

Step 1.   Go to **Configure > Controller Templates**.

Step 2.   Using the left sidebar menu, choose the category of templates to apply.

Step 3.   Select the box next to the template from the Template Name column that you want to apply to the controller. In Figure 18-6, you can see several WLAN templates.

Step 4.   Click the **Apply to Controllers** button. (You may need to scroll down to see it.)

Taking things a step further, you can create what is known as a configuration group. A *configuration group* is a way to apply configuration to many controllers as if they were one. The design here is for consistent configuration of a mobility group. A change in configuration changes all controllers in the group. You can also apply controller templates to a configuration group. You can access the configuration groups by selecting **Configure > Config Groups**. Figure 18-7 shows the Config Groups page. Notice that the group name **Config** is applied to one controller and 105 templates are applied to it. The 105 templates applied represent a great deal of manual configuration that was not necessary because templates were used.

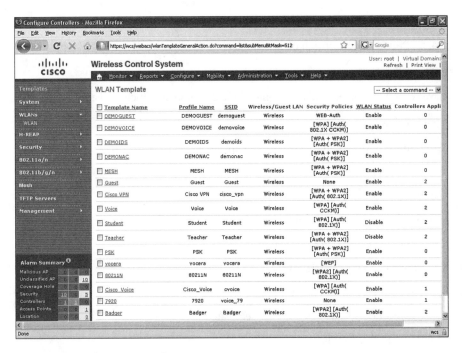

Figure 18-6 *WLAN Templates*

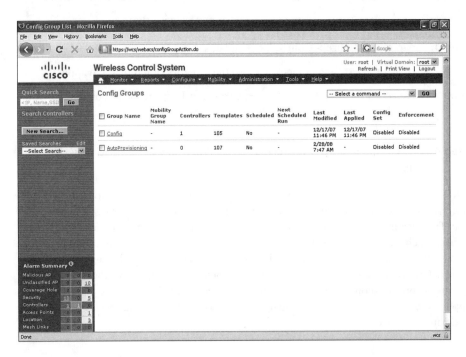

Figure 18-7 *Config Groups*

Auto Provisioning

You can configure auto provisioning to simplify deployments when you have many controllers. To set up auto provisioning, browse to **Configure > Auto Provisioning** to access the page shown in Figure 18-8.

Start by creating a filter to define which devices will be auto provisioned. To do this, use the **Select a command** drop-down and select **Add Filter**. Then click **Go**.

Next, select the desired filter properties.

After the filter is created, configure how the controller is detected on the network. You do this from the Auto Provisioning Setting page, the link for which you can find on the left side of the Auto Provisioning page. When you click on the Auto Provisioning Setting link, you are taken to the Auto Provisioning Primary Search Key Setting page, shown in Figure 18-9.

What happens when auto provisioning is configured? When a controller running version 5.0 or later is connected to the network for the first time, if it does not have a valid configuration, it first gets an IP address from a DHCP server. The DHCP server then returns through option 150, the IP address of a server with the configuration file of the controller. The server address is the WCS server.

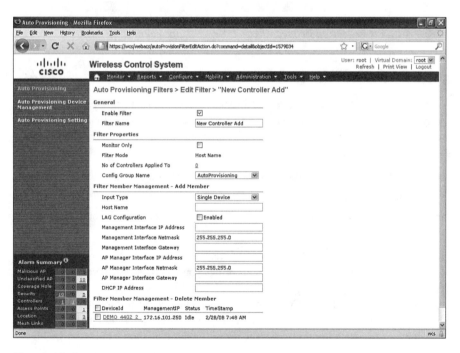

Figure 18-8   *Auto Provisioning*

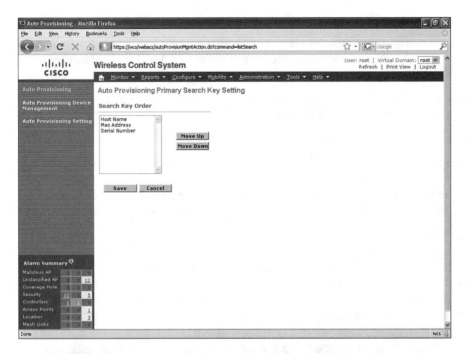

Figure 18-9   *Auto Provisioning Primary Search Key Setting Page*

Maps and APs in the WCS

Maps in the WCS are designed to give you a visual representation of the wireless network. Not only do maps help with monitoring after a deployment, but they help in the implementation and deployment process. You can use planning mode to determine how many APs you need in an area and where to place them.

To access the maps, browse to **Monitor > Maps**. From here you can see a list of maps, as illustrated in Figure 18-10.

You start by adding a building and then adding floors. After you have the building and floors, you add APs.

The maps begin in the context of a campus. To create a new campus, use the drop-down and select **New Campus**. Then click **GO**. This brings you to a page where you enter the campus name and contact and browse to the image file. After you have created the campus, it appears in the list of maps. You can now add a building to the campus; however, buildings do not necessarily need to be added to a campus. They can be standalone. To add a building, select **New Building** from the drop-down list, as shown in Figure 18-11.

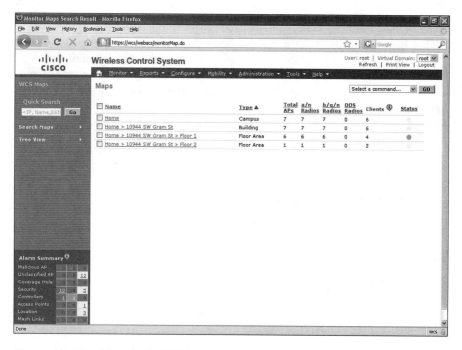

Figure 18-10 *Maps in the WCS*

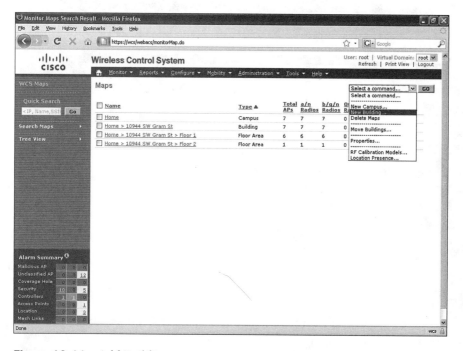

Figure 18-11 *Add Building*

Note: When adding buildings to a campus map, consider that the horizontal and vertical span should be larger than or the same size as any floors that you might add later. This can be a problem later when you build a map for the basement of a building and then work your way up to the first floor. If the first floor is larger than the basement, you cannot create the first floor. In fact, you cannot create any floor if it is larger than the basement. The WCS will not allow the larger level to then be added. You can find more information in the section "Adding and Using Maps" in the *Cisco Wireless Control System Configuration Guide, Release 4.1* at http://tinyurl.com/6f8apm.

When you add a building, you need to enter the following information:

- Building name

- Contact

- Number of floors

- Number of basements

- Horizontal and vertical dimensions in feet

Figure 18-12 shows a two-floor building.

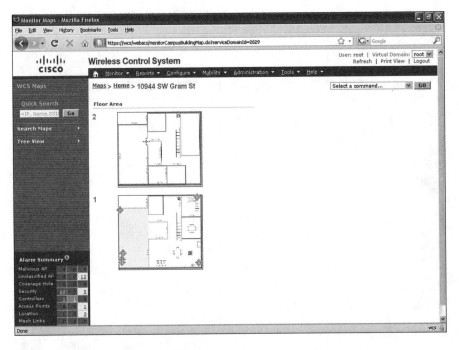

Figure 18-12   *Two Floor Building*

You can add a new floor area from the drop-down list. A floor area is what gives you a view of the environment and lets you add valuable information such as the floor type, the height, and the image file. Figure 18-13 shows this configuration page. The floor types include Cubes and Walled Offices, Drywall Office Only, and Outdoor Open Space. This is important because it assists the WCS with RF modeling.

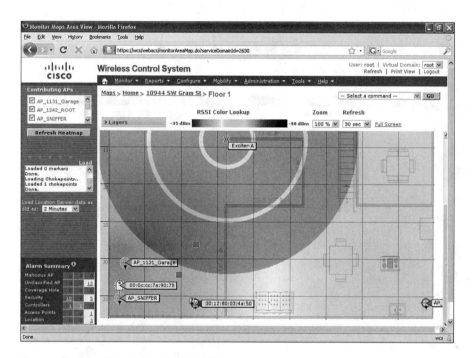

Key
Topic

Figure 18-13   *Heat Maps in the WCS*

After you have created the floor area, you can add APs to it. As you can tell, each element is layered on top of the prior (for example, Campus > Building > Floor Area > AP). It is really a logical method. Now when you add the AP, take care in your accuracy. Make sure you add them as the correct AP type, antenna configuration, location, and so on. When you place each AP on the floor area, RF prediction can take place. RF prediction generates heat maps and includes APs, clients, and rogues.

When you create the map as an administrator, you add obstructions, walls, windows, and doors. This information as well as the placement of the APs is used for RF prediction. The usage of the heat map created by RF prediction is to accurately display coverage. You can click on elements of the map to get more information. Figure 18-13 shows a sample of a heat map.

You might be wondering what the difference is between the RF prediction and the site survey. It is simple really. A *site survey* is a measurement of a certain point in time. That point in time is when you did the site survey. The values you determine from the site survey can change as influences to RF are added to the area where you performed the site survey.

In contrast, the WCS *RF prediction* uses information entered in the map and the map editor to predict how the AP will react in the environment. The WCS can base its information on what you tell it the environment *will* look like.

Using the drop-down list, you can access the map editor, as shown in Figure 18-14.

The map editor loads as shown in Figure 18-15.

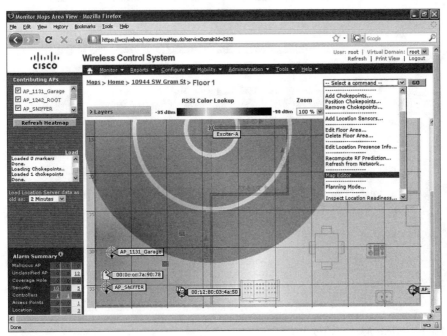

Figure 18-14 *Accessing the Map Editor*

Planning Mode

WCS Planning Mode lets you determine how many APs you need for a given coverage area. It places hypothetical APs on the map and lets you view the coverage area based on the placement of the hypothetical APs. From the **Monitor > Maps** page, use the **Select a command** drop-down to select Planning Mode. Click on **Add APs** to add the hypothetical APs to the map. When you do so, a blue dotted line appears on the map.

Note: If you do not want to use the square blue dotted area, you can select **perimeter** and then trace the exact area that you want to model off of.

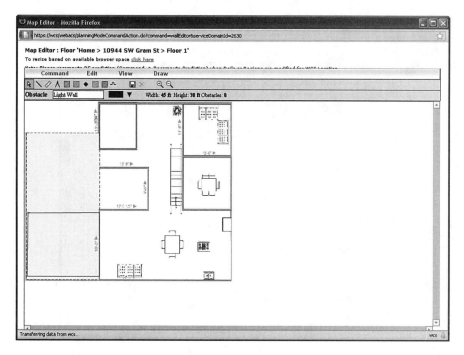

Figure 18-15 *Map Editor*

You move this around to determine the coverage area. You probably do not want it to trace the outer edge of the floor because it might place APs on the edge walls. This extends coverage beyond the outside of the building. If you want to extend the capabilities for radio frequency identification (RFID) and asset tracking, this might be something you want to do. It does help more accurately pinpoint the location of assets. However, if you are just talking about a WLAN used for employee or guest access, you would not want to extend the coverage to the outside.

In the menu on the left, select the AP type along with other criteria to be used and click the **Calculate** button. You can see this in Figure 18-16, where the AP type selected is a 1250 and "N" support is enabled.

You must also select at least one service type. The service type in the figure is Data/Coverage. Clicking the **Calculate** button shows that one AP is recommended, and clicking the **Apply** button displays a heat map identifying the coverage areas, as shown in Figure 18-17.

Now that you have an AP placed on the map and an accurate heat map depicting the coverage area, you can generate a proposal by clicking the **Generate Proposal** link at the top of the page in Figure 18-17. As Figure 18-18 shows, you first select the protocols you want to support and click **Generate**. This creates the proposal in Figure 18-19.

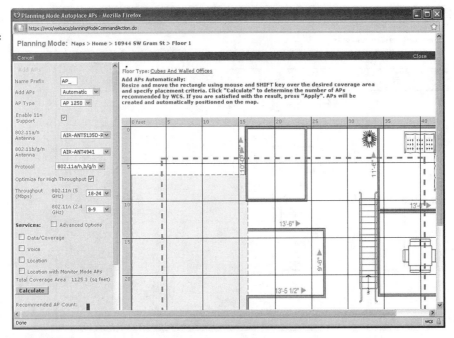

Figure 18-16   *Adding APs to the Map in Planning Mode*

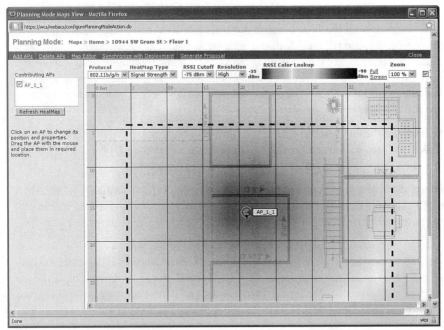

Figure 18-17   *Heat Map in Planning Mode*

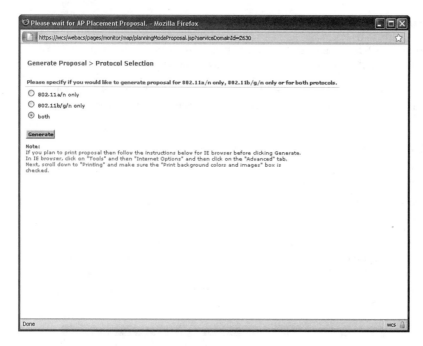

Figure 18-18 *Generating a Proposal*

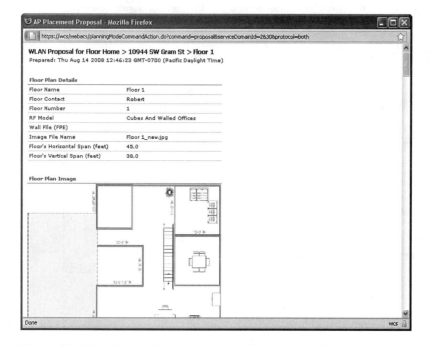

Figure 18-19 *Viewing the First Portion of the Proposal*

Monitoring with the WCS

You can use the WCS to monitor the wireless network. You can use the monitoring pages to view controllers, APs, and more. Figure 18-20 shows the Monitor menu.

An alarm summary, shown in Figure 18-20, is available and refreshes every 15 seconds. Fields that are clear indicate no alarms. Red is critical, orange is a major alarm, and yellow is a minor alarm.

By clicking an alarm, you can get more details on the situation.

Another valuable resource in the WCS is the capability to troubleshoot clients. Select **Monitor > Clients**. Next, place a Client MAC address into the **Client MacAddress** field and click the **Troubleshoot** button, as shown in Figure 18-21. This allows you to focus your troubleshooting efforts on the specified client.

You can also monitor rogue APs, security settings, and Radio Resource Management (RRM). In addition, you can monitor Location Appliances. The Location Appliance tightly integrates with the WCS and can provide real-time location tracking within about 30 feet. This is an added benefit when troubleshooting issues related to interference and rogues.

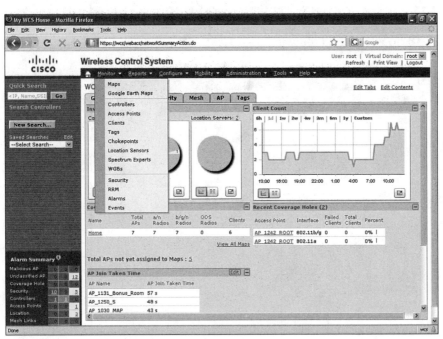

Figure 18-20   *Monitor Menu*

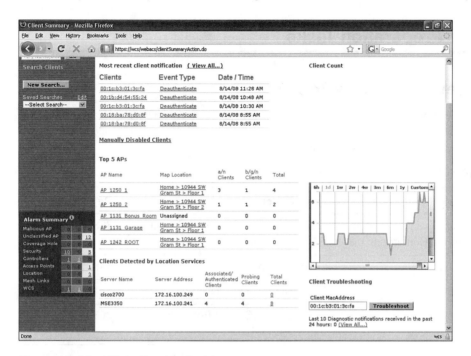

Figure 18-21 *Client Troubleshooting*

Exam Preparation Tasks

Review All the Key Topics

Review the most important topics from this chapter, noted with the Key Topics icon in the outer margin of the page. Table 18-3 lists a reference of these key topics and the page number where you can find each one.

Table 18-3 *Key Topics for Chapter 18*

Key Topic Item	Description	Page Number
Paragraph from the section "Installing and Configuring the WCS"	Lists detailing the requirements for install	358
Table 18-2	WCS ports	359
Figure 18-1	The WCS interface	361
Figure 18-3	Configuring controllers in the WCS	363
Paragraph from the section "Working with Templates"	Steps to create a template	364
Paragraph from the section "Working with Templates"	Steps to apply a template to a controller	365
Figure 18-10	Maps in the WCS	369
Figure 18-13	Heat maps in the WCS	371
Figure 18-14	Accessing the map editor	372
Figure 18-16	Adding APs to the map in Planning Mode	374
Figure 18-17	Heat map in Planning Mode	374
Figure 18-20	Monitor menu	376
Figure 18-21	Client troubleshooting	377

Complete the Tables and Lists from Memory

Print a copy of Appendix B, "Memory Tables" (found on the CD) or at least the section for this chapter, and complete the tables and lists from memory. Appendix C, "Memory Tables Answer Key," also on the CD, includes completed tables and lists to check your work.

Definition of Key Terms

Define the following key terms from this chapter, and check your answers in the Glossary:

WCS, Cisco Wireless Location Appliance, WCS templates, auto provisioning, site survey, WCS RF prediction, WCS Planning Mode

References

Chapter 10, "Using Templates," from the *Cisco Wireless Control System Configuration Guide, Release 5.0:* http://tinyurl.com/5ust42.

This chapter covers the following subjects:

Upgrading a Controller: Describes how to upgrade a Cisco controller.

Upgrading an AP: Looks at how an AP upgrades its image.

Upgrading WCS: Describes how to manage an upgrade of WCS.

Managing Configurations: Covers how to manage configuration files with the controller.

CHAPTER 19

Maintaining Wireless Networks

Part of the day-to-day management of a wireless network involves working with images of the controllers and access points (AP). Cisco recommends that all controllers run the same version of code. In turn, the APs associated with a controller run the same version of code as the controller. Hence, upgrading or downgrading a controller puts all the APs on the same version as well. In this chapter, you will learn the steps required to upgrade a controller, upgrade an AP, upgrade the Wireless Control System (WCS), and manage configuration files.

You should do the "Do I Know This Already?" quiz first. If you score 80 percent or higher, you may want to skip to the section "Exam Preparation Tasks." If you score below 80 percent, you should spend the time reviewing the entire chapter.

"Do I Know This Already?" Quiz

The "Do I Know This Already?" quiz helps you determine your level of knowledge of this chapter's topics before you begin. Table 19-1 details the major topics discussed in this chapter and their corresponding quiz questions.

Table 19-1 *"Do I Know This Already?" Section-to-Question Mapping*

Foundation Topics Section	Questions
Upgrading a Controller	1–5
Upgrading an AP	6–7
Upgrading WCS	8
Managing Configurations	9–11

1. According to the following figure, what version of controller code is in use?

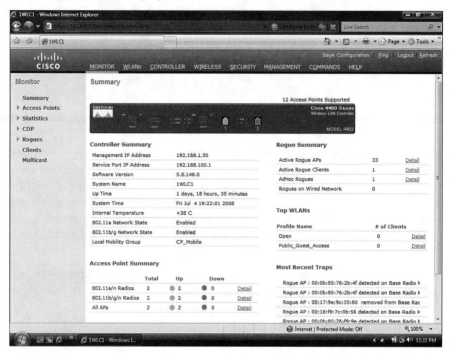

a. 5.0.148.0

b. 192.168.1.50

c. +38 C

d. 4.1.2.60 (Mesh)

2. What do you choose to verify the version of hardware?

a. Controller > General

b. Controller > Inventory

c. Management > Summary

d. Monitor > Summary

3. Which statement about the following figure is true?

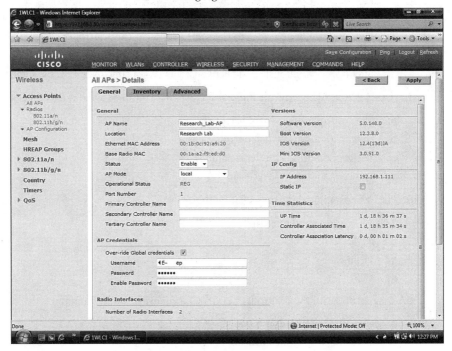

- **a.** The AP being viewed is the Lobby-AP.
- **b.** The AP is running in autonomous mode.
- **c.** The AP has a static IP address.
- **d.** The AP is running software version 5.0.148.0.

4. Which extension is used in controller upgrade files?

- **a.** .bin
- **b.** .exe
- **c.** .cfg
- **d.** .aes

5. Which protocols are used to upgrade a controller? (Choose two.)

- **a.** FTP
- **b.** TFTP
- **c.** HTTP
- **d.** SCP

6. What does an AP do if a controller is running a higher version of software?

    a. It does nothing; they don't need to be the same.

    b. It automatically upgrades to the same version as the controller.

    c. It causes the controller to downgrade to the same version as the AP.

    d. It reboots continuously and keeps searching for a controller with the same version.

7. If an AP leaves one controller and associates with another, what does it check?

    a. The controller's hardware version

    b. How many licenses the controller has

    c. The version the controller is running

    d. The version that other APs are running

8. The WCS is upgraded using what method?

    a. WCS code upgrade script

    b. FTP

    c. TFTP

    d. SCP

9. How do you save the controller's configuration using the web interface?

    a. Choose **Commands > Save.**

    b. Click the Save **Configuration** link.

    c. Choose **Commands > Copy-Run-Start.**

    d. Choose **Controllers > Save.**

10. If you clicked the **Upload** button on the page shown in the following figure, what would happen?

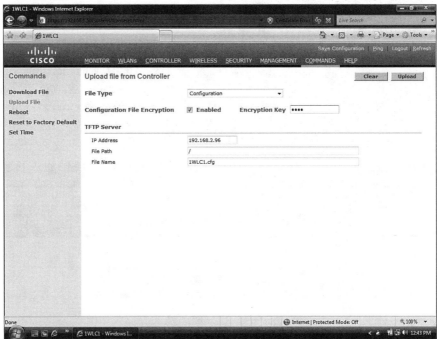

   a. The controller software would get backed up to an FTP server.

   b. The controller configuration would be archived to an NFS server at the IP address 192.168.2.96.

   c. The controller configuration would be uploaded in clear text using a TFTP server.

   d. The controller configuration would be encrypted and uploaded to 192.168.2.96 using TFTP.

11. In what format is the controller configuration file?

   a. XML

   b. XHTML

   c. DHTML

   d. Clear text

Foundation Topics

Upgrading a Controller

Management tasks in the controller involve upgrading or downgrading images as well as managing configuration files. You can begin working with these files by verifying the version currently running on the controller. Figure 19-1 shows the **MONITOR > Summary** page, which indicates that the version of code on this particular controller is software version 4.1.192.17M (Mesh). 5.x is the current version of code, so you need to obtain the version you want to have loaded before performing the upgrade.

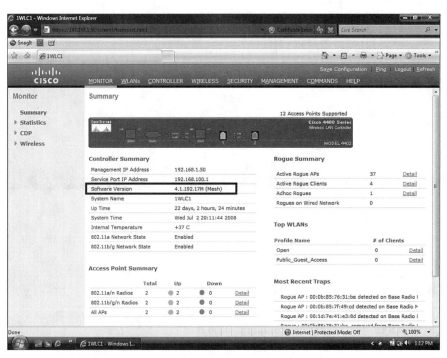

Figure 19-1   *Verify the Controller Software Version*

You also need to know the hardware with which you are working. You can find the hardware information by choosing **CONTROLLER > Inventory** and verifying the platform. The platform used in this example is an AIR-WLC4402-12-K9, as shown in Figure 19-2.

For the record, you might as well verify the AP hardware being used. To verify the AP software version, choose **WIRELESS > All APs**, and click the AP name you want to verify. In Figure 19-3, the Lobby-AP has been selected. You see a configuration page with four tabs:

- General
- Inventory

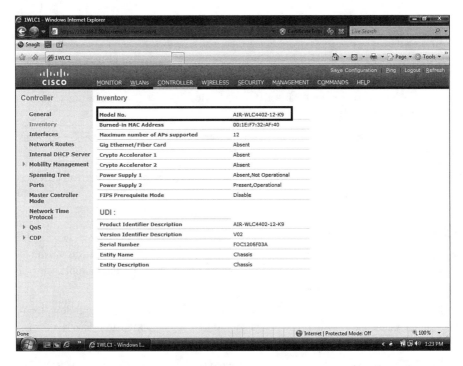

Figure 19-2   *Verify the Hardware Version*

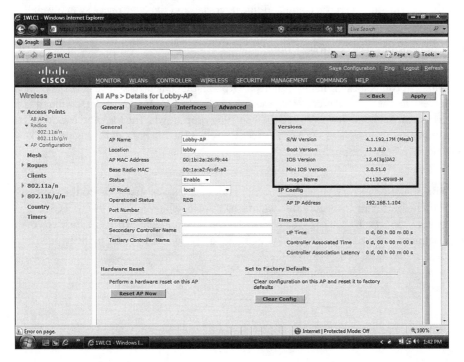

Figure 19-3   *General Details for the Lobby-AP*

- Interfaces

- Advanced

The General tab displays the software (S/W) version, as shown in Figure 19-3.

In the figure, the version on the AP is 4.1.192.17M (Mesh), which is the same version that is running on the controller.

Selecting the Inventory tab displays the hardware version. In this case, the Lobby-AP is an AIR-AP1131AG-A-K9, as shown in Figure 19-4.

Now you have all the version information you need to upgrade the controller software version. The next step is to determine which upgrade approach you will take.

Controller Upgrade Approaches

You can take two approaches when upgrading the controller. You can use the command-line interface (CLI), or you can use the web-based interface. To keep things simple, we will focus on the web interface method.

 Key Topic

Start by going to the Cisco Software Center (www.cisco.com/go/software) and downloading the image you want to install. The image should have an .aes extension. This is a compressed archive file. Three files are included in the .aes compressed file:

- **RTOS:** The controller's Real-Time Operating System

- **CODE:** Airwave Director, command-line interface, and the controller's switch web interface

- **ppcboot.bin:** The controller's bootloader

The next step is to place the .aes file on a TFTP server. Tftpd32 is a common TFTP server program that can you can obtain from http://tftpd32.jounin.net. As soon as the file is on the server, and the controller can reach the server, choose **COMMANDS > Download File**, as shown in Figure 19-5. You see the File Type drop-down. The file type is **Code**. Next, enter the IP address of the TFTP server, as well as the file path and filename. Click **Download** to begin the process.

> **Note**   Sometimes you have to upgrade through prior releases of software up to the version you ultimately want. This is because the older versions of code have a built-in TFTP client that does not support file transfers greater than 32 MB. The following URL is a good reference for helping network engineers or administrators determine an upgrade path: http://www.cisco.com/en/US/tech/tk722/tk809/technologies_configuration_example09186a00805f381f.shtml.

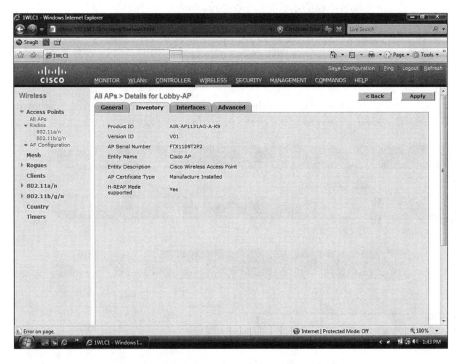

Figure 19-4 *AP Hardware Version*

Key
Topic

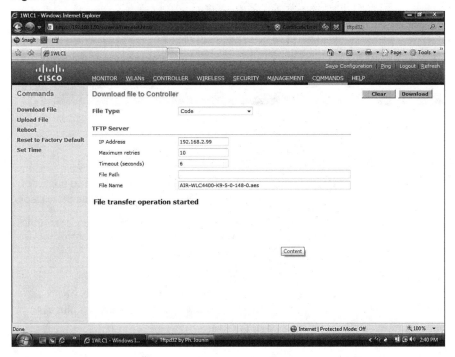

Figure 19-5 *Upgrade the Controller via the Web Interface*

As the transfer begins, the page continues to refresh every few seconds. The controller copies the file to RAM. When it's finished, the controller puts the file in flash. The existing image then becomes the backup image. As soon as the transfer is complete, you need to reboot the controller. You can click the link displayed on the Download file to Controller page. This redirects you to the Reboot page.

After the reboot, log back in, and verify that the new code has been transferred. As shown in Figure 19-6, the software version has been successfully upgraded.

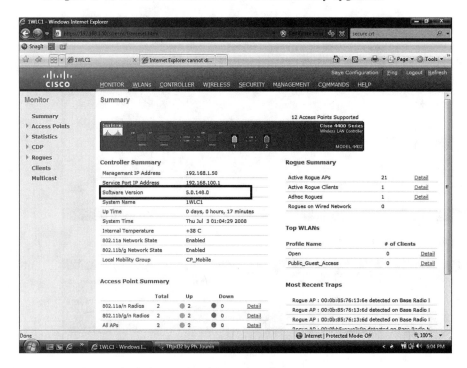

Figure 19-6 *Verify the Upgrade of the Controller*

Upgrade Using WCS

You can also use WCS to upgrade the controller. Upgrading the controller also upgrades the APs, because they sync to the same code. To perform the upgrade, follow these steps:

Step 1. Verify connectivity before you start the upgrade process. Use the ping utility from the WCS to be sure that the WCS server can contact the controller. Also, if you use an external TFTP server, ping it as well.

Note The ping utility is a Windows function, not a function or utility in WCS. To access the ping utility, you need to open a command prompt in Windows and enter the **ping** command followed by the address you want to ping.

Step 2.   Click **Configure > Controllers** to navigate to the All Controllers page.

Step 3.   Select the check box of the controller you want to upgrade. Choose **Select a Command > Download Software**, and click **GO**. WCS displays the Download Software to Controller page.

Step 4.   If you use the built-in WCS TFTP server, check the **TFTP Server on WCS System** check box. If you use an external TFTP server, uncheck this check box and add the external TFTP server IP address.

Step 5.   Click **Browse** and navigate to the software update file. The files are uploaded to the root directory that was configured for use by the TFTP server. You can change to a different directory.

> **Note**   You should always double-check the software file you plan to use for your controller. Selecting the wrong file can cause problems. Be sure that you have the correct software file for your controller.

Step 6.   Click **Download**. WCS downloads the software to the controller, and the controller writes the code to flash RAM. As WCS performs this function, it displays its progress in the Status field.

Upgrading an AP

Upgrading an AP is pretty easy. In fact, if you followed the process described in the preceding section, you are already done, because the AP synchronizes to the controller. Recall that in Figure 19-3 you verified the version of AP software, and it was the same as the controller—version 4.1.192.17M (Mesh). After upgrading the controller to software version 5.0.148.0, you can again verify the client by choosing **WIRELESS > All APs** and clicking the AP name that you want to verify. In Figure 19-7, the Lobby-AP has been selected. According to the information in the Software Version field, it has been upgraded to version 5.0.148.0, matching that of the controller. Remember that after upgrading the software on the controller, the APs automatically upgrade their software as well, but only 20 APs can upgrade at any given time.

Remember that APs synchronize to the controller. This means the following:

Key Topic

■   If the controller is a higher version, the AP upgrades.

■   If the controller is a lower version, the AP downgrades.

■   If the AP leaves one controller and associates with another, the AP checks the controller version and upgrades/downgrades as needed.

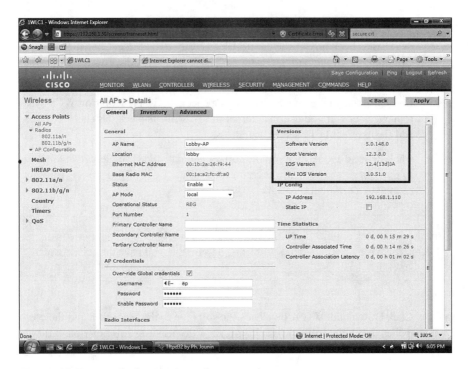

Figure 19-7 *Verify the AP Upgrade*

Upgrading WCS

Beginning in WCS version 4.2, the WCS code upgrade script made it possible to upgrade the WCS while retaining the directories, root password, and license information. The operation is automated and simply involves downloading the install file from the Cisco website and running it on the machine on which the WCS is installed. During the install process, you are informed that a previous install has been detected, and you're asked to choose between upgrading and installing. Upgrading retains all the information from the previous install. If you choose the install option, it will be as if WCS was not previously there; in other words, it's a fresh install.

Managing Configurations

When working in the Cisco Unified Wireless Environment, you deal with a number of configuration files. You potentially have numerous controller configurations as well as AP configurations. When you're working with the controller, it's a good idea to save your configuration often. Clicking the Save Configuration link can save a controller's configuration. It is found in the top-right corner of the web interface, as shown in Figure 19-8.

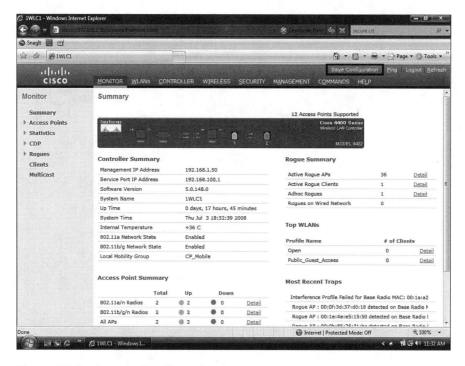

Figure 19-8   *Save the Configuration*

In addition to saving the configuration to NVRAM, you can back up the configuration on a remote TFTP server. Saving to a TFTP server is similar to how you upgraded the controller, only this time you are moving a file in the opposite direction. The setup requires the use of TFTP server software installed on the destination computer where you want to back up the file. TFTP uses UDP port 69, so make sure that nothing in the transit path, such as a firewall, might block that type of traffic. If you have already upgraded from the TFTP server, you probably won't have any issues.

The next step is to choose **COMMANDS > Upload File**. In the drop-down box, choose **Configuration**. Select the option to encrypt the file is you want, enter the server's address and configuration file name, and click upload. If you don't choose to encrypt it, you get a pop-up warning when you click **Upload**.

After you upload the configuration file, you can download this file to other controllers. However, you cannot read it as you would a configuration file from a router or switch, because it is an XML file.

Suppose you wanted to back up the controller configuration to 192.168.2.99. Simply enter the IP address 192.168.2.99 in the IP Address field and give it a name, as shown in Figure 19-9. In this example, the file name is 1WLC1.cfg.

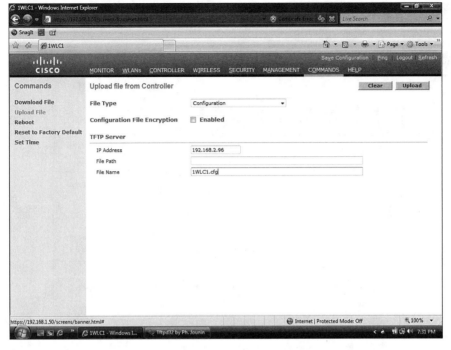

Figure 19-9   *Backing Up the Controller Configuration to TFTP*

Click the Upload button to begin the process. This takes a short time. After completion, you can verify by viewing the directory on the TFTP server where the files are stored, as shown in Figure 19-10. After viewing the directory on the TFTP server, you can see that the upload was successful. The file has been backed up and can now be used on other controllers.

Further exploration shows that the file can be opened and viewed but is not very readable, as shown in Figure 19-11.

If you do want to view the configuration in a readable format, you could issue the **show running-config** command from the CLI on the controller. In Example 19-1, the **show running-config** command has been entered on the controller. Using this command you can see line by line how the controller is configured. It's important to note the difference between this command and the **show run-config** command, because they produce very different output. **show running-config** displays the contents of the configuration line by line. **show run-config** provides information about the state of the system.

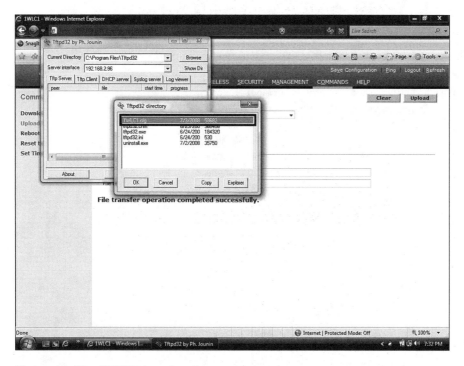

Figure 19-10   *TFTP Directory*

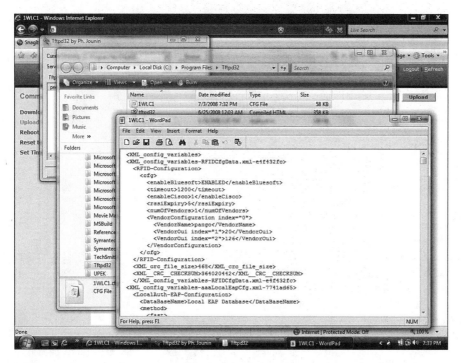

Figure 19-11   *Viewing the File on the TFTP Server*

Example 19-1   show running-config *Command Output*

```
(Cisco Controller) > show running-config

 802.11a 11nSupport a-mpdu tx priority 0 disable
 802.11a cac voice tspec-inactivity-timeout ignore
 802.11a cac video tspec-inactivity-timeout ignore
 802.11a cac voice stream-size 84000 max-streams 2
 802.11b 11nSupport a-mpdu tx priority 0 disable
 802.11b cac voice tspec-inactivity-timeout ignore
 802.11b cac video tspec-inactivity-timeout ignore
 802.11b cac voice stream-size 84000 max-streams 2
 aaa auth mgmt local radius
 advanced 802.11a receiver pico-cell-V2 rx_sense_thrld 0 0 0
 advanced 802.11a receiver pico-cell-V2 cca_sense_thrld 0 0 0
advanced 802.11a receiver pico-cell-V2 sta_tx_pwr 0 0 0
 Location Summary
 Algorithm used:              Average
 Client
        RSSI expiry timeout: 150 sec
        Half life:              60 sec
        Notify Threshold:       0 db
 Calibrating Client
        RSSI expiry timeout: 30 sec
        Half life:              0 sec
 Rogue AP
        RSSI expiry timeout:   120 sec
        Half life:              0 sec
        Notify Threshold:       0 db
 RFID Tag
        RSSI expiry timeout: 5 sec
        Half life:              0 sec
        Notify Threshold:       0 db
 location rssi-half-life tags 0
location rssi-half-life rogue-aps 0
 location expiry tags 5
 location expiry client 150
 location expiry calibrating-client 30
 location expiry rogue-aps 120
 advanced eap identity-request-timeout 1
 advanced eap identity-request-retries 20
 advanced eap request-timeout 1
 ap syslog host global 255.255.255.255
interface create guest_lan 80
interface address ap-manager 192.168.1.51 255.255.255.0 192.168.1.1
interface address dynamic-interface guest_lan 172.30.1.50 255.255.255.0 172.30.1.1
interface address management 192.168.1.50 255.255.255.0 192.168.1.1
```

```
interface address service-port 192.168.100.1 255.255.255.0
interface address virtual 1.1.1.1
interface dhcp ap-manager primary 192.168.1.1
interface dhcp dynamic-interface guest_lan primary 172.30.1.1
interface dhcp management primary 192.168.1.1
interface dhcp service-port disable
interface vlan ap-manager 1
interface vlan guest_lan 80
interface vlan management 1
interface port ap-manager 1
interface port guest_lan 1
interface port management 1
 load-balancing window 5
 logging buffered 1
 mesh security eap
 mgmtuser add admin **** read-write
 mobility group domain CP_Mobile
 mobility group anchor wlan add 2 192.168.1.50
 mobility dscp value for inter-controller mobility packets 0
 network webmode enable
 network rf-network-name CP_Mobile
 radius fallback-test mode off
 radius fallback-test username cisco-probe
 radius fallback-test interval 300
 snmp version v2c enable
 snmp version v3 enable
 sysname 1WLC1
 wlan create 1 Open Open
 wlan create 2 Public_Guest_Access GUESTNET
 wlan interface 2 guest_lan
 wlan session-timeout 1 1800
 wlan session-timeout 2 disable
 wlan wmm allow 1
 wlan wmm allow 2
 wlan security wpa disable 2
 wlan security web-auth server-precedence 1
 wlan security web-auth server-precedence 2
 wlan security wpa akm ft reassociation-time 0 1
 wlan security wpa akm ft over-the-air disable 1
 wlan security wpa akm ft over-the-ds disable 1
 wlan security wpa akm ft reassociation-time 0 2
 wlan security wpa akm ft over-the-air disable 2
 wlan security wpa akm ft over-the-ds disable 2
 wlan enable 1
 wlan enable 2
```

Working with AP Configuration Files

Keeping in mind that the AP gets its configuration from the controller should make it clear that you don't really have to do much to manage AP configurations. However, you might encounter scenarios where you want to reset an AP to its factory default. You can do this at the AP itself, but you require physical access to the AP. To reset the AP from the controller, simply choose **WIRELESS**, choose the AP you want to reset, and scroll to the bottom. You have two options, as shown in Figure 19-12. You can click **Clear All Config** or **Clear Config Except Static IP**. The choice depends on what you want to happen. If you use static IPs and want to reset the AP and remove it from the network, choose the second option.

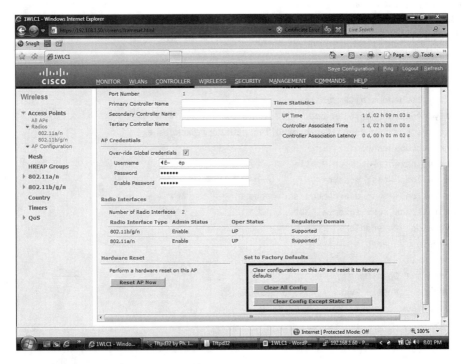

Figure 19-12 *Options for Resetting the AP*

Resetting the Controller to the Defaults

Finally, if you decide to reset the controller to its factory defaults, you can choose **COMMANDS > Reset to Factory Default**. This page presents a message similar to the one shown in Figure 19-13; it explains what happens when you reset the controller to the defaults. The controller needs to reboot for this to occur, because the configuration is not only stored in NVRAM, but it is also active in RAM and is cleared only with a reboot. You will lose connectivity when you do this.

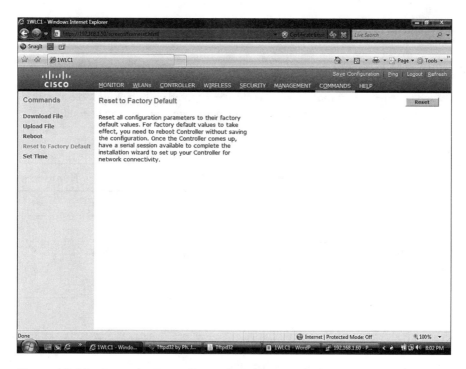

Figure 19-13   *Reset the Controller to the Factory Defaults*

Exam Preparation Tasks

Review All the Key Topics

Review the most important topics from this chapter, denoted with the Key Topic icon. Table 19-2 lists these key topics and the page number where each one can be found.

Table 19-2   *Key Topics for Chapter 19*

Key Topic Item	Description	Page Number
Figure 19-1	Verifying the software version	386
Figure 19-3	General details for the Lobby-AP	387
Paragraph from the section "Controller Upgrade Approaches"	A list of files contained in the compressed upgrade file	388
Figure 19-5	Upgrading the controller via the web interface	389
Paragraph from the section "Upgrading an AP"	Bullet points about AP upgrades and downgrades	391
Figure 19-9	Backing up the controller configuration to TFTP	394

Definition of Key Terms

Define the following key terms from this chapter, and check your answers in the Glossary:

RTOS, RAM, NVRAM, TFTP

References

Cisco Wireless Control System Configuration Guide, Release 5.0: http://www.cisco.com/en/US/docs/wireless/wcs/5.0/configuration/guide/wcstasks.html#wp1076844

Cisco Wireless LAN Controller Configuration Guide, Release 5.0: http://www.cisco.com/en/US/docs/wireless/controller/5.0/configuration/guide/c5mfw.html

This chapter covers the following subjects:

Physical Connections and LEDs: A look at troubleshooting using physical features of the network.

Common Client-Side Issues: A discussion of common client issues.

Using the CLI to Troubleshoot: A look at CLI commands for viewing and debugging using the CLI.

Using the Controller Interface: Details of troubleshooting using various web interface pages.

Using WCS Version 5.x to Troubleshoot Clients: Overview of techniques used to troubleshoot clients using WCS.

Using the Cisco Spectrum Expert: A brief introduction to the Cisco Spectrum Expert and its use.

CHAPTER 20

Troubleshooting Wireless Networks

Trouble tends to be something everyone runs into at some point in time. People make typos. Cables mysteriously go bad. Stuff happens. This chapter discusses numerous issues that can happen in a wireless network along with some of the techniques, commands, configuration pages, and methods that you can use to correct them. Although everyone has a unique style, this chapter helps you hone your skills at recognizing misconfigurations and making corrections, using the command-line interface (CLI), the controller interface, and the Wireless Control System (WCS).

You should do the "Do I Know This Already?" quiz first. If you score 80 percent or higher, you might want to skip to the section "Exam Preparation Tasks." If you score below 80 percent, you should spend the time reviewing the entire chapter. Refer to Appendix A, "Answers to the 'Do I Know This Already?' Quizzes," to confirm your answers.

"Do I Know This Already?" Quiz

The "Do I Know This Already?" quiz helps you determine your level of knowledge of this chapter's topics before you begin. Table 20-1 details the major topics discussed in this chapter and their corresponding quiz questions.

Table 20-1 *"Do I Know This Already?" Section-to-Question Mapping*

Foundation Topics Section	Questions
Physical Connections and LEDs	1–2
Common Client-Side Issues	3–5
Using the CLI to Troubleshoot	6–11
Using the Controller Interface	12–13
Using WCS Version 5.x to Troubleshoot Clients	14
Using the Cisco Spectrum Expert	15

1. At what layers of the OSI model does trouble happen most often?

   a. Layer 1

   b. Layers 1 through 3

   c. Layers 2 through 6

   d. Above Layer 7

2. What are some actions regarding physical characteristics that you can use for troubleshooting? (Choose all that apply.)

   a. Analyze port LEDs

   b. Verify wiring

   c. Check the internal fans

   d. View debugs

3. Which of the following accurately describes the hidden node issue?

   a. A node is hidden under a desk and used to attack the wireless network.

   b. A node is accessing the network from the parking lot.

   c. Two nodes are attempting to send at the same time. They are out of range of each other but not of the AP.

   d. Nodes on the network access hidden APs.

4. Which of the following best describes the exposed node issue?

   a. Two nodes are sending on the same channel to different APs. The cells are too close, so a collision occurs.

   b. A node is attacking the network in plain view.

   c. A node is on the wireless network without antivirus software.

   d. A node is listening on undesired ports.

5. When an AP has a greater RF range than a client, the client can see the AP but annot associate with it because the client frames do not reach the AP. What is this situation known as?

   a. The Weak Antenna syndrome

   b. The Weak Link issue

   c. The Half Duplex situation

   d. The Near/Far issue

6. From where can you execute **debug** commands?

   a. The GUI

   b. The CLI

   c. The GUI and the CLI

   d. The WCS only

7. What command provides a summary of clients?

   a. show clients

   b. show client summary

   c. show summary

   d. show ap client summary

8. Examine the following output and then answer the question.

```
(Cisco Controller) >show client detail 00:15:af:0a:0b:71
Client MAC Address............................... 00:15:af:0a:0b:71
Client Username ................................. N/A
AP MAC Address................................... 00:1a:a2:fc:df:a0
Client State..................................... Probing
Wireless LAN Id.................................. N/A
BSSID............................................ 00:1a:a2:fc:df:9f
Channel.......................................... 11
IP Address....................................... Unknown
Association Id................................... 0
Authentication Algorithm......................... Open System
Reason Code...................................... 0
Status Code...................................... 0
Session Timeout.................................. 0
Client CCX version............................... No CCX support
Mirroring........................................ Disabled
QoS Level........................................ Silver
Diff Serv Code Point (DSCP)...................... disabled
802.1P Priority Tag.............................. disabled
WMM Support...................................... Disabled
Mobility State................................... None
Mobility Move Count.............................. 0
Security Policy Completed........................ No
--More-- or (q)uit
Policy Manager State............................. START
Policy Manager Rule Created...................... Yes
NPU Fast Fast Notified........................... No
Policy Type...................................... N/A
```

Based on this output, does the client have full IP connectivity?

   a. Yes.

   b. No, the client has partial connectivity but no DNS.

   c. No, the client has no IP connectivity because he has no IP address.

   d. Yes, but the network is down.

9. If you leave a debug turned on, what happens?

    a. It consumes all the resources on the controller.

    b. It runs continuously.

    c. It turns off when the controller reloads.

    d. It becomes disabled when the session times out.

10. Look at the following output and answer the question.

```
(Cisco Controller) >debug ?

aaa Configures the AAA debug options.
airewave-director Configures the Airewave Director debug options
ap Configures debug of Cisco AP.
arp Configures debug of ARP.
bcast Configures debug of broadcast.
cac Configures the call admission control (CAC) debug options.
cdp Configures debug of cdp.
crypto Configures the Hardware Crypto debug options.
dhcp Configures the DHCP debug options.
client Enables debugs for common client problems.
disable-all Disables all debug messages.
dot11 Configures the 802.11 events debug options.
dot1x Configures the 802.1X debug options.
iapp Configures the IAPP debug options.
ccxrm Configures the CCX_RM debug options.
ccxdiag Configures the CCX Diagnostic debug options.
```

Which debug would be used to troubleshoot issues with port-based authentication?

    a. arp

    b. cdp

    c. dot11

    d. dot1x

11. How do you enable client troubleshooting?

    a. Issue the CLI command **debug mac addr** *mac_address_of_client*.

    b. Click the **Troubleshoot** button from the Clients Summary page of the WCS.

    c. Select the client from the **Clients** drop-down menu.

    d. Use an access list to match a client and tie it to a debug.

12. Where would you find information equivalent to the **show client summary** command within the controller interface?

    a. MANAGEMENT > Clients

    b. CONTROLLER > Clients

    c. MONITOR > Clients > Detail

    d. WLANs > Clients

13. Facility Level 5 is what?

    a. USENET

    b. SYSLOG

    c. FTP DAEMONS

    d. KERNEL

14. WCS is used to troubleshoot client-to-AP connectivity. True or false?

    a. True

    b. False

15. Which of the following devices does the Cisco Spectrum Expert provide information about?

    a. Microwave ovens

    b. RC cars

    c. Controllers

    d. Wired clients

Foundation Topics

Physical Connections and LEDs

Trouble usually happens between Layer 1 and Layer 3 of the OSI reference model. That is not to say that trouble does not occur at Layers 4 through 7, but Layers 1 through 3 are the layers where network administrators have the most hands on. Working your way up can often prove to be a time saver. Starting at Layer 1, physical connectivity can often save valuable time. You can begin by visually examining the physical connections. Keep in mind all that is involved in the path of your traffic. This can include areas related to the following:

- AP to switch

- Switch to switch

- Switch to controller

- Controller to distribution

While you are examining the physical connectivity, note the port LED status of each device. What do the LEDs indicate? Are they green? Are they amber? Are they red? Each device has different LEDs; for example, the LEDs on a controller are different from the LEDs on an AP, yet they all have somewhat of a common color coding. Usually red is bad, amber is not so good, and green is okay. Look up the Cisco documentation for details for each product that you work with. The "References" section at the end of this chapter includes some valuable links that can help you determine issues in the network and correct them, some using the port LEDs for verification.

After you have verified the physical connections, you can work in one of two directions:

- Verification from the client back to the controller

- Verification from the controller to the client

In either case, common issues arise. You might find that connectivity issues are not related to the wireless network at all, but rather the distribution network, gateway, or Internet service provider (ISP). Regardless, the ability to isolate problems is a requirement of those seeking the CCNA Wireless certification. The next section explores some common client-side issues.

Common Client-Side Issues

Client-side issues arise frequently and are often expressed in vague ways, for example, "I cannot get to the Internet." "Okay," you might think, "What does that mean?" The answer might not always be clear, but you can verify some values to quickly restore connectivity for end users.

Note: When I worked for a large service provider, we went through a transition from bridges to switches. During the initial deployment, none of the administrators on the local-area network knew about the Spanning Tree Protocol (STP) or the effects it had when a device was connected to a switchport.

I recall that first week, sitting in my little cubicle at 7:55 a.m. and hearing the voices of my colleagues say, "The Internet is down." And then, of course, someone would call IT and say that *nobody* could get to the Internet and that he thought the Internet was down. I felt sorry for the IT guys, because nobody called them and said, "When I came in this morning and turned on my computer, Spanning Tree put all the ports into a blocking mode while verifying that there was no loop, so none of us could get to the Internet for about one minute." Had someone done that, the IT guys could have simply enabled PortFast on all the client ports and solved the problem. My point? Users do not call and give you the answer to the problem. Instead, they give you a symptom, and it is up to you to decipher the true issue regardless of how vague the symptom they described is. Now enough of my reminiscing. What can you do to isolate these issues?

Some of the more common issues that you can verify include the following:

- Check that the client card is enabled. Many laptops have a hardware switch that disables the wireless card internally, which can cause issues.

- Check that service set identifiers (SSIDs) are not incorrectly configured.

- Verify whether the client is using a radio that is not enabled on the AP.

- Verify whether the MAC address of the client is being "blacklisted" on the network.

- If using 802.1x, verify whether the client side is configured to support the network method, such as Extensible Authentication Protocol-Transport Layer Security (EAP-TLS) with certificates.

- Verify whether the client is getting an IP address that is blocked by an access control list (ACL) somewhere else in the network.

- Check the client firewall or antivirus software, because it might be blocking access. There might not be much you can do other than asking the client to turn each of these off temporarily for testing.

- If performing Network Access Control (NAC), check whether the client is posturing properly. Check the Authentication, Authorization, and Accounting (AAA) server or the Monitoring, Analysis, and Response System (MARS) logs to determine this. From a wireless perspective, there is not much you can do except have the users access a "Guest" type of network that does not require security posturing.

Note: Cisco Security MARS provides security monitoring for network devices and host applications supporting both Cisco and other vendors. You can find out more about it at http://tinyurl.com/bfr64.

- If you are using preshared keys for wireless authentication, verify that they are correctly configured on the client side. Also, verify that they are configured for the correct length.

Checking these common issues can shorten the time that you spend troubleshooting.

Other problems, however, include one issue called the *Hidden Node issue*. This happens when more than one client tries to send on the same channel at the same time. This issue arises because the two clients are in range of the AP but not each other. The result is that they both send, and a collision occurs.

Methods of mitigating this issue include reducing the maximum frame size, forcing a request to send/clear to send (RTS/CTS), and reducing the transmit power of the AP and shrinking the cell. In some cases, obstacles cause the devices not to see each other. In these scenarios, you might need to remove the obstacle; however, sometimes removing a wall is not an option. In these cases, take the other measures mentioned. The goal is to either get the clients to hear each other (or an RTS/CTS) so they do not sent at the same time or to get them onto different APs and operating on different channels. By shrinking the cell, you get the clients on different channels, but by lowering the transmit power, you might need to add more APs to fully cover the area. By forcing an RTS/CTS, the clients still might be on the same channel, but at least they are not stepping on the toes of the other.

Another common issue is called the *Exposed Node issue*, which occurs when you have two wireless cells on the same channel and they are too close to each other. This happens often in Wireless B/G networks because only three nonoverlapping channels exist. If clients in either of the overlapping cells transmit packets, a collision can occur. The simple fix to this is to change your topology, or at least the channel allocation. In some cases this is not a possibility, so you might consider a change to an 802.11a deployment, where more channels are available for allocation.

Another issue that happens between clients and APs is the *Near/Far issue*, which is caused by an AP transmitter being more powerful than the client transmitter. When a client sees an AP, because of its strong signal, it attempts to associate with it. Because the client transmitter is weaker than the AP, it does not have the range that the AP does. This means that the client transmission does not reach the AP, and the association fails. You can solve this problem using features of the controller. The controller can help monitor the client signal and adjust the radio resources as needed.

Additionally, as you might have been expecting, backward compatibility is an issue. This issue occurs when an 802.11b client joins the 802.11g cell and when an 802.11b/g/a client enters an 802.11n cell. The normal symptom is overall degraded data rates. To solve this issue, you can lock in a G-only cell for G clients.

Using the CLI to Troubleshoot

Sometimes resolving the common issues is not easy and they require further research. In these cases, you can use the CLI or the GUI tool to gather additional information. From the CLI, you have a few options for troubleshooting. First, you can use **show** commands on the CLI to gain valuable information related to the operational status of the controller, the APs, and the clients. Many of these **show** commands are available in various pages of the GUI tool, as you will see in later sections of this chapter.

Some of the **show** commands you should be familiar with include the following:

- **show client summary**

- **show client detail**

Example 20-1 shows the output from a **show client summary** command. In this output, you can see clients that are associated or trying to associate to the network. The example has an 802.11b client with the MAC address 0:13:e8:a9:e1:29 that is probing but not associated with an AP. Furthermore, the client is seen by the AP "Lobby-AP."

Example 20-1 *Viewing the Client Summary*

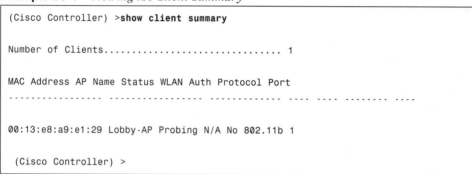

```
(Cisco Controller) >show client summary


Number of Clients................................ 1


MAC Address AP Name Status WLAN Auth Protocol Port
--------------- ----------------- ------------- ---- ---- -------- ----


00:13:e8:a9:e1:29 Lobby-AP Probing N/A No 802.11b 1


(Cisco Controller) >
```

How can this assist you in the troubleshooting process? Well, suppose that a client reports a problem associating, and as you further research the issue, you find that the AP MAC address is seen by the Lobby-AP, and it is usually associated with the Research-Lab AP. You might then ask if the client is trying to connect while in the lobby. Who knows where this might lead you, but at least you have more information than when you started—information that might lead to a resolution.

If you wanted to dig even deeper into the client information, you might use the **show client detail** command. Example 20-2 shows the output of this command. Note the additional information you can gain there. Information includes the client username if applicable, mobility information if applicable, and much more.

Example 20-2 *Viewing Client Details*

```
(Cisco Controller) >show client detail 00:15:af:0a:0b:71
Client MAC Address.............................. 00:15:af:0a:0b:71
Client Username ................................ N/A
AP MAC Address.................................. 00:1a:a2:fc:df:a0
Client State................................... Probing
Wireless LAN Id................................. N/A
BSSID.......................................... 00:1a:a2:fc:df:9f
Channel........................................ 11
IP Address..................................... Unknown
Association Id................................. 0
Authentication Algorithm....................... Open System
Reason Code.................................... 0
```

continues

Example 20-2 *Viewing Client Details (continued)*

```
Status Code...................................... 0
Session Timeout.................................. 0
Client CCX version.............................. No CCX support
Mirroring....................................... Disabled
QoS Level....................................... Silver
Diff Serv Code Point (DSCP)..................... disabled
802.1P Priority Tag............................. disabled
WMM Support..................................... Disabled
Mobility State.................................. None
Mobility Move Count............................. 0
Security Policy Completed....................... No
—More— or (q)uit
Policy Manager State............................ START
Policy Manager Rule Created..................... Yes
NPU Fast Fast Notified.......................... No
Policy Type..................................... N/A
Encryption Cipher............................... None
Management Frame Protection..................... No
EAP Type........................................ Unknown
Interface....................................... management
VLAN............................................ 0
Client Capabilities:
CF Pollable............................... Not implemented
CF Poll Request........................... Not implemented
Short Preamble............................ Not implemented
PBCC...................................... Not implemented
Channel Agility........................... Not implemented
Listen Interval........................... 0
Client Statistics:
Number of Bytes Received.................. 0
Number of Bytes Sent...................... 0
Number of Packets Received................ 0
Number of Packets Sent.................... 0
Number of Policy Errors................... 0
Radio Signal Strength Indicator........... Unavailable
—More— or (q)uit
Signal to Noise Ratio..................... Unavailable
Nearby AP Statistics:
TxExcessiveRetries: 0
TxRetries: 0
RtsSuccessCnt: 0
RtsFailCnt: 0
TxFiltered: 0
TxRateProfile: [0,0,0,0,0,0,0,0,0,0,0]
Research_Lab-AP(slot 0) ...................
```

Example 20-2   *Viewing Client Details   (continued)*

```
antenna0: 5 seconds ago -93 dBm................. antenna1: 4293918453 seconds ago
-128 dBm
Lobby-AP(slot 0) .........................
antenna0: 4293918453 seconds ago -128 dBm........ antenna1: 5 seconds ago -94 dBm
```

Although this information is valuable, it is important to note that it is static. In other words, the information you gain from **show** commands gives you the state or the conditions of the network at the time that you enter the command. If you require real-time information, debugs come in handy.

If you have come from the routing world, you are probably familiar with the use of **debug** commands and how invaluable they are in troubleshooting. If you are working your way through the certification program, and you are doing it in order (CCNA > CCNA Wireless), then you learned in the CCNA curriculum how a **debug** command is used in some basic troubleshooting scenarios. The concept of **debug** commands carries over here to the wireless space. Available only from the CLI, **debug** commands can be used on the controller to help troubleshoot issues. The principle in the use of **debug** commands is the same:

■   Do not leave them on, because they are CPU intensive.

■   Be prepared to turn them off. Sometimes the output is overwhelming.

■   **Debug** commands take priority over other processes on the controller.

If you think that some **debug** commands might already be enabled, use the **show debug** command to verify that notion. One fail-safe that is in place is that if you do turn on a **debug** command and forget about it, the **debug** becomes disabled when the CLI session times out. Although this is a good fail-safe, you should still turn your **debug** commands off when you are done with them. To see a list of the available **debug** commands, use the **debug ?** command, as seen in Example 20-3. You can use this to determine which **debug** command is appropriate for the situation; for example, if you are troubleshooting a port-based authentication problem, you might enable **debug dot1x**.

Example 20-3   *Viewing Available* **debug** *Commands*

```
(Cisco Controller) >debug ?

aaa Configures the AAA debug options.
airewave-director Configures the Airewave Director debug options
ap Configures debug of Cisco AP.
arp Configures debug of ARP.
bcast Configures debug of broadcast.
cac Configures the call admission control (CAC) debug options.
cdp Configures debug of cdp.
crypto Configures the Hardware Crypto debug options.
dhcp Configures the DHCP debug options.
client Enables debugs for common client problems.
disable-all Disables all debug messages.
```

continues

Example 20-3 *Viewing Available* **debug** *Commands* *(continued)*

```
dot11 Configures the 802.11 events debug options.
dot1x Configures the 802.1X debug options.
iapp Configures the IAPP debug options.
ccxrm Configures the CCX_RM debug options.
ccxdiag Configures the CCX Diagnostic debug options.
locp Configures the LOCP debug options.
l2roam Configures the L2 Roam debug options.
l2age Configures debug of Layer 2 Ago Timeout Messages.
lwapp Configures the LWAPP debug options
mac Configures MAC debugging
--More-- or (q)uit
```

To really hone in on where the issues are, you can use **debug** commands for a specific AP or a specific client. This requires placing the controller into client troubleshooting mode. To do this, begin by telling the controller, by way of a CLI command, that you want to debug for a specific MAC address. For example, to tell the controller that it will be debugging for MAC address 00:1a:a2:f9:ed:d0, enter the following:

```
(Cisco Controller) >debug mac addr 00:1a:a2:f9:ed:d0
```
The next step is to tell the controller which debug to use for that particular MAC address. For example, if you want to debug LWAPP events for the MAC address 00:1a:a2:f9:ed:d0, use the **debug lwapp** command as shown here:

```
(Cisco Controller) >debug lwapp events enable
```
To verify that the **debug** command is enabled, use the **show debug** command, as seen in Example 20-4.

Example 20-4 *Verifying Enabled Debugs*

```
(Cisco Controller) >show debug
MAC address ............................. 00:1a:a2:f9:ed:d0

Debug Flags Enabled:
arp error enabled.
bcast error enabled.
lwapp events enabled.
lwapp errors enabled.
```

Then you wait for an LWAPP event to occur. In Example 20-5, an LWAPP event has occurred, and a message has been sent to the console.

Example 20-5 *Controller Debug Output*

```
(Cisco Controller) >Wed Jun 25 19:50:50 2008: 00:1a:a2:f9:ed:d0 Received LWAPP
  ECHO_REQUEST from AP 00:1a:a2:f9:ed:d0
Wed Jun 25 19:50:50 2008: 00:1a:a2:f9:ed:d0 Successfully transmission of LWAPP
  Echo-Response to AP 00:1a:a2:f9:ed:d0
Wed Jun 25 19:50:50 2008: 00:1a:a2:f9:ed:d0 Received LWAPP PRIMARY_DISCOVERY_REQ
  from AP 00:1a:a2:f9:ed:d0
```

Example 20-5 *Controller Debug Output   (continued)*

```
Wed Jun 25 19:50:50 2008: 00:1a:a2:f9:ed:d0 Received LWAPP RRM_DATA_REQ from AP
  00:1a:a2:f9:ed:d0
Wed Jun 25 19:50:50 2008: 00:1a:a2:f9:ed:d0 Successfully transmission of LWAPP
  Airewave-Director-Data Response to AP 00:1a:a2:f9:ed:d0
Wed Jun 25 19:51:14 2008: 00:1a:a2:f9:ed:d0 Received LWAPP RRM_DATA_REQ from AP
  00:1a:a2:f9:ed:d0
Wed Jun 25 19:51:14 2008: 00:1a:a2:f9:ed:d0 Successfully transmission of LWAPP
  Airewave-Director-Data Response to AP 00:1a:a2:f9:ed:d0
```

The actual output of the debug in the example is pretty normal. What is important, however, is that you understand how to enable the debug process, verify it, and turn it off. To
disable the debug process, use the **debug disable-all** command, as seen in Example 20-6.
First the debug process was verified with the **show debug** command, and then it was disabled. After the debug process was disabled, the command **show debug** was again used to
verify that it was in fact disabled.

Example 20-6 *Verify the Enabled Debugs*

```
(Cisco Controller) >show debug
MAC address ............................. 00:1a:a2:f9:ed:d0

Debug Flags Enabled:
arp error enabled.
bcast error enabled.
lwapp events enabled.
lwapp errors enabled.


(Cisco Controller) >debug disable-all

 (Cisco Controller) >show debug
MAC debugging ........................... disabled

Debug Flags Enabled:


 (Cisco Controller) >
```

When you let the session time out, even though it turns off the **debug** command, it still
leaves the command to perform client troubleshooting, as seen in Example 20-7. This
means that if you enable a new **debug** command, it only debugs for the client you specify.

Example 20-7 *Command to Perform Client Troubleshooting Remains*

```
Connection to 192.168.1.50 closed.
terminal$:
terminal$:
terminal$:ssh 192.168.1.50
```

continues

Example 20-5   *Command to Perform Client Troubleshooting Remains   (continued)*

```
(Cisco Controller)
User: admin
Password:*****
(Cisco Controller) >show debug
MAC address ............................... 00:1a:a2:f9:ed:d0

Debug Flags Enabled:
```

As you can see, the connection was closed, essentially timing out. After authenticating again to the CLI of the controller, the **show debug** command was entered. This command output indicates that the MAC address 00:1a:a2:f9:ed:d0 is still enabled for client debugging. The point here is that it is always best to turn off **debug** commands when you are finished using them. You can also turn off a specific **debug** command using the **disable** option at the end of the command. For example, to turn off the LWAPP debug that was used in the previous examples, you would use the **debug lwapp events disable** command.

When you are comfortable turning **debug** commands on and off, you can explore **debug** commands such as **debug dot11**. The **debug dot11** command helps you troubleshoot 802.11 parameters, such as these:

- Mobility

- Rogue detection

- Load balancing events

In Example 20-8, you can see a client that has successfully associated.

Example 20-8   *A Successful Association*

```
Fri Aug 8 15:32:54 2008: 00:1e:c2:ab:14:26 apfPemAddUser2 (apf_policy.c:209)
  Changing state for mobile 00:1e:c2:ab:14:26 on AP 00:1a:a2:f9:ed:d0 from
  Associated to Associated

Fri Aug 8 15:32:54 2008: 00:1e:c2:ab:14:26 New client (policy)

Fri Aug 8 15:32:54 2008: 00:1e:c2:ab:14:26 Stopping deletion of Mobile Station:
  (callerId: 48)

Fri Aug 8 15:32:54 2008: 00:1e:c2:ab:14:26 Sending Assoc Response to station on
  BSSID 00:1a:a2:f9:ed:d0 (status 0)

Fri Aug 8 15:32:54 2008: 00:1e:c2:ab:14:26 apfProcessAssocReq (apf_80211.c:4149)
  Changing state for mobile 00:1e:c2:ab:14:26 on AP 00:1a:a2:f9:ed:d0 from
  Associated to Associated

Fri Aug 8 15:32:54 2008: 00:1e:c2:ab:14:26 802 new client 00:1e:c2:ab:14:26
```

Example 20-8   *A Successful Association*   *(continued)*

```
Fri Aug 8 15:32:55 2008: 00:1e:c2:ab:14:26 LBS Client data rcvd from AP
00:1a:a2:f9:ed:d0(0) with RSSI (A -128, B -36), SNR 57

Fri Aug 8 15:32:55 2008: 00:1e:c2:ab:14:26 LBS change cur RSSI B -44 , prev -47,
  send notify
```

In this small output, you can see that the client has become associated. One aspect of troubleshooting might involve connectivity. With this output, you can see that the client is in fact associated. If the client still has connectivity issues, you would want to start looking at the wired network, working your way from the controller, then to the switch, then to the next hop router, and so on.

You can also use debugs such as **debug dhcp** if you are having issues with clients obtaining IP addresses. If you are having authentication issues, you might use the **debug aaa** or **debug dot1x** commands.

Using the Controller Interface

The controller has several tools to help troubleshoot. From the controller interface, you can use controller logs, SNMP to alert administrators to current issues, and the Tech Support Pages. In the section "Using the CLI to Troubleshoot," you looked at output of a client that was trying to associate. You can see a web interface equivalent to the **show client summary** command in Figure 20-1.

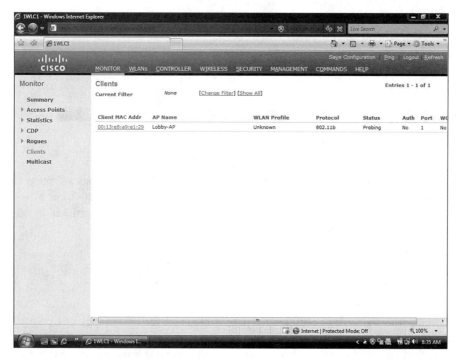

Figure 20-1   *Viewing the Client Summary*

Here you can gain information about the client, the WLAN the client is on, and other valuable information for troubleshooting.

Using the Controller Logs

Another valuable resource is the controller logs. Controller logs allow you to see events that have occurred at various levels. You probably want to send these to a Syslog server, but you can view them on the controller by going to **MANAGEMENT > Logs > Message logs**. Figure 20-2 shows just a sample of the information that you can obtain here.

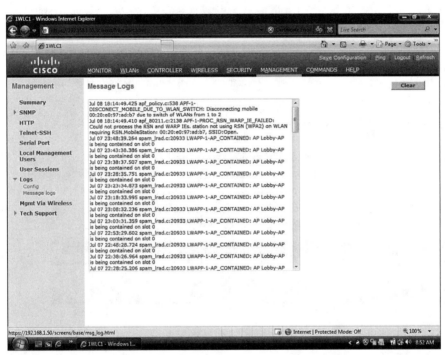

Figure 20-2   *Viewing the Controller Logs*

To change the way logging is configured, browse to **MANAGEMENT > Logs > Config**. This configuration page is shown in Figure 20-3. You cant see it inf Figure 20-3, but by selecting the **Syslog** check box, you can point to an external server by entering the address in the Syslog Server IP Address field.

> **Note:**   If you do not already have a Syslog server, you can download kiwi from http:/ /www.kiwisyslog.com. Kiwi is a free Syslog server that many people use.

In addition, from the Syslog Configuration page, you can set the level of logging by changing the facility levels. These levels control how much information is captured. In general, the larger the facility number, the more information that is recorded; however, this is not always the case. Table 20-2 shows the available facility levels.

Table 20-2   *Available Facility Levels*

Facility Name	Facility Level
Kernel	0
User Process	1
Mail	2
System Daemons	3
Authorization	4
Syslog	5
Line Printer	6
USENET	7
Unix-to-Unix Copy	8
Cron	9
—	10
FTP Daemons	11
System Use 1	12
System Use 2	13
System Use 3	14
System Use 4	15
Local Use 0	16
Local Use 1	17
Local Use 2	18
Local Use 3	19
Local Use 4	20
Local Use 5	21
Local Use 6	22
Local Use 7	23

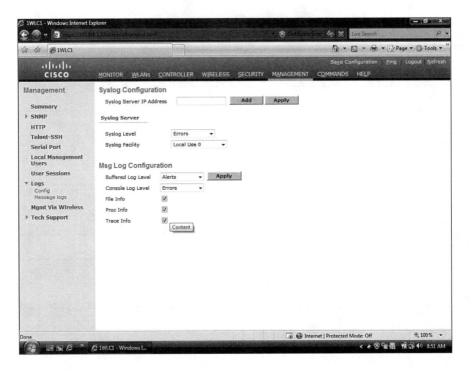

Figure 20-3   *Configuring Syslog*

You can locally view the logs by selecting **MANAGEMENT > Logs > Message logs**. The message logs include information related to the network infrastructure, client issues, authentication issues, and AP association issues. These have relevance to the controller.

Using SNMP

When using SNMP gets/sets, you can obtain information about the status of the controller and allows you to remotely manage the controller. To set up SNMP, go to **MANAGEMENT > SNMP > General**. Here you configure the following parameters, as shown in Figure 20-4:

- Name

- Location

- Contact

- System Description

- System Object ID

- SNMP Port Number

- Trap Port Number

- SNMP v1 Mode

- SNMP v2c Mode

- SNMP v3 Mode

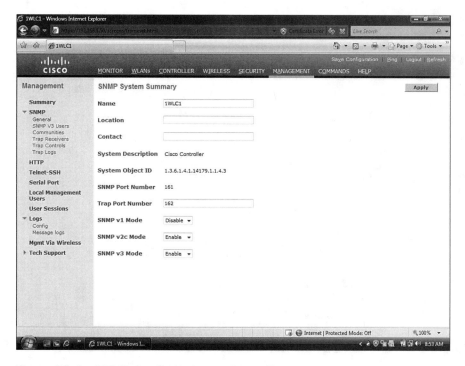

Figure 20-4   *SNMP Configuration on Controllers*

Configuring the Community Strings

When you set up SNMP, two community names exist by default. Public is for read-only access, and Private is for read/write access. If you have any involvement in security, you already know that you should change these values. They are well-known values that an attacker can use to gain control of your controller. You can modify the values in the controller by choosing **MANAGEMENT > SNMP > Communities**.

You can also set the SNMPv3 users and trap receivers. Although it is not covered here, it is recommended that you use SNMPv3, because it is the most secure method at the moment.

To view the SNMP trap logs, go to **MANAGEMENT > SNMP > Trap Logs**. Figure 20-5 shows a sample of the SNMP trap logs.

You can use these trap logs to troubleshoot client association failures and AP association failures. The trap logs generate a reason code that can point you in the right direction to correct the issue. Another way to refine the information you receive is by using the Trap Controls found at **MANAGEMENT > SNMP > Trap Controls**. Here you can control what events generate a trap.

Figure 20-5 *SNMP Trap Logs*

Using Tech Support

You might also find the Tech Support Pages, found at **MANAGEMENT > Tech Support**, to be of benefit. Although Cisco TAC uses most of what you do here, you might find it beneficial information for troubleshooting.

Crash logs, which the controller maintains, are created when a system fails. You cannot use most of the information found in the logs without Cisco TAC assistance. If Cisco TAC request these logs, you can access them by going to **MANAGEMENT > Tech Support > Controller Crash**. Five crash dump files can be stored on a controller at any given time.

APs also create a crash log file that the controller can download. Go to **MANAGEMENT > Tech Support >AP Crash Log > Get Log** to retrieve it. TAC also uses the AP crash logs.

Using WCS Version 5.x to Troubleshoot Clients

You can use WCS to troubleshoot wireless deployments. Use the **Monitor > Client** page to troubleshoot clients. You can see this page in Figure 20-6. When you use this tool, you get a Summary page with a list of problems and corresponding solutions. The page also has a log analysis and a detailed event history.

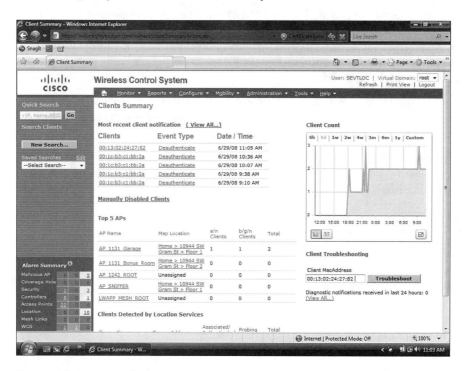

Figure 20-6 *Critical Alarms*

You can use the alarms to troubleshoot. In the Clients Summary page, click the numerous alarms in the lower left to be taken to that Alarm page. Figure 20-6 shows several critical alarms.

Using the Cisco Spectrum Expert

Cisco Spectrum Expert addresses the problem of RF interference in wireless networks. With Cisco Spectrum Expert, you can detect, classify, locate, and manually mitigate sources of wireless interference.

The Cisco Spectrum Expert Wi-Fi is the industry-leading spectrum intelligence product for Wi-Fi networks. Cisco Spectrum Expert Wi-Fi offers complete visibility into the RF physical layer in the 2.4-GHz and 5-GHz frequencies, allowing for enhanced performance, security, and reliability of WLAN services.

The Cisco Spectrum Expert Wi-Fi includes the following components:

■   Cisco Spectrum Expert Wi-Fi sensor

■   Cisco Spectrum Expert software

■   Cisco Spectrum Expert antenna

The Cisco Spectrum Expert Wi-Fi sensor is a sensor in the CardBus card form factor for notebooks. It is supported on Microsoft Windows–based laptops and delivers comprehensive spectrum intelligence. Network administrators can streamline wireless network troubleshooting with better visibility into the RF spectrum and can easily identify and detect sources of wireless interference.

Cisco Spectrum Expert provides a comprehensive list of all access points, ad hoc networks, and interferer devices (for example, microwave ovens, cordless phones, wireless security cameras, Bluetooth devices, and RF jammers).

Cisco Spectrum Expert also gives you a Channel Summary that provides visibility of RF activity—such as power levels and presence of 802.11 and interferer devices—on a channel-by-channel basis.

The Devices View provides a deeper look at each device and its impact to the wireless network, including power level, channel coverage, and other data.

A Device Finder tracks down the location of devices, causing wireless interference throughout your enterprise. The Device Classifier offers the most comprehensive classification of the RF devices, which include the following:

■   Wi-Fi access points

■   In-network devices

■   Known devices

■   Unknown devices

■   Ad hoc devices

■   Wi-Fi stations

■   A variety of Bluetooth devices

■   A variety of cordless phones[1]

■   Microwave ovens

■   Generic fixed-frequency devices

■   Generic frequency-hopped devices

■   Generic continuous transmitters (for example, FM phones, NTSC video devices)

■   RF jamming devices

■   802.11FH devices

■   Analog video devices

The Spectrum Views create plots and charts for a direct view into the RF spectrum, including measurements of RF power and network device activity. The plots are especially useful to trained RF engineers, and the charts are informative for both the expert RF engineer and the generalist network engineer.

An Alarms Setting configures enterprise-specific alerts and alarm triggers to notify you when wireless network is at critical utilization points.

All this is integrated with Cisco WCS and is based on obtaining a license to integrate it.

Exam Preparation Tasks

Review All the Key Topics

Review the most important topics from this chapter, noted with the Key Topics icon in the outer margin of the page. Table 20-3 lists a reference of these key topics and the page number where you can find each one.

Table 20-3 *Key Topics for Chapter 20*

Key Topic Item	Description	Page Number
Paragraph from the section "Common Client-Side Issues"	Discussion of the Hidden Node issue	410
Paragraph from the section "Common Client-Side Issues"	Discussion of the Exposed Node issue	410
Paragraph from the section "Common Client-Side Issues"	Discussion of the Near/Far issue	410
Example 20-1	Viewing the client summary	411
Example 20-2	Viewing client details	411
Command syntax	Enable client troubleshooting	414
Command syntax	Debug LWAPP events	414
Example 20-4	Verify enabled debugs	414
Figure 20-1	Viewing the client summary	417
Figure 20-2	Viewing the controller logs	418

Complete the Tables and Lists from Memory

Print a copy of Appendix B, "Memory Tables," (found on the CD) or at least the section for this chapter, and complete the tables and lists from memory. Appendix C, "Memory Tables Answer Key," also on the CD, includes completed tables and lists to check your work.

Definition of Key Terms

Define the following key terms from this chapter, and check your answers in the Glossary:

Hidden Node issue, Exposed Node issue

References

"Troubleshooting TechNotes" at Cisco.com: http://tinyurl.com/6dqxj2

"Troubleshooting Connectivity in a Wireless LAN Network" at Cisco.com: http://tinyurl.com/6l2ob2

The Cisco Spectrum Expert at Cisco.com: http://tinyurl.com/5eja7f

Part IV: Final Preparation

Chapter 21   **Final Preparation**

Final Preparation

This book has covered the technologies, protocols, commands, and features required for you to be prepared to pass the CCNA Wireless exam. Although this book supplies detailed information, most people need more preparation than simply reading a book. This chapter details a set of tools and a study plan that can help you complete your preparation for the exam.

If you're preparing for the CCNA Wireless exam, you should have already passed the CCNA level exams, either the CCNA exam or the ICND1 and ICND2 exams. For information on passing the CCNA exams, refer to *CCENT/CCNA ICND1 Official Exam Certification Guide* or *CCNA ICND2 Official Exam Certification Guide*, or go to http://www.cisco.com/go/ccna.

This short chapter has two main sections. The first lists the exam preparation tools that are useful at this point in your study process. The second section lists a suggested study plan now that you have completed the rest of the chapters.

Note: This chapter refers to many of the chapters and appendixes included with this book, as well as tools available on the CD. Appendixes B and C are included only on the CD that comes with this book. To access those, just insert the CD and make the appropriate selection from the opening interface.

Tools for Final Preparation

This section describes the available tools and how to access them.

Exam Engine and Questions on the CD

The CD in the back of the book includes an exam engine—software that displays and grades a set of exam-realistic questions. The question database includes simulation (sim) questions, drag-and-drop questions, and many scenario-based questions that require the same level of analysis as the questions on the CCNA Wireless exam. Using the exam engine, you can either study by practicing using the questions in Study Mode, or take a simulated (timed) CCNA Wireless exam.

The installation process has two major steps. The CD in the back of this book has a recent copy of the exam engine software, supplied by Boson Software (http://www.boson.com). The practice exam—the database of CCNA Wireless exam questions—is not on the CD. Instead, the practice exam resides on the www.boson.com web server, so the second major step is to activate and download the practice exam.

Note: The cardboard CD case in the back of this book includes the CD and a piece of paper. The paper lists the activation key for the practice exam associated with this book. *Do not lose this activation key.*

Install the Software from the CD

The software installation process is pretty routine as compared with other software installation processes. The following list outlines the steps:

Step 1. Insert the CD into your PC.

Step 2. The software that automatically runs is the Cisco Press software to access and use all CD-based features, including the exam engine, viewing a PDF of this book, and viewing the CD-only appendixes. From the main menu, click the option to **Install the Exam Engine**.

Step 3. Respond to the prompt windows as you would with any typical software installation process.

The installation process might give you the option to register the software. This process requires that you establish a login at the www.boson.com website. You need this login to activate the exam, so feel free to register when prompted.

Activate and Download the Practice Exam

After the exam engine is installed, you should activate the exam associated with this book:

Step 1. Start the Boson Exam Engine (BEE) software from the Start menu.

Step 2. The first time you start the software, it should ask you to either log in or register an account. If you do not already have an account with Boson, select the option to register a new account. (You must register to download and use the exam.)

Step 3. After you are registered, the software might prompt you to download the latest version of the software, which you should do. Note that this process updates the exam engine software (formally called the Boson Exam Environment), not the practice exam.

Step 4. To activate and download the exam associated with this book, from the exam engine main window, click the **Exam Wizard** button.

Step 5. From the Exam Wizard pop-up window, select **Activate a purchased exam** and click the **Next** button. (Although you did not purchase the exam directly, you purchased it indirectly when you bought the book.)

Step 6. At the next screen, enter the Activation Key from the paper inside the cardboard CD holder in the back of the book and click the **Next** button.

Step 7.   The activation process downloads the practice exam. When it is done, the main exam engine menu should list a new exam, with a name like "ExSim for Cisco Press CCNA Wireless ECG." If you do not see the exam, make sure you have selected the My Exams tab on the menu. You may need to click the plus sign icon (+) to expand the menu and see the exam.

At this point, the software and practice exam are ready to use.

Activating Other Exams

You need to install the exam software and register only once. Then, for each new exam, only a few steps will be required. For instance, if you bought both this book along with *CCENT/CCNA ICND1 Official Exam Certification Guide* or *CCNA ICND2 Official Exam Certification Guide*, you could follow the steps listed on the last page or so to install the software and activate the exam associated with this book. Then, for the practice exam associated with the ICND1 book and ICND2 book, you would need to follow only a few more steps. All you have to do is start the exam engine (if it's not still up and running) and follow Steps 4 and 5 in the preceding list. If fact, if you purchase other Cisco Press books, or purchase a practice exam from Boson, you just need to activate each new exam as described in Steps 4 and 5.

You can also purchase additional practice exams from Boson directly from its website. When you purchase an exam, you receive an activation key, and then you can activate and download the exam—again without requiring any additional software installation.

Cisco Learning Network

Cisco provides a wide variety of CCNA wireless preparation tools at a Cisco Systems website called the Cisco Learning Network. The Cisco Learning Network includes Quick Learning Modules, interviews with Cisco's Portfolio Manager for Wireless Certifications, documents that give you a sneak peek of what's included in the Instructor-Led Training Course, and blogs and discussion forums to help you on your way.

To use the Cisco Learning Network, you do not need a registered login at http://www. cisco.com, but you can register as a member of the learning network. This gives you access to additional content. To register, simply go to https://cisco.hosted.jivesoftware.com/create-account.jspa and supply some information. (You do not need to work for Cisco or one of its Partners to get a login.)

After you have registered, proceed to the Certifications area, and look for the link to the CCNA Wireless pages.

Study Plan

You could simply study using all the available tools, as mentioned earlier in this chapter. However, this section suggests a particular study plan, with a sequence of tasks that may work better than just using the tools randomly. However, feel free to use the tools in any way and at any time that helps you get fully prepared for the exam.

The suggested study plan separates the tasks into three categories:

- **Recall the facts:** Activities that help you remember all the details from this book.

- **Practice configurations:** You must master configurations on various devices to pass the CCNA Wireless exam. This category lists the items you can use to master configuration skills.

- **Use the exam engine to practice realistic questions:** You can use the exam engine on the CD to study using a bank of unique exam-realistic questions available only with this book.

Recall the Facts

As with most exams, you must recall many facts, concepts, and definitions to do well on the test. This section suggests a couple of tasks that should help you remember all the details:

- Review and repeat, as needed, the activities in the Exam Preparation Tasks section at the end of each chapter. Most of these activities help refine your knowledge of a topic while also helping you memorize the facts.

- Using the Exam Engine, answer all the questions in the Book database. This question database includes all the questions at the beginning of each chapter. Although some of the questions may be familiar, repeating them will help improve your recall of the topics covered in the questions.

Practice Configurations

A large part of CCNA wireless involves performing configurations on various devices. You might need to work on a controller, AP, or even WCS. Understanding these interfaces and various configurations is a must. This means that hands-on experience can take you over the edge to confidently and accurately build or verify configurations.

There are a number of sources of lab access. Some of these sources include rack rentals from trusted Cisco Partners. If you are a Cisco Partner, you might even have access to the Partner E-learning Connection (PEC). If you have access to a lab provided by your company, take advantage of it. Nothing beats hands-on experience.

Additionally, you can review the key topics in each chapter. These often refer to key configuration elements.

Use the Exam Engine

The exam engine includes two basic modes:

- **Study mode:** Study mode is most useful when you want to use the questions to learn and practice. In study mode, you can select options such as whether you want to randomize the order of the questions, randomize the order of the answers, automatically see the answers, and many other options.

- **Simulation mode:** Simulation mode simulates an actual CCNA Wireless exam by either requiring or allowing a set number of questions and a set time period. These timed exams not only allow you to study for the actual exam, but they also help you simulate the time pressure that can occur on the actual exam.

Choosing Study or Simulation Mode

Both study mode and simulation mode are useful for preparing for the exams. Picking the correct mode from the exam engine's user interface is pretty obvious, but you should still spend some time experimenting with the exam engine.

Passing Scores for the Cisco CCNA Wireless Exams

When scoring your simulated exam using this book's exam engine, you should strive to get a score of 85 percent or better. However, the scoring on the book's exam engine does not match how Cisco scores the actual CCNA Wireless exam. As it turns out, Cisco does not publish many details about how the actual exam is scored. Therefore, you cannot reasonably deduce which questions you got right or wrong, and how many points are assigned to each question.

Cisco does publish some specific guidance about how it scores the exam, and other details have been mentioned by Cisco personnel during public presentations about the CCNA Wireless exam. Here are some key facts about scoring:

- Cisco does give partial credit on simulation questions, so complete as much of a simulation question as you can.

- Cisco may or may not give more weight to some questions.

- The test does not adapt based on your answers to early questions in the test. For example, if you miss a RIP question, and it is question 1, the test does not start giving you more RIP questions.

- Cisco's scores range from 300 to 1000, with a passing grade usually (but not always) around 849 for the CCNA Wireless exam.

- The 849 out of 1000 does not necessarily mean that you got 84.9 percent of the questions correct.

Part V: Appendixes

Answers to the "Do I Know This Already?" Quizzes

Chapter 1

1. A
2. D
3. B and C
4. A
5. B
6. C and D
7. A, D, and E
8. A and C
9. A
10. C

Chapter 2

1. A
2. B
3. A and C
4. A
5. A, B, and E
6. B
7. A
8. A
9. C
10. A and C

Chapter 3

1. D
2. D
3. A
4. C
5. D
6. B
7. A
8. B and D
9. A
10. C
11. B and D

Chapter 4

1. C
2. B
3. C
4. B and D
5. A
6. B
7. B
8. B and C
9. D
10. A
11. A
12. B
13. B
14. A
15. D
16. D
17. A
18. A
19. C
20. B
21. B
22. A and C

23. C

24. C

25. B

26. A

Chapter 5

1. A, B, and D

2. A

3. C

4. D

5. B

6. C

7. B

8. A and C

9. B

10. B

11. A

12. D

13. A, C, and D

14. B

15. A

16. A

17. B and C

18. B

19. A

20. B

Chapter 6

1. B

2. C

3. A and D

4. D

5. A

6. D

7. B

8. A and C

9. A and B

10. A, C, and D

11. A and B

12. C

13. D

14. A and C

15. B

16. A

17. C

18. C

19. A and B

20. A and B

21. A

22. A

23. A

24. C

25. B

Chapter 7

1. A, B, and C

2. A

3. B

4. A and D

5. C

6. D

7. A

8. D

9. A

10. D

11. A

12. B

Chapter 8

1. D

2. C

3. D

4. D

5. A

6. B

7. B

8. A, B, and D

9. A

10. B

11. A

12. B

13. A

14. A

15. A and B

Chapter 9

1. A

2. D

3. D

4. D

5. A and B. A VLAN is used to define a logical broadcast domain and isolate a subnet.

6. B

7. D

8. C

9. C

10. A

11. D

12. C

Chapter 10

1. A

2. D

3. C

4. B

5. A, B, and C

6. A, C, and D

7. C

8. A

9. A and B
10. A
11. B
12. B
13. A
14. C
15. C
16. D
17. C

Chapter 11

1. A and D
2. D
3. A
4. D
5. C
6. B
7. B
8. D
9. A
10. A
11. A
12. C
13. A
14. C

Chapter 12

1. C
2. D
3. A
4. A
5. B
6. A and C
7. D
8. C
9. B

10. A
11. B

Chapter 13

1. B
2. D
3. A
4. A
5. D
6. A
7. C
8. D
9. D
10. A
11. A and B
12. B
13. C
14. D
15. A, B, and D
16. C
17. A
18. C
19. C

Chapter 14

1. A
2. A and B
3. B, C, and D
4. A, B, and D
5. B
6. B
7. A and D
8. D
9. B
10. A

Chapter 15

1. B
2. C
3. D
4. B, C, and D
5. A
6. B, C, and D
7. D
8. A
9. D
10. A

Chapter 16

1. D
2. A and C
3. B
4. B
5. B
6. B
7. A and B
8. A
9. A
10. C
11. A and B
12. A

Chapter 17

1. A and B
2. A and C
3. B
4. C
5. D
6. B
7. A
8. D
9. D

10. A

11. C

12. A

13. D

14. A

Chapter 18

1. A, B, and C

2. B

3. B

4. A and B

5. D

6. B

7. C and D

8. A

9. B

10. A and B

11. A

12. D

13. A

14. A and C

15. C

16. C

17. D

18. B. There are AP templates as well.

19. D

20. A

21. A, B, and C

22. A, B, and C

23. A

24. C

25. C

Chapter 19

1. A
2. B
3. D
4. D
5. A and B
6. B
7. C
8. A
9. B
10. D
11. A

Chapter 20

1. B
2. A and B
3. C
4. A
5. D
6. B
7. B
8. C
9. D
10. D
11. A
12. C
13. B
14. A
15. A

GLOSSARY

This glossary defines many of the terms, abbreviations, and acronyms related to networking. It includes all the key terms used throughout the book. As with any growing technical field, some terms evolve and take on several meanings. Where necessary, multiple definitions and abbreviation expansions are provided.

Numbers

802.1q   An IEEE form of trunking.

802.1x   An IEEE definition of port-based authentication.

802.15.1   An IEEE definition of personal-area networks.

802.15.1-2005   An IEEE definition of personal-area networks that includes additions incorporated in Bluetooth v1.2.

802.16e   An IEEE standard defining point-to-multipoint broadband wireless definitions and an amendment to 802.16.

A

absorption   Removes amplitude from a wave, essentially reducing the distance it can travel.

access port   A port connected to a host rather than to another switch and normally on only one VLAN.

acknowledged (ACK)   A response to some form of request.

active scan   The process of actively scanning for available wireless networks.

Adaptive Frequency Hopping Spread Spectrum Technology   A spread spectrum method used to improve resistance to RF, often used in Bluetooth technology.

ad hoc   When two computers communicate directly with one another.

Advanced Encryption Standard (AES)   Also known as Rijndael. A block cipher adopted as an encryption standard by the U.S. government.

Aironet Client Administration Utility (ACAU)   A Cisco software utility designed to configure the Aironet Desktop Utility before deployment.

Aironet Desktop Utility (ADU)   Cisco software used to manage a single a/b/g wireless card.

Airport Extreme   The MAC-OSX wireless client.

amplifier   Added between the AP and the antenna to strengthen the signal.

amplitude   The volume of the signal.

anchor   The original controller.

Announcement Traffic Indication Message (ATIM)   Used in IEEE 802.11 ad hoc or independent BSS networks to announce the existence of buffered frames when a client is in sleep mode.

AP priming   After the AP is associated with at least one controller, the AP gets a list of other controllers it can associate with from the one that is already associated with.

ARP   Address Resolution Protocol. Used to resolve a MAC address to an IP address.

association request   A request from a client to the AP for association.

association response   A response from an AP to a client during open association.

asymmetric tunneling   Traffic from the client is routed to the destination, regardless of its source address. The return traffic is sent to its original controller, called an anchor, and is tunneled to the new controller.

attenuator   Reduces the signal if there is too much signal, causing bleed-over into other networks.

authentication request   A request from a client to an AP during open authentication.

authentication response   A response from an AP to a client during open authentication.

authentication server   An AAA server that has a list of users in one form or another that can verify the supplicant.

authenticator   The switch.

Autonomous Workgroup Bridge (aWGB)   A wireless bridge operating autonomously.

autoprovisioning   Simplifies deployments when you have a large number of controllers.

azimuth   The angle measured in degrees between a reference plane and a point.

B

backoff timer   A random number that begins a countdown process while listening.

bandwidth   The frequency spectrum, measured in Hertz. Bandwidth can refer to data rates or the width of an RF channel.

barker code   Defines the use of 11 chips when encoding data.

Basic Service Area (BSA)   The coverage area of the AP.

Basic Service Set (BSS)   One device sets a network name and radio parameters, and the other uses it to connect.

Basic Service Set Identifier (BSSID)   Only one network that an AP is offering service for.

beacon   An announcement of services from an AP.

Binary Phase Shift Keying (BPSK)   A modulation technique used in 802.11 networks.

block acknowledgment   The confirmation from the recipient station, stating which frames have been received. Used in 802.11n networks.

Bluetooth   A personal-area technology.

bridge mode   A mode that an AP can operate in, in which it bridges traffic from source to destination.

C

Carrier Sense Multiple Access/Collision Avoidance (CSMA/CA)   When a device wants to send, it must listen first. Similar to CSMA/CD.

channel   A defined frequency range.

Channel State Information (CSI)   If the receiver is moving, the reflection characteristics change, and the beamforming can no longer be coordinated.

chipping code   A code used to represent bits.

circular polarization   Indicates that the wave circles as it moves forward.

Cisco Client Extension Program (CCX)   A no-cost licensing of technology for use in WLAN adapters and devices.

Cisco Configuration Assistant (CCA)   A software application used to set up mobility express networks.

Cisco Discovery Protocol (CDP)   A Cisco-proprietary protocol that can gain information about directly connected Cisco devices.

Cisco Site Survey Utility (CSSU)   The optional software set that you select with a check-box during installation.

Cisco Smart Business Communication System (SBCS)   The Cisco solution for voice, video, and wireless for the small business.

Cisco Wireless Location Appliance   Maps clients and helps enforce security policies.

Cisco Wizard Configuration Tool   A wizard-type menu used to perform basic configuration.

Clear Channel Assessment (CCA)   A function found within physical layers that determines the current state of use of a wireless medium.

Clear-To-Send (CTS)   A message indicating that it is clear to send data on the wireless medium.

Clear-To-Send to self (CTS to self)   A method indicating that it is clear to send data on a wireless network.

client MFP   If the client is running CCX 5 or better, it can actually talk to the AP and find out what the MIC is.

co-channel interference   Crosstalk between channels that are next to each other.

Code Division Multiple Access (CDMA)   A channel access method.

community   A group name for your mobility express network.

Complementary Code Keying (CCK)   Uses a series of codes called complementary sequences.

contention window   The total amount of time that Station A waits before sending.

control frame   Used to acknowledge when data frames are received.

CSSC   Cisco Secure Services Client software.

D

data frame   A frame that contains data.

deauthentication message   When a client is connected to a wireless cell, either the client or the AP can leave the connection by sending this message. This message has information in the body about why it is leaving.

deauthentication response   A response to a deauthentication message.

destination address (DA)   A frame's final destination.

Digital Enhanced Cordless Telecommunications (DECT)   An ETSI standard for digital portable phones. Found in cordless technology that is deployed in homes or business.

dipole   See rubber duck.

directional antenna   Mounted on a wall. Its radiation pattern is focused in a certain direction.

Direct Sequence Spread Spectrum (DSSS)   The modulation technique used by 802.11b devices to send data. The transmitted signal is spread across the entire frequency spectrum that is being used.

disassociation message   Disassociates from the cell but keeps the client authenticated.

disassociation response   A response to a disassociation message.

Distributed Coordination Function (DCF)   Each station is responsible for coordinating the sending of its data.

Distributed Interframe Space (DIFS)   Each sending station must wait after a frame is sent before sending the next frame.

distribution system   The AP connects to a distribution system to get to server farms, the Internet, and other subnets.

diversity vertical polarization   The use of two antennas for each radio to increase the odds of receiving a better signal on either of the antennas.

dual-patch "omnidirectional"   Two patch directional antennas are placed back to back, making it "omnidirectional."

Dynamic Frequency Control (DFC)   The ability to change frequency to avoid radar signals.

dynamic interface   Includes the user-defined list.

Dynamic Rate Shifting (DRS)   The capability of a wireless network to shift to a lower rate as a client moves farther away from the AP.

E

Effective Isotropic Radiated Power (EIRP)   Used to estimate the service area of a device. The formula is as follows:

EIRP = transmitter − cable loss + antenna gain

elevation plane (E-plane)   The vertical pattern does not propagate evenly.

Enhanced Data Rate (EDR)   A Bluetooth 2.0 feature providing up to three times the bandwidth for Bluetooth clients.

exposed node issue   When there are two wireless cells on the same channel and they are too close to each other.

Extended Rate Physical (ERP)   Devices that have extended data rates.

Extended Service Area (ESA)   More than one AP is connected to a common distribution system.

Extensible Authentication Protocol (EAP)   Controls the authentication process under the premise that no matter what EAP method you use, the basic steps will reamain the same.

Extensible Authentication Protocol-Flexible Authentication via Secure Tunnel (EAP-FAST)   Created to address weaknesses in Lightweight Extensible Authentication Protocol (LEAP). Uses PAC, not PKI.

Extensible Authentication Protocol-Transport Layer Security (EAP-TLS)   A commonly used EAP method for wireless networks.

European Telecommunications Standards Institute (ETSI)   Produces globally applicable standards for Information and Communications Technologies (ICT), including fixed, mobile, radio, converged, broadcast, and Internet technologies.

F

Federal Communications Commission (FCC)   An independent U.S. government agency established by the Communications Act of 1934. It regulates interstate and international communications by radio, television, wire, satellite, and cable. The FCC's jurisdiction covers the 50 states, the District of Columbia, and U.S. possessions.

Frame Check Sequence (FCS)   Extra checksum characters added to a frame in a communication protocol for error detection and correction.

free path loss   The loss in signal strength of an electromagnetic wave that results from a line-of-sight path through free space, where no obstacles are nearby to cause reflection or diffraction.

frequency   The pitch of the signal.

Frequency Division Multiple Access (FDMA)   An access technology that radio systems use to share the radio spectrum, commonly found in 802.11 networks.

Frequency Hopping Spread Spectrum (FHSS)   A spread spectrum method in which the signal hops between channels. If a channel experiences interference, it can be skipped.

G

Generic Token Card (GTC)   Authenticates the user inside an encrypted tunnel.

Global System for Mobile Communication (GSM)   A digital mobile telephony system that uses a variation of time-division multiple access (TDMA). The most widely used of the three digital wireless telephony technologies (TDMA, GSM, and CDMA). GSM operates at either the 900-MHz or 1800-MHz frequency band.

Group Master Key (GMK)   Used by the AP to generate a group random number.

Group Temporal Key (GTK)   Generated by the GMK random number. Provides a group key and a MIC. This key changes when it times out or when a client leaves the network.

Group Transient Key (GTK)   Used to decrypt broadcast and multicast.

H

Hertz (Hz)   Used to measure bandwidth. Hertz measures the number of cycles per second. One Hertz is one cycle per second.

hidden node issue   When more than one client tries to send on the same channel at the same time. They are in range of the AP but not each other.

hidden node problem   When two devices cannot hear each other.

horizontal plane (H-plane)   The horizontal plane of an omnidirectional polarized antenna, opposite the E-plane.

horizontal polarization   The wave goes left and right in a linear way.

hybrid REAP mode   Hybrid Remote Edge Access Point (H-REAP) is a solution for branch office and remote office deployments. It lets you configure access points (AP) in a branch or remote office from the corporate office through a wide-area network (WAN) link without the need to deploy a controller in each office.

I

Independent Basic Service Set (IBSS)   When two machines do not need a central device to speak to each other.

Industry, Scientific, and Medical (ISM) frequency bands   Use of spread spectrum in the commercial market.

infrastructure   Refers to assets that support a network.

infrastructure device   The access point (AP).

infrastructure MFP   Management Frame Protection performed by APs.

initialization vector (IV)   A block of bits that is used to produce a unique encryption key.

Institute for Electrical and Electronics Engineers (IEEE)   A nonprofit organization, IEEE is the world's leading professional association for the advancement of technology.

intercontroller roaming   When a user roams from one controller to another but remains on the same VLAN.

interface   The logical, dynamic, or static port of a network device. Also refers to VLANs.

interframe spacing (IFS)   A period of time that a station has to wait before it can send.

intracontroller roaming   When roaming is handled within a single controller.

IP Setup utility   Takes the MAC address of the AP and resolves the IP address associated with it.

isotropic radiator   A reference that assumes that the signal is propagated evenly in all directions. This would be a perfect 360-degree sphere in all directions, on the H- and E-planes.

iwconfig   The command-line tool for Linux to work with WLANs.

J–K

join request message   A message sent by an AP to join a wireless controller.

L

Layer 3 LWAPP mode   The default LWAPP mode on most Cisco devices.

lightning arrestor   Prevents surges from reaching the RF equipment by the device's shunting effect.

Lightweight Access Point Protocol (LWAPP)   A protocol used for communication between a lightweight AP and a wireless controller.

lightweight AP   An AP that receives configuration from a controller and cannot function without the controller.

Lightweight Extensible Authentication Protocol (LEAP)   Uses a proprietary algorithm to create the initial session key.

Line-of-Sight (LOS)   The signal between the two points that appears to be a straight shot.

link budget   A value that accounts for all the gains and losses between sender and receiver. It accounts for attenuation, antenna gain, and other miscellaneous losses that may occur.

local mode   The standard operating mode of an access point.

LWAPP discovery request   An LWAPP message used to discover a controller.

LWAPP discovery response   A response from a controller to an AP during discovery.

M

management frame   Used to join and leave a wireless cell.

Management Frame Protection (MFP)   A method used to detect spoofed management frames in which valid frames contain a hash that spoofed frames would not.

master controller   Configured in the GUI interface by choosing CONTROLLER > Advanced > Master Controller Mode.

Maximum Transmission Unit (MTU)   The largest frame size supported on an interface.

Message Integrity Check (MIC)   A cryptographic hash in each management frame used to ensure that data is not tampered with.

Microsoft Challenge Handshake Authentication Protocol version 2 (MS-CHAPv2)   A protocol used to authenticate the user inside an encrypted tunnel in Microsoft Windows Active Directory.

mobility anchor   A feature in which all the client traffic that belongs to a WLAN (especially the guest WLAN) is tunneled to a predefined WLC or a set of controllers that are configured as an anchor for that specific WLAN. Also called guest tunneling or auto-anchor mobility.

mobility domain   A controller can be aware of another controller in a different mobility group.

mobility group   A setting that defines the controller as a member of a group.

monitor mode   A mode that an AP can operate in where it constantly scans all channels to perform rouge detection. When in this mode, the AP cannot service clients.

multipath   Defines when portions of signals are reflected and then arrive out of order at the receiver.

Multiple Basic Service Set Identifier (MBSSID)   Used when the AP has more than one network.

Multiple-Input Multiple-Output (MIMO)   A technology that is used in the new 802.11n specification. A device that uses MIMO technology uses multiple antennas to receive signals, usually two or three, as well as multiple antennas to send signals.

N

N+1   A method of controller redundancy—a controller plus one for backup.

N+N   Two active controllers that can back each other up.

N+N+1   Two controllers backing each other up, with a dedicated backup as a last resort.

native VLAN   The VLAN on a trunk that does not get tagged.

NAV   Norton AntiVirus.

N connector   A type of antenna connector.

network manager   A graphical user interface (GUI) tool that enables the creation of wireless profiles in Linux.

node   Another term for an access point in a mesh network.

null function frame   The client wakes up after a certain period of time, during which the AP buffers any traffic for it.

NVRAM   Nonvolatile RAM. A storage location used to keep configuration files.

O

omnidirectional antenna   An antenna type that does not focus a signal in one direction.

one-floor concept   The signal propagates wider from side to side than from top to bottom. Therefore, the signal can offer coverage to the floor it is placed on rather than to the floor above or below the AP.

Orthogonal Frequency Division Multiplexing (OFDM)   Defines a number of channels in a frequency range. Not considered a spread spectrum technology but is used for modulation in a wireless network.

Over-the-Air Provisioning (OTAP)   A method for APs to discover the management IP of a controller over the air.

P

Pairwise Master Key (PMK)   A wireless security key.

Pairwise Transient Key (PTK)   This type of key confirms the PMK between two devices, establishes a temporal key to be used for message encryption, authenticates the negotiated parameters, and creates keying material for the next phase, called the two-way group key handshake.

parabolic dish   Has a very narrow path and is very focused in its radiation pattern.

passive scan   A scan in which wireless clients mark the channels on which a beacon is heard.

phase   The timing of the signal between peaks.

Point Coordination Function (PCF)   The AP is responsible for coordinating the sending of its data.

polarity   The direction in which the RF is sent from an antenna—horizontal or vertical.

port   A physical interface on your controller.

precoding   A function that takes advantage of multiple antennas and the multipath issue.

probe request   A client request for an AP.

probe response   A response to a probe request.

protected EAP (PEAP)   Only a server-side certificate is used to create a tunnel, and then the real authentication takes place inside.

PS-poll   Power-save poll.

Q–R

Quadrature Phase Shift Keying (QPSK)   A version of frequency modulation in which the phase of the carrier wave is modulated to encode bits of digital information in each phase change.

radiation pattern   The direction of the RF propagation.

Radio Resource Management (RRM)   A software feature of the Cisco controller that acts as a built-in RF engineer to consistently provide real-time RF management of your wireless network.

RAM   Random-access memory, used during operation. Lost when the system reloads.

Real-Time Operating System (RTOS)   The controller's operating system.

Receiving Address (RA)   The address of the direct station that this frame is sent to.

Reduced Interframe Space (RIFS)   A smaller interframe space, reducing delay and overhead.

reflection   Happens when a signal bounces off something and travels in a different direction.

refraction   The change in direction or the bending of a waveform as it passes through something that has a different density.

repeater   A device that repeats a signal to extend distance.

Request-To-Send (RTS)   A request to send on a wireless network.

response   In a wireless LAN, a response to a request for connectivity.

Reverse-Polarity Threaded Neill-Concelman (RP-TNC)   A type of antenna connector.

roaming   A client moving from one AP to another AP, overlapping.

rogue detector mode   A mode an AP can operate in to look for rogue devices. When operating in this mode, an AP looks on the wireless network for ARP messages from rogue devices.

rubber duck   A common wireless antenna in a rubber sheath.

S

scattering   The signal is sent in many different directions. This can be caused by an object that has reflective yet jagged edges, or dust particles in the air and water.

Secure Services Client Administration Utilities (SSCAU)   A component of Cisco Secure Services Client (SSC) client software that enables the administrator to create complex profiles.

Service Set Identifier (SSID)   The name of a wireless network.

Short Interframe Space (SIFS)   For higher priority. Used for ACKs, among other things.

Signal-to-Noise Ratio (SNR)   How much stronger the signal is compared to the surrounding noise that corrupts it.

site survey   A measurement of a certain point in time—the time when you did the site survey.

slottime   The speed at which the backoff timer countdown occurs.

Small to Mid-Size Business (SMB)   A business that has customers seeking to gain a competitive edge without having to compromise between price and sophistication.

sniffer mode   A mode that an AP can operate in to capture data and forward 802.11 packets to an application such as Wireshark for analysis.

sniff subrating   Increases battery life up to five times.

source address (SA)   The stations that sent the frame.

spatial multiplexing   Takes a signal, splits it into a bunch of lower-rate streams, and then sends each one out different antennas.

Special Interest Group (SIG)   A Bluetooth group.

splitter   Used in outdoor wireless deployments to split in two a signal coming from a cable, and send it in two directions.

static interface   Includes management interface, AP-Manager, service port.

station (STA)   The client on a network.

supplicant   A device that can use an EAP method to prove its identity to the authentication server.

symmetric tunneling   All traffic is tunneled from the client to the anchor controller, sent to the destination, returned to the anchor controller, and then tunneled back to the client via the foreign controller.

T

Temporal Key Integrity Protocol (TKIP)   A method of automatically changing the keys.

TFTP   Trivial File Transfer Protocol. Used to copy files between a client and server using UDP port 69.

Time Division Multiple Access (TDMA)   An access method that allocates time slots to access the network.

Traffic Indication Map (TIM)   This field indicates whether the AP is buffering traffic for clients in power-save mode.

Transmit Beamforming (TxBF)   A technique that is used when there is more than one transmit antenna. The signal is coordinated and sent from each antenna so that the signal at the receiver is dramatically improved, even if it is far from the sender.

Transmit Power Control (TPC)   The ability to adjust power dynamically, and a requirement for use in the UNII bands.

Transmitter Address (TA)   The address of the station that is emitting the frame.

trunk port   A port that carries traffic for multiple VLANs by tagging traffic from each VLAN.

U

Universal Workgroup Bridge (uWGB)   A wireless bridge.

Unlicensed National Information Infrastructure (UNII)   Frequency ranges used in wireless networks that don't require licensing.

upgrade tool   A Windows application that converts the device to lightweight mode.

V

vertical polarization   The wave moves up and down in a linear way.

virtual carrier sense   A method of verifying link integrity.

virtual local-area network (VLAN)   A concept in switched networks that allows segmentation of users at a logical level.

W

wavelength   The distance between successive crests of a wave.

WCS planning mode   Determines how many APs are needed for a given coverage area by placing hypothetical APs on the map. Lets you view the coverage area.

WCS RF prediction   Uses information entered into the map and the map editor to predict how the AP will react in the environment.

WCS template   Allows administrators to save time by configuring it once and then being able to apply it to more than one device.

Wi-Fi Alliance   A nonprofit organization that certifies the interoperability of more than 4200 products.

Wi-Fi Protected Access (WPA)   Uses the Temporal Key Integrity Protocol (TKIP) as a way to automatically change the keys.

Wi-Fi Protected Access 2 (WPA2)   Allows for the AES/CCMP variant and allows keys to be cached for faster connections.

Windows Wireless Zero Configuration Utility (WZC)   The wireless configuration tool for Microsoft Windows.

Wireless Control System (WCS)   A browser-based software application control element that offers the ability to manage multicontroller deployments through a single interface.

Wireless LAN Controller (WLC)   A Cisco wireless controller used to configure wireless networks and deliver configurations to lightweight APs.

wireless local-area network (WLAN)   The wireless portion of a local-area network.

wireless metropolitan-area network (WMAN)   A wireless network that encompasses a metropolitan area.

wireless personal-area network (WPAN)   A wireless network covering a very small area.

wireless wide-area network (WWAN)   A wireless network that covers a wide area.

workgroup bridge (WGB)   A device that bridges traffic.

Worldwide Interoperability for Microwave Access (WiMax)   A method of wide-area or last-mile wireless access.

WPA   A Wi-Fi protected access, authentication, and encryption method using the TKIP protocol.

WPA2   A Wi-Fi protected access, authentication, and encryption method using AES encryption.

X–Y–Z

Yagi-Uda   A directional antenna that offers a very direct radiation pattern.

ZigBee   A technology consisting of small, low-power digital radios based on the IEEE 802.15.4 standard for wireless personal-area networks.

Index

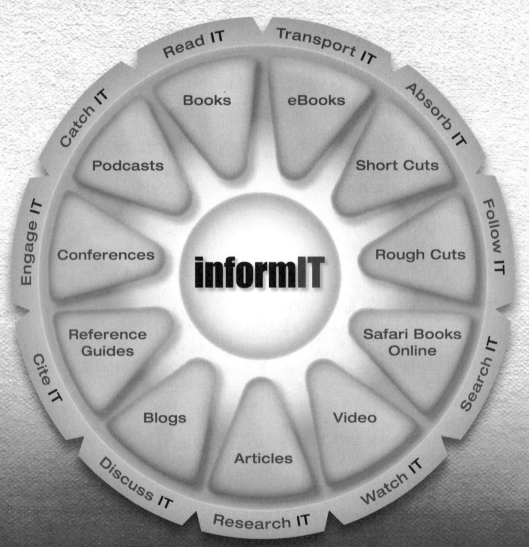

LearnIT at InformIT

Go Beyond the Book

Read IT
Transport IT
Catch IT
Absorb IT
Books
eBooks
Short Cuts
Podcasts
Engage IT
Follow IT
Conferences
informIT
Rough Cuts
Reference Guides
Safari Books Online
Cite IT
Search IT
Blogs
Video
Discuss IT
Articles
Watch IT
Research IT

11 WAYS TO LEARN IT at **www.informIT.com/learn**

The digital network for the publishing imprints of Pearson Education

 Addison
Cisco Press
EXAM/CRAM
 IBM
 que
  SAMS

FREE Online Edition

Your purchase of **CCNA Wireless Official Exam Certification Guide** includes access to a free online edition for 45 days through the Safari Books Online subscription service. Nearly every Cisco Press book is available online through Safari Books Online, along with over 5,000 other technical books and videos from publishers such as Addison-Wesley Professional, Exam Cram, IBM Press, O'Reilly, Prentice Hall, Que, and Sams.

SAFARI BOOKS ONLINE allows you to search for a specific answer, cut and paste code, download chapters, and stay current with emerging technologies.

Activate your FREE Online Edition at www.informit.com/safarifree

> **STEP 1:** Enter the coupon code: HTNRYCB.

> **STEP 2:** New Safari users, complete the brief registration form. Safari subscribers, just login.

If you have difficulty registering on Safari or accessing the online edition, please e-mail customer-service@safaribooksonline.com